ALTRUISM, SYMPATHY, AND HELPING

Psychological and Sociological Principles

Sponsored by the Society for the Psychological Study of Social Issues

ALTRUISM, SYMPATHY, AND HELPING
Psychological and Sociological Principles

Edited by

LAUREN WISPÉ

Departments of Communications and Psychology
University of Oklahoma
Norman, Oklahoma

ACADEMIC PRESS   New York   San Francisco   London   1978

A Subsidiary of Harcourt Brace Jovanovich, Publishers

ACADEMIC PRESS, INC.
111 Fifth Avenue, New York, New York 10003

United Kingdom Edition published by
ACADEMIC PRESS, INC. (LONDON) LTD.
24/28 Oval Road, London NW1 7DX

Library of Congress Cataloging in Publication Data

Main entry under title:

Altruism, sympathy, and helping.

Includes bibliographies.
1. Altruism. I. Wispé, Lauren. [DNLM:
1. Altruism. 2. Social behavior. 3. Psychological
theory. BJ1474 A469]
BF637.H4A47   171.8   78–3350
ISBN 0–12–760450–2

Contents

II PSYCHOLOGICAL AND SOCIOLOGICAL EXPLANATIONS

III SOME CRITICAL CONSIDERATIONS

List of Contributors

Numbers in parentheses indicate the pages on which the authors' contributions begin.

DONALD T. CAMPBELL (39), Department of Psychology, Northwestern University, Evanston, Illinois 60201

RONALD COHEN (79), Department of Anthropology, Northwestern University, Evanston, Illinois 60202

RUDOLF EKSTEIN (165), Clinical Professor of Medical Psychology, University of California at Los Angeles, UCLA, and Training Analyst, Los Angeles Psychoanalytic Institute and Southern California Training Institute

ELAINE HATFIELD (115), Department of Sociology, University of Wisconsin, Madison, Wisconsin 53706

HARVEY A. HORNSTEIN (177), Teachers' College, Columbia University, New York, New York 10027

JOHN KAPLAN (291), Stanford University Law School, Stanford, California 94305

DENNIS KREBS (141), Center for Advanced Study in the Behavioral Sciences,

202 Junipero Serra Boulevard, Stanford, California 94305 and Department of Psychology, Simon Fraser University, Burnaby, B.C.

PETER LENROW (263), Department of Psychiatry, Harvard Medical School, Cambridge, Massachusetts 02138 and McLean Hospital Program in School Consultation

HELMUT E. LÜCK (209), Gesamthochschule Duisburg, Psychologie, 4100 Duisburg 1, Postfach 919, Federal Republic of Germany

ROGER D. MASTERS (59), Department of Government, Dartmouth College, Hanover, New Hampshire 03755

JANE ALLYN PILIAVIN (115), Department of Sociology, University of Wisconsin, Madison 53706

D. L. ROSENHAN (101), Department of Psychology, Stanford University, Stanford, California 94305

B. F. SKINNER (249), Psychology Department, Harvard University, Cambridge, Massachusetts 02138

G. WILLIAM WALSTER (115), Department of Sociology, University of Wisconsin, Madison, Wisconsin 53706

SASHA R. WEITMAN (229), Department of Sociology and Anthropology, Tel Aviv University, Ramat Aviv, Tel Aviv, Israel

EDWARD O. WILSON (11), Museum of Comparative Zoology, Harvard University, Cambridge, Massachusetts 02138

LAUREN WISPÉ (1, 303), Departments of Communications and Psychology, Room 134, Building 158, South Campus, University of Oklahoma, Norman, Oklahoma 73069

Preface

What is there about the human predicament that we are constrained, under certain conditions, to attend to the suffering and the safety of our fellows? Why is it that we subject ourselves to others' pain and anguish when we so actively avoid such sensations for ourselves? What is the name of the impulse that draws some men to be concerned about the misfortunes of others, to share their grief, to defend them at the risk of bodily harm, to try to rescue them even in the face of death itself? And all of this when there is nothing personally to be gained?

Such behavior has been attributed to many impulses, called at different times by such names as altruism, benevolence, compassion, empathy, fellow feeling, sympathy, and love. Whatever the distinctions among them, these terms all refer to behavior that has as its aim to produce, maintain, or improve the physical or psychological welfare and integrity of other persons. In sum: These terms describe behavior that is other-directed in a positive sense. For lack of a better descriptive phrase, let us agree to call it, generically, "positive social behavior."

Whatever the reasons, research and theorizing about positive social behavior is burgeoning. Perhaps this trend is in response to the troubles of our times, perhaps to the tumult of the 1960s, or perhaps to the realization that behavioral scientists have too long been concerned almost exclusively with antisocial behaviors. Whatever the causes, it is important to point out that areas of human behavior are now being investigated that might have led in the past to the expulsion of the researcher from the scientific community. Indeed, this research is being rewarded. The prestigious American Association for the Advancement of Science prize was awarded in 1968 to Latané and Darley for their work on bystander intervention and in 1969 to Zick Rubin for his study of romantic love. It would be premature to try to predict the outcome of this trend, but there can be no doubt that a more positive orientation is taking place in the behavioral sciences. The title of this volume was chosen, in part, to reflect this fact.

The title also indicates those disciplines in which most of the work to date has been done. "Altruism" is the favorite term of the biologists, and Wilson's (1975) work, *Sociobiology*, has revitalized and enlivened it. The biologists have, in their own manner, contributed one of the most important theoretical explanations for altruistic behavior. It is, predictably, a genetic explanation, not a psychological one. Their fundamental concern is whether altruism can be explained by natural selection. Behavioral scientists will find in this volume one of the clearest presentations of the current interest in the biological as opposed to the social basis for altruism. Anthropologists and philosophers opt for the concept of "sympathy." This is the only serious explanatory contender, though perhaps it is complementary to the genetic explanation for positive behavior. Interestingly enough, Darwin (1871) used the concept of sympathy, but it found its way into the behavioral sciences probably through Hume (1739) and Adam Smith (1759). Psychologists have preferred the term "empathy" to sympathy, probably because it was used originally by Titchener (1909), but the two terms are very similar (Wispé, 1968). And social philosophers like Nagle (1970) and Mercer (1972) have expanded the concept of sympathy as a basis for social life. This brings us to the third word in the title, "helping." Experimental psychologists and sociologists have researched seemingly all manner of positive behaviors, including "aiding," "donating," and "intervening," to mention only a few. The term "helping" was chosen to cover all of these, since "helping" refers generally to doing whatever is necessary to assist or relieve someone in need. "Altruism" refers to self-sacrificial behavior in the grand manner; "helping" research has investigated those bits of everyday behavior by which social bonds are reinforced, the theoretical explanation for which one finds in the concept of "sympathy."

Because of the somewhat tripartite division of labor in this area, there has been more than the usual amount of benign neglect of interdisciplinary research and theorizing. With the exception of Trivers' (1971) article, one finds no more than an occasional reference to work in other disciplines. The explicit purpose of this volume, therefore, is to bring to bear different theoretical viewpoints upon the general area of altruism, sympathy, and helping. The authors are all established, senior investigators with sterling credentials in their own fields. Several, like Wilson (Chapter 1), Hatfield, Walster, and Piliavin (Chapter 6), and Hornstein (Chapter 9), offer comprehensive—albeit widely differing—theoretical interpretations for helping behavior. Others, like Masters (Chapter 3), Rosenhan (Chapter 5), and Krebs (Chapter 7), adopt a more critical stance toward one or another of the theoretical explanations of helping. Still others like Cohen (Chapter 4), Ekstein (Chapter 8), and Lück (Chapter 10) discuss some aspect of the problem in light of their particular areas of expertise. To the best of my knowledge, an endeavor of this kind is nowhere else to be found.

It is not the purpose of this book to present the final, definitive explanation for altruistic, sympathetic, helping behavior. Indeed, premature conclusions in this area could be disastrous. At this juncture, all ports of intellectual entry must remain open. Some important lessons are learned when a wide variety of theoretical viewpoints are brought to bear upon this particular topic. One finds, for example, that, with regard to fundamental assumptions, each theoretical position has a kind of private existence. Adherents may research and extend the position, but there is little profound self-criticism, and few comparisons with disparate approaches are made. Each has its own empirical operations and uses its own language. This kind of laissez-faire theorizing and research provides some unexpected benefits, although it inestimably complicates the attempt to find points of agreement and frustrates conceptual confrontations. It does serve, however, to illuminate implicit assumptions in one theory that are made explicit in another and to suggest ways in which different approaches can complement each other. These possibilities are considered in various chapters in this volume.

This volume will have served its purpose if it raises important questions about the various theories that have tried to explain helping behavior—"helping" in the broadest sense. The final chapter raises some important, integrative questions. What are the underlying assumptions in the various theories of helping behavior, altruism, and sympathy? What predictions can these theories make? And for which do they have empirical support? Which data are hard for the theories to handle? Finally, do we need a special theory of helping behavior, or can this phenomenon be integrated into one of the existing behavioral science theories? And, most important of all, how can this process lead to new questions and new attempts at empirical resolutions?

Perhaps this book has another purpose, too. Perhaps a review of what the behavioral sciences have to say about altruism, sympathy, and helping will cause a reappraisal of what the behavioral sciences have to say about the behavioral sciences and the quality of social life.

REFERENCES

Darwin, C. *The descent of man and selection in relation to sex.* New York: Appleton, 1871. (Reprinted New York: Modern Library, no date given.)

Hume, D. *A treatise of human nature.* London, 1739. (Reprinted London: Oxford University Press, 1968.)

Nagle, T. *The possibility of altruism.* Oxford: Clarendon, 1970.

Mercer, P. *Sympathy and ethics.* Oxford: Clarendon, 1972.

Smith, A. The theory of moral sentiments. In H. Schneider (Ed.), *Adam Smith's moral and political philosophy.* New York: Hafner, 1948.

Titchener, E. *Lectures on the experimental psychology of the thought processes.* New York: Macmillan, 1909.

Trivers, R. The evolution of reciprocal altruism. *Quarterly Review of Biology,* 1971, *46,* 35–57.

Wilson, E. *Sociobiology: The new synthesis.* Cambridge: Harvard University Press, 1975.

Wispé, L. Sympathy and empathy. In E. Shills (Ed.), *International encyclopedia of the social sciences,* Vol. 15. New York: Macmillan & Free Press, 1968.

ALTRUISM, SYMPATHY, AND HELPING

Psychological and Sociological Principles

Introduction

LAUREN WISPÉ

Let us face the issue squarely. At one's own peril is the power of hedonism denied. Most people most of the time, given the opportunity to choose and knowing the consequences of their actions, will choose to avoid pain, suffering, and discomfort. The roots of psychological learning theory are firmly planted in the dictum that "pleasure stamps in, and pain stamps out." Only when the consequences of pain presently endured are such that they are expected to lead to a more advantageous state of affairs in the future will that alternative be selected. Otherwise we consider a person who chooses pain over pleasure, discomfort over comfort, suffering over contentment, to be neurotic, a fool, a saint—or in love. But this argument offers us an immediate, and too facile, explanation for all the kinds of behaviors subsumed by the title of this volume. William James long ago dispatched this point of view. "Some form of sympathy," he wrote, "that of mother with child, for example, are surely primitive, and not intelligent forecasts of board and lodging

1

and other support to be reaped in old age [1950, p. 410]." In other words, not all altruistic behavior is motivated by ulterior motives.

But let us consider history. There is still another hedonistic explanation for altruistic, sympathetic helping behavior—the desire to be morally superior. Self-righteousness is a powerful goad. And exceeding the moral norms is an automatic way to achieve moral one-up-manship. This explanation is usually couched in terms of "self-reward," but the mechanisms are similar, if not identical. In Chapter 5 of the present volume, however, Rosenhan questions the value of the "self-reward" concept. It may explain more than is observed, he says, and so it may be circular. Therefore, "self-rewards," or the knowledge that one has done a good deed, may also not be sufficient explanations for altruistic, sympathetic behavior.

There is, however, another approach to explaining selfless behavior; accept it at face value. Psychological hedonism—briefly argued above— maintains that altruism is an epiphenomenon. What appears to be self-less behavior is really motivated by self-interests. For the True Believer, all behavior is self-oriented, and proving otherwise can be as frustrating as trying to prove the Null hypothesis. Hedonism is the natural enemy of altruism. Moreover, for quite some time (Wispé, 1974) there was little empirical research and few theoretical discussions with which to counter the hedonistic arguments. Of course, anthropologists (see Cohen, Chapter 4) and sociologists have long acknowledged that even the most primitive forms of society are marked by some kind of cooperation and that some ameliorative institutions are necessary for social survival. Cohen notes that the Hobbesian idea of a "war of all against all" is an idea, not a fact. But psychological hedonism has had an enormous influence in the behavioral sciences (Allport, 1968), especially in America. Parenthetically, one reason for this influence might be worth mentioning. Hedonism—in the form of pleasure and pain—lent itself readily to any drive-reduction theory, and these kinds of theories became the most important ones in American experimental psychology. Although it is difficult to interpret events going on before one's very eyes, this situation seems to be changing.

In the first place, there was in one decade the happy confluence of the works of six major behavioral scientists concerned with positive forms of social behavior: Gouldner (1960), with his classic article on "reciprocity norms"; Berkowitz (for example, Berkowitz & Daniels, 1963; Daniels & Berkowitz, 1963), with references too numerous to mention, who established the legitimacy of investigating helping behavior in the psychological laboratory; Campbell (1965), who had the temerity to use the term "altruism" in psychology; Aronfreed's (1968) thorough study of sympathy in children; and Latané and Darley (1970), whose ingenious work on the unresponsive bystander captured the imagination of scores of scientists in all the behavioral science fields. In the second place, there were also important social forces operating at about the same time; to mention only a few, there was the period of political activism by both students and their professors, various experiments in communal living, a resurgence of the peace movement, the impact of humanistic philosophies, and a growing emphasis upon cognitive psychology. By the end of the 1960s, therefore, the names in the game had begun to change. There had always been studies of sympathy (e.g., Murphy, 1937) and cooperation (e.g., Mead, 1937), but now terms like "aiding," "attraction," "charity," "friendship," "helping," "sharing," and "trust" began appearing in the literature. Trying to find a word to characterize this research can be a sticky wick, but, in order to avoid jargon, let us agree to call it research on "positive" social behavior—without any connotations that research on positive behavior is better than research on negative behavior (Wispé, 1972).

In addition to the works mentioned above, there are two excellent collections. The book by Macaulay and Berkowitz (1970) admirably presented "the state of the art" at that time. And the book by Likona (1976) emphasizes aspects of moral development. The mission of the present volume is different from that of any of the books mentioned. It began with the *Journal of Social Issues*, Volume 28, Number 3 (1972), which dealt with "Positive Forms of Social Behavior," some of which has been used and modified. The purpose of this book is to bring to bear on the area of positive behavior—altruism, sympathy, and helping–quite different theoretical analyses and explanations. These theoretical confrontations, and the reinterpretation of considerable empirical data, will lead, hopefully, to further research and even to a more integrative theory within which altruism, sympathy, and helping will have a more central role.

It would not be possible, obviously, to include in one volume all the current theories of helping behavior. Many of these theories, such as the Just World hypothesis and bystander intervention research, have already been summarized, and little would be gained by yet another presentation. Nevertheless, both of these theories are briefly discussed. There are also several other theories that have not yet had time to generate enough research to warrant an inclusive, critical chapter. Any endeavor of this kind must be selective. But the most important motivational theories of helping behavior are presented in this volume, and among these chapters are several interesting and unique developments, some of which are discussed below. In fact, this volume can be read as a detailed analysis of the reasons, research, and theories about *why* people help.

This volume offers a discussion at three levels. Part I examines the possibilities for the origins of altruism. Part II moves to a more sociological and psychological discussion of the development and maintenance of positive behaviors. Part III presents some of the social and legal implications of helping. By way of briefly summarizing each of the chapters, let us turn to an overview of each of these parts.

The chapters in Part I juxtapose some arguments and some evidence for the biological as opposed to the sociocultural basis for altruism and cooperation. The basic theoretical question was first examined by Haldane (1932) and Wright (1945), but there has been a recrudescence of the question with Wilson's (1975) work. Wilson argues for the possibility of some kind of genetic evolution of altruism, because altruism in some way increases the genetic fitness of the species. Although developments in this field have been rapid, Wilson's position remains intact. The rest of the chapters in Part I—by a psychologist (Campbell), a political scientist (Masters), and an anthropologist (Cohen)—all take issue with Wilson in one way or another. Campbell argues cogently for the social evolution of altruism. The factor of genetic competition for procreative opportunities, Campbell reasons, cannot provide the felicitous occasion for the furtherance of altruism. Masters maintains that Campbell's analogizing is in error. Natural selection can account for altruism, because the traits that make for intraspecies dominance and reproductive success can include at least some forms of altruism. Masters's chapter (Chapter 3) has another side to it, too. He also points out that this is an old problem for political scientists; namely, what is the nature of human nature? If evil, what kinds of social institutions are necessary to contain man's essential hedonism? Interestingly enough, Kaplan, a lawyer, re-engages this problem in Chapter 14. Finally Cohen, in Chapter 4, supports Campbell. Cohen feels that sympathy and altruism are culturally determined, and he offers several cross-cultural analyses of both phenomena. For some reason, altruism, sympathy, and helping have not been considered cross-culturally. Cohen's discussion is a rich source for instances of cultural differences in helping behavior. And he makes an especially important point in this connection; that is, that all helping is not necessarily altruistic or sympathetic. It is clear in Part I, and it becomes increasingly clear throughout this volume, that the authors are often talking about different aspects of the altruism—helping problem. And in Part I, this difficulty is compounded by differences between human and lower forms of behavior. But for the most part, the focus of the discussion, the theorizing, is at the genetic level.

The chapters in Part II try to redress the balance. They offer various psychologically-oriented explanations for altruism, sympathy, and helping. Rosenhan (Chapter 5) explores some of the problems inherent in a learning-theory explanation of helping. From Ward (1883) he borrows the phrase "altruistic paradox" to explore what rewards behavior that is supposed to be selfless. He refers to affective amplification and self-rewards. The latter are a particularly difficult problem. Self-rewards, as he says, can explain more than is observed. The same problem arises again in the Hatfield, Walster, and Piliavin (Chapter 6) discussion of Equity theory, for there is a hidden reinforcement in Equity theory. This chapter presents a subtle denial of the basic definition of altruism while at the same time explaining—or Rosenhan would probably say, explaining away—so many of the empirical results. In Chapter 7, Krebs takes a more cognitive–developmental approach to helping, but only after a strong criticism of approaches—like learning theory—which fail to consider the meaning of the situation for the actor. In some ways, Kreb's chapter and Chapter 8 by Ekstein offer a short, but trenchant, discussion of the deficiencies in the positions advocated by both Rosenhan and Hatfield *et al.* Hornstein (Chapter 9) adapts Lewinian theory to present his Promotive Tension theory of helping. Like Krebs, Hornstein is considerably more cognitively oriented. But, unlike Krebs, he does not criticize the noncognitive approaches. Rather, in a step-like manner he develops the conditions that facilitate helping behavior. This involves the perception of the person in need of help as included in a social categorization such that the needs or goals of the needy person can be internalized by the potential helper. Hornstein refers to these as "we groups." Some of the factors predisposing a person to the perception of "we groups" are discussed by Ekstein. Ekstein especially stresses the importance of early childhood parental support. Lück in Chapter 10 discusses the generalizability of some research in this area. This is important, because culture has not been included as a variable in many of these studies. It is assumed, but never tested, that these results can be replicated in other cultures. Social psychology has done too little of this kind of transnational, cross-cultural research, and Lück presents a needed discussion of some of the difficulties, as well as some of the empirical results, of research done in Germany. The important point is how transnational research can enrich our understanding of helping behavior.

Into this happy confluence Part III introduces some contradictory and embarrassing argument. The chapters in Part III are more sociologically oriented, although the problems begin in Part II with Weitman, the only one who is identifiable as a sociologist. Weitman (Chapter 11) is concerned with acts of social exclusion. Every act of social inclusion, he says, involves reciprocally an act of social exclusion. Helping some people means that others are not being helped. Unless properly channeled, Weitman argues, the inevitable frustrations of being excluded can lead to violent outrage.

Every book which tries to focus a collective attack upon a particular problem needs several chapters which question the fundamental premises upon which the book is based. Implicit in the chapters so far has been the notion that "helping is good and we ought to learn how to make more of it." Good sociologists must see immediately the difficulty in this position. Ever since the research on relative deprivation, they have realized that the opportunities for status disequilibrium are almost limitless. And so Weitman turns the argument around. Helping, he maintains, is not always and absolutely good. Skinner, in Chapter 12, turns the argument on its head; not only is helping not always a good thing, but, indeed, it can be a bad thing. Helping, Skinner argues, leads to a sense of possessiveness, rather than a sense of acquisition. It will not do just to help people. Society should institute programs to help people help themselves. Totalitarian governments, Skinner says, provide for their citizens the necessities of life; but the price, loss of freedom, is too high. This chapter will probably earn Skinner a few more angry reprisals from those who disagree with his philosophy, his psychology, or both. But he steadfastly refuses to disabuse himself of the notion that behavioral scientists have a responsibility for the world in which they live.

The remaining two chapters in Part III move to a practical level. Lenrow critically examines institutionalized helping roles, and Kaplan provides some sparkling and informative comments on the legal aspects of helping. Both chapters are unique. In Chapter 13, Lenrow returns to the analysis of folk helping roles begun by Cohen in Chapter 4. But Lenrow's purpose is different. His analysis of folk helping provides an informed basis for some critical comments on current ameliorative programs. In this regard he is like Skinner. Such programs, Lenrow says, may provide certain necessities, but they preclude the emergence of self-respect, without which the very point of helping is lost. Lenrow then extends his analysis. From folk helping roles one can learn techniques and procedures for more efficacious professional helping by psychotherapists, social workers, remedial specialists, even physicians. There is one particular aspect of Lenrow's analysis that must be mentioned. Whether in folk or in professional helping roles, there are certain inevitable tensions. Deriving, perhaps, from the asymmetrical distribution of power on the one hand and need on the other, the equality (Lenrow) or the equity (Hatfield *et al.*) that is necessary in genuine—as opposed to neurotic (Ekstein, Chapter 8)—helping is always precariously balanced. Finally, in Chapter 14, Kaplan, trained as a lawyer, raises some provocative questions about helping and the law. The message is that a person can get into trouble for helping someone else. When difficult social problems arise, America seems to have two knee-jerk responses— pass a law, and then throw a lot of money at it. Lenrow and Skinner, especially, speak to the danger of misappropriating resources. Kaplan's chapter is intended to speak to those who imagine that Good Samaritan and similar laws will reduce crime and increase good will. It won't work, says Kaplan; at least, not the way one expects. And finally, as if to return full circle to the title of this volume, Kaplan asks, if laws were passed to make helping obligatory, would it any longer be altruistic? A nice question.

By now it should be clear that no single theoretical approach fully explains the phenomenon under discussion. Nor is the time ripe for an integrative theory of positive behaviors. But perhaps some new questions will arise, or old questions will be put in new ways, by using altruism, sympathy, and helping as focal points for an integrative discussion. Chapter 15 makes a few steps in this direction. In this chapter, the various thoretical contributions are juxtaposed, examined, and compared in detail. The strengths and weakness of various empirical results are considered. And, perhaps, things are seen in a slightly different way. Chapter 15 also emphasizes the importance of cognition in theories where this has not been clear. Finally, this chapter discusses again the importance of the topic—altruism, sympathy, and helping—for the behavioral sciences.

REFERENCES

Allport, G. The historical background of modern social psychology. In G. Lindzey & E. Aronson (Eds.), *The handbook of social psychology*. Reading, Mass.: Addison-Wesley, 1968, Pp. 1–80.

Aronfreed, J. *Conduct and conscience*. New York: Academic, 1968.

Berkowitz, L., & Daniels, L. Responsibility and dependency. *Journal of Abnormal and Social Psychology*, 1963, *66*, 429–437.

Campbell, D. Ethnocentrism and other altruistic motives. In D. Levine (Ed.), *Nebraska symposium on motivation*. Lincoln: Nebraska Press, 1965.

Daniels, L., & Berkowitz, L. Liking and response to dependency relations. *Human Relations*, 1963, *16*, 141–148.

Gouldner, A. The norm of reciprocity: A preliminary statement. *American Sociological Review*, 1960, *25*, 161–178.

Haldane, J. *The causes of evolution*. London: Longmans, Greene, 1932.

James, W. *The principles of psychology.* New York: Holt, 1890. (Reprinted, New York: Dover Publications, 1950)

Latané, B., & Darley, J. *The unresponsive bystander: Why doesn't he help?* New York: Appleton, 1970.

Likona, T. (Ed.). *Moral development and behavior.* New York: Holt, Rinehart and Winston, 1976.

Macaulay, J., & Berkowitz, L. (Eds.). *Altruism and helping behavior.* New York: Academic, 1970.

Mead, M. *Cooperation and competition among primitive people.* New York: McGraw-Hill, 1937.

Murphy, M. *Social behavior and child personality.* New York: Columbia, 1937.

Ward, L. *Dynamic sociology: Or applied social science as based on statistical sociology and the less complex sciences.* New York: Appleton, 1883.

Wilson, E. *Sociobiology: The new synthesis.* Cambridge: Harvard Press, 1975.

Wispé, L. Positive forms of social behavior: An overview. *The Journal of Social Issues,* 1972, *28,* 1–19.

Wispé, L. The yin and yang of psychological research: An analysis of studies of positive and negative forms of social behavior. Paper presented at the American Psychological Association meetings, New Orleans, 1974.

Wright, G. Tempo and mode in evolution: A critical review. *Ecology,* 1945, *26,* 415–419.

I

BIOLOGICAL AND SOCIAL BASES OF ALTRUISM AND SYMPATHY

1

The Genetic Evolution of Altruism[1]

EDWARD O. WILSON

Altruism is ordinarily defined as self-destructive behavior performed for the benefit of others. Evolutionary biologists define it more strictly as behavior that enhances the personal genetic fitness of others at the cost of genetic fitness on the part of the altruist; the altruist either reduces its own survival capacity, or curtails its own reproduction, or both. The theoretical problem created by the existence of widespread altruism is the following: How can the genes determining an altruistic trait, or at least permitting the development of the trait, persist in a species if they are seemingly disadvantageous? The answer in a nutshell is that they are not really at a disadvantage. So long as the beneficiaries of the

[1] Adapted by the author and reprinted by permission of the publishers from *Sociobiology: The New Synthesis* by Edward O. Wilson, Cambridge, Massachusetts: The Belknap Press of Harvard University Press, copyright © 1975 by the President and Fellows of Harvard College. The author's personal research has been supported by National Science Foundation Grant No. GB 40247.

altruism themselves carry some of the altruistic genes, and so long as the benefit they receive permits them to multiply those genes to a more than compensating degree, the genes will increase in the population as a whole, and the altruistic behavior will spread. In short, altruism can be most readily evolved by some form of group selection. This simple proposition has been ramified by biologists to explain a wide array of previously disparate behavioral phenomena.

KIN AND INTERPOPULATION SELECTION

Selection is often called *group selection* when it affects sets of individuals beyond parents and their progeny. We can delimit various of these groups at a lower level of organization: a set of sibs, parents, and their offspring; a close-knit tribe of families related by at least the degree of third cousin; and so on. If selection operates in such a way as to affect the frequency of genes shared by common descent in relatives, the process is referred to as kin selection. The defining requirement is that the action of an individual affects not only its own survival and reproduction but, in ways that may be complex and highly specific, the survival and reproduction of other members of the population who share identical genes by common descent, that is, kin. It is rather imprecise to refer to this particular process as group selection, since what is involved is not the extinction and reproduction of the kin as a discrete group in opposition to other such groups, but rather the differential multiplication of genes shared by common descent through the kin-directed actions of individuals. At a higher level, an entire breeding population may be the unit, so that populations possessing different genotypes are extinguished differentially, or disseminate different numbers of colonists, in which case we speak of interpopulation (or inter-demic) selection. The expression *interdemic* should be used only where the population is in fact considered a deme, that is, where breeding occurs randomly throughout the population. The ascending levels of selection are visualized in Figure 1. The concept of group selection was introduced by Darwin in *The Origin of Species* to account for the evolution of sterile castes in social insects. The term *intergroup selection*, in the sense of interpopulation selection as defined here, was used by Sewall Wright in 1945. Essentially the same expression (*Gruppenauslese*) was used independently and with the same meaning by Olavi Kalela (1954, 1957), whereas the phrase *kin selection* was coined by J. Maynard Smith (1964). The classification adopted here is approximately that recommended by J. L. Brown (1966). Selection can also operate at the

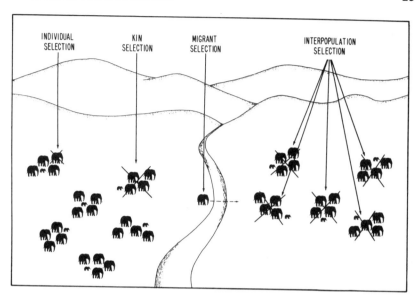

Figure 1. Ascending levels of selection. Selection beyond the level of the individual, sometimes referred to loosely as group selection, consists of either kin selection, in which the unit is a set of related individuals, or interpopulation selection, in which entire populations are diminished or extinguished at different rates. The differential tendency to disperse is referred to as migrant selection. (From Wilson, 1975.)

level of species or entire clusters of related species. This process, well known to paleontologists and biogeographers, is responsible for the familiar patterns of dynastic succession of major groups such as ammonites, sharks, graptolites, and dinosaurs through geologic time (Darlington, 1971; Simpson, 1953). It is even possible to conceive of the differential extinction of entire ecosystems, involving all trophic levels (Dunbar, 1960, 1972). However, selection at these highest levels is not likely to be important in the evolution of altruism, for the following simple reason. In order to counteract individual selection, it is necessary to have population extinction rates of comparable magnitude. New species are not created at a sufficiently fast pace to be tested in this manner, at least not when the species are so genetically divergent as those ordinarily studied by the biogeographers. The same restriction applies a fortiori to ecosystems.

Pure kin and pure interdemic selection are the two poles at the ends of a gradient of selection of ever-enlarging nested sets of related individuals. They are sufficiently different as to require different forms of mathematical models, and their outcomes are qualitatively different.

Depending on the behavior of the individual organisms and their rate of dispersal between societies, the transition zone between kin selection and interpopulation selection for most species probably occurs when the group is large enough to contain somewhere on the order of 10 to 100 individuals. At that range one reaches the upper limit of family size and passes to groups of families. One also finds the upper bound in the number of group members one animal can remember and with whom it can therefore establish personal bonds. Finally, 10 to 100 is the range in which the effective population numbers of a great many vertebrate species fall. Thus, aggregations of more than 100 are genetically fragmented, and the geometry of their distribution is important to their microevolution.

INTERPOPULATION SELECTION

A cluster of populations belonging to the same species may be called a metapopulation. The metapopulation is most fruitfully conceived of as an amebalike entity spread over a fixed number of patches (Levins, 1970). At any moment of time a given patch may contain a population or not; empty patches are occasionally colonized by immigrants that form new populations, and old populations occasionally become extinct, leaving empty patches. If $P(t)$ is the proportion of patches which support populations at time t, m is the proportion receiving migrants in an instant of time (whether already occupied or not), and $\overline{E}$ is the proportion of populations becoming extinct in an instant of time:

$$dP/dt = mg(P) - \overline{E}P.$$

The function $g(P)$ must decrease with the proportion of sites already occupied, a relation that can exist in the simple logistic form

$$dP/dt = mP(1 - P) - \overline{E}P.$$

At equilibrium the proportion of occupied patches is

$$P = 1 - (\overline{E}/m),$$

where the metapopulation as a whole can persist only if $\overline{E} < m$. Thus the system is metaphorically viewed through evolutionary time as a nexus of patches, each patch winking into life as a population colonizes it and winking out again as extinction occurs. At equilibrium the rate of winking and the number of occupied sites are constant, despite the fact that the pattern of occupancy is constantly shifting. This imagery can be translated into reality only when the observer is able to delimit real Mendelian populations in the system.

In considering interpopulation selection, it is important to distinguish the timing of the extinction event in the history of the populations (Figure 2). There are two moments at which extinction is most likely: at the very beginning, when the colonists are struggling to establish a hold on the site, and soon after the population has reached (or exceeded) the carrying capacity of the site, when it is in most danger of crashing from starvation or destruction of the habitat. The former event can be called r extinction and the latter K extinction. This is in appreciation of the close parallel to the dichotomy between r and K selection, in which r selection refers to an opportunistic strategy and K selection to certain steady, stable characteristics. When populations are more subject to r extinction, altruist traits favored by group selection are likely to be of the "pioneer" variety. They will lead to clustering of the little population, mutual defense against enemies, and cooperative foraging and nest building. The ruling principle will be the maximum *average* survival and fertility of the group as a whole; in other words, the maximization of r. In K extinction the opposite is true. The premium is now on "urban qualities" that keep population size below dangerous levels. Extreme pressure from density-dependent controls of an external nature is avoided. Mutual aid is minimized, and personal restraint in the forms of underutilization of the habitat and birth control comes to the fore (see Gadgil, 1975).

Very young, growing populations are likely to consist of individuals

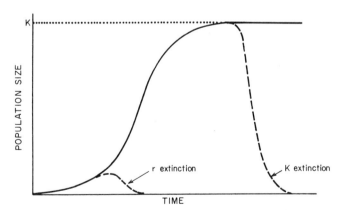

Figure 2. Extinction of a population probably most commonly occurs at an early stage of its growth, particularly when the first colonists are trying to establish a foothold (r extinction), or after the capacity of the environment has been reached or exceeded and a crash occurs (K extinction). The consequences in evolution are potentially radically different. (From Wilson, 1973.)

who are closely related. Interpopulation selection by r extinction is therefore intrinsically difficult to separate from kin selection, and in extreme cases it is probably identical with it. A second phenomenon that makes the process difficult to analyze is genetic drift, which is the random fluctuation in gene frequencies during the segregation and recombination of genes in the sexual process. In populations of 10 or so individuals drift can completely swamp out the overall effect of differential extinction within the metapopulation. For these reasons analysis has been concentrated on larger populations, and the most general results obtained are more easily applicable to interpopulation selection by K extinction.

Our current understanding of counteracting interpopulation selection can be most clearly understood if approached through its historical development. In 1932 Haldane constructed a general theory with a few elements that are equally applicable to kin and interpopulation selection. He thought he could dimly see how altruistic traits increase in populations.

> A study of these traits involves the consideration of small groups. For a character of this type can only spread through the population if the genes determining it are borne by a group of related individuals whose chances of leaving offspring are increased by the presence of these genes in an individual member of the group whose own private viability they lower [p. 207].

Haldane went on to prove that the process is feasible if the groups are small enough for altruists to confer a quick advantage. He saw that the altruism could be stable in a metapopulation if the genes were fixed in individual groups by drift made possible by the small size of the groups or at least of the new populations founded by some of their emigrants. For some reason Haldane overlooked the role of differential population extinction, which might have led him to the next logical step in developing a full theory.

A separate thread of thought winds from Wahlund's principle (1926) to the development by Sewall Wright in the 1930s and 1940s of the "island model" of population genetics. For a formal, comprehensive review of the subject the reader is referred to the second volume of Wright's recent treatise (1969). The island model was related explicitly to the evolution of altruistic behavior by Wright in his 1945 essay review of G. G. Simpson's *Tempo and Mode in Evolution*. The formulation was nearly identical to that of Haldane, although made independently of it. Wright conceived of a set of populations diverging by genetic drift and adaptation to local environments but exchanging genes with one another. The pattern is that which Wright has persistently argued to be the greatest creative factor of all in evolution. In the special case considered here, the disadvantageous (for example, altruistic) genes can prevail over all the metapopulation if the populations they aid are small enough to allow them to drift to high values and if the aided populations thereby send out a disproportionate number of emigrants. Like Haldane, Wright did not consider the effect of differential extinction on the equilibrial metapopulation. Nor did the model come any closer to a full theory of altruistic evolution. It is a curious twist that when W. D. Hamilton re-initiated group selection theory 20 years later, he was inspired not by the island model but by Wright's studies of relationship and inbreeding, which led to the topic of kin selection.

The next step in the study of interpopulation selection was taken by ecologists largely unaware of genetic theory. Kalela (1954, 1957) postu-lated group selection as the mechanism responsible for reproductive restraint in subarctic vole populations. He saw food shortages as the ulti-mate controlling factor but believed that self-control of the populations during times of food plenty prevented starvation during food shortages. Kalela correctly deduced that self-control in matters of individual fitness can only be evolved if the groups not possessing the genes for self-control are periodically decimated or extinguished as a direct consequence of their lack of self-control. Kalela added one more feature to his scheme that substantially increased its plausibility. He suggested that rodent populations in many cases really consist of expanded family groups, so that self-restraint is the way for genetically allied tribes to hold their ground while other tribes of the same species eat themselves into extinc-tion. In other words, the most forceful mode of interpopulation selection is one that approaches a special form of kin selection. Kalela believed that the same kind of population structure and group selection might characterize many other rodents, ungulates, and primates. Independent but similar views were briefly expressed by Snyder (1961) and by Brere-ton (1962).

It remained for Wynne-Edwards in his book *Animal Dispersion in Relation to Social Behaviour* (1962) to bring the subject to the attention of a wide audience of biologists. Wynne-Edwards' contribution was to carry the theory of self-control by group selection to its extreme—some of his critics would say to the reductio ad absurdum—thereby forcing an evaluation of its strengths and weaknesses.

> Food may be the *ultimate* factor, but it cannot be invoked as the *proximate* agent in chopping the numbers, without disastrous consequences. By analogy with human experience we should therefore look to see whether there is not some natural counterpart of the limitation-agreements that provide man with his only known remedy against over-fishing—some kind of density-dependent convention, it would have to be, based on the

quantity of food available but "artificially" preventing the intensity of exploitation from rising above the optimum level. Such a convention, if it existed, would have not only to be closely linked with the food situation, and highly (or better still perfectly) density-dependent in its operation, but, thirdly, also capable of eliminating the direct contest in hunting which has proved so destructive and extravagant in human experience [p. 11].

The governing phrases in this scheme are "limitation-agreements" and "conventions." Social conventions are devices by which individual animals curtail their own individual fitness, that is, their survivorship or fertility or both, to promote group survival. The density-dependent effects cited by Wynne-Edwards as involving social conventions run virtually the entire gamut: lowered fertility, reduced status in hierarchies, abandonment or direct killing of offspring, endocrine stress, deferment of growth and maturity. Sacrifice in each of these categories is viewed as an individual contribution to maintain populations below crash levels. Much of social behavior was reinterpreted by Wynne-Edwards to be epideictic displays, which he defined as the modes of communication by which members of populations inform each other of the density of the population as a whole and therefore the degree to which each member should decrease its own individual fitness. Examples of epideictic displays (which are distinguished from the epigamic displays by which animals court one another in the breeding season) include the formation of mating swarms by insects, flocking in birds, and even the vertical migration of zooplankton. The displays, then, are the most evolved communicative part of social conventions.

There has been a good deal of confusion, especially among nonbiologists, over just what Wynne-Edwards had said that was different. He himself later stated (1971), "Seven years ago I put forward the hypothesis that social behavior plays an essential part in the natural regulation of animal numbers [p. 267]." That is not correct. The role of social behavior in population regulation is an old one and was never in dispute. What Wynne-Edwards proposed was the specific hypothesis that animals voluntarily sacrifice personal survival and fertility in order to help control population growth. He also postulated that this is a very widespread phenomenon among all kinds of animals. Furthermore, he did not stop at kin groups, as had Kalela, but suggested that the mechanism operates in Mendelian populations of all sizes, representing all breeding structures. Alternative hypotheses explaining social phenomena, such as nuptial synchronization, antipredation, and increased feeding efficiency, were either summarily dismissed or altogether ignored.

Wynne-Edwards' book had considerable value as the stalking-horse that drew forth large numbers of biologists, including theoreticians, who addressed themselves at last to the serious issues of group selection and genetic social evolution. It is also fair to say that in the long series of reviews and fresh studies that followed, culminating in G. C. Williams' *Adaptation and Natural Selection* (1966), one after another of Wynne-Edwards' propositions about specific conventions and epideictic displays was knocked down on evidential grounds or at least matched with competing hypotheses of equal plausibility drawn from models of individual selection. But for a long time neither critics nor sympathizers could answer the main theoretical question raised by this controversy. What are the deme sizes, interdemic migration rates, and differential deme survival probabilities necessary to counter the effects of individual selection? Only when population genetics was extended this far could we hope to evaluate the significance of extinction rates and to rule out one or the other of the various competing hypotheses in particular cases. Substantial progress toward construction of a rigorous dynamic theory has been made only in the past decade.

The Levins Model

As we have seen, Levins (1970) conceived of a metapopulation occupying various fractions of a fixed number of habitable sites. Each population is subject to extinction but also has the opportunity to send forth N propagules to colonize previously empty sites. Now suppose there is an altruist gene occurring at a variable frequency x in each of the occupied sites. The proportion of populations containing exactly x altruist genes at time t will be denoted as $F(x, t)$, the overall gene frequency for the metapopulation as $\bar{x}$, the extinction rate of a population with x altruist genes as $E(x)$, and the mean extinction rate for all the populations as $\bar{E}$. Also, the frequency of the altruist gene in a founding group of N individuals is indicated as $N(x, \bar{x})$, and the rate at which individual selection reduces the gene frequency within a population as $M(x)$. The rate at which the proportion of populations with x gene changes through time is

$$dF(x, t)/dt = -E(x)F(x, t) + \bar{E}N(x, \bar{x}) + d/dx\,[M(x)F(x, t)].$$

This equation says that the proportion of populations in the metapopulation containing x altruist genes is declining because of extinction of such populations at the rate $-E(x)F(x, t)$, where $E(x)$ is a generally declining function of x; that is, the more altruist genes there are, the lower the extinction rate. The equation also states that $F(x, t)$ is simultaneously changing because of new sites being colonized by groups of propagules with gene frequency x. When the proportion of sites occupied is at equilibrium, the proportion being newly occupied in each instant of time is $\overline{E}$, the proportion becoming extinct. Each population is founded by N individuals; the frequency of the altruist gene in these founder populations, which we designate $N(x, \overline{x})$, varies at random according to a binomial distribution around the metapopulation mean $\overline{x}$. In other words, the metapopulation is the source of the N migrants who found each new colony, and x, the frequency of the altruist genes among these founders, is a random variable dependent on N and $\overline{x}$. $N(x, \overline{x})$ is the binomial distribution (which can be approximated by the normal) of the gene frequencies in all founding populations, and the rate at which the altruist gene is changing because of colony foundation is therefore $\overline{E}N(x, \overline{x})$. $F(x, t)$ is also decreasing because of individual selection. By itself, each population has its gene frequency reduced toward zero by individual selection.

The rate of change of the frequency of the altruist gene through the entire metapopulation is the mean of rates of change in all the constituent populations:

$$\frac{d\overline{x}}{dt} = \int_0^1 x \, \frac{dF(x, t)}{dt} \, dx$$

Levins' approach to the problem was to write parallel equations for the variance and higher central moments of the populations with reference to the gene frequency. Then $E(x)$ was expanded in Taylor series to obtain $E(0)$, the extinction rate of populations containing no altruists, and $E'(0)$, the rate at which the extinction rate declines as the first altruist genes are added. The easiest procedure was next to analyze the set of simultaneous equations for stability, where $x = 0$ and $E(x) = E(0)$. If a set of values for the individual selection intensity and other parameters yields instability in the ensuing matrix analysis, the implication is that x will move away from zero. In other words, the altruist gene will increase in frequency.

When selection is additive, the system is stable near $\overline{x} = 0$ if

$$-E'(0) < (N - 1)s + [2Ns^2/E(0)].$$

Analysis of this inequality shows that even if group selection, measured by $E'(0)$, is stronger than individual selection, measured by s, the selection coefficient, the best it can do is to establish the altruist gene in a polymorphic state within the metapopulation. Prospects are better if the altruist gene is dominant. When the altruist gene is fixed to start with

$(\bar{x} = 1)$, then stability is achieved, and the gene remains fixed, provided that

$$-E'(1) > s,$$

in other words, if the rate at which the altruist gene improves group survival as $\bar{x}$ approaches fixation is greater than the selection coefficient (see Figure 3). When $\bar{x} = 0$, stability is abolished, and the altruist gene begins to increase in frequency, provided that the following inequality exists:

$$E'(0) > (N - 2)s + [2Ns^2/E(\bar{x})].$$

In general, if $E' < s$ for any initial value of x, individual selection will prevail, and the altruist gene will be reduced toward zero or at least toward the mutational equilibrium. It is also necessary, in both the additive and dominance cases, to have a sufficiently high overall population extinction rate, measured by $E(0)$ or $E(\bar{x})$, to compensate for $2Ns^2$ in the righthand term of the inequality.

The Levins model advanced theory fundamentally by identifying and formalizing the parameters of extinction, relating them to migrant and individual selection, and introducing the technique of stability

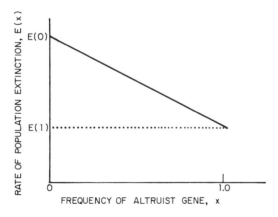

Figure 3. Group selection favoring an altruist gene. In this simplest possible model the rate of population extinction declines linearly as the frequency of the altruist gene in each population increases. The intensity of group selection is measured in two ways: first, by the extinction rates at various values of x, for example $E(x) = E(0)$, or $E(x) = E(\bar{x})$, the average extinction rate for all values of x; second, by the rate at which an increase in x lowers $E(x)$. In the elementary case depicted here, $E'(0) = E'(1)$. (From Wilson, 1973.)

analysis to provide broad qualitative results. Recently, B. R. Levin and W. L. Kilmer (1974) extended Richard Levins' model by studying similar island-model metapopulations with computer simulations. They realized that only by specifying the actual frequency distributions through time $(F(x, t))$ would it be possible to design studies of real populations. Their experimental runs are stochastic processes in which fixed values are assigned to the individual selection coefficients, the extinction rates of the populations, and the rates at which individuals migrate between populations. The populations were specified as being either fixed or allowed to grow. The results so far are at least qualitatively consistent with the inequalities produced by Richard Levins' model. The advantage of the stimulation technique is its potential realism—it is rather easily modified to accommodate special properties encountered in actual populations. The disadvantage, as in most simulation procedures, is the difficulty in defining the boundary conditions within which the phenomenon of interest can occur.

The Boorman–Levitt Model

S. A. Boorman and P. R. Levitt (1972, 1973a) made a second study with the same goal of predicting the outcome of evolution by group selection. In order to characterize analytically the full course of evolution, they envisaged a particular metapopulation structure different from that of Levins, consisting of a large, enduring central population and a set of marginal populations more liable to extinction. The altruist genes present in the marginal populations do not come to affect the population extinction rates until the populations have reached their demographically stable size and individual selection does not operate in the marginal populations. Hence the Boorman–Levitt system allows for K extinction, whereas the Levins system more closely approximates the conditions that promote r extinction. Although Boorman and Levitt chose this particular structure in part for its analytic tractability, it was a biologically happy choice as well. Many real metapopulations do in fact consist of large, stable "source" populations occupying the ecologically favorable portion of the range and groups of smaller, semiisolated populations near the periphery of the range. The peripheral populations are more liable to extinction not only because of their smaller size but also because they more often exist in less favorable habitats.

The Boorman–Levitt model can be regarded as the mode of pure populational selection by means of K extinction that is the most likely to counteract individual selection. Its principal result is the demonstration that extinction of a severe and peculiar form is required to elevate significantly the frequencies of altruist genes—or of any other kinds of genes favored by group selection and opposed by individual selection. In particular, the extinction operator $E(x)$ must approach a step function, of the kind illustrated in Figure 4, in order to work. When it does work, the achievement comes after a close race between the rise of the frequency of the altruist gene in the metapopulation and the total extinction of the metapopulation. In order for the altruist gene to approach a frequency of 20 or 30%, most of the constituent populations must become extinct. Also, as suggested by Levins' model, the best the metapopulation can attain when starting from low frequencies is polymorphism between the altruist and nonaltruist genes.

In summary, deductions from these two special models agree, thus pointing to the conclusion that evolution of an altruist gene by means of pure interpopulation selection based on differential population extinction is an improbable event. The metapopulation must pass through a very narrow "window" framed by strict parameter values: steeply descending extinction functions, preferably approaching a step function with a threshold value of the frequency of the altruist gene; high extinction rates comparable in magnitude (in populations per generation) to the opposing individual selection (in individuals per population per generation); and the existence of moderately large metapopulations broken into many semiisolated populations. Even after achieving all these conditions the metapopulation is likely to be no more than polymorphic for the gene.

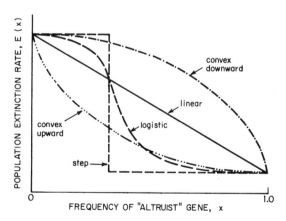

Figure 4. Various extinction rate functions that were applied in the Boorman–Levitt model. Only a steep logistic function or step function can produce a significant increase in the frequency of the altruist gene within the entire metapopulation as a result of pure interpopulation selection.

Other Models

Although the results of the formal models just summarized seem to suggest that altruistic evolution by interpopulation selection is unlikely, special circumstances are now being conceived of that might circumvent the unlikelihood. Gilpin (1975; see also May, 1975) showed that predator–prey systems can be destabilized and populations can head for quick extinction due to the appearance of only a few selfish individuals which transgress the density-dependent controls of the predator population. Thus, if in the beginning a population is stable on the basis of some form of altruistic behavior spread throughout the population, it can be eliminated by the "infection" of selfish genotypes, leaving the ground open for still-uncontaminated populations. Gilpin's system, if it exists in nature, provides the theoretical basis for high differential mortality of populations based directly on the frequency of altruistic genes. It might work in metapopulations of either the peripheral or the diffuse kinds.

There also exist special conditions under which interpopulation selection can proceed without differential population extinction and in a way that might spread altruist genes rapidly in a population. Maynard Smith (1964) suggested a model in which local populations are first segregated and then allowed to grow or to decline for a while in ways influenced by their genetic composition. Then individuals from different populations mix and interbreed to some extent before going on to form new populations. Suppose that the populations were mice in haystacks, with each haystack being colonized by a single fertilized female. If a/a are altruistic individuals, and A/A and A/a selfish individuals, the a allele would be eliminated in all haystacks where A-bearing individuals were present. But if pure a/a populations contributed more progeny in the mixing and colonizing phases, and if there were also a considerable amount of inbreeding (so that pure a/a populations were more numerous than expected by chance alone), the altruist gene would spread through the population. D. S. Wilson (1975) argues that many species in nature go through regular cycles of segregation and mixing and that altruist genes can be spread under a wide range of realistic conditions beyond the narrow one conceived by Maynard Smith. All that is required is that the absolute rate of increase of the altruists be greater. It does not matter that their rate of increase relative to the nonaltruists in the same population is (by definition) less during the period of isolation. Provided that the rate of increase of the population as a whole is enhanced enough by the presence of altruists, they will increase in frequency through the entire metapopulation. This process, which transcends the narrow restrictions of the group-extinction models, is potentially very important and needs to be investigated further both in theory and in field research.

What specific traits would interpopulation selection be expected to produce? Under some circumstances the altruism would oppose r selection. There is a fundamental tendency for genotypes that have the highest r to win in individual selection, and their advantage is enhanced in species that are opportunistic or otherwise undergo regular fluctuations in population size. But the greater the fluctuation, the higher the extinction rate. Thus interpopulation selection would tend to damp population cycles by lower fertility and by an early, altruistic sensitivity to density-dependent controls. There is also a fundamental tendency for genotypes that can sustain the highest density to prevail (K selection). But high density contaminates the environment, attracts predators, and promotes the spread of disease, all of which increase the extinction rates of entire populations. Altruism promoted by these effects might include a higher physiological sensitivity to crowding and a greater tendency to disperse, even at the cost of lowered fitness. Levins (1970) has pointed out that mixtures of genotypes in populations of fruit flies and crop plants often attain a higher equilibrium density than pure strains, but under a variety of conditions one strain excludes the others competitively. If higher densities result in the production of more propagules without incurring a greater risk of extinction to the mother population, an antagonism between group and individual selection will result. Also, genetic resistance to disease or predation often results in lowered fitness in another component, as exemplified by sickle-cell anemia. In the temporary absence of this pressure, individual selection "softens" the population as a whole, which will be disfavored in interpopulation selection when the pressure is exerted again.

It is also true, as Madhav Gadgil (1975) has pointed out, that pure interpopulation selection acting apart from kin selection can lead to exceptionally selfish and even spiteful behavior. Suppose, for example, that the particular circumstances of populational selection within a given species dictate a reduction in population growth. Then the altruist that curtails its personal reproduction might just as well spend its spare time cannibalizing other members of the population—also to the benefit of the deme as a whole. Another seemingly spiteful behavior that could be favored by K extinction is the maintenance of excessively large territories.

In spite of the broadening of interpopulation selection theory, it remains true that most of the wide array of social conventions hypothesized by Wynne-Edwards and other authors are probably nonexistent.

Moreover, self-restraint on behalf of the entire population is *least* likely in the largest, most stable populations, where social behavior is the most highly developed. Examples include the breeding colonies of seabirds, the communal roosts of starlings, the leks of grouse, the warrens of rabbits, and many of the other societal forms cited by Wynne-Edwards as the best examples of altruistic population control. In these cases one must favor alternative hypotheses that involve either kin selection or individual selection. Even so, mechanisms for the evolution of population-wide cooperation have been validated, and the hypothesis of social conventions must either be excluded or kept alive for each species considered in turn. One should also bear in mind that the real population is the unit whose members are freely interbreeding. Such a unit can exist firmly circumscribed in the midst of a seemingly vast population— which is really a metapopulation in evolutionary time. Consider a population of rodents in which tens of thousands of adults hold small territories over a continuous habitat of hundreds of square kilometers. The aggregation seems vast, yet each ridge of earth, each row of trees, and each streamlet could cut migration sufficiently to delimit a true population. The effective population size might be 10 or 100, despite the fact that a hawk's-eye view of the entire metapopulation makes it seem continuous. Not even the little habitat barriers are required. If the rodents move about very little, or return faithfully to the site of their birth to breed, the population neighborhood will be small, and the effective population size low. The delimitation of such local populations could be sharpened by the development of cultural idiosyncrasies such as the learned dialects of birds (Nottebohm, 1970) or the inherited burrow systems of social rodents. With increasing delimitation and reduction in population size, the selection involved also slides toward the kin-selection end of the scale. To evaluate definitively the potential intensity of interpopulation selection, it is necessary to estimate the size of the neighborhood, the effective size of the populations, and the rate at which the true populations become extinct.

The chief role of populational selection may turn out to lie not in forcing the evolution of altruistic density-dependent controls but rather in serving as a springboard from which other forms of altruistic evolution are launched. Suppose that the altruists also have a tendency to cooperate with one another in a way that ultimately benefits each altruist at the expense of the nonaltruists. Cliques and communes may require personal sacrifice, but if they are bonded by possession of one inherited trait, the trait can evolve as the groups triumph over otherwise comparable units of noncooperating groups. The bonding need not even require prolonged sacrifice, only the trade-offs of reciprocal altruism. The formation of such networks requires either a forbiddingly high starting gene frequency or a large number of random contacts with other individuals in which the opportunity for trade-offs exists (Trivers, 1971). These frequency thresholds might be reached by interpopulation selection that initially favors other aspects of the behavior that are not altruistic.

KIN SELECTION

Imagine within a population a network of individuals linked by kinship. One or more of these blood relatives cooperate or bestow altruistic favors in a way that increases the average genetic fitness of the members of the network as a whole, even when this behavior reduces the individual fitnesses of certain members of the group. The members may live together or be scattered throughout the population. The essential condition is that individuals behave in a way that benefits the others, multiplying the genes shared by common descent, while remaining in relatively close contact with the remainder of the population. This enhancement of kin-network fitness in the midst of a population is called *kin selection*. Note that kin selection can be viewed as an extension of individual selection. The effects can only be calculated as the outcome of kin-directed actions of individuals. Kin groups will not ordinarily be discrete enough or stable enough across generations to serve as true units of selection.

Kin selection can merge into populational selection by an appropriate spatial rearrangement. If the kin network settles into one physical location and becomes physically isolated from the rest of the species, it approaches the status of a true population. A closed society, or one so nearly closed that it exchanges only a small fraction of its members with other societies each generation, is a true Mendelian population. If in addition the members all treat one another without reference to genetic relationship, kin selection and interdemic selection are the same process. If the closed society is small, say with 10 members or less, we can analyze group selection by the theory of kin selection. If it is large, containing an effective breeding size of 100 or more members, or if the selection proceeds by the extinction of entire populations of any size, the theory of interpopulation selection is probably more appropriate.

The personal actions of one member toward another can be conveniently classified into three categories in a way that makes the analysis of kin selection more feasible. When a person (or animal) increases the fitness of another at the expense of his or her own fitness, this is called an act of *altruism*. Self-sacrifice for the benefit of offspring is altruism in the conventional but not in the strict genetic sense, because individual fitness is measured by the number of surviving offspring. But self-sacrifice on behalf of second cousins is true altruism at both levels, and when directed at total strangers such abnegating behavior is so surprising (that is, "noble") as to demand some kind of theoretical explanation. In contrast, a person who raises his or her own fitness by lowering that of others is engaged in *selfishness*. Whereas we cannot publicly approve of the selfish act, we do understand it thoroughly and may even sympathize. Finally, a person who gains nothing or even reduces his or her own fitness in order to diminish that of another has committed an act of *spite*. The action may be sane, and the perpetrator may seem gratified, but we find it difficult to imagine the rational motivation. We refer to the committing of a spiteful act as "all too human"—and then wonder what we meant.

The concept of kin selection to explain altruistic behavior was originated by Charles Darwin in *The Origin of Species*. Darwin had encountered in the social insects the "one special difficulty, which at first appeared to me insuperable, and actually fatal to my whole theory [p. 236]." How, he asked, could the worker castes of insect societies have evolved if they are sterile and leave no offspring? This paradox proved truly fatal to Lamarck's theory of evolution through the inheritance of acquired characteristics, for Darwin was quick to point out that the Lamarckian hypothesis requires characteristics to be developed by use or disuse of the organs of individual organisms and then to be passed directly to the next generation, an impossibility when the organisms are sterile. To save his own theory, Darwin introduced the idea of natural selection operating at the level of the family rather than of the single organism. In retrospect, his logic seems impeccable. If some of the individuals of the family are sterile and yet important to the welfare of fertile relatives, as in the case of insect colonies, selection at the family level is inevitable. With the entire family serving as the unit of selection, it is the capacity to generate sterile but altruistic relatives that becomes subject to genetic evolution. To quote Darwin:

> Thus, a well-flavoured vegetable is cooked, and the individual is destroyed; but the horticulturist sows seeds of the same stock, and confidently expects to get nearly the same variety; breeders of cattle wish the flesh and fat to be well marbled together; the animal has been slaughtered, but the breeder goes with confidence to the same family [*The Origin of Species*, 1859, p. 237].

Employing his familar style of argumentation, Darwin noted that intermediate stages found in some living species of social insects connect at least some of the extreme sterile castes, making it possible to trace the route along which they evolved. As he wrote,

> With these facts before me, I believe that natural selection, by acting on the fertile parents, could form a species which regularly produces neuters, either all of a large size with one form of jaw, or all of small size with jaws having a widely different structure, or lastly, and this is the climax of our difficulty, one set of workers of one size and structure, and simultaneously another set of workers of a different size and structure [*The Origin of Species*, 1859, p. 24].

Darwin was speaking here about the soldiers and minor workers of ants.

Family-level selection is of practical concern to plant and animal breeders, and the subject of kin selection was at first pursued from this narrow point of view. One of the principal contributions to such theory was provided by Jay L. Lush (1947), a geneticist who wished to devise a prescription for the choice of boars and gilts for use in breeding. It was necessary to give each pig "sib credits," determined by the average merit of its littermates. A quite reliable set of formulas was developed that incorporated the size of the family and the phenotypic correlations between and within families. This research provided a useful background but was not addressed directly to the evolution of social behavior in the manner envisaged by Darwin.

The modern genetic theory of altruism, selfishness, and spite was launched instead by William D. Hamilton in a series of important articles (1964, 1970, 1971a,b, 1972). Hamilton's pivotal concept is *inclusive fitness:* the sum of an individual's own fitness plus the sum of all the effects it causes to the related parts of the fitnesses of all its relatives. When an animal performs an altruistic act toward a brother, for example, the inclusive fitness is the animal's fitness (which has been lowered by the performance of the act) plus the increment in fitness enjoyed by that portion of the brother's hereditary constitution that is shared with the altruistic animal. The portion of shared heredity is the fraction of genes held by common descent by the two animals and is measured by the coefficient of relationship r. Thus, in the absence of inbreeding, the animal and its brother have $r = \frac{1}{2}$ of their genes identical by common descent. Hamilton's key result can be stated very simply as follows. A genetically based act of altruism, selfishness, or spite will evolve if the average inclusive fitness of individuals within networks displaying it is greater than the inclusive fitness of individuals in otherwise comparable networks that do not display it.

Consider, for example, a simplified network consisting solely of an individual and his brother (Figure 5). If the individual is altruistic, he

Figure 5. The basic conditions required for the evolution of altruism, selfishness, and spite by means of kin selection. The family has been reduced to an individual and his brother; the fraction of genes in the brother shared by common descent ($r = \frac{1}{2}$) is indicated by the shaded half of the body. A requisite of the environment (food, shelter, access to mate, and so on) is indicated by a vessel, and harmful behavior to another by an axe. *Altruism:* The altruist diminishes his own genetic fitness but raises his brother's fitness to the extent that the shared genes are actually increased in the next generation. *Selfishness:* The selfish individual reduces his brother's fitness but enlarges his own to an extent that more than compensates. *Spite:* The spiteful individual lowers the fitness of an unrelated competitor (the unshaded figure) while reducing that of his own or at least not improving it; however, the act increases the fitness of the brother to a degree that more than compensates.

will perform some sacrifice for the benefit of the brother. He may surrender needed food or shelter, or defer in the choice of a mate, or place himself between his brother and danger. The important result, from a purely evolutionary point of view, is loss of genetic fitness—a reduced mean life-span, fewer offspring, or both—which leads to less representation of the altruist's personal genes in the next generation. But at least half of the brother's genes are identical to those of the altruist by virtue of common descent. Suppose, in the extreme case, that the altruist leaves no offspring. If his altruistic act more than doubles the brother's personal representation in the next generation, it will ipso facto increase the one-half of the genes identical to those in the altruist, and the altruist will actually have gained representation in the next generation. Many of the genes shared by such brothers will be the ones that encode the tendency toward altruistic behavior. The inclusive fitness, in this case determined solely by the brother's contribution, will be great enough to cause the spread of the altruistic genes throughout the population, and hence the evolution of altruistic behavior.

The model can now be extended to include all relatives affected by the altruism. If only first cousins were benefited ($r = \frac{1}{8}$), the altruist who leaves no offspring would have to multiply a cousin's fitness eightfold;

an uncle ($r = \frac{1}{4}$) would have to be advanced fourfold; and so on. If combinations of relatives are benefited, the genetic effect of the altruism is simply weighted by the number of relatives of each kind who are affected and by their coefficients of relationship. In general, k, the ratio of gain in fitness to loss in fitness, must exceed the reciprocal of the average coefficient of relationship $(\bar{r})$ to the ensemble of relatives:

$$k > 1/\bar{r}.$$

Thus, in the extreme brother-to-brother case, $1/\bar{r} = 2$, and the loss in fitness for the altruist who leaves no offspring was said to be total (that is $= 1.0$). Therefore, in order for the shared altruistic genes to increase, k, the gain-to-loss ratio, must exceed 2. In other words, the brother's fitness must be more than doubled.

The evolution of selfishness can be treated by the same model. Intuitively it might seem that selfishness in any degree pays off so long as the result is the increase of one's personal genes in the next generation. But this is not the case if relatives are being harmed to the extent of losing too many of their genes shared with the selfish individual by common descent. Again, the inclusive fitness must exceed 1, but this time the result of exceeding that threshold is the spread of the selfish genes.

Finally, the evolution of spite is possible if it, too, raises inclusive fitness. The perpetrator must be able to discriminate relatives from nonrelatives, or close relatives from distant ones. If the spiteful behavior causes a relative to prosper to a compensatory degree, the genes favoring spite will increase in the population at large. True spite is a commonplace in human societies, undoubtedly because human beings are keenly aware of their own blood lines and have the intelligence to plot intrigue. Human beings are unique in the degree of their capacity to lie to other members of their own species. They typically do so in a way that deliberately diminishes outsiders while promoting relatives, even at the risk of their own personal welfare (Wallace, 1973). Examples of spite in animals may be rare and difficult to distinguish from purely selfish behavior. This is particularly true in the realm of false communication. Chimpanzees and gorillas, the brightest of the nonhuman primates, sometimes lie to one another (and to zookeepers) to obtain food or to attract company (Hediger, 1955, p. 150; van Lawick-Goodall, 1971). The mental capacity exists for spite, but if these animals lie for spiteful reasons, this fact has not yet been established. Even the simplest physical techniques of spite are ambiguous in animals. Male bowerbirds sometimes wreck the bowers of the neighbors, an act that appears spiteful at first (Marshall, 1954). But bowerbirds are polygynous, and the probability exists that the destructive bird is able to attract more females to his own bower. Hamilton (1970) has cited cannibalism in the corn ear worm (*Heliothis zea*) as a possible example of spite. The first caterpillar that penetrates an ear of corn eats all subsequent rivals, even though enough feed exists to see two or more of the caterpillars through to maturity. Yet even here, as Hamilton concedes, the trait might have evolved as pure selfishness at a time when the *Heliothis* fed on smaller flowerheads or small corn ears of the ancestral type. Many other examples of the killing of conspecifics have been demonstrated in insects, but almost invariably in circumstances where the food supply is limited and the aggressiveness is clearly selfish, as opposed to spiteful (Wilson, 1971).

The Hamilton models are beguiling in part because of their transparency and heuristic value. The coefficient of relationship, r, translates. easily into "blood," and the human mind, already sophisticated in the intuitive calculus of blood ties and proportionate altruism, races to apply the concept of inclusive fitness to a reevaluation of its own social impulses. But the Hamilton viewpoint is also unstructured. The conventional parameters of population genetics, allele frequencies, mutation rates, epistasis, migration, group size, and so forth are mostly omitted from the equations. As a result, Hamilton's mode of reasoning can be only loosely coupled with the remainder of genetic theory, and the number of predictions it can make is unnecessarily limited.

One of the most persuasive pieces of evidence for the operation of kin selection has been provided by the social insects. The insect order Hymenoptera, composed of bees, wasps, and ants, is among the few animal groups in which sex is determined by haplodiploidy; that is, unfertilized (haploid) eggs yield males, while fertilized (diploid) eggs yield females. As Hamilton first pointed out, one consequence is that sisters will be related to each other by $r = \frac{3}{4}$ but to their brothers by only $r = \frac{1}{4}$. Mothers and daughters remain related by $r = \frac{1}{2}$. Hamilton argued that the high frequency of advanced social life among hymenopterans (11 out of the 12 known evolutionary lines within the insects as a whole) is due to the fact that sisters are more closely related than mothers and daughters. It is to the advantage of a female to become an altruistic worker and rear sisters, a factor which will bias species toward social evolution but not necessarily drive them into it. Trivers and Hare (1975) extended this reasoning to produce some unexpected numerical results, the simplest and most dramatic of which is the following. In cases where the queen lays all of the eggs and the workers are in control of colony reproduction, the workers should try to invest more in females than in males. The ratio of investment, measured in dry weight of the newly produced virgin queens and males, should approach 3:1 in favor of the queens (sisters), since the workers trade $r = \frac{1}{4}$ for $r = \frac{3}{4}$ if they invest in a sister instead of a brother. Moreover, the equilibrium value of the ratio reached in evolution should be 3:1, since at that point the expected reproductive success of the scarcer males will then be three times that of the queen on a per-gram basis, balancing the one-third initial investment. For various species of ants thus far measured, the ratio is indeed significantly greater than 1:1, and in many cases it falls very close to 3:1 (Trivers & Hare, 1975).

RECIPROCAL ALTRUISM

The theory of kin selection has taken most of the good will out of altruism. When altruism is conceived of as the mechanism by which DNA multiplies itself through a network of relatives, spirituality becomes just one more Darwinian enabling device. The theory of natural selection can be extended still further into the complex set of relationships that Trivers (1971) has called *reciprocal altruism*. The paradigm offered by Trivers is "Good Samaritan" behavior in human beings. A man is drowning, let us say, and another man jumps in to save him, even though the two are not related and may not even have met previously. The reaction is typical of what human beings regard as "pure" altruism. However, upon reflection one can see that the Good Samaritan has much to gain by his act. Suppose that the drowning man has a one-half chance of drowning if he is not assisted, whereas the rescuer has a one-in-twenty chance of dying. Imagine further that when the rescuer drowns the victim also drowns, but when the rescuer lives the victim is always saved. If such episodes were extremely rare, the Darwinist calculus would predict little or no gain to the fitness of the rescuer for his attempt. But if the drowning man reciprocates at a future time, and the risks of drowning stay the same, the rescue will have benefited both individuals. Each man will have traded a one-half chance of dying for about a one-tenth chance. A population at large that enters into a series of such moral obligations, that is, reciprocally altruistic acts, will be a population of individuals with generally increased genetic fitness. The trade-off actually enhances personal fitness and is less purely altruistic than acts evolving out of interpopulation and kin selection.

In its elementary form the Good Samaritan model still contains an inconsistency. Why should the rescued individual bother to reciprocate? Why not cheat? The answer is that in an advanced, personalized society in which individuals are identified and the record of their acts is weighed by others it does not pay to cheat even in the purely Darwinist sense. Selection will discriminate against the individual if cheating has later adverse effects on his life and reproduction that outweigh the momentary advantage gained. Iago stated the essence of this fact in *Othello*: "Good name in man and woman, dear my Lord, is the immediate jewel of their souls."

Trivers has skillfully related his genetic model to a wide range of the most subtle human behaviors. Aggressively moralistic behavior, for example, keeps would-be cheaters in line—no less than hortatory sermons to the believers. Self-righteousness, gratitude, and sympathy enhance the probability of receiving an altruistic act by virtue of implying reciprocation. The all-important quality of sincerity is a metacommunication about the significance of these messages. The emotion of guilt may be favored in natural selection because it motivates the cheater to compensate for his misdeed and to provide convincing evidence that he does not plan to cheat again.

Human behavior abounds with reciprocal altruism consistent with genetic theory, but animal behavior seems to be almost devoid of it. Perhaps the reason is that in animals relationships are not sufficiently enduring, or memories of personal behavior reliable enough, to permit the highly personal contracts associated with the more human forms of reciprocal altruism. Almost the only exceptions I know of occur just where one would most expect to find them—in the more intelligent monkeys, such as rhesus macaques and baboons, and in the anthropoid apes. Members of troops are known to form coalitions or cliques and to aid one another reciprocally in disputes with other troop members. Chimpanzees, gibbons, African wild dogs, and wolves also beg food from one another in a reciprocal manner.

Granted a mechanism for sustaining reciprocal altruism, we are still left with the theoretical problem of how the evolution of the behavior gets started. Imagine a population in which a Good Samaritan appears for the first time as a rare mutant. He rescues but is not rescued in turn by any of the nonaltruists who surround him. Thus the genotype has low fitness and is maintained at no more than mutational equilibrium. Boorman and Levitt (1973b) have formally investigated the conditions necessary for the emergence of a genetically mediated cooperation network. They found that for each population size, for each component of fitness added by membership in a network as opposed to the reduced fitness of cooperators outside networks, and for each average number of individuals contacted in the network, there exists a critical frequency of the altruist gene above which the gene will spread explosively through the population and below which it will slowly recede to the mutational equilibrium. How critical frequencies are attained from scratch remains unknown. Cooperative individuals must play a version of the game of "Prisoner's Dilemma" (Hamilton, 1971b; Trivers, 1971). If they chance cooperation with a nonaltruist, they lose some fitness, and the nonaltruist gains. If they are lucky and contact a fellow cooperator, both gain. The critical gene frequency is simply that in which playing the game pays by virtue of a high enough probability of contacting another cooperator. The machinery for bringing the gene frequency up to the critical value must lie outside the game itself. It could be genetic drift in small populations, which is entirely feasible in semiclosed societies, or a concomitant of interpopulation or kin selection favoring other aspects of altruism displayed by the cooperator genotypes.

REFERENCES

Boorman, S. A., & Levitt, P. R. Group selection on the boundary of a stable population. *Proceedings of the National Academy of Sciences, U.S.A.*, 1972, *69*(9), 2711–2713.

Boorman, S. A., & Levitt, P. R. Group selection on the boundary of a stable population. *Theoretical Population Biology*, 1973, *4*(1), 85–128. (a)

Boorman, S. A., & Levitt, P. R. A frequency-dependent natural selection model for the evolution of social cooperation networks. *Proceedings of the National Academy of Sciences, U.S.A.*, 1973, *70*(1), 187–189. (b)

Brereton, J. L. G. Evolved regulatory mechanisms of population control. In G. W. Leeper (Ed.), *The evolution of living organisms.* Parksville, Victoria: Melbourne University Press, 1962, Pp. 81–93.

Brown, J. L. Types of group selection. *Nature*, 1966, *211*(5051), 870.

Darlington, P. J. Interconnected patterns of biogeography and evolution. *Proceedings of the National Academy of Sciences, U.S.A.*, 1971, *68*(6), 1254–1258.

Darwin, C. R. *On the origin of species by means of natural selection, or The preservation of favoured races in the struggle for life,* 1st ed. London, John Murray, 1859.

Dunbar, M. J. The evolution of stability in marine environments: Natural selection at the level of the ecosystem. *American Naturalist*, 1960, *94*(875), 129–136.

Dunbar, M. J. The ecosystem as a unit of natural selection. In E. S. Deevey (Ed.), *Growth by intussusception: Ecological essays in honor of G. Evelyn Hutchinson.* New Haven: Transactions of the Academy, Connecticut Academy of Arts and Sciences, 1972, *44*, Pp. 114–130.

Gadgil, M. Evolution of social behavior through interpopulation selection. *Proceedings of the National Academy of Sciences, U.S.A.*, 1975, *72*(3), 1199–1201.

Gilpin, M. *Group selection in predator-prey communities.* Princeton: Princeton University Press, 1975.

Haldane, J. B. S. *The causes of evolution.* London: Longmans, Green, 1932.

Hamilton, W. D. The genetical theory of social behaviour, I, II. *Journal of Theoretical Biology*, 1964, *7*(1), 1–52.

Hamilton, W. D. Selfish and spiteful behaviour in an evolutionary model. *Nature*, 1970, *228*, 1218–1220.

Hamilton, W. D. Geometry for the selfish herd. *Journal of Theoretical Biology*, 1971, *31*(2), 295–311. (a)

Hamilton, W. D. Selection of selfish and altruistic behavior in some extreme models. In J. F. Eisenberg & W. S. Dillon (Eds.), *Man and beast: Comparative social behavior*. Washington: Smithsonian Institution Press, 1971, Pp. 47–91. (b)

Hamilton, W. D. Altruism and related phenomena, mainly in social insects. *Annual Review of Ecology and Systematics*, 1972, *3*, 193–232.

Hediger, H. *Studies of the psychology and behaviour of captive animals in zoos and circuses*, trans. by G. Sircom. New York: Criterion Books, 1955.

Kalela, O. Über den Revierbesitz bei Vögeln und Säugetieren als populationsökologischer Faktor. *Annales Zoologici Societatis Zoologicae Botanicae Fennicae "Vanamo"* (Helsinki), 1954, *16*(2), 1–48.

Kalela, O. Regulation of reproductive rate in subarctic populations of the vole *Clethrionomys rufocanus* (Sund.). *Annales Academiae Scientiarum Fennicae* (Suomalaisen Tiedeakatemian Toimituksia), Ser. A (IV, Biological), 1957, *34*, 1–60.

Lawick-Goodall, Jane van. *In the shadow of man*. Boston: Houghton Mifflin Co., 1971.

Levin, B. R., & Kilmer, W. L. Interdemic selection and the evolution of altruism: A computer simulation study. *Evolution*, 1974, *28*(4), 527–545.

Levins, R. Extinction. In M. Gerstenhaber (Ed.), *Some mathematical questions in biology*. Providence, R.I.: Lectures on Mathematics in the Life Sciences, vol. 2. American Mathematical Society, 1970, Pp. 77–107.

Lush, J. L. Family merit and individual merit as bases for selection, I, II. *American Naturalist*, 1947, *81*(799), 241–261; *81*(800), 362–379.

Marshall, A. J. *Bower-birds, their displays and breeding cycles*. Oxford: Clarendon Press of Oxford University, 1954.

May, R. M. Group selection. *Nature*, 1975, *254*, 485.

Maynard Smith, J. Group selection and kin selection. *Nature*, 1964, *201*, 1145–1147.

Nottebohm, F. Ontogeny of bird song. *Science*, 1970, *167*, 950–956.

Simpson, G. G. *The major features of evolution*. New York: Columbia University Press, 1953.

Smith, J. Maynard. See under Maynard Smith, J.

Snyder, R. L. Evolution and integration of mechanisms that regulate population growth. *Proceedings of the National Academy of Sciences, U.S.A.*, 1961, *47*(4), 449–455.

Trivers, R. L. The evolution of reciprocal altruism. *Quarterly Review of Biology*, 1971, *46*(4), 35–57.

Trivers, R. L., & Hare, Hope. Haplodiploidy and the evolution of the social insects. *Science*, 1976, *191*, 243–263.

Wahlund, S. Zusammensetzung von Populationen und Korrelationserscheinungen von Standpunkt der Vererbungslehre aus Betrachtet. *Hereditas*, 1928, *11*, 65–106.

Wallace, B. Misinformation, fitness, and selection. *American Naturalist*, 1973, *107* (953), 1–7.

Williams, G. C. *Adaptation and natural selection: A critique of some current evolutionary thought*. Princeton, N.J.: Princeton University Press, 1966.

Wilson, D. S. A theory of group selection. *Proceedings of the National Academy of Sciences, U.S.A.*, 1975, *72*(1), 143–146.

Wilson, E. O. Competitive and aggressive behavior. In J. F. Eisenberg & W. Dillon

(Eds.), *Man and beast: Comparative social behavior*. Washington, D.C.: Smithsonian Institution Press, 1971, Pp. 183–217.

Wilson, E. O. *Sociobiology: The new synthesis*. Cambridge, Massachusetts: Belknap Press of Harvard University Press, 1975.

Wright, S. Tempo and mode in evolution: A critical review. *Ecology*, 1945, *26*(4), 415–419.

Wright, S. *Evolution and the genetics of populations*, Vol. 2, *The theory of gene frequencies*. Chicago: University of Chicago Press, 1969.

Wynne-Edwards, V. C. *Animal dispersion in relation to social behaviour*. Edinburgh: Oliver and Boyd, 1962.

Wynne-Edwards, V. C. Space use and the social community in animals and men. In A. H. Esser (Ed.), *Behavior and environment: The use of space by animals and men*. New York: Plenum Press, 1971, Pp. 267–280.

2

On the Genetics of Altruism and the Counterhedonic Components in Human Culture[1]

DONALD T. CAMPBELL

Civilization is a process in the service of Eros whose purpose is to combine single human individuals, and after that, families, then races, peoples, nations, into one great unity, the unity of mankind.... But man's natural aggressive instinct, the hostility of each against all and of all against each, opposes this program of civilization.... The struggle between Eros and Death, between the instinct of life and the instinct of destruction ... is what all life essentially consists of, and the evolution of civilization may therefore be simply described as the struggle for life of the human species [Freud, 1930, p. 122].

Why do our relatives the animals not exhibit any such cultural struggle? We do not know. (*Oh, wir wissen es nicht.*) Very probably some of them—the bees, the ants, the termites—strove for thousands of years before they arrived at the state institutions, the distribution of functions,

[1] The preparation of this chapter has been supported in part by a grant from the Carnegie Corporation of New York.

and the restrictions upon individuals, for which we admire them today. It is indicative of our present state that we should not think ourselves happy in any of these animal states, nor in any of the roles assigned by them to the individual [Freud, 1930, p. 123].

These verses of scripture from Freud set the problem for this essay. I believe Freud right in identifying the social insects as our most similar relatives insofar as complex social interdependence, *Kultur*, and self-sacrificial altruism are concerned. I believe he was also right in noting in man a profound ambivalence toward his social role, an ambivalence absent in the bees, and ants, and the termites. Current technical discussions in evolutionary genetics regarding the possibility of selecting traits that are good for the group but are costly for the procreational opportunities of the individual offer an explanation of that difference. It is a difference that mere evolutionary time will not cure, being a byproduct of the fact that among humans, unlike the social insects, there is genetic competition among the cooperators. (Among vertebrates each member produces offspring, potentially in different numbers. Among the social insects all of the cooperators are sterile and are thus not in genetic competition.) The major disagreement with Freud is as to the nature of the ambivalence. Rather than a death instinct, modern evolutionary genetics points to something closer to Freudian narcissism: self-serving aggressiveness in competition with co-workers for food, space, and mates; self-serving cowardice in war; self-serving dishonesty to fellow in-group members; cheating, greed, disobedience, etc. Freud's view of the pervasively counterhedonic content of culture is accepted and given a functional interpretation: Complex social coordination, with full division of labor, professional soldiers, and apartment-house living, has been achieved in man as a *social*-evolutionary product by inculcating behavioral dispositions directly counter to the selfish tendencies produced by genetic selection.

The occasion for this essay is not any special competence in these matters but rather a wish to correct certain misstatements made at a time when I was still less competent. That we psychologists as a whole need to be more informed on these matters is illustrated by the fact that our other major discussions of the genetics of altruism (e.g., Hebb, 1971; Hebb & Thompson, 1954; Krebs, 1970, 1971; Wright, 1971) have also been unaware of it—Aronfreed (1970) is a partial exception.

ETHNOCENTRIC ALTRUISM

In relation to this volume's theme, I now wish to reconsider an earlier article (Campbell, 1965b) that derived altruistic individual behavior from the superior survival value of group-organized complex social interdependence as compared with individualistic modes of adaption. Individual motivations, it was argued, are in substantial part what they are because they make group functioning possible. Most such motives are correctly classified as "altruistic." But although altruistic, not all are "positive," "wise," or "good." The willingness to die for group causes and related motives makes possible tribalism, nationalism, and war and are thus suicidal for modern man. Though the essay recognized that man's achievement of a termite-like degree of division of labor and social interdependence (far exceeding that of the chimpanzee or wolf) is preponderantly a matter of cultural cumulation or social evolution (Campbell, 1964a; Cohen, 1962), it nonetheless also argued that genetic tendencies would be accumulated around these social functions. It is on this point that I would now like to reconsider that essay.

The "realistic group conflict" theory there reviewed and propositionalized (see also LeVine & Campbell, 1972) is one of the most impressive convergences in social science theory, with extensive documentation and independent invention in political science, sociology, psychology, and economics. Opposing psychological theories that interpret intergroup conflicts as projective displacements or byproducts of intragroup or intraindividual conflicts, realistic group conflict theory assumes that intergroup conflicts are rational in that groups do have incompatible goals and are in competition for scarce resources. But although the theory is stated at the level of group function and process, 6 of the 10 propositions emerging posit individual-dispositional laws. These are laws of "altruism," of individual commitment to group survival. This group functionality of individual altruistic dispositions is still strongly recommended to the attention of psychologists. What I now wish to reconsider is the source of these dispositions. In greater continuity with the mainstream of social psychological thought, I now believe that these self-sacrificial dispositions, including especially the willingness to risk death in warfare, are, in man, a product of social indoctrination counter to rather than supported by genetically transmitted behavioral dispositions.

This line of thought must be sharply distinguished from the currently popular biological-evolutionary explanation of war. The concept of territoriality has added much to our understanding of aggression at the level of the individual fighting fish and gander (Lorenz, 1966). Realistic group conflict theory may be thought of as a theory of social group territoriality and social group aggression. But the relationship between these two levels of territoriality should be kept clear. Vertebrate territoriality as studied by the ethologists represents the behavioral syndrome of an individual male protecting a single female or harem and his offspring.

Realistic group conflict theory is not the same theory and does not explain intergroup conflict as an expression of this territorial instinct in individual males. Rather, it is an analogous theory at a different level of organization. Realistic group conflict theory refers to organized groups involving many males and many families. In terms of the behavioral dispositions of the individuals involved, the two levels of territoriality are in opposition rather than coterminous. Even though efforts to mobilize human ethnocentrism often make reference to protecting home and family, group-level territoriality has always required that the soldier abandon for extensive periods the protecting of his own wife, children, and home. Individual territoriality and aggression means *intra*group conflict and is regularly suppressed in the service of *inter*group conflict. Proposition 4 of realistic group conflict theory (Campbell, 1965b, p. 288) states that *real threat causes in-group solidarity*. In an early statement, Sumner (1906) says: "The exigencies of war with outsiders are what make peace inside, lest internal discord should weaken the we-group for war. These exigencies also make government and law in the ingroup, in order to prevent quarrels and enforce discipline [p. 12]." It is the "internal discord" and the "quarrels within" that are the aggressive manifestations of instinctive territoriality, if any. This is the most recurrent proposition in the many sources of realistic group conflict theory. The Sherifs (1953) make a major point of it. And with the help of reviewers such as Coser (1956), Berkowitz (1962), and Rosenblatt (1964) one can readily assemble several dozen citations affirming it. It is also a major theme of the anthropological description of pyramidal-segmental societies (LeVine & Campbell, 1972). Thus it is not mammalian or primate territoriality that explains war in this theory. It is instead an analogous function at a larger organizational level, and one that requires the inhibition of the lower-level individual mammalian territoriality. It is this discontinuity that makes the social insects rather than the higher apes the closest functional analogue for complex human social organization.

GENETICS OF ALTRUISM

Wynne-Edwards's book, *Animal Dispersion in Relation to Social Behavior* (1962; see also Wynne-Edwards, 1963, 1965), has assembled the evidence and has made the case for the natural selection of traits leading to the survival of breeding groups and whole species, even at the expense of individual procreational success. Although mechanisms for the restriction of population are the preponderant illustration, his viewpoint supports the genetic speculations of my earlier paper regarding altruism and certainly should have been cited, although that would not have altered my conclusions.

George Williams, in *Adaptation and Natural Selection* (1966), challenges Wynne-Edwards's major conclusions, arguing that mechanisms that inhibit the effective fertility of the individual are incompatible with the theory of natural selection in its most developed statistical form. In so doing, he applies an argument on the problem of "altruistic" genes first presented by J. B. S. Haldane (1932) in a special appendix to his pioneering book on the statistical theory of evolution. The prohibition is not against all altruistic tendencies, but rather against those that are altruistic at some risk to the individual and that thus impair to some degree the individual's chances for procreation, effectively diminishing the frequency of his genes in later generations.

Although the argument takes a mathematical form in Haldane, and briefly so in Williams's very readable book, its core concept can be stated simply. Let us suppose that mutations have produced a heterogeneity within a social group, so that there are some individuals with genes predisposing a self-sacrificial bravery that furthers group survival and other individuals with genes predisposing a self-saving cowardice. Let us suppose that, due to the presence of the bravery genes in some individuals, the group as a whole survives better. This increases the average reproductive opportunity of both the brave and the cowardly among the group members. The net gain for the brave is reduced to some degree because of the costs or the risks they incur. The net gain for the cowardly has no such subtraction. Thus, whereas all gain, the cowardly gain more, and their genes will gradually become more frequent as a result. There is no way in which the altruistic genetic tendencies could increase relative to the cowardly, to say nothing of becoming predominant, if there is a self-sacrificial component to the bravery.

Wynne-Edwards and others argue for a group-versus-group selection process that could, if strong enough, counter the individual-versus-individual selection processes within each group. Thus, if competing social groups of the same species varied greatly in the frequency of the altruistic bravery gene and if there were a strong group selection favoring altruistic bravery, this could counteract the selection against altruistic bravery within each group. Williams argues that such a process is virtually impossible. For breeding groups of expected sizes, the only way group-to-group differences in gene frequency can be achieved is by systematic selection on an individual-to-individual level within each group. Thus, the only way the groups with high frequency of the altruistic gene could have developed would be if they had migrated into an ecology where the trait was *not* self-sacrificial, and then migrated back into a common ecology. Even if this unlikely set of coincidences were to occur, if the brave group were to any extent heterozygous or if there were mutants back to the cowardly gene, the individual-versus-individual selection processes would erode the prevalence of the bravery gene in favor of the cowardly.

The one qualification to this argument follows Sewell Wright (1931) in pointing out that, if the breeding groups were very small and highly inbred, then by chance alone some groups would end up being homozygous in the gene for altruistic bravery. Williams plausibly argues that such genetic isolation of small groups could not persist and that in becoming heterozygous the individual-versus-individual selection would take over. When Wright's argument is extended to trait-complexes involving many genes, it becomes less likely to the nth power of the number of such genes.

Although reviewers have found Williams's book too extreme and one-sided (e.g., Lewontin, 1966), and although the issues it raises are far from settled within biology, I am tentatively persuaded to regard it as correct and to accept the fact that for us vertebrates and for others for whom there is genetic competition among the cooperators there are stringent restraints against genetic selection for self-sacrificial altruism.

The kind of "selfishness" selected needs to be spelled out in more detail. Self-sacrificial altruism in the defense of offspring is selected, as it is only through these offspring that the increase in gene frequency can be achieved. Sibling mutual defense is selected, since they share 50% of the same genes. But tendencies to sacrifice for the protection of more remote relatives such as cousins or nephews are rarely if ever advantageous. Williams accents this point by noting that parental defense of offspring only occurs in species in which parents can distinguish between their own and their neighbors' offspring. Thus, familial solidarity is selected for, but group solidarity on larger than family lines that involves much risk or sacrifice on the part of the cooperator is in general selected against. Much cooperative behavior involves a direct gain rather than risk or loss, and such cooperative behavior is positively selected. Williams uses the hunting of elks by groups of wolves as one of many examples. In other instances, the gains to the individual outweigh the losses, as Trivers (1971) argues for warning cries in birds. The degree of vertebrate sociality thus produced probably reaches its limit in that found within packs of wolves and chimpanzees that include several families, that is, a very limited degree of social interdependence.

The case of the social insects—the termites, ants, and bees—is fundamentally different. Among them, there is little or no "genetic competition" between the cooperators. A cowardly soldier within one nest will not have more offspring than a self-sacrificially brave one, for both are sterile. It is only the queen and the drones that have offspring—and their chances of offspring increase with the frequency of effectively brave soldiers. Likewise, the soldier termite that stands, fights, and dies is not in genetic competition with the also sterile worker whose conscience calls him to flee back into the nest when enemies are near. As a result, the social insects have achieved extreme degrees of complex social inter-dependence involving dramatic instances of self-sacrificial bravery and other extreme division-of-labor adaptations (Allee, Emerson, Park, Park, & Schmidt, 1949; Brian, 1965; Krishna & Weesner, 1969; Wilson, 1971b). Undoubtedly, the first prerequisite to this evolution was the development of a sterile caste. After that invention, the further evolution of a complex division of labor could take place. For the ants, wasps, and bees, this development was furthered by the fact that male drones are haploid, having only one set of chromosomes rather than pairs. They thus give all of their offspring an identical set of genes, with the result that females share ¾ of their genes with full sisters and only ½ of their genes with daughters. There is thus a selective advantage to furthering even over their own offspring the life chances of younger eggs from the same mother. As judged by the more primitively social forms, this furthers a first stage of social life lacking morphological differences between queen and worker, except for inhibited fertility. Wilson (1971b), building upon Hamilton (1964), presents the details. (He also provides evidence of some forms of genetic competition within the nest, using this to predict drone selfishness and other anomalies. These qualifications do not affect the arguments and illustrations that I have used above.) The achievement of the first sterile castes in termites is less well understood. It no doubt first involved a survival value for immature sibling assistance with brood care, upon which was superimposed a prolongation of the period of infantile infertility. Again, once an infertile worker caste was achieved, the subsequent development of complex multi-caste differentiation of structure and function was possible. The key step was elimination of genetic competition among the cooperators (Williams, 1966).

Parenthetically, it should be noted that Williams is worth reading by psychologists on many other grounds. His discussion of the genetic competition between males and females is fascinating and includes both the specification of how that competition leads to 50–50 sex ratios at the age of sexual maturity and a discussion of the genetics of coyness versus aggressive promiscuity. (It is the sexual partner who incurs the greater risks in childbearing who will be the coy and selective one. Usually this is the female, but not so among the pipefish-seahorse family, in which the eggs are incubated in a brood pouch in the male.) It should also be noted that Williams's main approach in attacking Wynne-Edwards's claims on group-selected population-restrictive mechanisms (postponement of fertility when food is short or conditions are crowded, decrease in brood size, postponement of age of fertility, territorial spacing, etc.) is to demonstrate how these mechanisms actually increase the effective fertility of the animals showing them and are thus achievable by individual selection. But some of Wynne-Edwards's facts he finds necessary to doubt or deny.

Although Williams (1966, 1971) has influenced me the most, it is only fair to note that an impressive group of evolutionary geneticists take a more moderate position, allowing a larger role to group selection and allowing for more selection for altruism even among us vertebrates. Adoption of their point of view would, however, modify only slightly the contrast that I have presented between the genetics of altruism in man and in the social insects. Lewontin (1965, 1970) accepts the existence of group selection under some conditions, but the examples he provides are unusual exceptions and not at all typical of Wynne-Edwards's illustrations: By and large, Lewontin endorses Williams's criticisms of Wynne-Edwards (Lewontin, 1966, 1970).

Hamilton (1964) has provided basic analyses and mathematical formulations upon which Williams has built his arguments. Hamilton's own conclusions, however, are more moderate. He emphasizes that the extremes of selfishness and spitefulness are also selected against, just as is extreme self-sacrificial altruism. He uses the Prisoner's Dilemma analysis to present the evolutionary predicament (Hamilton, 1971). If the preponderant tendency is to choose the cooperative alternative, then it is genetically advantageous to cheat; but if most choose the opportunistic selfish alternative, it is dysgenic. The more there are repeated interactions with the same other individuals, and the closer the genetic relation between those interacting, the stronger the selection pressure for cooperative dispositions. But once cooperation is well-established, there is genetic selection in favor of cheating. Under transient and random contacts, selfishness is favored.

Hamilton (1971) makes a statement on this crucial issue, one more in keeping with my earlier paper than with the present chapter:

> With still further increase in intelligence, with increase in ability to communicate (and hence also to organize), with invention of new weapons (primarily for hunting) and ability to transmit culturally the techniques acquired, and with increase in possessions that could be carried off or usurped and used in situ, I find no difficulty in imagining that it could

become advantageous for groups to make organized forcible incursions into the territory of weaker neighbors. In other words, I suggest that warfare was a natural development from the revolutionary trends taking part in the hominid stock. . . . If we accept that the elaborate instinctive patterns involved in the "war," "slavery," and "robbery" of the social insects are evolved by natural selection, can we consider it unlikely that in man also the corresponding phenomena have a natural basis [pp. 78–79]?

This is an off-hand conclusion to which he has not yet applied his own careful mathematics and computer simulations. When he does, I am sure he will find that there is a selection pressure favoring cowardly soldiers in man that has no counterpart in the social insects just because they have no genetic competition among the soldiers or between soldiers and workers. . . . I am sure that my conclusions are more loyal to Hamilton's overall analysis of the genetics of altruism than is this comment of his. I of course agree with the first two sentences quoted, if a social evolution rather than a purely genetic one is included. I feel that my conclusion on this point is one Williams would agree with, as well as would Wilson (1971a, 1971b), Lewontin, and Trivers. Probably, on second thought Hamilton would too.

Trivers's (1971) paper is one that psychologists should find of particular interest because he relates the psychological literature on altruism to the controversy in genetics. Following Hamilton (1971), he also uses the Prisoner's Dilemma paradigm. Still more than Hamilton, he emphasizes selection pressures for disguised cheating and sham cooperation. He posits a selection pressure for a contingent cooperation with cooperators, made possible by long interaction with the same specific others. His paper is full of valuable sutble considerations that cannot be treated here but should eventually be incorporated into psychology's literature on this topic. But his paper will not be the final word and may be internally inconsistent. For example, his two animal examples fail to illustrate his principle. Symbiotic cleaning relations involve no genetic competitions of the type under consideration, because the two cooperators are of different species. Furthermore, it is to the direct survival advantage of the cleaned fish not to eat the cleaner; it is selfishly motivated, as Trivers makes clear. Similarly, he persuasively argues that, although the bird that utters a warning cry increases his risks, his own chances of survival are more than compensated for by the advantages of keeping the predator from being sustained by a meal and from learning to eat his type in his locale. In Trivers's discussion of human reciprocal altruism (the term "clique selfishness" would be equally appropriate) he makes use of learned individual tendencies as well as genetic ones, but he fails to give explicit consideration to the social evolution of reward and punishment customs and tends to consider all personality and behavioral dispositions as genetically inherited. Although he uses the mathematical models of evolutionary genetics, he has not developed these for many of his most crucial speculations on human altruism.

One of Trivers's major conceptual contributions is to raise the issue of genetic selection for *moralistic aggression* against cheaters. Genes favoring such tendencies are unambivalently selected for. Insofar as such action changes the cheater's behavior in a more altruistic direction or eliminates his genes through ostracism and death, such genes benefit those holding them, unlike genes for own altruism. Trivers focuses unnecessarily on the effects of such action (and sham moralistic aggression) as a two-party interaction initiated by the one cheated and producing specific restitution to him by the cheater. Most important would seem the "altruistic" eagerness to see cheaters punished even when one has not been directly harmed or will not directly benefit from their punishment. Ranulf (1938) has portrayed such tendencies, although mistakenly identifying them with middle-class psychology rather than with complex division of labor society. Such tendencies can be selected by group selection, because they benefit the whole group without special costs to the individuals holding the genes. The case is similar for tendencies to applaud and reinforce altruists.

In my earlier paper (1956b), I wrote of "ambivalence as optimal compromise." In it, with ample quotes from William James on the ambivalent balance of curiosity about and fear of new objects, I argued that natural selection could produce opposed genetic tendencies and that ambivalence was a better resolution of opposed utilities than was an averaged indifference to novel objects. I argued that in man (but not in the social insects) genetically determined altruism or bravery were in a similar ambivalent balance with genetically determined selfishness or cowardice. Trivers's and Hamilton's analyses support this view. What I argue for in the present chapter is an ambivalence between socially induced altruistic bravery and a genetically induced selfish cowardice. Although, both for reasons of conviction and of clarity, I stick to this position in the present chapter, a mixture of both sources of ambivalence is of course possible.

The literature of evolutionary genetics on altruism and group selection is mushrooming. A major contributor has been E. O. Wilson (1973, 1975, and Chapter 1 in this volume). The general trend of these newer contributions has been to stress the possibility of group selection for self-sacrificial altruistic traits under carefully specified conditions (see also Gadgil, 1975; D. S. Wilson, 1975). Williams (1966), on whom I depend so heavily, though praised for his effective criticisms of Wynne-Edwards's excesses, is also chided by Wilson (1975) for going too far in the opposite direction:

> Nevertheless Williams's distaste for group-selection hypotheses wrongly led him to urge the loading of the dice in favor of individual selection.... Group selection and higher levels of organization, however intuitively improbable they may seem, are at least theoretically possible under a wide range of conditions [p. 30].

Counter to this general trend, Ghiselin (1974) has produced a thoroughly documented book fully committed to explaining all traits, including complex social coordination, by selection for individual procreational advantage. His major achievement is that of making clear how the obvious costs of bisexual reproduction may be overcome in many ecologies by its individual procreational advantages in competition with parthenogenesis, asexual budding, and hermaphroditism, compellingly assembling evidence from species that have the ability to reproduce by either of two means. Especially relevant to the present discussion are his chapters on "The Antisocial Contract" and "A New Theory of Moral Sentiments." Whereas I regard Ghiselin's book as supporting the discussion of the genetics of altruism as presented earlier, it is doubtful that he, any more than Williams, would endorse the use I make of it in the following section.

Of all the contributors to this book, Wilson is the only one who has earned scientific authority on the genetics of altruism. In his magnificent book, *Sociobiology* (1975), he has just founded the discipline to which this chapter attempts to contribute. However, because the background tone of his writing (e.g., "the theoretical problem created by the existence of widespread altruism," Chapter 1 of this volume, p. 11) may seem to contradict my argument, I would like to restate the essential points of my argument that remain intact after accepting his views.

Unlike most ethologists and the other contributors to this volume, Wilson (1975) accepts the social insects as well as the social vertebrates as relevant comparisons in developing a biology of social life that includes human sociality. Although his tendencies to present social insect and vertebrate examples together on a given topic and to emphasize any cooperative or altruistic traits found among vertebrates may obscure the point, a careful reading reinforces the conclusion that the complex social coordination, communication, division of labor, and self-sacrificial altruism exhibited by the sterile castes of the higher social insects greatly exceeds that of any nonhuman vertebrate, be it wolf, chimpanzee, hamadryas baboon, savanna baboon, chacma baboon, howler monkey, langur monkey, rhesus monkey, marmot, turkey, California woodpecker, Mexican freetail bat, or grey seal.

Wilson (1975) recognizes that the special genetic advantages that predispose the social insects to self-sacrificial altruism and complex division of labor lie in selection for "fitness of the colony as a whole and particularly of the progenitrix queen, with reference to whom the non-reproductive members can be regarded as a somatic extension [p. 15]." He emphasizes the fact that, in 11 out of the 12 times that social insects have independently evolved complex social systems, this has been supported by the presence of haploid males with the concomitant fact that sisters share more genes than do mothers and daughter (1975, p. 33, and Chapter 1 in this volume). For all the social insects—ants, bees, wasps, and termites—there are early-evolved mechanisms that produced sterile or usually sterile castes. Those castes most characterized by self-sacrificial altruism (all varieties of soldiers and such rarities as the honey-storage-vat caste) are never fertile. The course of evolution of every complex caste system starts with a sterile worker caste morphologically undifferentiated from the fertile mother or queen. This sterility is maintained in the subsequent elaboration of complex specializations, and this inhibition of genetic competition among the cooperators is reasonably claimed as a prerequisite for the extremes of specialization and self-sacrificial altruism. Wilson emphasizes the "narrow window" through which a species must pass if group selection is to overcome the negative effects of individual selection for self-sacrificial altruism, a window that is particularly narrow for vertebrates.

It will probably be conceded by all that urban social humanity exceeds all other vertebrates, and overlaps the social insects, for complex social interdependence, division of labor, and self-sacrificial altruism. Human urban populations achieve this in spite of being further removed than other vertebrates from the special conditions laid out by Wilson (1975, Chapter 5, and Chapter 1 in this volume) for group selection. I can agree that early humankind in the small hunting-band condition could exceed other vertebrates in the selection of self-sacrificial altruism for some or all of the following reasons: The capacity to recognize other individuals, repeated interaction with the same others, good memory, and long life all support reciprocal altruism, which no doubt stabilized as in-group loyalty and out-group hostility. Disperson as small groups, with the frequent extinction of whole groups, augmented by traditions of victors exterminating the vanquished, plus high rates of inbreeding, all support group selection for self-sacrificial altruism. But even if careful study shows that humankind at this level was in a selective system supporting more self-sacrificial altruism than the ecologies of the wolf and the baboon this does not plausibly hold for urban agricultural man, for whom most of these features are greatly weakened or eliminated.

On all these points, which are its essential foundation, my argument remains unscathed by Wilson and, indeed, by the other chapters in this volume. Where my argument is unsupported at the present time is in the conception that social and biological evolution are in conflict insofar as altruistic traits are concerned and in my willingness to use the traditional moralizings of urban social systems (which uniformly scold human selfishness and cowardice) as evidence of that conflict. (For further expansion of this last argument and reactions to it, see Campbell, 1975 and reactions to it in Wispé and Thompson, 1976 and in Burhoe, 1976.)

ON THE CONFLICT BETWEEN SOCIAL AND BIOLOGICAL EVOLUTION IN MAN

Human complex social interdependence greatly exceeds that of wolves and chimpanzees. If animal counterparts are to be found at all, it is among the social insects. And though the ambivalence Freud noted is present, along with uneven execution of the self-sacrificial roles in the social machine, in many ways civilized man even exceeds the social insects in his complex social interdependency.

Man and the social insects demonstrate the great survival value of extreme social interdependence. The case of the social insects shows that some complex forms of it can be achieved on a genetic base. That wolves and chimpanzees have never achieved it is due to the evolutionary trap or conflict produced by genetic competition among the cooperators. Man is in the same genetic predicament. The conclusion seems to me inevitable that man can have achieved his social-insect-like degree of complex social interdependence only through his social and cultural evolution, through the historical selection and cumulation of educational systems, intragroup sanctions, supernatural (superpersonal, superfamilial) purposes, etc. A detailed discussion of the selective-retention evolution of social customs and artifacts has been provided elsewhere (Campbell, 1965a; Cohen, 1962).

Not only must man's complex social interdependence be a product of social evolution, but the evolved socially induced dispositions must also have directly opposed the selfish dispositional tendencies continually selected for by the concurrent biological evolution. It is this opposition between the dispositional products of biological and social evolution that explains Freud's observations on man's ambivalence toward his social roles and man's contrast to the unambivalent insects. But Freud was wrong in believing that length of *time* in evolutionary history is the problem; it is rather the more fundamental fact of the evolutionary *route* toward social complexity.

This suggestion goes far beyond Williams in its emphasis on the role of social evolution (note, however, Auger, 1952, pp. 122–123). But the conclusion provides for me, as a social scientist interested in the puzzles of his own cultural background, a strong reason for accepting Williams's point of view. For it makes evolutionary sense out of the otherwise anomalous or incomprehensible preoccupation with sin and temptation in the folk morality that our religious traditions provide. The commandments, the proverbs, the religious "law" represent social evolutionary products directed at inculcating tendencies that are in direct opposition to the "temptations" representing, for the most part, the dispositional tendencies produced by biological evolution. For every commandment, we may reasonably hypothesize an opposite tendency that runs counter to some social-systemic optimum.

This hypothesis predicts certain uniformities in the popular moralizings of all complex societies, a scholarly investigation that I have not yet undertaken. All should preach against cowardice in battle. (Inspection of fragments of the anthropological literature leads me to expect this to be nearly universal, even among societies without a full-time division of labor or storable food stuffs. The very ubiquity of this morality may account for its being assumed rather than preached anew in the written ethics of the more complex societies.) All should preach against lying for personal gain (if not lying for group advantage), in-group theft, greed, murderous rage, and arrogant self-pride. Industry, abstemiousness, doing one's unique duty, group loyalty—all these should be praised. A detailed study of this aspect of the moralizings of the presumably independently developed complex societies (such as ancient China, the valleys of the Indus and the Ganges, the Aztecs, Mayas, and Incas) is called for. For these purposes, shame cultures and guilt cultures (if such differences exist) share a functional equivalence.

Caveat

This is a shallow overview for which even detailed and disciplined speculation is lacking, to say nothing of research. If these issues are important, meticulous examination of both the genetic and the social selection processes is required. For example, it must be made clearer than I have done how a social transmission could avoid the restrictions that genetic transmission encounters. Attention has recently been focused on the fact that in social exchange processes the optimizing of individual well-being is often or even usually destructive of the collective good (Crowe, 1969; Frohlich & Oppenheimer, 1970; Hardin, 1968; Olson, 1968; Schelling, 1971). These cross-interests are directly analogous to those involved in the genetics of altruism. How can a social evolution not only have avoided them but also have gone further and have counteracted their genetic product? If the socialization process were predominantly from parent to child, social evolution could not produce self-sacrificial altruism. The predicament would be the same as for genetic inheritance. Childe (1951), Ginsberg (1961), and Waddington (1961) are among the astute commentators on social evolution who have noted the important disanalogy between biological and social evolution, in that social evolution permits cross-lineage borrowing. Whereas their focus was on group-to-group borrowing, this also applies to lineage-to-lineage borrowing within a group. Thus, effective group indoctrination to self-sacrificing bravery, if resulting in group success, would perhaps avoid the differential propagation that genetic transmission runs into. But if there were genetic differences in indoctrinability, potentiality for identification with group purposes, etc. and if warfare were the main selective system operating, then there would be genetic selection against indoctrinability and capacity for identification.

No doubt there is positive genetic selection for gregariousness and fear of ostracism. Indoctrinability makes possible cultural cumulation and hence is probably in general positively selected for at the individual level, as Waddington in his remarkable *The Ethical Animal* (1960) argues. Probably the overall adaptive advantage for indoctrinability, group identification, and fear of ostracism is strong enough to outweigh the negative selection produced when the most indoctrinable incur greater fatality rates in wartime. Looking at the individual's role as an indoctrinator and enforcer of group-adaptive altruistic behavior on the part of others, such tendencies would be selected for at both social and genetic levels as long as these others were not in one's own family. There could be a *social* selection for customs granting extra procreational opportunities to surviving heroes, but a *genetic* tendency for women to be most attracted to the altruistically brave would be weeded out through the diminished survival rate of these women's sons. There is probably positive selection for heroic bluff that persists as long as successful but turns into cowardly retreat when the odds become overwhelming; such a pattern is not, in Haldane's usage, technically altruistic.

Expanding the perspective only slightly reveals still more problems. The moralizings in the Old Testament against onanism, homosexuality, and the temptation to sacrifice one's firstborn son (Bakan, 1966; Wellisch,

1954) must be directed against socially produced dispositions, since these tendencies would be genetically self-eliminating. How can one account for effective individual commitment to ideals and future social arrangements when these run counter to the survival of both one's own genes and one's own current social system? To label such positive self-sacrificial altruism "masochism" or "ethnophobia" merely provides a disparaging description, not an explanation, unless one can specify a plausible genetic or social selective system that would provide it. . . . If we are to take this problem area seriously, we should make the issues and the alternatives explicit and test out their joint effects in the disciplined speculation of mathematical and computer simulation.

Implications for Peace

Skipping the doubts of the last paragraph and accepting the conclusion that man's termite- and ant-like capacity for military heroism is in culturally transmitted dispositions, not genetic ones, make me more optimistic about the possibilities of social inventions eliminating war, for such developments will have the temptations of biological selfishness on their side. However resistant culture is to change, it is probably less so than is the gene pool. I have argued (1965b) that intransigent public leaders in the United States had a popular advantage over peacemakers, as exemplified in the competition between Nixon and Kennedy for the most bellicose stand in the 1960 campaign, the public pillorying after the Cuban crisis of 1962 of Kennedy's more conciliatory advisors rather than the more warlike ones, etc. Perhaps the Johnson–Goldwater campaign, Johnson's decision not to run in 1968, and the public acceptance of conscientious objection and draft resistance show a shift in public preference so that the apparent peacemaker now has the popular advantage. These optimistic observations do not, of course, imply optimism about the organizational future of those societies that are first to lose the archaic capacity to fight wars; for, until all nations have achieved this state of intelligent cultural decay, those that achieve it first will be at a decided disadvantage in international competition. We should note, too, that our great cities and large populations are also manifestations of our termite-like capacity for complex social interdependence; they are thus also in jeopardy as we tear down the belief systems of the past and the altruistic purposes and dispositions they provided. What are grounds for optimism with regard to the problem of war may also be grounds for pessimism about our capacity to maintain the still functional aspects of complex social interdependence.

SUMMARY

Man is more similar to the social insects than to the wolf and the chimpanzee in regard to complex social coordination, division of labor, and self-sacrificial altruism. In the social insects, the behavioral dispositions involved are genetically determined, an evolution made possible by the absence of genetic competition among the cooperators. In man, genetic competition precludes the evolution of such genetic altruism. The behavioral dispositions that produce complex social interdependence and self-sacrificial altruism must instead be products of culturally evolved indoctrination that has had to counter self-serving genetic tendencies. Thus, unlike the social insect, man is profoundly ambivalent in his social role—as Freud noted.

REFERENCES

Allee, W. C., Emerson, A. E., Park, O., Park, T., & Schmidt, K. P. *Principles of animal ecology.* Philadelphia: Saunders, 1949.

Aronfreed, J. The socialization of altruistic and sympathetic behavior: Some theoretical and experimental analyses. In J. Macaulay & L. Berkowitz (Eds.), *Altruism and helping behavior.* New York: Academic Press, 1970, Pp. 103–126.

Auger, P. *L'homme microscopique: Essai de monodologie.* Paris: Flammarion, 1952.

Bakan, D. *The duality of human existence.* Chicago: Rand McNally, 1966.

Berkowitz, L. *Aggression: A social psychological analysis.* New York: McGraw-Hill, 1962.

Brian, M. V. *Social insect populations.* New York: Academic Press, 1965.

Burhoe, R. W. (Ed.). Religion's role in the context of genetic and cultural evolution: Campbell's hypotheses and some evaluative responses. *Zygon,* 1976, *11*(3), 156–303.

Campbell, D. T. Variation and selective retention in sociocultural evolution. In R. W. Mack, G. I. Blanksten, & H. R. Barringer (Eds.), *Social change in underdeveloped areas: A reinterpretation of evolutionary theory.* Cambridge, Mass.: Schenkman, 1965. (a)

Campbell, D. T. Ethnocentric and other altruistic motives. In D. Levine (Ed.), *Nebraska symposium on motivation: 1965.* Lincoln: University of Nebraska Press, 1965. (b)

Campbell, D. T. On the conflicts between biological and social evolution and between psychology and moral tradition. *American Psychologist,* 1975, *30,* 1103–1126. Reprinted in *Zygon,* 1976, *11*(3), 167–208.

Childe, V. G. *Social evolution.* London: Watts, 1951.

Cohen, R. The strategy of social evolution. *Anthropologica,* 1962, *4,* 321–348.

Coser, L. A. *The functions of social conflict.* Glencoe, Ill.: Free Press, 1956.

Crowe, B. L. The tragedy of the commons revisited. *Science,* 1969, *166,* 1103–1107.

Freud, S. *Civilization and its discontents.* London: Hogarth, 1930. (Standard ed., Vol. 21, 1961.)

Frohlich, N., & Oppenheimer, J. A. I get by with a little help from my friends: The "free-rider" problem. *World Politics*, 1970, *23*, 104–120.

Gadgil, M. Evolution of social behavior through interpopulation selection. *Proceedings of the National Academy of Sciences (U.S.A.)*, 1975, *72*, 1199–1201.

Ghiselin, M. T. *The economy of nature and the evolution of sex*. Berkeley: University of California Press, 1974.

Ginsberg, M. Social evolution. In M. Banton (Ed.), *Darwinism and the study of society*. Chicago: Quadrangle Books, 1961, Pp. 95–127.

Haldane, J. B. S. *The cause of evolution*. London: Longmans, 1932.

Hamilton, W. D. The genetical evolution of social behavior. *Journal of Theoretical Biology*, 1964, *7*, 1–51.

Hamilton, W. D. Selection of selfish and altruistic behavior in some extreme models. In J. F. Eisenberg & W. S. Dillon (Eds.), *Man and beast: Comparative social behavior*. Washington, D.C.: Smithsonian Institution Press, 1971, Pp. 57–91.

Hardin, G. The tragedy of the commons. *Science*, 1968, *162*, 1243–1248.

Hebb, D. O. Comment on altruism: The comparative evidence. *Psychological Bulletin*, 1971, *76*, 409–410.

Hebb, D. O., & Thompson, W. R. The social significance of animal studies. In G. Lindzey (Ed.), *Handbook of social psychology*, Vol. 1. Cambridge, Mass.: Addison Wesley, 1954, Pp. 532–561. Reprinted in G. Lindzey & E. Aronson (Eds.), *Handbook of social psychology* (2nd ed), Vol. 2, 1968, Pp. 729–774.

Krebs, D. L. Altruism: An examination of the concept and a review of the literature. *Psychological Bulletin*, 1970, *73*, 258–302.

Krebs, D. L. Infrahuman altruism. *Psychological Bulletin*, 1971, *76*, 411–414.

Krishna, K., & Weesner, F. M. (Eds.). *Biology of termites*. New York: Academic Press, 1969.

LeVine, R. A., & Campbell, D. T. *Ethnocentrism: Theories of conflict, ethnic attitudes and group behavior*. New York: Wiley & Sons, 1972.

Lewontin, R. C. Selection in and of populations. In J. A. Moore (Ed.), *Ideas in modern biology*. Garden City, N.Y.: Natural History Press, 1965, Pp. 297–311.

Lewontin, R. C. Review of G. C. Williams, *Adaptation and natural selection*. *Science*, 1966, *152*, 338–339.

Lewontin, R. C. The units of selection. *Annual Review of Ecology and Systematics*, 1970, *1*, 1–18.

Lorenz, K. *On aggression*. New York: Harcourt, Brace, and World, 1966.

Olson, M. *The logic of collective action*. New York: Schocken, 1968.

Ranulf, S. *Moral indignation and middle class psychology*. Copenhagen: Levin & Munksgaard, 1938.

Rosenblatt, P. C. Origins and effects of group ethnocentrism and nationalism. *Journal of Conflict Resolution*, 1964, *8*, 131–146.

Schelling, T. C. On the ecology of micromotives. *The Public Interest*, 1971, *25*, 61–98.

Sherif, M., & Sherif, C. W. *Groups in harmony and tension*. New York: Harper, 1953.

Sumner, W. G. *Folkways*. New York: Ginn, 1906.

Trivers, R. L. The evolution of reciprocal altruism. *Quarterly Review of Biology*, 1971, *46*, 35–37.

Waddington, C. H. *The ethical animal*. London: Allen & Unwin, 1960.

Waddington, C. H. The human evolutionary system. In M. Banton (Ed.), *Darwinism and the study of society*. Chicago: Quadrangle Books, 1961, Pp. 63–81.

Wellisch, E. *Isaac and Oedipus: A study in biblical psychology of the sacrifice of Isaac, the Akedah.* London: Routledge and Kegan Paul, 1954.

Williams, G. C. *Adaptation and natural selection.* Princeton, New Jersey: Princeton University Press, 1966.

Williams, G. C. (Ed.). *Group selection.* Chicago: Aldine-Atherton, 1971.

Wilson, D. S. A theory of group selection. *Proceedings of the National Academy of Science,* 1975, *72*(1), 143–146.

Wilson, E. O. The prospects for a unified sociobiology. *American Scientist,* 1971, *59*, 400–403. (a)

Wilson, E. O. *The insect societies.* Cambridge, Mass.: Belknap Press, 1971. (b)

Wilson, E. O. Group selection and its significance for ecology. *BioScience,* 1973, *23*, 631–638.

Wilson, E. O. *Sociobiology: The new synthesis.* Cambridge, Mass.: Belknap Press of Harvard University Press, 1975.

Wispé, L. G., & Thompson, J. N. Jr. (Eds.). The war between the words; Biological versus social evolution and some related issues. *American Psychologist,* 1976, *31*(5), 341–384.

Wright, D. *The psychology of moral behaviour.* Harmondsworth, England: Penguin, 1971.

Wright, E. Evolution in Mendelian populations. *Genetics,* 1931, *16*, 97–159.

Wynne-Edwards, V. C. *Animal dispersion in relation to social behavior.* Edinburgh: Oliver & Boyd, 1962.

Wynne-Edwards, V. C. Intergroup selection in the evolution of social systems. *Nature,* 1963, *200*, 623–626.

Wynne-Edwards, V. C. Self-regulating systems in populations of animals. *Science,* 1965, *147*, 1543–1547.

3

Of Marmots and Men:
Animal Behavior
and Human Altruism

ROGER D. MASTERS

HEDONISM AND ALTRUISM IN WESTERN THOUGHT

Are human beings by nature cooperative and altruistic, or is human nature intrinsically egoistic and competitive? This fundamental issue is as old, or older than, the Western tradition of political theory. For the pre-Socratic philosophers, as for moderns like Hobbes, men are naturally oriented to individual gain; for these thinkers, altruistic behavior is merely a culturally acquired restraint on the desires of competitive individuals. In contrast, Plato and Aristotle as well as Hegel and Marx view human beings as naturally social, so that cooperation and altruism are at least as natural for our species as rivalry.

In ancient Greece, the question was therefore already posed with clarity. The pre-Socratics developed a frankly egoistic or hedonistic theory of human nature, in which cooperative or altruistic behaviors are merely necessary evils for calculating, selfish individuals. Best known from the speeches of Thrasymachus in Plato's *Republic,* this hedonistic view treats human laws or customs as "restraints" on nature. As Antiphon the Sophist puts it in *On Truth:*

> Men draw life from the things that are advantageous to them: they incur death from the things that are disadvantageous to them. But the things which are established as advantageous in the view of the law are restraints on nature, whereas the things established by nature as advantageous are free. Therefore things which cause pain do not, on a right view, benefit nature more than things which cause pleasure; and therefore, again, things which cause suffering would not be more advantageous than things which cause happiness—for things which are really [i.e., truly or in truth] advantageous ought not to cause detriment, but gain.... Take the case of those who retaliate only after suffering injury, and are never themselves the aggressors; or those who behave well to their parents, though their parents behave badly to them; or those, again, who allow others to prefer charges on oath, and bring no such charges themselves. Of the actions here mentioned one would find many to be inimical to nature. They involve more suffering when less is possible, less pleasure when more is possible, and injury when freedom from injury is possible [Barker, 1960, pp. 96–97].

In short, since humans naturally follow individual gain or pleasure, altruism can only be explained as the result of social custom or convention—and thus is essentially learned.

Both Plato and Aristotle, following the tradition apparently inaugurated by Socrates, contest this position. For example, when Aristotle asserts that man is by nature a "political animal," he directly challenges the Sophists' assertion that human society rests on contractual or conventional obligations among calculating individuals. Aristotle's view rests on a developmental or evolutionary account of social cooperation:

> The family is the association established by nature for the supply of men's everyday wants.... But when several families are united,... the first society to be formed is the village. And the most natural form of the village appears to be that of a colony from the family.... When several villages are united in a single complete community, large enough to be nearly or quite self-sufficing, the state [*polis*] comes into existence, originating in the bare needs of life, and continuing in existence for the sake of a good life. And therefore, if the earlier forms of society are natural, so is the state [*polis*], for it is the end of them, and the nature of a thing is its end. For what each thing is when fully developed, we call its nature, whether we are speaking of a man, a horse, or a family.... Hence it is evident that the state [*polis*] is a creation of nature, and that man is by nature a political animal. And he who by nature and not by mere accident is without a state [*polis*] is either a bad man or above humanity [*Politics,* I.1252 b 27–1253 a 4; ed. McKeon, 1941, pp. 1128–29].

When some men rule others for their common benefit, Aristotle maintains, this situation is natural and in the interest of all; hence, not only is altruism or sharing virtuous, but such moral virtue is also the development of human nature, not merely a conventional restraint on individual pleasure or gain.

Among moderns, the same issue separates individual hedonists like Hobbes and Locke (Macpherson, 1962; Strauss, 1953) from the continental tradition stemming from Hegel and Marx (see Masters, 1977). As these examples suggest, the perennial question of altruism and selfishness has immense consequences for one's understanding of the origins and limits of political and social obligation. Opposed views tend to suggest different psychological theories as well as different ethical and legal ideals.

Theories of human nature are thus not merely normative preferences unrelated to scientific inquiry. The great thinkers of the past always took into consideration the science of their time, just as empirical science inevitably raises moral and philosophical questions (Masters, 1978). Hence it is of the greatest importance to assess the bearing of contemporary scientific evidence on this persistent problem of political philosophy and psychology.

SOCIOBIOLOGY AND HUMAN NATURE

Over the last generation, prodigious advances in the biological sciences have led to renewed debates concerning human nature. Comparisons between humans and other species, though still criticized in some quarters, have been shown to be possible—and even essential—provided they are drawn with adequate care and specificity (Lorenz, 1974; von Cranach, 1976). In particular, research in population genetics and ethology, recently described globally as "sociobiology" (Wilson, 1975), casts new light on the issue of human altruism and competitiveness.

In the late nineteenth and the early twentieth century, Darwin's theory of evolution was interpreted to mean that natural selection favored the "survival of the fittest." Social Darwinists thus used a conception of natural competition to justify laissez-faire capitalism. Contemporary biologists have of course abandoned such a view of natural selection, not to mention its transformation into an ideological defense of free enterprise.

Since "fitness" is now defined as the capacity to transmit genes to succeeding generations, it is usually said that evolution merely favors those organisms producing more than the average number of offspring—

and hence exhibiting an "advantage in differential reproduction [Simpson, 1967, pp. 221–224]." As a result, it is "simply the fit, rather than the 'fittest,' who survive [Dobzhansky, 1955, p. 112]." In the last few years, this approach has been redefined as "inclusive fitness." According to this concept, animals tend to maximize the proportion of their own genes transmitted to subsequent generations (whether or not these genes are carried by their own offspring).

On the surface, there is a striking similarity between the logic of hedonists like Antiphon the Sophist and of biologists like Hamilton (1964), Trivers (1971), and Wilson (1975, pp. 118–121, 341–344, 415–417, et passim). For Antiphon, the proof that men are naturally selfish is that when individuals are unobserved, they violate the laws: "A man, therefore, who transgresses legal rules, is free from shame and punishment whenever he is unobserved by those who made the covenant, and is subject to shame and punishment only when he is observed [Barker, 1960, p. 95; cf. Plato, Republic, II.359c–360d]." Genetic theorists use exactly the same argument with reference to animal behavior when describing the selective advantage of "disguised cheating and sham cooperation [Campbell, 1972, p. 30]."

Clearly, the Sophist tradition—and its modern equivalent in Hobbes and his followers—was an extremely insightful analysis of the theoretical issue posed by cooperation among individually competing organisms. But modern biology leads one to question whether this problem is appropriately viewed from the perspective of the individual *organism* (or phenotype); now biologists speak of *genes*, not individuals, as "selfish" (Dawkins, 1976). Despite similarities in logic, the Sophist perspective is very different from one according to which an organism's "advantage" or "interest" is measured by the fate of its genes rather than by its immediate pleasures and pains. Hence the Sophists did not conclude that it is *natural* to sacrifice in favor of one's child (Gernet, 1923, p. 182), let alone to prefer one's sister's offspring to one's own. In contrast, theories of inclusive fitness show how such apparent "self-sacrifice" can be the most effective way of increasing the proportion of an individual's genes in the next generation.

Whatever the limitations of sociobiology, it is a major error to confuse contemporary theories of inclusive fitness with the outmoded individualism of Social Darwinists. True, some population biologists have concluded that altruism is highly unlikely to be favored by natural selection, due to a number of theoretical constraints. Following this interpretation, Campbell, in Chapter 2 in this volume, presents the argument that humans are naturally hedonistic or selfish and that our social cooperation results from cultural or learned mechanisms. But others have argued that altruistic behavior can be favored by natural selection, at least under specifiable conditions (see Wilson, 1975 and Chapter 1 in this volume).

The concept of "inclusive fitness" thus does not solve the question of whether or not humans are naturally selfish or naturally altruistic (cf. Barkow, 1978). On the contrary, theoretical arguments based on the presumed "selfish" competition between isolated genes have been challenged on the grounds that they ignore the importance of evolution at the level of the genome as a whole (Alexander & Sherman, 1977). Indeed, the latest work at the molecular level suggests that genetic sequences can overlap, so that the concept of the gene as a totally discrete unit may not always be consistent with the physical properties of DNA strings (Kolata, 1977).

It follows that the debate on altruism is not likely to be resolved solely on the basis of abstract genetic theories; in particular, consideration of empirical data from ethology is also necessary. This is especially so because arguments derived from population genetics often focus on a presumed gene for altruistic bravery (e.g., Wilson and Campbell, Chapters 1 and 2 in this volume). That is, the question is posed as if cooperative behaviors detrimental to individual survival would only be transmitted genetically if there existed a distinct gene for them. Yet this assumption is not merely debatable, but contrary to a wide range of research in animal behavior.

ANIMAL BEHAVIOR AND SOCIAL COOPERATION

One of the most obvious examples of "altruistic" self-sacrifice occurs when an individual fights—and dies—in defense of his group. This behavior is often taken as a test of human altruism, on the assumption that fighting *within* a group is a sign of individual competitiveness or hedonism, whereas fighting *between* groups is evidence of altruism. As a result, Campbell sharply contrasts territorial defense by individuals— presumably "selfish" or competitive—with "real group conflicts," in which altruistic individuals cooperate to defend their group's territory against another group (e.g., Campbell, 1972, p. 24).

Ethology shows, however, that *inter*group rivalry is not simply the opposite of *intra*group conflict, such as establishment and defense of individual territory or social dominance. On the one hand, competition within the group is not merely "selfish"; on the other, defense of the group is not a pure case of "altruism." In many social vertebrates, and especially in the primates, physical traits or behaviors can satisfy *more than one* function, depending on circumstances (see Appendix).

This multifunctionality of behavior deserves examination. Competition is often related to rivalry for dominance, whether in the form of status in a dominance hierarchy or as control over territory (Lorenz & Ley-hausen, 1973, pp. 120–136). In many species, including primates, such dominance seems to be correlated with reproductive success (Hall & DeVore, 1965, pp. 72–77; Southwick, 1965). In these cases, highly dominant males leave behind a disproportionate percentage of offspring in each generation. Hence a trait that gives its possessor an adaptive advantage in sexual encounters often has effects on other social behaviors as well.

Assume that dominance behaviors, including privileged access to re-ceptive females and a tendency to serve as the focus of group "attention structure" (Chance, 1967), are individually beneficial traits. Classical theories of population genetics account for the natural selection of the competitive behaviors usually associated with dominance. But in differ-ent settings these very behavioral traits can also produce altruistic de-fense against predators or other groups of the same species. For example, dominant baboon males move rapidly to counter any threat to the band as soon as they are alerted by the warning signals of peripheral juveniles (Bert *et al.*, 1967; DeVore & Hall, 1965; Kummer, 1971). Since such behaviors are conventionally described as "altruistic bravery," a tradi-tional selective process easily accounts for the possibility of an "ambi-valence" between hedonism and social cooperation.

If the selection pressure in favor of traits associated with intragroup dominance is high enough, these traits will have a selective advantage even if some of their possessors die or do not reproduce because of in-creased vulnerability to predators or to other groups of the same species. Natural selection could simultaneously favor *both* the adult males' traits of size, strength, or intragroup aggressiveness *and* their "altruistic brav-ery" in defense of the group. The "cost" of these traits to those who are wounded or killed would be less than the average "benefit" they confer on those who are not. This is, in fact, what is meant by evolutionary "fitness."

In other words, studies of animal behavior show that natural selec-tion can account for what is conventionally called altruistic behavior among individuals who compete for reproductive success. Given the multifunctionality of bodily or behavioral traits in complex vertebrates like the primates, theoretical discussions in terms of a "gene for altru-ism" are misleading. There is every reason to assume that *both* hedonis-tic *and* cooperative behaviors are favored to some extent by selection among primate species with relatively elaborate patterns of socialization and group structure. And, if so, it is hardly unreasonable to hypothesize that similar genetic factors are present in *Homo sapiens*.

It may be objected that population genetics establishes strict limits to the altruism possible among primates like ourselves. Campbell, for example, argues that genetic competition limits the innate social cooperation possible among vertebrates. In this view, only social insects with sterile worker and soldier castes can develop complex social systems comparable to a human civilization but based on an instinctively programmed altruism. According to this argument, vertebrate sociality may reach its limit with packs of wolves and troupes of chimpanzees, which include at best only several families.

This conclusion is questionable. If one measures "sociality" in terms of complexity, it could be argued that hamadryas baboons have a more intricate social structure than wolves or chimpanzees (cf. Kummer, 1971 and Reynolds, 1967, 1968). And if one defines "sociality" as the degree of cooperative behavior, chimpanzees seem somewhat more individualistic and less "social" than baboons or rhesus monkeys, who form lasting structured groups and exhibit such potentially "altruistic" behaviors as "vigilance," dispute settlement, and defense against predators (Southwick et al., 1965). In some cases, two or three dominant males actually form coalitions and mutually assist each other in maintaining their status (Altmann, 1967). Indeed, even such an apparently "hedonic" behavior as primate grooming is in part social and cooperative, controlling parasitic disease and maintaining the dominance structure (Sparks, 1969).

One could, of course, dismiss these details as minor corrections. When arguing that "human complex social interdependence greatly exceeds that of wolves and chimpanzees," Campbell has in mind civilizations like "Ancient China, the valleys of the Indus and the Ganges, the Aztecs, Mayas, and Incas [see Chapter 2, this volume, pp. 51 and 52]." Such large-scale societies are crucial for those who argue that human altruism is sociocultural rather than genetic in origin. Since this view is shared by many social scientists, it is worth examination.

Clearly, Campbell cannot merely be saying that empires and large-scale civilizations were produced by cultural evolution. Were that the case, there would be less to his argument than meets the eye. Obviously, this form of human culture was the result of cultural evolution. The argument appears to go beyond such circular reasoning to suggest that genetic competition places a narrow limit on natural cooperation in *any* human group. If so, altruism is "socially induced" even in the smaller human societies that antedated the emergence of civilized empires and survived alongside them until the twentieth century.

Such an argument equates "complexity" with "civilization" in a way that is doubly vulnerable to criticism. On the one hand, the cultural complexity of preliterate human hunter–gatherers now appears to be far greater than was assumed by those dismissing such peoples as "primitive" (Lévi-Strauss, 1962). And, on the other hand, it is probably a serious mistake to equate the size or stratification pattern of an animal society with its "social interdependence." Quite to the contrary, contemporary sociobiology points to a wide variety of social patterns as alternate strategies for species survival, often in response to the ecological setting. Hence the structure of social behavior need not be considered solely, or even primarily, in terms of the "altruism" or "competitiveness" of individuals.

OF MARMOTS AND MEN

Recent work in sociobiology has begun to explain the difference between species whose members live in isolation and those living in colonies as a function of their typical environments. Rather than attributing the apparent complexity of social structures to the "instincts" of individual animals, sociobiologists are looking at the ecological niche of different species—or of populations of a single species. The results of this approach show the error of assuming that vertebrate social complexity is caused by individual traits.

For example, Barash (1974) has presented a general theory of the evolution of marmot societies. Marmots (the genus *Marmota*) are rodents, of which the most familiar is the woodchuck. Different species of this genus have highly varied patterns of social organization.

> The woodchuck, M. *monax*, is best known east of the Mississippi, where it most commonly inhabits fields and forest ecotones at low elevations. . . . In this comparatively equitable environment, woodchucks are solitary and aggressive; the association between adult male and female is essentially limited to copulation, the only lasting social tie being the mother-young nexus, which itself terminates at weaning when the young disperse [Barash, 1974, p. 415].

Apart from aggressive encounters between adult males, M. *monax* thus seems to approximate Rousseau's famous description of the "state of nature" in which humans originally were solitary, "wandering in the forests, without industry, without speech, without war and without liaisons [Masters, 1964b, p. 137]."

Although these woodchucks seem to illustrate the minimum of "sociability" in the natural world, not all marmots have this mode of life:

> by contrast, the Olympic marmot (M. *olympus*) is highly social, living in distinct, closely organized colonies usually composed of several adults (most commonly one male and two females), 2 year olds, yearlings, and

the young of the year. This species is highly tolerant and playful, commonly feeding in social groups of three to six individuals. No territories or even distinct individual home ranges are maintained; all parts of the colony are equally available to all colony members. Dominance relationships are generally indistinct and nonpunitive. Olympic marmot social life is characterized by a high frequency of 'greeting behaviors'... apparently associated with individual recognition [Barash, 1974, p. 415].

As Barash's analysis makes clear, the difference between the "individualistic" woodchucks and the "sociable" Olympic marmot is strongly correlated with their environmental niches. M. Monax benefits from "a relatively long vegetative growing season" and exploits its favorable environment by population dispersion. M. olympus inhabits "the alpine meadows in Olympic National Park, Washington . . . at or above timberline where they experience very short growing seasons of 40 to 70 days [ibid., p. 415]." Under these harsher conditions, a more elaborate colony structure has selective advantages.

It would make relatively little sense to attribute this difference in social organization to "learning" on the part of Olympic marmots, though undoubtedly some components of marmot behavior are learned. Moreover, it is not even clear that M. olympus is more "social" than M. monax. Rather, different social patterns are best understood as species-specific adaptations to varied ecological niches (cf. Martin, 1972, p. 429). The isolated individuals of M. monax represent an effective means by which the species has adapted to the environment of fields and low level forests, just as the colonies of M. olympus are an adaptive response to the harsher conditions of alpine meadows.

Barash is able to provide convincing evidence for such an interpretation. For example, he shows that another species, the yellow-bellied marmot (M. flaviventris), not only inhabits environments intermediate to those of M. monax and M. olympus but also exhibits social behaviors intermediate to these more extreme cases. Indeed, within this one species, variations in social structure can be correlated to ecological niche (Barash, 1974, p. 419). Far from attributing the more complex social structure of M. olympus to "genetic altruism" or the solitary life of M. monax to innate "hedonism," Barash thus shows how various marmot species and populations have evolved social structures adapted to their environments. From this perspective, one can speak theoretically of the "strategy" of a gene pool or population instead of postulating attributes of individual organisms (Ehrlich et al., 1975; Slobodkin, 1964).

Three major points follow from Barash's work. First, at least one behavioral trait of the Olympic marmot is unusual and difficult to explain on narrowly "hedonic" grounds. As an adaptation to environmental

severity, M. *olympus* females "produce litters in alternate years only."
After careful examination, Barash concluded that "biennial breeding is
thus apparently a genetically determined characteristic of this species,
just like annual breeding in the woodchuck [1974, p. 418]." This form of
birth control sharply contrasts with the generally prolific breeding of
other rodents and might superficially be described as "altruistic" self-
restraint.

Second, as Barash insists specifically, Wynne-Edwards's (1962) theory
of group selection is "unnecessary as an explanation of . . . the unique
reproductive strategy exhibited by the Olympic marmot." All that need
be assumed is that "traditional" natural selection operates "upon each
individual" and produces "the reproductive performance likely to generate the maximum number of surviving offspring [Barash, 1974,
p. 418]." Although "kin selection" and "interdemic selection" may be
more important than Barash suggests (Wilson, Chapter 1 in this volume),
verification of such theories is not indispensable for demonstrating the
existence of genetically controlled cooperation or altruism among vertebrates.

Third, and perhaps most important of all, the isolated adults of the
woodchuck M. *monax* do not represent the absence of social life (cf.
Lorenz & Leyhausen, 1973, p. 120). This is perhaps most difficult for us
to understand, since it is tempting to conclude that Olympic marmots
are "social" whereas woodchucks are "solitary" or asocial. Such a
Rousseauistic interpretation ignores the behavioral mechanisms required
for the *dispersal of the young*, who are forced to leave their mothers in
both species. The difference, on closer inspection, is that different marmot species have evolved different tolerances for a persisting bond
between maturing young and adults.

Apparently aggressive interactions between members of a species must
therefore be understood as fundamentally *social* behavior (cf. Masters,
1964a). Maturing infants in both woodchucks and Olympic marmots are
rejected by their mothers after a certain stage of development. When
young Olympic marmots were experimentally removed from their home
colony and later reintroduced, they were received "in an unusually aggressive manner" similar to contacts between woodchucks (Barash,
1974, p. 417). The degree of rejection would thus not seem to be a
measure of "individualism," but rather an aspect of behavioral development and population structure characterizing a species in its ecological
niche.

Similarly, primate mothers are often observed to reject their maturing
infants at the stage when infant peer groups begin to form. Although
the precise details vary in different species, one researcher concludes

that, in general, "the more the mother rejects the infant, the more dependent does the infant become [Kaufman, 1974, p. 60]." Even where increased maternal hostility to an infant does not prolong the mother–infant bond, one could hardly conclude that the behavior involved is antisocial: "Rejection increases the tendency to attachment ... at the same time as it progressively denies the person of the mother as the object for attachment thus leading to major attachments to *other* objects, an essential requirement of advanced societal living [*ibid.*, p. 59]."

The same primate species often exhibits different social patterns in different settings (e.g., Jay, 1965; Ripley, 1967; Sugiyama, 1967). Beyond the complexity and variety of the behavioral adaptations of marmots, monkeys, and humans, we thus see different solutions to the ubiquitous problem of the survival of species as breeding units. When observers identify some of these behaviors as "cooperative" and "altruistic"—or describe animals as "hedonistic"—they are thus classifying forms of interaction, *not* discovering a fundamental natural trait of individuals that causes species to form more or less complex groups.

Social behavior cannot be reduced to or entirely derived from individual traits without reference to the complex interplay of species and their environments. Campbell was probably correct when he originally suggested (1965) that it is insufficient to derive social structures from a psychology of individual motivations. To be sure, it would also be inaccurate to deduce individual motivations from characteristics of groups or species. Contemporary biology stresses the importance of distinct levels of analysis and the danger of reductionism in relating one level to another (Anderson, 1972; Jacob, 1977; Masters, 1973). There is no easy answer to the study of complexity.

THE EVOLUTION OF HUMAN ALTRUISM

The behavior of species as diverse as marmots and primates thus provides evidence that altruistic or cooperative social behavior can be genetically transmitted in vertebrates without postulating group selection. There are excellent reasons for reasserting the view that human competition and cooperation are both in part innate and in part learned (Eibl-Eibesfeldt, 1971). Further evidence of this ambivalence might be found not only in modern biological principles, which reveal the inadequacy of a sharp dichotomy between nature and nurture (Masters, 1975a), but also in the convergence of studies of animal behavior based on the traditions of American experimental behaviorism and European ethological description (Masters, 1976).

There is every reason to believe that we have evolved from early hominids, like *Australopithecus africanus*, who lived in small groups characterized by a combination of cooperation and rivalry (Coppens *et al.*, 1976, esp. p. 548; Humphrey, 1976, pp. 310–312; Thompson, 1976; Isaac, 1978). And such studies of our evolutionary origins are confirmed by careful research into the mixtures of aggressive and cooperative behaviors in very young children (e.g., Montagner, 1977)—as well as by the combination of innate and acquired elements in human emotional and social behavior (e.g., Ekman, 1978). Recent evolutionary anthropology thus agrees with the emerging field of human ethology: Both genetic and cultural causal processes contribute to both human cooperation and human competition.

Such research puts a new light on Freud's treatment of social taboos as restraints on the pleasurable drives of individuals. Without endorsing Freud's poetic dichotomy of "eros" and "thanatos," something like this ambivalence does indeed seem to be natural. To be sure, some taboos are purely cultural in origin. But consider incest, which—even if not absolutely universal—is probably the most widespread of these cultural prohibitions. There is good evidence to believe that the avoidance of interbreeding with close kin has a biological element (Bischoff, 1972).

It has been said that "Freud was wrong in believing that length of *time* in evolutionary history is the problem" underlying the duality of competition and cooperation in humans (Campbell, 1972, p. 32). Let me conclude by suggesting that Freud may well have been correct after all. Assuming that both hedonism and altruism are partly innate and partly learned in our species, could human evolution have altered the balance in a potentially dangerous way?

Prior to the neolithic revolution, hominids lived for at least several million years in small hunting and gathering groups (Morin, 1973; Thompson, 1976). If primate sociology and anthropology give us a clue, dominance and group defense would probably have become more advantageous (and hence the selective pressure in favor of them more marked) as population densities increased the frequency of group interaction. Sometime in the 3 million years or more of hominid evolution prior to the emergence of civilization, humans developed languages. By the time of the oldest cave paintings, 40,000 to 50,000 years ago, some forms of ritual and magic were in existence. Hence, since the Pleistocene, we can assume something like a "culture" as a complex symbolic system for social coordination.

As long as the size of human groups remained relatively small, the ambivalence between altruism and selfishness, of which baboons and rhesus monkeys would be examples, need not have been a serious problem for the species. A high proportion of all males in the early human populations would exercise dominant behaviors if, as among many baboon and rhesus groups, 2 or 3 out of 10 to 15 males formed a dominant alliance coordinating group behavior. It would not be hard to explain genetic as well as cultural selection for traits that produced dominance within the band, an ability to lead the hunt, and "altruistic bravery" in defending the group.

In this hypothesis, rapid evolution to very large populations over the last 10,000 years—made possible by agricultural food surpluses—has required an enlarged *scope* of altruism or cooperation and an equally enlarged arena of in-group competition or threat behavior. This extension of both human cooperation and human competition to broader objects was, of course, only possible through cultural means. But in so doing, the rapid sociocultural evolution we call "history" has put enormous strains on our species.

From this perspective, time is indeed a major variable. Large-scale human civilizations are superimposed on a species with a long history of cooperative competition in small bands. Even within modern societies, groups of 10 to 15 males have persisted as key units—boards of directors, cabinets or councils of ministers, sports teams . . . (Tiger, 1969). Success in agonistic or aggressive behavior within such a small cooperative group seems to correlate with reproductive success in many primates. The persistence of similar groups within modern civilizations suggests that humans retain an analogous primate heritage even within large-scale social systems. What is different in modern civilization is the scope of the society with which individuals identify. And that difference is clearly cultural, necessitating very strong social "indoctrination"—including on occasion a heavy dose of xenophobia, not to mention run-of-the-mill ethnocentrism (Campbell, 1965).

Cultural norms must therefore play a very strong role in reinforcing the appropriate behaviors in human societies. Depending on the cultural context, however, these norms may reinforce either competition (selfishness) or cooperation (altruism). All that we know of cultural variability, especially between Eastern and Western civilizations, would confirm this connection between the evolution of more complex sociopolitical units and the extraordinary differences in behavior patterns from one population to another. But this means that wide cultural variability in our species is a sign of stress, insofar as our primate heritage has ill prepared the human animal to live in enormous, impersonal social systems. Indeed, the relatively transient character of political communities during recorded history underlines the instability of very large units in which the subtle mixtures of competition and cooperation—well-adapted for small groups—are easily destroyed.

It is in this context that political philosophy can be understood as a response to the predicament facing human civilization. Precisely because the ambiguity of cooperation and competition is natural to humans, it is never completely clear how we should relate to each other. And because both selfishness and altruism have a natural root that has been transformed by cultural change, it is rare that political institutions are universally acceptable and stable. Hence, humans are continually led to seek the "right" or "just" way of organizing their social life in the hopes of establishing standards for justifying, improving, or criticizing existing institutions.

As these reflections indicate, research in comparative animal behavior can ultimately contribute to the debates that have traditionally engaged philosophers (Masters, 1975b, 1978). In particular, the conception of natural justice—once at the center of political philosophy (Strauss, 1953)—would seem to be rehabilitated by contemporary ethology. Just as Aristotle rejected the relativism of the Sophists on the grounds that good or just behavior combines both conventional and natural elements, ethologists are coming to view varied cultural practices and norms in a naturalistic framework (Bischoff, 1972; Eibl-Eibesfeldt, 1971; Tiger & Fox, 1969; Wickler, 1972).

There is, of course, a risk in such speculations. The history of Social Darwinist doctrines should be ample warning that the attribution of "natural" status to a definition of justice can easily become ideological. Simplistic teleology in human affairs is dangerous, since it can readily be transformed into a defense of particularistic social opinions and class or national prejudices. Nonetheless, the refusal to consider the biological roots of human political and social life is untenable; rejecting a natural component in human altruism can be as ideological as was Social Darwinism.

We are thus led back to the perennial problems of political philosophy as a legitimate focus for the social sciences. Discussion of the relationship between human selfishness and altruism cannot ignore the character as well as the structure of society. But, to be fruitful, such a philosophical inquiry must be illuminated by the empirical findings and theories of natural science.

Elsewhere (Masters, 1977), I argue that the tradition of political thought represented by Aristotle, Hegel, and Marx—which assumes that society is a natural consequence of human evolution—is generally sounder than the hedonism of the Sophists and of those moderns who returned to their individualistic premises. Similarly, I suggest that Plato and Aristotle seem superior to moderns like Marx and Hegel because the latter assume a historical progress no longer guaranteed in our understanding of evolutionary theory (Jacob, 1977; Masters, 1978).

This assessment of the Western tradition is, however, another matter. For present purposes, it is enough to have shown that contemporary biology supports the view that the human ambivalence between selfishness and altruism is in part genetic and in part cultural. Some may find this conclusion frustrating, since it does not "solve" anything. But the evolution of the tension between cooperation and competition does illustrate one important point: Humans cannot understand their own humanity without asking what kinds of society are truly just, in accordance with nature.

APPENDIX

Many will be unconvinced by the foregoing argument. Comparisons of humans with other animals seem to ignore the most important feature of our species—namely, the large human brain, with its attendant capacity for learning, symbolic communication, and self-consciousness. But this generally accepted view ignores a crucial scientific problem. Where did our big brains come from?

At first glance, the increased cranial capacity of *Homo sapiens* would seem to be an unambiguously adaptive trait: Larger brain capacity could be associated with more complex learning abilities, the capacity to cope with "problems of interpersonal relationships" (Humphrey, 1976), and hence better probabilities of survival and reproduction for the mutants that first carried this trait. Reflection indicates, however, that larger head size at birth also increases the danger that mother, infant, or both might die during childbirth (cf. Montagu, 1968).

The adaptive advantages of increased cranial capacity thus had correlative disadvantages. Moreover, it is far from certain why this particular evolutionary trend occurred when it did in hominid evolution. The fossil record suggests that the earliest hominids maintained a brain size of approximately 800 cc for up to three million years after the initiation of toolmaking. Suddenly, approximately 500,000 years ago, brain size increased rapidly. Since this evolutionary change is not correlated with other known developments in technology, life style, or bodily structure, the emergence of the large human brain (averaging 1400 cc) has never really been explained (cf. Caspari, 1968; Holloway, 1968; Mettler, 1962).

One possibility, rarely discussed, is that changes in hominid proto-culture occurred *before* the increase in brain size and made it possible (cf. Isaac, 1978). If our small-brained ancestors extended their coopera-tion to childbirth, at least to the extent of providing assistance to mothers in cases of difficulty, the increased mother/child mortality in case of a large-brained fetus would have been counterbalanced for the first time. If so, a pattern of social cooperation would have shifted the cost–benefit ratio, permitting the obvious adult adaptiveness of the large brain to come into play (cf. Morin, 1973). Without some such factor, it is hard to see how the increased size of the infant head would not have continued to be a selective disadvantage.

Observations of childbirth in free-ranging primates seem relatively rare, suggesting that it is not a social event for other primates (e.g., van Lawick-Goodall, 1969, p. 370). Chimpanzee females seem to give birth more easily than humans (DeVore, personal communication). When a female baboon was seen immediately after childbirth, "none of the other animals in the group actually approached her. On the contrary, on several occasions she tried to move close to some of them, and these sometimes moved away from her [Hall & DeVore, 1965, p. 85]."

True, childbirth in some existing preliterate tribes is also not a social event. But the human mother can be instructed on delivery, and social assistance is available in case of complications. It would, of course, be necessary to spell out and examine in detail the hypothesis that new forms of social cooperation between the pregnant mother and other members of the group became feasible about 500,000 years ago. But surely it is possible that positive feedback between increased social cooperation and the benefits of larger brains might account for the puzzling way in which the hominid brain increased to its present average size of 1400 cc.

This hypothesis is worth mentioning because the generally assumed relationship of human brain size to complex social systems is in fact debatable. Very often, it has been found that behavioral changes occur before physiological ones. Although bodily mutations sometimes influ-ence behavior, behavioral changes can create the selective advantage for bodily mutations (cf. Mayr, 1958). It is usually argued that humans cooperate in society because they have big brains. Perhaps the truth is that we have big brains because we cooperate in society.

REFERENCES

Alexander, Richard D., & Sherman, Paul D. Local mate competition and parental investment in social insects. *Science*, 1977, *196*, 494–500.

Altmann, Stuart (Ed.). *Social communication among primates.* Chicago: University of Chicago Press, 1967.

Anderson, P. W. More is different. *Science*, 1972, *177*, 393–396.

Barash, David. The evolution of marmot societies: A general theory. *Science*, 1974, *185*, 415–420.

Barker, Ernest. *Greek political theory.* New York: Barnes & Noble, 1960.

Barkow, Jerome H. Culture and sociobiology. *American Anthropologist*, 1978, *80*, 5–20.

Bert, J., Ayats, H., Martin, A., & Collumb, H. Notes sur l'organisation de la vigilance sociale chez le babouin Papio papio dans l'Est Senegalais. *Folia Primat.*, 1967, *6*, 44–47.

Bischoff, N. Biological foundations of the incest taboo. *Social Science Information*, 1972, *6*, 7–36.

Campbell, Donald. Ethnocentric and other altruistic motives. In D. Levine (Ed.), *Nebraska symposium on motivation.* Lincoln: University of Nebraska Press, 1965, Pp. 283–311.

Campbell, Donald. On the genetics of altruism and the counterhedonic components in human culture. *Journal of Social Issues*, 1972, *28*, 21–37.

Caspari, Ernest. Selective forces in the evolution of man. In M. F. A. Montagu (Ed.), *Culture: Man's adaptive dimension.* New York: Oxford, 1968, Pp. 159–169.

Chance, M. R. A. Attention structure as the basis of primate rank orders. *Man*, 1967, *2*, 503–518.

Coppens, Yves, Howell, F. Clark, Isaac, Glynn L., & Leakey, Richard E. F. *Earliest man and environments in the Lake Rudolf basin.* Chicago: University of Chicago Press, 1976.

Dawkins, Richard. *The selfish gene.* New York: Oxford University Press, 1976.

Dobzhansky, Theodosius. *Evolution, genetics, and man.* New York: Wiley, 1955.

Eibl-Eibesfeldt, Irenaus. *Love and hate.* New York: Holt, Rinehart, & Winston, 1971.

Ekman, Paul. Biological and cultural contributions to body and facial movement. In John Blacking (Ed.), *Anthropology of the body.* New York: Academic Press, 1978, Pp. 39–84.

Erlich, Paul, White, Raymond, Singer, Michael, McKechnie, Stephen, & Gilbert, Lawrence. Checkerspot butterflies: A historical perspective. *Science*, 1975, *188*, 221–228.

Gernet, Louis (Ed.). *Antiphon: Discours suivi des fragments d'Antiphon le Sophiste.* Paris: Editions Les Belles Lettres, 1923.

Hall, K. R. L., & DeVore, Irven. Baboon social behavior. In Irven DeVore (Ed.), *Primate behavior.* New York: Holt, Rinehart, & Winston, 1965, Pp. 52–110.

Hamilton, W. D. The genetical theory of social behavior. *Journal of Theoretical Biology*, 1964, *7*, 1–52.

Holloway, Ralph. Cranial capacity and the evolution of the human brain. In M. F. A. Montague (Ed.). *Culture: Man's adaptive dimension.* New York: Oxford, 1968, Pp. 170–196.

Humphrey, N. K. The function of intellect. In P. P. G. Bateson & R. A. Hinde (Eds.). *Growing points in ethology.* Cambridge: Cambridge University Press, 1976, Pp. 303–317.

Isaac, Glynn. The food-sharing behavior of protohuman hominids. *Scientific American*, 1978, *238*, 90–108.

Jacob, François. Evolution and tinkering. *Science*, 1977, *196*, 1161–1166.

Jay, Phyllis. The Common Langur of North India. In Irven DeVore (Ed.), *Primate behavior*. New York: Holt, Rinehart & Winston, 1965, Pp. 197–249.

Kaufman, I. Charles. Mother/Infant relationships in monkeys and humans: A reply to Professor Hinde. In Norman White (Ed.), *Ethology and psychiatry*. Toronto: University of Toronto Press, 1974, Pp. 47–68.

Kolata, Gina Bari. Overlapping genes: More than anomalies? *Science*, 1977, *196*, 1187–1188.

Kummer, Hans. *Primate societies*. Chicago: Aldine-Atherton, 1971.

Lévi-Strauss, Claude. *La pensée sauvage*. Paris: Plon, 1962.

Lorenz, Konrad. Analogy as a source of knowledge. *Science*, 1974, *185*, 229–234.

Lorenz, Konrad, & Leyhausen, Paul. *Motivation of human and animal behavior*. New York: Van Nostrand Reinhold, 1973.

Macpherson, C. B. *The political theory of possessive individualism*. Oxford: Clarendon Press, 1962.

Martin, R. D. Concepts of human territoriality. In Peter Ucko, Ruth Tringham, & G. W. Dimbley (Eds.), *Man, settlement and urbanism*. Cambridge, Mass.: Schenkman, 1972, Pp. 427–445.

Masters, Roger. World politics as a primitive political system. *World Politics*, 1964, *16*, 595–619. (a)

Masters, Roger (Ed.). *Rousseau's First and Second Discourses*. New York: St. Martin's Press, 1964. (b)

Masters, Roger. Functional approaches to analogical comparisons between species. *Social Science Information*, 1973, *12*, 7–35.

Masters, Roger. Politics as a biological phenomenon. *Social Science Information*, 1975, *14*, 7–63. (a)

Masters, Roger. Vers une science? *Contrepoint*, 1975, *16*, 109–122. (b)

Masters, Roger. The impact of ethology on political science. In Albert Somit (Ed.), *Biology and politics*. The Hague: Mouton, 1976.

Masters, Roger. Nature, human nature, and political thought. In Roland Pennock & John Chapman (Eds.), *Human nature in politics*. New York: New York University Press, 1977, Pp. 69–110.

Masters, Roger. Classical political philosophy and contemporary biology. Paper presented at the Conference for the Study of Political Thought. Chicago, Ill., April 7, 1978.

Mayr, Ernst. Behavior and systematics. In Anne Roe & George Simpson (Eds.), *Behavior and evolution*. New Haven: Yale University Press, 1958, Pp. 341–362.

McKeon, Richard (Ed.). *The basic works of Aristotle*. New York: Random House, 1941.

Mettler, Fred A. Culture and the structural evolution of the central nervous system. In M. F. A. Montagu (Ed.), *Culture and the evolution of man*. New York: Oxford University Press, 1962, Pp. 155–201.

Montagner, Hubert. Silent speech. *Horizon—BBC2* (videotape), July 28, 1977.

Montagu, M. F. Ashley. Brains, genes, culture, immaturity, and gestation. In M. F. A. Montagu (Ed.), *Culture: Man's adaptive dimension*. New York: Oxford University Press, 1968, Pp. 102–113.

Morin, Edgar. *Le paradigme perdu*. Paris: Le Seuil, 1973.

Reynolds, Vernon. *The apes*. New York: Harper Colophon, 1967.

Reynolds, Vernon. Kinship and the family in monkeys, apes and man. *Man*, 1968, *3*, 209–223.

Ripley, Suzanne. Intertroop encounters among Ceylon Grey Langurs. In Stuart

Altmann (Ed.), *Social communication among primates.* Chicago: University of Chicago Press, 1967, Pp. 237–253.

Simpson, George Gaylord. *The meaning of evolution* (rev. ed.). New Haven: Yale University Press, 1967.

Slobodkin, Lawrence. The strategy of evolution. *American Scientist,* 1964; *52,* 342–357.

Southwick, Charles, Beg, Mirza Azhar, & Siddiqi, M. Rafiq. Rhesus monkeys in North India. In Irven DeVore (Ed.), *Primate behavior.* New York: Holt, Rinehart & Winston, 1965, Pp. 111–159.

Sparks, John. Allogrooming in primates: A review. In Desmond Morris (Ed.), *Primate ethology.* New York: Doubleday Anchor, 1969, Pp. 190–225.

Strauss, Leo. *Natural right and history.* Chicago: University of Chicago Press, 1953.

Sugiyama, Yokimaru. Social organization of Hanuman Langurs. In Stuart Altmann (Ed.), *Social communication among primates.* Chicago: University of Chicago Press, 1967, Pp. 221–236.

Thompson, Philip R. A behavior model for *Australopithecus africanus. Journal of Human Evolution,* 1976, *5,* 547–558.

Tiger, Lionel. *Men in groups.* New York: Random House, 1969.

Tiger, Lionel, & Fox, Robin. The zoological perspective in social science. *Man,* 1969, *1,* 75–81.

Trivers, R. L. The evolution of reciprocal altruism. *Quarterly Review of Biology,* 1971, *46,* 35–57.

van Lawick-Goodall, Jane. Mother–Offspring relationships in free-ranging chimpanzees. In Desmond Morris (Ed.), *Primate ethology.* New York: Doubleday Anchor, 1969, Pp. 365–436.

von Cranach, Mario (Ed.). *Methods of inference from animal to human behavior.* The Hague: Mouton, 1976.

Wickler, Wolfgang. *The biology of the Ten Commandments.* New York: McGraw Hill, 1972.

Wilson, Edward O. *Sociobiology.* Cambridge, Mass.: Harvard University Press, 1975.

Wynne-Edwards, A. C. *Animal dispersion in relation to social behavior.* Edinburgh: Oliver & Boyd, 1962.

4

Altruism: Human, Cultural, or What?

RONALD COHEN

Some years ago I roomed with a German who had been assigned on his first tour of duty during World War II to a concentration camp—a phenomenon he did not fully believe existed until he got there. One night he told me of a strange event at the camp that nearly drove him mad. Another, older, more seasoned guard was assigning every tenth person to die. When he got to a particular tenth one, instead of telling him to step forward for execution, the guard raised his eyebrows almost imperceptibly and chose the eleventh. The tenth, he explained later, was a *Landsmann* from the same town, and they had known each other before the Hitler period. In other words, while engaged dutifully in mass murder, the guard was merciful and evidently sympathetic with one particular member of the victimized group. I was reminded of this experience during the recent war in Vietnam, when the press often reported quite touching kindness by U.S. military personnel toward individual Vietnamese. At the same time, these soldiers were engaged in delivering indiscriminate death and destruction on the land and people of this small country.

What is it about man that he can often act so cruelly and, at one and the same time, so empathically toward his fellows? I have decided to call this quality the "altruistic paradox," and it is to an understanding of this phenomenon that I wish to address myself in this essay. The examples just alluded to suggest the first attempt at an answer. Man by himself may be good or bad and capable of kindness or cruelty, but, as a member of a system, a society, he is sometimes forced to carry out what we call "inhuman" as well as humane acts. In its optimistic mode (the idea that man is good), I would call it the Rousseauesque tradition of explanation. Man is essentially good and capable of kind and noble thoughts and acts. However, evil results when man is caught within bad societies that stimulate and create bestial, selfish, and "inhuman" behavior. A similar set of assumptions appears in Marxist and environmentalist approaches, in which individuals are considered to be morally neutral but determined by unjust and exploitative "relations of production" or by evil and unsatisfactory social environments. Man's evil is the result of evil surroundings. The opposite and more pessimistic tradition (that man is bad) runs in a line from Machiavelli to Hobbes to Freud. Within this context, man is said to possess basically animalistic and bestial qualities that must be controlled by a society and its laws or else he will become savagely worse than animals of prey.

It is interesting that both these traditions use comparative materials from other cultures to prove the truth of their arguments. Early writers knew of other cultures in a rudimentary way and used cross-cultural comparisons to point out differences and uniquenesses in their own society as well as to provide insights into "human nature." Some viewed their own Western European societies as essentially centrally organized nation states that functioned to provide civilized law and order. Without such a social contract man's basic and brutish nature would assert itself, and life would be horrible, cruel, incestuous, and savage. According to Hobbes, this was in fact the way of life of the American Indian. Other writers (Rousseau and Engels) saw their own society to be corrupt and evil. By comparison, non-Western societies, especially the less complex ones, allowed man's "true," noble nature to express itself in freedom from the evils of contemporary Europe. Therefore they preached reform, indeed fundamental radical change, in order to create new societies that could, like primitive ones, unfetter man's goodness instead of demeaning, corrupting, and exploiting him. Both of these traditions still affect our thinking and theorizing about man's essential nature and about his innate capacity for good, evil, sympathy, callousness, justice, and injustice. In order to get these "innate" qualities, it is necessary to show that man manifests them despite the context in which he develops and lives. Therefore, to ask about altruism or any other feature said to be a quality of human nature we must examine whether or not it persists despite cultural differences.

THE LOGICAL BASES OF ALTRUISM

In order to find out whether man is this or that *by nature*, we must obtain some operationally useful conception of the attribute we are studying. By operationally useful I mean that it can be indicated variously but validly across cultures as well as within the one from which it originated conceptually. For such purposes, altruism can be defined as an act or desire to give something gratuitously to another person or group because he, she, they, or it needs it or wants it. It does not matter whether the thing is oneself or one's power or possessions, only that one can give it. It follows by deduction that, from the individual's point of view, altruism depends upon the ego's knowing and caring about the needs of alter and their satisfaction. Furthermore, although this is probably somewhat more controversial because it is so difficult to demonstrate, altruism also seems to involve the idea of gratuitousness. Altruistic acts are, if you like, their own reward. No reward is or should be sought from alter directly. The person who altruistically picks up spilled groceries for an elderly woman does not do so for a tip or for a share of the groceries. Thus by definition and logical extension, altruism is composed of three elements—giving or the desire to do so, empathy, and no motives of reward from the object of the altruistic behavior. These ideas are discussed by Wispé (1968), who defines the most difficult term here—empathy—as "the self-conscious awareness of the consciousness of the other."

But the definition is just that—a statement of what altruism is. As such it says nothing about the circumstances in which it occurs, or whether it occurs at all. If one or another of these attributes is not clearly present in an act, it would be difficult to label it as altruistic. For example, giving for no reward but without empathy could be done for reasons of obligation tied to a role or status, or because a person is foolishly generous. To obtain some theoretical conception of altruism, we must therefore look at the conditions upon which these components depend.

PSYCHOLOGICAL, CULTURAL, AND
SOCIAL CONDITIONS

Cooley (1902), as discussed by Wispé (1968), tended to obscure these issues in ways that could prove attractive to psychologists. By looking at sympathy from the point of view of both society and the individual and by then saying that society and the individual are the *same* set of phenomena viewed from different perspectives, Cooley was giving the psychologists (*a*) power to generalize beyond the scope of their data; (*b*) help in producing a kind of psychologistic myopia that says, in effect, that the individual is the key to understanding; and (*c*) a solution to the altruistic paradox by saying that it is not real that there is no conflict real or potential between society and the individual, since these are abstractions from a common set of observations.

I have only introduced the Cooley ideas in order to clearly state my own, since to disprove them in detail would take more time than the subject is worth. Like Freud and almost every other serious social theorist of the twentieth century, I accept the idea that the psychological, the cultural, and the social realms or domains are overlapping but significantly independent (and therefore potentially conflicting) aspects of human activity. The Oedipus myth (culture) is similar to but different from the interaction conflicts and coalitions within a Western nuclear family (social), and both of these are related to but distinguishable from the feelings, cognitions, and motivations (psychological) of the persons concerned.

To state this position does not simply upset the Cooley position noted above; it makes every research problem, and all human problems, many, many times more complex than Cooley seems to have hoped they might be. It means that any behavioral output has a psychological, a cultural, and a social side to it. And until we know what each of these realms contribute to occurrences like altruistic acts, it is impossible to understand such complex phenomena from a truly human or cross-cultural perspective. For purposes of space, I will separate the psychological very strictly from the social and the cultural, especially since separating social from cultural is less relevant to this paper and more controversial theoretically.

ALTRUISM AS A PSYCHOLOGICAL PHENOMENON

From the psychological point of view, altruism is not in a strong position either logically or empirically. Logically, the reason is an old philosophical chestnut called the "hedonistic paradox," which states that even the most unselfish act may produce a psychological reward for the actor. Gide, in his novel *Lafcadio's Adventures* (1960), tries to point out that a truly gratuitous act is impossible; either good or bad, rewarding or punishing effects will always result, so that we must simply accept the idea that as we act we must, whether we will it or not, hinder or help ourselves. Since I can never fully get into the mind of another, I can always assume that my giving produces some feelings of satisfaction and well-being, but I can never confidently argue that the desire to give of my efforts, time, or resources is not in terms of real or imagined rewards rather than in terms of some innate helping or altruistic impulse. This means that, in effect, the hedonistic paradox makes a good logical basis for postulating man's essentially hedonistic nature, although it obviously neither proves nor disproves such a postulate or its opposite—namely, that man can act from purely altruistic motives.

What I wish to know from the vantage point of the anthropologist is that altruism as it is known empirically is a complex result of socio-cultural evolution. Psychologically, it is not real, unreal, or absurd. As morality, it has survival value for the population as a whole, and therefore it is learned, selectively retained—and manipulated.

ALTRUISM IN CROSS–CULTURAL PERSPECTIVE

In most, possibly all, cultures, altruism in the form of giving functions to express and maintain group membership and personal identity. At the same time, it can be manipulated to maintain or create prestige and influence. *Giving* in the anthropological literature is generally described under two categories, reciprocity and redistribution. The former involves mutuality or equivalence to gift-giving, whereas the latter denotes non-equivalence, in which some persons give more than others. The empathy–sympathy component of altruism assumes that the capability to feel for others is a constant. In my view, the cross-cultural materials do not support such a notion, by which I mean that the capacity for altruism varies across cultures.

Reciprocal Giving

From the point of view of "human nature," the best place to begin is at the simplest level of sociocultural organization. This is represented by the hunting bands, whose mode of adaptation is by far the longest-lasting in human and human-like history. In this sense, such a state possibly represents man's most "natural" mode of sociocultural and psychological development. Furthermore, the hunting-band stage of adaptation is man's first level of achievement after his emergence from the nonhuman primate background.

Hunting and gathering societies generally involve very low population densities and small local groups. One set of characteristics that decisively differentiates such societies from those of nonhuman groups is that of mutual cooperation and obligatory sharing of food. Role differentiation, longer nurturance of the young, and, more generally, sexual dimorphism are probably at the root of this development. But whatever the cause, obligatory giving is an essential element in the step from the nonhuman to the human phase of evolution. Our closest nonhuman relatives simply do not have the inhibitory capabilities to sustain food-sharing practices.

Reciprocal sharing of food and other gifts defines the network of social relations making up the group of people with whom an individual is meaningfully related. The giving and receiving of these gifts, therefore, also helps to define a person's identity. I am a member of such and such a group. Why? Because we look after each other. Once a person leaves the group, he or she may return once in a while—bringing gifts that are in turn reciprocated—but continuous, obligatory food-sharing is transferred to his or her new group. In this sense, sharing and gift-giving express the network of social relations that a person belongs to.

At the psychological level, this feature has been observed closely, and writers report that its use is primarily to enhance personal power and to create imbalances in interpersonal influence and power. As one writer on obligatory sharing among hunters and gatherers puts it:

> In a reciprocal distributive system in hunting societies an imbalance of production and distribution achieves balance and hence stability through a counterflow of esteem and influence to the person who contributes most. According esteem to the excessive producer results in many people striving to overproduce in order to acquire social esteem. This situation generates competition among hunters for the acquisition of game in order to distribute, i.e., give it [Dowling, 1968, p. 505].

The writer goes on to explain that conflict among hunters over which one actually killed some game is, therefore, not over food but over the right to give it away—to distribute it and thus to acquire the prestige that goes with such giving. This is why strict rules develop to determine who the owner (i.e., the killer) of the dead animal really is (Dowling, 1968). In this same vein, I have witnessed a Hare Indian near the arctic circle of Canada in a near frenzy of decision making because he had killed a moose and was plotting how to give it away for both prestige purposes *and* revenge against those who had up to now slighted him. This latter quality is well-documented by Ridington (1968) in his description of a Beaver Indian who, after making a splendid kill of three moose, could not resist capitalizing on it and therefore gave some very good meat to the leader of a competing faction in the band with whom there was an agreement *not to share* food. The successful hunter broke this custom of:

> tacit nonexchange of meat by taking a box of meat from his kill to Baptiste's camp and shed crocodile tears of mock pity and generosity. Baptiste, obviously put out at his rival's coup, complained that Jonathan had given him bad meat, a form of accusation [Ridington, 1968, p. 1158].

Notice here the ungratefulness (in Western terms) of the recipient, who knows full well the underlying intention of the giver and therefore honestly aims his retort not at the act of giving but at the psychological motivation of prestige-making and shaming that he feels underlies this "generosity."

Redistributive Giving

I emphasize giving among hunters and gatherers because of the great length of time that man has spent in such societies. Compared to the many thousands of years he has been a hunter, he has lived in more complex societies briefly, between five and twelve millennia, and in some places for much less time than that. Thus, as organisms, we are still carrying about many adaptations developed during the earlier hunting phase of evolution. However, it is also true that since neolithic times most of mankind has lived in more compact and more densely populated communities and has had greater control over food production and ever greater control over the environment in general.

This change has produced a concomitant change in giving. Whereas giving is reciprocal among hunters, it is both reciprocal and progressively more redistributive after the hunting stage, among people who farm, keep cattle, or both. Redistributive giving involves the differentiation and institutionalization (culturizing, if you like) of the prestige-seeking hunter-as-giver. It means that differences in status in a household, in a village, or among a set of villages are kept clear and are maintained through unequal giving.[1] Enhancement of status (social mobility) can be

---

[1] As Rosman and Rubel (1974) point out, individuals, especially high status "big men" or chiefs, may be involved in both reciprocal gift-giving with equals and redistributive gift-giving nonequals. This maintains and expresses their chiefly status vis-à-vis other chiefs and their status as big men vis-à-vis followers.

achieved through changing one's giving patterns from reciprocal ones to redistributive ones.

I have observed both successful and unsuccessful attempts at such change-overs in northern Nigeria. High-status men, political leaders, or very wealthy men validate and make real their status by giving more at ceremonies than anyone else does and more than the ceremony giver would ever return to this particular giver. Ordinary people simply go to ceremonies held by those who come to theirs, and giving in such cases is reciprocal. Thus A gives to B what he would expect from B on a similar occasion. But if A is trying to improve his social position, then he goes to many more ceremonies and gives more than he would normally receive on such occasions. If he has the new-found status and wealth to support this change from reciprocity to redistribution, then he can permanently raise his social standing; if not, then he fails and is referred to as a "ceremonies man" or what we would call a spendthrift who uses his wealth foolishly (Cohen, 1970). People who give in this way are in no way deluded about the exchanges involved. They can stipulate what is being given *in exchange* for what and why the actor wishes to obtain such a return. If an interviewer asks from very many different points of view—as I have—why someone should not give of himself or his possessions for the sheer gratification obtained by giving, the informant simply cannot understand the question. "Why do such a thing? If you say there is no reason and this is true, then you should not do it; if this is not true, then you are hiding the real reason and you are an untruthful and untrustworthy person." Although this is a theoretical answer, I have had many intimations of such a view from Kanuri (Nigerian) informants. Either I am going to receive esteem and influence or, if I have acted generously to someone, I want something in particular and will state its as soon as it is diplomatic to do so. This is the Kanuri way (Cohen, 1967) and, as far as I know, it is the way among most people of this world in their everyday behavior—no matter what their ideology may happen to be.

In effect, what this means is that, at the individual psychological level, the hedonistic paradox proclaims a profound truth. Man operates, in a motivational sense, from the point of view of self-interest. At some level of his awareness he can calculate rewards for his action even when the action involves giving away time, energy, wealth, even life itself for others or for a cause. In general, giving is never a simple act. As Mauss, Durkheim, Gouldner, Lévi-Strauss, and a host of writers in sociology and anthropology have claimed and documented, *giving creates obligation or meets it*. Therefore, it is an aspect of power-seeking, of status validation, and of the other factors that enter into social stratification, political organization, and other kinds of organized behavior.

Affective Aspects

On the dimensions of altruism dealing with empathy and sympathy, we move from the cognitive and evaluative aspects of altruism to the affective ones. Feeling what another person feels and suffering with him requires, in my view, a social and cultural setting that rewards such an orientation and the concomitant emotions.

Human beings are capable of enormous callousness. Where death, disease, hunger, and privation are common everyday occurrences, as they still are in most of the world, the individual must adapt to such an environment. He must learn not to be too upset if people close to him disappear suddenly or die slowly and horribly. To become too involved would be maladaptive. Thus people become fatalistic or they say, "He (or she) was (is) just a person," thereby affirming that an individual does not count that much. Instead, the group (lineage, clan, household, etc.) becomes the crucial unit of survival. How else could some of the untold thousands of deaths like those experienced recently in Pakistan be withstood and adapted to? Like all other psychological experiences, misfortune, disaster, and suffering produce rapid adaptation and fatigue, with a concomitant raising of thresholds of sensitivity.

More accurately, the technologically advanced nations can protect individuals from the harsher experiences of human existence, so that thresholds of empathy can be lowered and sympathies "refined" and more widely applied. This does not in any sense mean that people in more developed countries behave more humanely. Hiroshima or Buchenwald are, in my view, infinitely more terrible than Iroquois prisoner torture, in which very few were involved and in which the prisoner redeemed his pride through his reaction to pain. However, like American funerals, modern warfare sanitizes and makes abstract and impersonal the horrors of the cruelty and death we are now capable of delivering to our fellow creatures. Only as a Western-trained anthropologist living in a small African village did I for the first time experience death as an ordinary everyday occurrence. And although shocked at first, by the end of 2 years I, like my fellow villagers, also took it to be sad and avowedly regrettable—but normal.

But the matter is much more complex than this. Empathy and sympathy are affective responses, and two contradictory theoretical positions are applicable in thinking about affect. The most widely held view assumes that all human populations have similar ranges and intensities of affective response; those societies that manifest less are "repressing," and those that show more in the way of feelings and emotions are more "expressive." This assumption is based on the belief that affect itself is fairly constant across populations but that culture determines how it is to be acceptably expressed.

I have no argument with the idea that all human populations manifest similar types of affect. But I am unaware of any research that supports (or negates) the notion of a constancy of affect-intensity across all cultures. Contrarily, I would argue that it is both sensible and theoretically fruitful to assume that intensity of affect varies across human populations. Populations that do not manifest much affect may be assumed to have developed socialization patterns in which affect responses are inhibited through experience. Adults in such populations can be viewed not as *repressing* affect but simply as having less to express because it is simply less developed among the individuals of the society.

My own field experience in Africa and in the Arctic region as well as my reading of the ethnographic literature leads me to postulate a more intense degree of affect among persons in European cultures. For example, Kanuri informants in Nigeria find our concept of romantic love to be a wrong-headed way of forming heterosexual relationships. Admittedly, deep emotional attachments between the sexes do occur. However, these are evaluated as deviant and, in terms of local lore, they are said to be psychologically abnormal. To them it is quite clearly wrong to have such feelings. Indeed, deep emotional involvement with any other person is very uncommon. People do not manifest such affect, and the ease and grace with which this is accomplished lead me to believe that there is not much "repression" in such situations.

Determinants of Affective Intensity

Given the validity of the above observation, we can now ask questions about the determinants of higher and lower ranges of affective intensity among various human societies. Put another way, why are European cultures and their derivatives associated with high affect and many other cultures with much lower degrees of this same quality? I would hypothesize that the major differentiating factors are those of family and household composition and their effects on socialization.

Emotional intensity develops when there are social conditions that allow for durable and frequent interaction between persons. If for some reason social conditions inhibit such interactions, especially during the growth and maturation of the individual, then the amount of affect available for interpersonal relations is less than it is when such early relations are stable, frequent, and durable. In effect, durable parent–child relations produce, develop, and magnify emotional capacities. This is especially so if there are stable monogamous parents rather than a group of "parents" defined as such by the culture. It is more difficult to focus on one parent of each sex in a group, and therefore it is the norm of relating that becomes important rather than the actual person being related to.

In the dominant white American family situation, there are only two parents in a single household, and they have relatively low divorce expectation—only one in about three or four unions end in divorce, a very low rate as compared with other cultures (Cohen, 1971; Goode, 1963). Our traditional and still predominant family pattern is one of intensive, frequent, and durable relations among members, especially when the children are small. Under such conditions affective responses develop and indeed are fostered, so that deep emotional attachments can be part of social relations between persons who are "close to" each other.

It is interesting as a corollary of this idea to note that within such comparatively intense family relations we develop strong superego structures so that, among other things, social control operates through feelings of guilt. In effect, as Freud put it, we internalize not some general notion of authority, but a parent figure and the parental way of doing and feeling about things. Where such family conditions do not hold, then superego feelings are much less intense, and wrongdoing is more a matter of getting caught.

The high affect component in Western social relations also affects our reaction to wider-scaled social relations outside the family. We cannot express such emotions too easily at work or with the taxi driver, so we theorize that society is alienative to the individual. In response, the younger generation—in commenting on social, not psychological, forces—asks not that we gain better understanding of social and political events but that we have more love! Our family system and our socialization procedures have created a cathection for affect that is not common cross-culturally—just as the combination of our family, isolated household, and socialization procedures are not common. This has adaptive features, but, as implied here, it also has maladaptive aspects that should be seriously considered by social reformers.

If for contrast we take the family and household systems most like our own, we must look at people like the Eskimos or the northern Athabascans. They too have bilateral kin groups, and there is a tendency for nuclear family life, although not a definite prescription for such a structure. Traditionally, camp groups often included some other families that were not necessarily related; however, often the heads of these families were brothers. Monogamy was statistically most common (and is now the invariant rule), but both polyandry and polygyny were known among the Eskimos. Marital dissolution by breakup, desertion, sickness, and death has always been quite common, affecting as many marriages as not. However, under the influence of the church, more settled ways, and modern medicine, a number of forces are converging to create conditions that lead to more stable unions.

Given an increase in durable monogamous families, one theory would be to predict kinds of affect development similar to those described here for our own society. However, to a Westerner's eyes these people are inordinately self-controlled and they also tend to show "control" on psychological tests. This control has been interpreted among the Eskimo as a necessity for group survival. A hunter must wait patiently for hours next to a hole in the ice for his and his family's food. If he gets nothing and starvation begins to occur, the group must maintain some form of control—with very little law, no chiefs, no police, only through individual and interpersonal control. As one writer puts it in discussing Eskimo Rorschach responses:

> It is apparent that the Great Whale Eskimo place a very high value on outward poise and community equanimity...where people are so closely thrown together and environmental pressures are so great, emotional control may be essential for survival. It is possible, then, that underlying the affable, fun loving behavior so typical of the Great Whale River Eskimo, there is an habitual disinclination for emotional involvement [Honigmann, 1962, p. 85].

But how are such controls achieved? In another publication on a structurally similar hunting and gathering group (the Kaska), Honigmann (1949) suggests that the inhibitory mechanism is emotional rejection by the mother. For the first 2 or 3 years, the Kaska child is indulged; after that, the child is summarily rejected. This is quickly followed by a regressive reaction in which the child tries to act younger than he or she now is in order to get a replay of the indulgence. Continued reactions, however, simply fail to achieve any response from the mother. This leads to a trauma of disappointment in which the child is finally taught not to cathect love objects. Ultimately, the adult becomes emotionally aloof and fearful of all love relationships. "Realistically regression is impossible; so the person comes to perceive one avenue of safety in the maintenance of personal inviolability and self-sufficiency [Honigmann, 1949, p. 308]." In effect, the demands of an extremely rigorous environment and the child-training practices tend to reinforce one another. We, on the other hand, utilize nuclear family relations to nurture and expand the emotional components of interpersonal relations. Hunters and gatherers of the arctic, although with a similar familial structure, have several distinct differences in the way this pattern is used in that very harsh environment. They have a history of greater marital instability, so that durable parent–child relations have not been as common; they have child-training practices that inhibit emotional development; and they live in a physical environment that favors the resulting personality patterns.

Finally, here is an African example that represents one of the most common forms of family organization in world history. In northern Nigeria the Kanuri live in polygynous compounds with their father, his wives, clients, brothers, brothers' wives, full siblings, half siblings, cousins (also siblings), grandparents, etc. Divorce rates vary from 58 to 99% of all completed marriages (Cohen, 1971). Children, therefore, generally lose their mothers even though fertility lowers the probability of divorce. Furthermore, children often live in a number of households as they grow up. People say it is good for them because it teaches them proper respect for authority. In their own household there are many "fathers" and "mothers." All must be respected and acted properly toward. High affect is negatively regarded. But proper behavior in superior–subordinate relations is highly valued. The growing child is taught by experience, especially by the high turnover of people in his young life, to cathect not particular persons, but *proper behavior*—until finally he or she knows how to use norms of subordination and superordination for personal advantage, indeed, as a kind of currency (Cohen, 1965). To become emotionally involved with people is, therefore, to weaken or lessen one's capacity to cathect roles, norms, and rules rather than the individual who is filling any particular slot. Thus, a man says, "You are my father" to a perfect stranger because he is hoping for a father–son-like relationship vis-à-vis status and material gain. If I would like such a follower, then I treat him like a son, and the relationship has begun; if it is unsatisfactory, we end it; to be emotionally involved would limit our capacities for mobility. So, the lack of emotional content in relationships that is taught by early experiences is adaptive.

It is my hypothesis that these are not isolated cases. Highly developed emotional capacities as parts of interpersonal relationships are, I contend, limited to nuclear family systems in which there are long-term nonrejecting stable relationships with parents who do not share the household with any other adults. This welds emotional qualities to interpersonal relations in a very intense way. And it is under these conditions that the empathy and sympathy necessary for altruism can develop. Thus, psychologically, I would suggest that altruism is culture-dependent and not part of some theoretical notion of human nature.

ALTRUISM AND SOCIOCULTURAL REALITY

As we have seen, individuals as persons can best be viewed as seeking their own self-interest. Even if that self-interest involves drastic danger or self-destruction, we can often interpret the act as one in which the person seeks to create or maintain either real material returns or a good opinion of himself. As we shall see, altruism, as in social giving, is primarily not so much a function of empathy and sympathy but of the sociocultural reality in which an individual finds himself. Sociocultural reality is like psychological levels in that it contains elements and forces that are both conscious and unconscious. Thus, white Americans may know that the black American population has a higher relative percentage of unemployed and a lower average annual income than they do, but they are not aware in any detailed way about the effects of such inequities even though such effects are real forces in their social environment. At the strictly cultural level there are values and ideology and products of behavior that either state outright or symbolize and evaluate desirable actions and beliefs that should be held by the population. Individuals may or may not share or practice such ideological positions, but the position itself exists above and beyond the person and his or her individual life-span. It is in this sense that I speak of the traditions of a people.

A good example of such an ideology is that of Nibbanic Buddhism—the theological tradition of nirvana or nothingness (Spiro, 1970). This well-known tradition teaches that sympathy and empathy are very desirable attributes and must be sought after constantly if man is to achieve nirvana, a salvation of eternal rest. In Buddhist terms, this is defined as the end of individual existence, manifest by a total conjunction of the person with the infinite.

In order to achieve nirvana and destroy one's eternal birth–rebirth cycling, one must learn to love as a basis for moral action. Such "love" is broken down into three parts (a) mettā or loving-kindess, which is a generalized friendliness for all creatures; (b) karunā or pity for those who suffer; and (c) muditā or empathic joy, which is a pleasure felt for the happiness of others. Only after achieving these states can one achieve the emotional detachment necessary for salvation. In other words, Buddhist teaching claims that involvement in everyone and everything is the road to lack of attachment in any particular thing or person (Spiro, 1970). The important point for this present discussion is that very few human beings other than Buddha himself *ever* achieve such a desirable end in their actual personalities; thus, goes the tradition, they must face eternal reincarnation rather than eternal rest. The ideal is one thing, the practice another. In other words, persons may be variously socialized into the ideological traditions of their society so that the two—ideology and its achievement—are not simply the same thing from different perspectives, but are quite independently variable entities.

What, then, determines sociocultural reality if not the *aggregated* thoughts and feelings of individuals? Obviously, the individual attributes have some effect, but I prefer to separate levels of analysis and look upon them from an evolutionary perspective. Thus, a tradition is a semi-independent aspect of reality that evolves through time in response to internal variation and selective factors in the environment. Just as there are problems in functionalist statements, so too there are tautological aspects to evolutionary epistemology.[2] However, in the end I find the latter arguments more persuasive and convincing. In my view, sociocultural phenomena persist through time because they have survival value; that is, they tend to aid in group survival more adequately than does some other set of contending traditions. The presence and persistence of altruistic values or elements of altruism have survival value for the group that maintains such beliefs. In other words, there is in human nature no genetic basis for altruism (as defined here) except for some biological capacity to learn it. Whether or not altruism exists, and to what exent, lie in the nature and evolution of the sociocultural system, which then in turn has effects on the motivations and behaviors of individuals.

To follow this through by looking at the elements of altruism is a fairly simple task. The prestige and obligatory concomitants of meat-sharing among hunters has obvious survival value for the group. Hunting capabilities are never evenly distributed, yet through sharing patterns the entire breeding population benefits equally in a survival sense.

But the patterns can become more complex than this. In Australia there are extremely complicated kinship and marital exchange systems that have been studied by anthropologists for years. Recently, on reviewing this material, I have concluded that a more materialistic and political

---

[2] Alland and McCay (1973, pp. 144–156) ably explain the problem. Adaptation is inferred from survival, and survival is said to occur because of adaptation. Nevertheless, these same authors, after reviewing the literature in biology and anthropology, demonstrate that the concept of adaptation is both operationally and theoretically useful and necessary. I agree.

interpretation is the most powerful theoretical approach. These people have territorial rights over water holes. But each "tribal" territory does not have continuous sustaining features and, if the people had to stay within the territory in perpetuity, there would be random starvation. The separately located groups allow neighbors to come onto their own territory when grave shortages appear. Concomitantly these hunters and gatherers are the only people at this level of development to have exogamy rules based on the territorially based groups. In other words, marriage and mutual sharing of resources and exogamy all cohere into a system of mutual giving that provides for the survival of the entire group. It may not be the only system that could work in such an environment (there is another in the Kalahari, also based on much mutual giving), but many, many systems we could think of would fail. For man at his most primitive level of adaptation—the level he has occupied for well over 90% of the species' history—the selective advantage of altruistic behavior is clear. Obviously, norms of morality develop quickly to turn these statistically frequent patterns into moral prescriptions and rules that then become part of the cultural tradition of a particular set of peoples.

At "higher" or more complex levels of social life, social cohesion and integration are maintained, activated, and dramatized by the giving and receiving of presents, women, and/or tributes on innumerable occasions. Across all cultures the ubiquity of giving, whether it is reciprocal or redistributive, indicates the adaptive nature of this almost universal practice. Does it indicate something else about culture and social life if it is a constant across all of them? Possibly—but the evidence on man as a hedonistic, self-gratifying creature is so strong that I would rather interpret giving as a social act and a cultural tradition. I see it as just that, an aspect of sociocultural rather than of psychological reality. After all, who has not felt at some time in his life that he would just rather not give so-and-so a gift at this time, but does so anyway. "It is better to give than to receive," "Do unto others," etc. are not psychological statements but cultural traditions that act as stimuli from our sociocultural envelope, no matter what we as persons think or feel.

In this regard, let us look for a moment at Buddhism. Spiro (1970) shows how giving is the central concept of merit acquisition in Buddhism. Thus, one earns points for a better future life through altruistic acts. Everyone knows this and tries to offset bad acts with meritorious ones involving giving. Thus, the cultural admonition to act altruistically is seen in terms of personal gain at the psychological level. At the sociocultural level the major recipients of giving are the religious institutions and their personnel. Therefore, the religion, a cultural–ideological system, has developed a high value for altruistic giving, most of which seems to be directed toward its own organization. A circular but effective survival device!

Empathy and sympathy as human qualities are not ubiquitously stressed outside of the great religious traditions (e.g., Hinduism, Buddhism, Judaism, Christianity, and Islam). Probably the great religions—having long traditions of recorded philosophical and theological specialization, writing, and reflection—have reached out in many directions not generally included in the thought of other religions. In these great traditions, teachers and thinkers preach the functionality of altruism. They see it as a necessary part of the good life or as a requisite for salvation. But here again it is a tradition and not a psychological reality.

On the other hand, as an anthropologist I am continually struck by the cultural limitations of our ideas of empathy and sympathy. In Africa I soon learned that feeling for others was not always considered a profitable or even a proper way to behave. Upon expressing my concern over the fate and feelings of a newcomer to my little village, the leaders of the town said "Why are you doing all this; after all, this is just a person!" The implication was very clear. In their culture, relationships, especially kinship and hierarchical (patron–client) relations, are the most important things in life. A mere individual outside such relations—as this man was—is of no importance, nor is his fate, whatever it might be. For me not to understand this point was not to see things their way and was, therefore, ethnocentric. From their point of view, the only thing that was operating was *my* cultural background, which strongly impelled me to worry about what would happen to this alone and friendless man if I did not support him against the village. Ultimately, culture won out, and I gave in—squelching my Western ways and accepting the local verdict that the man must leave the village because "He was only a person" with no connections, no group to be responsible for him if he did something wrong.

The Africans I lived with had no problem over such feelings. We, although we have myths about friends dying for one another, lovers committing suicide together, etc., can dismiss a young colleague whom we like very much personally but whose promise as a scholar is not up to some abstract standard of achievement. Thus, we often behave as if "He is just a person," but we have cultural traditions of empathy and sympathy as well as socialization patterns that make such actions very upsetting and difficult. My African (Kanuri) friends would not bat an eye at such a task.

The lesson I am trying to teach is a simple one. As with giving, feelings for others are culture-bound. All cultures have some of this quality;

our culture has a great deal. Some writers, for example Lerner (1958), go so far as to say that empathy is a feature of modernization, but even Lerner accepts the idea that empathy is culturally relative in intensity and frequency.

SUMMARY AND DISCUSSION

I began this essay accepting the idea that altruism is a function of giving, of empathy, and of sympathy. Using this definition, I have tried to ask questions about the appearance of these qualities in other cultures and about whether or not we can assume or suggest the presence of altruism as an innate psychological feature in human beings. Giving, obligatory sharing, and other forms of exchanges are universal in human experience. They provide expression and identity to individuals and maintain cohesion and boundaries in social groupings. They also provide a means to gain prestige, increase status, and shame or humiliate one's enemies. In short, giving provides avenues for achieving personal gratification, and I have argued that man, like most other creatures, operates hedonistically, in terms of rewards and punishments. This often leads him to manipulate for his own advantage the norms of giving. The giving component in altruism is not organismic. Rather, it originates as a learned response to sociocultural norms in a person's environment. Because giving is such an adaptive feature for the maintenance of social life, it is ubiquitous among human societies.

However, altruism as it is defined in the Western cultural tradition and in those of the great world religions is dependent upon a high level of affect intensity. For such an outcome to occur, there must be a rather rare concatenation of socialization and family structures present. Because these conditions are not widespread, the emotional components of altruism as psychological attributes of individuals are also not very common across cultures.

Finally, what about the altruistic paradox? How can a person sometimes be kind and cruel at the same time? The answer I would now give is somewhat ethnocentric. That is, in many cultures my German friend would have had less difficulty in selecting a prior acquaintance for execution. His capacity for empathy and sympathy would simply be less intensively developed. Western man has produced family conditions and cultural traditions that leave potentially large gaps between the individual, his feelings, and the general requirements of the social system. Out of this comes the possibility of severe conflicts between the individual and society, which in my view are of greater frequency and intensity within our Western tradition and its correlated conditions for altruism.

The conflicts occur because self-interest in interaction with societal interest results in tension within the individual. Altruism as defined here is fundamentally a survival device or adaptation at the level of socio-cultural evolution. Reward-seeking individuals learn such norms and must then integrate innate hedonistic self-interest with learned (and variably intense across cultures) altruism. No wonder, then, that altruism is often manipulated for self-interest. At least, both demands are met under such conditions. A further complication and solution to the conflict lies in the fact that, once learned as a personal good as well as a social norm, altruism may become its own reward. This latter condition is what confuses the issue—making it seem plausible to argue that altruism emerges from innate psychological features. But it is not a single chicken-and-egg problem. Altruism, as we have seen, is much more adequately explained as an adaptive outcome of sociocultural evolution. Furthermore, it varies across cultures as a function of socialization and family structure.

The altruistic paradox does, I believe, ennoble man and reflects a profound truth: We are not instinctual servants of society and culture. We can change our sociocultural environment and our traditions of altruism. As we have seen, other conditions (such as a low divorce rate and the nuclear family) actually produce and vary this tension between self-seeking individuals and the altruism taught by culture—which in turn produces tension, conflict, and ultimately the capacity for greatness through surmounting these obstacles.

On a more theoretical level, it is important to note that the congruence or lack of it among psychological, social, and cultural spheres is one of the measures of adaptive capacity. Congruence means that people are socialized in such a way that they internalize the values and practices of society, with little deviation from expected norms, whereas lack of congruence is just the reverse. As Eisenstadt (1965) has shown, lack of conflict among these spheres, that is, a lessening of the grounds for the altruistic paradox, produces unidirectional or rigid adjustments to the environment, whereas lesser amounts of integration (above some limiting threshold) produce more flexibility. Culture says one thing, society and its practices and social forces suggest another set of ideas, and individuals may vary even more widely. In an evolutionary sense, this situation is the most flexible and adaptive one. Thus, the altruistic paradox is in fact a result of man's living in society and being provided with conditions for his own survival. Without it we would become more consistent, more integrated, more predictable—and probably extinct.

ACKNOWLEDGMENTS

I wish to thank Johnnes Fabian, Paul Friesma, Donald Sade, Donald Strickland, and Polly VanStone for helpful comments and criticisms. In addition, these views, although my own, have been enriched and strengthened in discussions with Donald Campbell during a seminar on evolution and social change held at Northwestern University in Spring 1971.

REFERENCES

Alland, A. Jr., & McCay, B. The concept of adaptation in biological and cultural evolution, J. J. Honigmann (Ed.), *Handbook of social and cultural anthropology.* Chicago, Rand McNally, 1973, Pp. 143–178.
Cohen, R. Some aspects of institutionalized exchange: A Kanuri example. *Cahiers d'Etudes Africaines,* 1965, *19*, 353–369. (Reprinted as #4, *Northwestern University Program of African Studies* reprint series)
Cohen, R. *The Kanuri of Bornu.* New York: Holt, Rinehart, and Winston, 1967.
Cohen, R. Social stratification in Bornu. In A. Tuden & L. Plotnicov (Eds.), *Social stratification in Africa.* New York: Free Press, 1970, Pp. 225–267.
Cohen, R. *Dominance and defiance.* Washington, D.C.: American Anthropological Association Monograph Series, November 6, 1971.
Cooley, C. H. *Human nature and the social order.* Glencoe, Ill.: Free Press, 1902.
Dowling, J. H. Individual ownership and the sharing of game in hunting societies. *American Anthropologist,* 1968, *70*, 502–507.
Eisenstadt, S. N. Transformation of social, political and cultural orders in modernization. *American Sociological Review,* 1965, *5*, 659–673.
Gide, A. *Lafcadio's adventures* (translated by D. Bussy). New York: Random House, 1960.
Goode, W. J. *World revolution and family patterns.* New York: Free Press, 1963.
Honigmann, J. J. *Culture and ethos of Kaska society.* Yale Publications in Anthropology, 1949, *10*.
Honigmann, J. J. Social networks in Great Whale River. *Bulletin of the National Museum of Canada,* 1962, *178*.
Lerner, D. *The passing of traditional society.* Glencoe, Ill.: The Free Press, 1958.
Ridington, R. The medicine fight: An instrument of political process among the Beaver Indians. *American Anthropologist,* 1968, *70*, 1152–1160.
Rosman, A., & Rubel, P. G. Big man structure and exchange systems in New Guinea. Paper presented at the American Anthropological Meetings in Mexico City, November 1974.
Spiro, M. *Buddhism and society: A great tradition and its Burmese vicissitudes.* New York: Harper & Row, 1970.
Wispé, L. G. Sympathy and empathy. In D. L. Sills (Eds.), *International encyclopedia of the social sciences,* Vol. 15. New York: Macmillan, 1968, Pp. 415–420.

II

PSYCHOLOGICAL AND
SOCIOLOGICAL EXPLANATIONS

5

Toward Resolving the Altruism Paradox: Affect, Self-Reinforcement, and Cognition[1]

D. L. ROSENHAN

To speak of learning theory in relation to altruistic prosocial behavior is to acknowledge an odd paradox; for learning involves reward, and altruism appears to involve none. How then, according to learning theory, are altruistic behaviors acquired, and why do we engage in them?

Nearly all theories of learning implicate the concept of *reinforcement*, by which is commonly meant some form of direct "reward" or the avoidance of pain. Pavlov's dogs, for example, salivated at the sound of the bell (much as we tend to get hungry around five in the afternoon) because they knew that food was coming; the bell signaled the coming of a reward. Skinner's rats pressed the bar to obtain a pellet or to terminate a shock. However complex the kind of behavior one considers, the basic rule is the same: Behavior occurs because it is rewarded or because it is instrumental in avoiding pain.

[1] Supported by NIMH 16462 and by the H. & K. Montgomery Fund.

Now consider the behaviors that are involved in dramatic forms of altruism, such as when a person risks or, indeed, loses his or her life in order to save another person. Although such behavior is not common, neither is it unknown. We now have careful documentation on the histories of many individuals who risked their lives to save Jews and Gypsies during World War II (London, 1970). Often the rescuers did not even know the names of the rescued, much less obtain rewards from them. No tangible evidence of personal gain, much less the avoidance of punishment or risk, is available to account for these behaviors. But if all behavior is elicited by its rewards, how *do* we account for such behaviors?

Lest it seem that the paradox arises only with regard to rare and dramatic instances of courage, consider some of the common impulses to prosocial behaviors that occur in all of us. Fund-raisers say that a considerable amount of charity is given anonymously by people of modest means, simply because they want to remain anonymous (and not because they have income tax problems!). Occasionally one hears of poor people who have received substantial gifts from benefactors who remain anonymous. Often the experience of being in love is accompanied by a desire to give everything or nearly everything to the beloved, quite out of proportion to, and without regard for, what one might in turn receive. Clearly, love is a complex example, for it can be argued that the lover gives all in order to gain his beloved. But the disproportionality in giving and the phenomenological experience of being willing to give without return raise problems for theories that assert that all behavior is dominated by actual or anticipated reward.

In a sense, the altruistic paradox parallels the neurotic paradox that Mowrer (1950) brought to our attention. Mowrer asked: If organisms seek to maximize their own rewards and to minimize their pain, how do we account for the presence of neurotic, self-defeating, and self-punishing behaviors that persist long after the initial elicitors should have extinguished it? In a similar sense, we ask here: If organisms seek to maximize reward and minimize pain, how shall we account for altruistic phenomena that take their very definition from the willingness and ability of organisms to forgo obvious and often significant rewards, even to give them up entirely?

Prosocial Behavior

Let me make clear what I mean by prosocial behavior. For theoretical reasons, I take a narrower view of prosocial behavior than that often taken by other theorists. I exclude, for example, all acts that are delivered with the clear expectation of quid pro quo. That I help you paint your house with the clear or tacit understanding that you will help me paint mine (or install my cabinets or fix my radio, etc.) is, in some sense, socially useful behavior, for what would society be like without such cooperative engagements? Yet, in general, I exclude from consideration such cooperative acts and all others wherein there is a clear or presumptive expectation of external or reciprocal reward.

The kind of prosocial behavior that is theoretically challenging and more difficult to understand is that in which a person seems to give up rewards without gaining any in return. Such prosocial behavior implies that something other than the lure of external reward is operating to promote the behavior. Thus, the bounds of prosocial behavior incorporate those behaviors in which the emphasis is, as Auguste Comte would describe it, upon actual *concern* for others. They include those acts of helpfulness, charitability, self-sacrifice, and courage in which the possibility of reward from the recipient is presumed to be minimal or nonexistent and in which, on the face of it, the prosocial behavior is engaged in for its own sake.

In this essay, three variables that seem to be deeply implicated in the elicitation of altruistic behavior are examined. They are *affect, self-reinforcement,* and *cognition.* Together, and sometimes alone, these processes seem sufficiently potent to resolve the altruism paradox.

THE ROLE OF AFFECT

Empathic Conditioning

To the extent that prosocial behavior involves forgoing personal rewards while alleviating the distress of others or promoting their gain, it can be argued that something must replace, or be more powerful than, external reward for the actor. External consequences are strong motivating forces, but subjective consequences in the form of affect or cognition or both may, at times, be equally strong. In order to forgo reward or to suffer punishment on behalf of another, there must be some enlargement of affect, an intensification of feeling for another person or cause. That amplification of feeling, often called empathy or sympathy, is frequently considered to be the basis for altruistic acts (Aronfreed, 1968; Lenrow, 1965; Rosenhan, 1969b; Tomkins, 1963).

Miller and his associates (Miller, Banks, & Ogawa, 1963; Miller, Caul, & Mirsky, 1967) have demonstrated that a weak form of empathy can be elicited in monkeys through training. After first training the monkeys to avoid shock in response to nonsocial cues, these authors observed that one monkey will respond to the distress cues of the other in order to avoid giving shock to himself and the other. The primitive empathy that is observed here consists of recognizing that the behavior that distresses the other way may have similar consequences for the actor, and vice versa.

A more advanced form of empathy is demonstrated in the experiments of Masserman, Wechkin, and Terris (1964). In these experiments a monkey avoided pulling a chain that provided him with food while simultaneously shocking another monkey. (A second chain, which provided him food without inflicting suffering on the other, was available to the monkey.) Although the definitive demonstration of empathy would have occurred if the animal had only the first chain to pull (since in that case he would have had to forsake his own reward in order to spare the other animal pain), it can nevertheless be held that a certain form of empathy negotiated the choice between the two chains.

A strong form of altruistic empathy would, of course, be demonstrated if the organism forsook his own reward in order to spare another pain or to promote gain for another. This kind of empathy allows us to speculate that the consequences that arise in connection with another's gain are greater for the organism than the material rewards that might have accrued to him.

Several experiments with children have demonstrated the power of empathic affect in promoting the forsaking of material rewards. In the first, conducted by Aronfreed and Paskal (1965; see also Aronfreed, 1968), young children were exposed to a conditioning paradigm wherein an experimenter responded joyfully to the onset of a red light. Joy was manifested by expressive cues (a broad smile, coupled with appropriate verbalizations) and affectional ones (a hug for the child). Subsequently, the child operated a choice apparatus on which she could either produce the red light (and joy for the experimenter) or candy for herself. Compared to control children who had experienced only the affectional *or* the expressive cues, children in the combined condition chose to turn on the light more often; indeed, more often than they chose to gain candies. Both sets of experimenter behaviors were found to be critical in the formation of this altruistic response. *Expressive* cues from the experimenter served as a subsequent signaling function that the experimenter was experiencing "joy." *Affectional* cues evoke that experience in the child and, by conditioning, enable the child to experience the experimenter's joy even in the experimenter's absence. Each set of cues by itself had considerably less effect on the willingness of children to forgo their own sweet rewards than did the combination.

A subsequent experiment by Midlarsky and Bryan (1967) supported these findings and also demonstrated that the actual sequence of affectional and expressive cues made little difference in the acquisition of the altruistic disposition. This is to say that, during the training period, whether hugs preceded smiles or smiles preceded hugs had no differential effect on the child's subsequent disposition to turn on the red light and forgo candies. Moreover, these investigators demonstrated that the conditioning paradigms remain powerful during the subsequent test condition regardless of whether the experimenter continues to display expressive and affectional cues.

The conditioning paradigm also illuminates the empathic response to suffering. Paskal and Aronfreed (1965) conducted a three-phase experiment to demonstrate these mechanisms. During the first phase, both the child and the experimenter heard an aversive noise through earphones. The experimenter evidenced her distress by placing her head in her hands. During the second phase, only the child wore the earphones and heard the aversive noise. The experimenter moved quickly to terminate the noise in the child's earphones. In the process of so doing, the experimenter forsook the opportunity to make a correct choice on a discrimination task and to gain rewards. The third phase tested whether the child had acquired the disposition to reproduce the experimenter's response, this time with another child who was distressed by the aversive noise.

The experiment offered strong evidence for the efficacy of empathic conditioning (Phase I) and modeling (Phase II) in the production of sympathetic responses. Control conditions, which eliminated the conditioning in Phase I or which varied the intensity of the noise signal in Phase II, yielded significantly weaker responses than the three-phase combination just described. It is interesting to observe, however, that when the distressed child failed to emit distress signals, the empathically conditioned child continued to offer nearly as much help as in the original, more emphatic sequence. Such actions on the part of the conditioned child suggest the operation of cognitive, as well as affective, components in the elicitation of distress-terminating behavior.

Note, however, that this experiment provided neither a test of empathic conditioning in the absence of modeling nor a test of the effects of modeling in the absence of empathic conditioning. Conceivably, one or the other of these variables might have been sufficiently powerful to meet the standard set by their combined action.

We know very little about the durability of empathic conditioning, but there is reason to suspect that its long-term effects are in some way controlled by the nature of the cues that elicit empathic responses.

Weiss, Buchanan, Alstatt, and Lombardo (1971), for example, have found that adults will rapidly learn to decrease the latency of a button-pressing response that is designed to terminate the shock received by a confederate. In this experiment, the confederate was suffering before the subject's very eyes. Lenrow (1965), on the other hand, found that adults had quite weak sympathetic responses to stories about others in distress unless the listener had previously role-played a distressing role. Such role playing might serve to reintegrate or "reinstate" (Campbell & Jaynes, 1966) earlier empathic conditionings and so promote greater sympathetic responsiveness.

Naturalistic Studies

The view that affect may mediate altruism is supported by existing research, including naturalistic studies that indicate the importance of feeling as a basis for helping others. In a retrospective study of the abolitionists, for example, Tomkins (1965) found affect to be strongly implicated in their courageous behavior. Similarly, London (1970) observed that sympathy for the victims appeared to motivate many of the people who attempted to rescue Jews, Gypsies, and American servicemen from the Nazis during World War II.

Thus, the presence of affect, sympathetic or empathic, directed toward a potential recipient of prosocial activity seems to be fairly well documented and can possibly be understood through the empathic conditioning model. There is, however, a kind of affect that is not so well understood, in this model or in any other. Various forms of prosocial behavior have been shown, in both naturalistic and laboratory settings, to arise from positive affect that resides within the donor and is not directed toward the recipient. In a naturalistic study of early civil rights workers, Rosenhan (1970) observed a strong correlation between sustained engagement on the behalf of black people in the South and the characteristic affective relationship between the actor and his parents. People who were deeply committed to political education and to the registration of black voters in the South and who had revealed that commitment by giving up the comforts of home and job in order to go South for a long period of time were found to have had and to have continued to maintain with their parents relationships characterized by strong positive feelings. And although this is only a correlational finding, the possibility that positive affect precedes and promotes prosocial behavior is supported by laboratory investigations.

A series of studies by Berkowitz and Connor (1966), Isen (1970), and

Isen, Horn, and Rosenhan (1973) have found that the prior experience of success promotes helpfulness and charitability in a wide variety of contexts. It would seem that the critical component here is the affect that is generated by success, rather than the cognitive or competence aspects of that experience. Thus, Isen and Levin (1972) found that experiences such as finding coins in a phone booth or being offered a cookie similarly serve to promote helpfulness and charitability. Moreover, studies by Moore, Underwood, and Rosenhan (1973) and Rosenhan, Underwood, and Moore (1974) have shown that the direct experience of positive affect (as by reminiscing on past experiences that made one happy) has a powerful facilitating effect on generosity. Correspondingly, reminiscing on unhappy experiences generates negative affect that retards generosity.

OBSERVATIONAL LEARNING AND SELF–REINFORCEMENT

There is ample evidence that the acquisition of altruistic behavior can be mediated through observation of altruistic models (Aronfreed, 1968; Bryan, 1970; Midlarsky & Bryan, 1967; Rosenhan, 1969b; Rosenhan & White, 1967; White, 1972). But much as experimental studies of altruism place a heavy burden on traditional theories of reinforcement to explain these phenomena, so do they place a similar burden on theories that attempt to explain observational learning. Consider first the theories of Baer and his associates (Baer, Peterson, & Sherman, 1967; Baer & Sherman, 1964). These investigators invoke the notion of "generalized imitation" to account for all modeling phenomena. According to their view, imitation is a matter of conditioned reinforcement. They theorize that, when aspects of the model's behavior have been reinforced, being similar to the model in itself gradually becomes sufficient reinforcement, even when no particular and discrete reinforcers are being emitted by the model. Bandura (1969a) has argued cogently that this theory describes more than has been observed. If it were the case that conditioned reinforcement operates to promote generalized imitation, then children and adults would imitate indiscriminately. The fact, however, is that both children and adults manifest considerable discrimination in matters of imitation. They pick and choose the people, the behaviors, and the times when they will imitate.

Gewirtz and Stingle (1968) hold that observational learning is maintained solely by the presence of extrinsic reinforcers. Although this may be the case for many behaviors, it clearly cannot be applied to any situation in which an individual behaves in the *relative absence* of social controls. And, indeed, a number of laboratory experiments have been carried out precisely to elicit and maintain observational altruistic learning *without* extrinsic reinforcers. Studies by Hartup and Coates (1967), Bryan (1970), Bryan and Walbek (1970), Rosenhan and White (1967), Rosenhan, (1969a,b,c), and White (1972) seem direct refutations of the position of Gewirtz and Stingle. In all of them, subjects contributed anonymously, with no expectation of either a future reward or of subsequent contact with the experimenter.

Yet another theory of imitative learning is that put forth by Bandura (1969a,b). It holds that observational learning is essentially regulated by its anticipated consequences. On its face, it serves no better than the earlier ones in explaining altruistic phenomena. In the familar case in which a child observes a model contributing to a charity, what are the anticipated consequences? That the imitating child will have much less money than he might ordinarily have had at his disposal? In what sense might this be reinforcing? How might the anticipated consequences of this act be so palatable to the child that they would overcome his understandable reluctance to part with his money?

One possibility, which is compatible with Bandura's view, holds that being charitable is *self-reinforcing*. In the course of observing a model, children acquire standards for their own behavior. Meeting or violating those standards has subjective consequences. In the context of imitating a model who has just been charitable, children tell themselves that they are "good" because they have contributed, and experience positive affect as a result. Correspondingly, the failure to contribute would signal failure to meet the acquired standard and would engender subjective distress.

The notion of self-reinforcement as an internal event is increasingly attracting attention and empirical support. Recent studies summarized by Bandura (1971) and Mahoney (1974) indicate that children and adults establish and maintain behaviors in a variety of contexts through the administration of self-reward and self-punishment. Attention to behavioral and/or symbolic models plays a major role in the acquisition of such standards. Very likely, their maintenance depends, among other things, on their consistency with the person's other standards and values. What are not yet fully understood are the decision processes by which conflicts are resolved. This is an especially critical problem for altruisic behavior, since the acquisition of material rewards may also be supported by internalized values and standards.

Internalized standards for one kind of altruistic behavior may or may not support the performance of other kinds, depending on the breadth of the acquired standard. Thus, Weissbrod (1976) found no relationship between donating and rescuing among children who had been exposed to charitable (but not rescuing) models. The spectrum of altruistic behaviors in which people engage should be related to the spectrum of modeled behaviors to which they have been exposed or, alternately, to the breadth and consistency of the values to which those behaviors have been linked (cf. Bem & Allen, 1974).

THE ROLE OF COGNITIVE FACTORS

It is clear that cognition plays some considerable role in the elicitation of altruistic behavior, but the nature and limits of that role are not well understood. Coates and Hartup (1969) have offered evidence that observational learning, which itself is heavily implicated in prosocial phenomena, is related to cognitive development. Moreover, there is ample evidence that the acquisition and elicitation of generous behavior increases with age (Handlon & Gross, 1959; Midlarsky & Bryan, 1967; Rosenhan, 1969a; Ugurel-Semin, 1952; Wright, 1942), and age is related to cognitive development. Younger children would likely have difficulty placing themselves in the role of a needy other (Flavell, 1968; Piaget, 1926), which may be a prerequisite for empathic and sympathetic affect. Finally, there is evidence that amplifying cognition within an experimental context increases altruistic behavior. Children who have been told about the experimental consequences of being orphaned elevate their contributions to an Orphans' Fund (Rosenhan, 1969a).

All of these studies assess or amplify cognitions regarding the needy other. And it is likely that cognition of the needy other plays a very strong role in altruistic behavior. But amplifying cognitions about the virtues of altruism per se, rather than about the object of the altruistic act, seems to have little effect. In a series of illuminating experiments, Bryan (1970) presented children with a model who, on the one hand, gives to a charity, but, on the other hand, verbally decries charitability. Or, in the opposite instance, is behaviorally niggardly, but verbally preaches the virtues of charitability. This series of experiments has yielded one powerful finding, which is that children are consistently much more impressed by, and imitative of, behavior than they are by the model's preaching. When the model gives to charity, the child gives, regardless of what the model says. And, similarly, when the model himself fails to give to charity, the child also fails, regardless of how the model *preaches* the virtues of charitability.

Similar findings have been observed in a naturalistic context. In the study of civil rights workers mentioned earlier (Rosenhan, 1970), it was found that those individuals whose involvements in civil rights activities had been transient and peripheral offered a much more elaborate rationale for civil rights efforts than did those whose involvement had been relatively more enduring and committed. It seemed in this instance that cognitive elaboration served the purpose of muting prosocial involvement. At the very least, it seemed negatively correlated with it.

These findings promote the speculation that cognitive factors play a role in the elicitation of altruistic behavior when and only when they amplify empathic and sympathetic affect. Thus, cognition about orphans would likely increase one's contributions to them, much as role playing in Lenrow's studies (1965) increased sympathetic activities. When, however, the cognition is addressed to the altruistic act rather than to the object of the beneficence, the likely outcome is either no material increase in altruistic propensities, or even *reactance* (Brehm, 1966).

SUMMARY

Insofar as theories of learning and behavior are dominated by conceptions that state that they are motivated by external reward, altruism is and remains a paradox, for altruism frequently involves giving up cherished possessions, even life itself. However, once we begin to attend to psychological processes within the individual, some progress can be made in unraveling that paradox. These intrapsychic processes seem especially significant for illuminating altruism. First, the likelihood of altruistic behavior is enhanced when the person is experiencing positive *affect*. Second, altruism may satisfy standards of behavior that an individual has internalized and may thus lead to covert *self-reinforcement*. And, third, *cognitive processes*, and especially attentional ones, may facilitate the performance of altruistic behavior.

It is one thing to specify the processes that promote altruism, and quite another to stipulate precisely the mechanisms that are involved, as well as their limits. Why, for example, does positive affect promote altruism? Precisely what mechanisms join "feeling good" to prosocial behavior? These are questions for which answers are not readily available. Nor do we yet understand the decision processes that allow an individual to mediate between conflicting values and standards in cases in which altruism is concerned. Although these processes are germane to a full understanding of altruism, they are processes that are of interest in their own right. That fact augurs well for the future. As the processes of affect, self-reinforcement, and attention are unraveled, so also will our understanding of altruistic phenomena deepen.

REFERENCES

Aronfreed, J. *Conduct and conscience: The socialization of internalized control over behavior.* New York: Academic Press, 1968.

Aronfreed, J., & Paskal, V. Altruism, empathy, and the conditioning of positive affect. Unpublished manuscript, University of Pennsylvania, 1965.

Baer, D. M., Peterson, R. F., & Sherman, J. A. The development of imitation by reinforcing behavioral similarity to a model. *Journal of Experimental Analysis of Behavior,* 1967, *10,* 405–416.

Baer, D. M., & Sherman, J. A. Reinforcement control of generalized imitation in young children. *Journal of Experimental Child Psychology,* 1964, *1,* 37–49.

Bandura, A. Social-learning theory of identification processes. In D. A. Goslin (Ed.), *Handbook of socialization theory and research.* Chicago: Rand McNally, 1969, Pp. 213–262. (a)

Bandura, A. *Principles of behavior modification.* New York: Holt, Rinehart & Winston, 1969. (b)

Bandura, A. Vicarious and self-reinforcement processes. In R. Glaser (Ed.), *The nature of reinforcement.* New York: Academic Press, 1971, Pp. 228–278.

Bem, D. J., & Allen, A. On predicting some of the people some of the time: The search for cross-situational consistencies in behavior. *Psychological Review,* 1974, *81,* 506–520.

Berkowitz, L., & Conner, W. H. Success, failure and social responsibility. *Journal of Personality and Social Psychology,* 1966, *4,* 664–669.

Brehm, J. W. *A theory of psychological reactance.* New York: Academic Press, 1966.

Bryan, J. H. Children's reactions to helpers. In J. R. Macaulay & L. Berkowitz (Eds.), *Altruism and helping behavior.* New York: Academic Press, 1970, Pp. 61–73.

Bryan, J. H., & Walbek, N. Preaching and practicing generosity: Children's actions and reactions. *Child Development,* 1970, *41,* 329–353.

Campbell, B. A., & Jaynes, J. Reinstatement. *Psychological Review,* 1966, *73,* 478–480.

Coates, B., & Hartup, W. W. Age and verbalization in observational learning. *Developmental Psychology,* 1969, *1,* 556–562.

Flavell, J. H. *The development of communication and role-taking skills in children.* New York: John Wiley, 1968.

Gewirtz, J. L., & Stingle, K. C. The learning of generalized imitation as the basis for identification. *Psychological Review,* 1968, *75,* 374–397.

Handlon, B. J., & Gross, P. The development of sharing behavior. *Journal of Abnormal and Social Psychology,* 1959, *59,* 425–428.

Hartup, W. W., & Coates, B. Imitation of a peer as a function of reinforcement from the peer group and rewardingness of the model. *Child Development,* 1967, *38,* 1003–1016.

Isen, A. M. Success, failure, attention and reaction to others: The warm glow of success. *Journal of Personality and Social Psychology,* 1970, *15,* 294–301.

Isen, A. M., Horn, N., & Rosenhan, D. L. Effects of success and failure on children's generosity. *Journal of Personality and Social Psychology*, 1973, 27, 239–247.

Isen, A. M., & Levin, P. F. Effect of feeling good on helping: Cookies and kindness. *Journal of Personality and Social Psychology*, 1972, 21, 384–388.

Lenrow, P. B. Studies in sympathy. In S. S. Tomkins & C. E. Izard (Eds.), *Affect, cognition and personality*. New York: Springer, 1965, Pp. 264–294.

London, P. The rescuers: Motivational hypotheses about Christians who saved Jews from the Nazis. In J. Macauley & L. Berkowitz (Eds.), *Altruism and helping behavior*. New York: Academic Press, 1970, Pp. 241–250.

Mahoney, M. J. *Cognition and behavior modification*. Cambridge, Mass.: Ballinger, 1974.

Masserman, J. H., Wechkin, S., & Terris, W. "Altruistic" behavior in rhesus monkeys. *American Journal of Psychiatry*, 1964, 121, 584–585.

Midlarsky, E., & Bryan, J. Training charity in children. *Journal of Personality and Social Psychology*, 1967, 5, 408–415.

Miller, R. E., Banks, J. H., & Ogawa, N. Role of facial expression in "cooperative avoidance conditioning" in monkeys. *Journal of Abnormal and Social Psychology*, 1963, 67, 24–30.

Miller, R. E., Caul, W. F., & Mirsky, I. F. Communication of affects between feral and socially isolated monkeys. *Journal of Personality and Social Psychology*, 1967, 7, 231–239.

Moore, B. S., Underwood, B., Rosenhan, D. L. Affect and altruism. *Developmental Psychology*, 1973, 8, 99–104.

Mowrer, O. H. *Learning theory and behavior*. New York: Wiley, 1950.

Orne, M. T. Hypnosis, motivation and the ecological validity of the psychological experiment. In W. J. Arnold & M. M. Page (Eds.), *Nebraska symposium on motivation*. Lincoln, Neb.: University of Nebraska Press, 1970, Pp. 187–265.

Paskal, V., & Aronfreed, J. The development of sympathetic behavior in children: An experimental test of a two-phase hypothesis. Paper presented at the meetings of *The Society for Research in Child Development*, 1965.

Piaget, J. *The language and thought of the child*. New York: Harcourt, Brace, 1926.

Rosenhan, D. L. Studies in altruistic behavior: Developmental and naturalistic variables associated with charitability. Paper presented at the meetings of *The Society for Research in Child Development*, 1969. (a)

Rosenhan, D. L. Some origins of concern for others. In P. Mussen, M. Covington, & J. Langer (Eds.), *Trends and issues in developmental psychology*. New York: Holt, Rinehart and Winston, 1969, Pp. 132–153. (b)

Rosenhan, D. L. The kindness of children. *Young Children*, 1969, 25, 30–44. (c)

Rosenhan, D. L. The natural socialization of altruistic autonomy. In J. Macaulay & L. Berkowitz (Eds.), *Altruism and helping behavior*. New York: Academic Press, 1970, Pp. 251–268.

Rosenhan, D. L., Underwood, B., & Moore, B. S. Affect moderatse altruism and self-gratification. *Journal of Personality and Social Psychology*, 1974, 30, 546–552.

Rosenhan, D. L., & White, G. M. Observation and rehearsal as determinants of prosocial behavior. *Journal of Personality and Social Psychology*, 1967, 5, 424–431.

Tomkins, S. S. *Affect, imagery, consciousness, Vol II: The negative affects*. New York: Springer, 1963.

Tomkins, S. S. The psychology of commitment, Part 1: The constructive role of violence and suffering for the individual and for his society. In S. S. Tomkins

& C. E. Izard (Eds.), *Affect, cognition and personality.* New York: Springer, 1965, Pp. 148–171.

Ugurel-Semin, R. Moral behavior and moral judgment of children. *Journal of Abnormal and Social Psychology,* 1952, *47,* 463–474.

Weiss, R. F., Buchanan, W., Altstatt, L., & Lombardo, J. P. Altruism is rewarding. *Science,* 1971, *171,* 1262–1263.

Weissbrod, C. S. Noncontingent warmth induction, cognitive style, and children's imitative donation and rescue effort behaviors. *Journal of Personality and Social Psychology,* 1976, *34,* 274–281.

White, G. M. Immediate and deferred effects of model observation and guided and unguided rehearsal on donating and stealing. *Journal of Personality and Social Psychology,* 1972, *21,* 139–148.

Wright, B. Altruism in children and perceived conduct of others. *Journal of Abnormal and Social Psychology,* 1942, *37,* 218–233.

6

Equity Theory and Helping Relationships[1]

ELAINE HATFIELD, G. WILLIAM WALSTER, AND JANE ALLYN PILIAVIN

Equity theory is intended to be a general theory, useful for predicting human behavior in a wide array of social interactions (Berkowitz & Walster, 1976). To date, Equity theory has been applied to predict people's responses in such diverse areas as exploiter–victim relationships, industrial relationships, and intimate relationships. In this chapter, we shall explore the possibility that Equity theory can provide an orderly framework for the understanding of philanthropist–recipient relationships as well. In the first section we shall briefly review Equity theory. In the second section we shall consider some possible applications of Equity theory in three different types of helping relationships: (a) relationships that might best be labeled *exploitative* or *excessively profitable* relationships; (b) reciprocal relationships; and (c) true "altruis-

[1] This research was supported in part by the National Institute of Mental Health, Grant MH 26681.

tic" relationships. In the second section we shall take the *helper's* point of view in probing these three relationships; in the third section we shall take the *recipient's* point of view.

THEORETICAL BACKGROUND: THE EQUITY FORMULATION [2]

Equity theory is a strikingly simple theory. Essentially it consists of four propositions:

> Proposition I: *Individuals will try to maximize their outcomes (where outcomes equals rewards minus costs).*
> Proposition II: *Groups can maximize collective reward by evolving accepted systems for "equitably" apportioning rewards and costs among members. Thus, members will evolve such systems of equity and will attempt to induce members to accept and adhere to these systems.*
> *Groups will generally reward members who treat others equitably and generally punish (increase the costs for) members who treat others inequitably.*

Equity theorists define an "equitable relationship" to exist when the person scrutinizing the relationship (i.e., the scrutineer–who could be Participant A, Participant B, or an outside observer) perceives that all participants are receiving equal relative gains from the relationship:

$$\frac{\text{Outcomes}_A - \text{Inputs}_A}{(|\text{Inputs}_A|)^{k_A}} = \frac{\text{Outcomes}_B - \text{Inputs}_B}{(|\text{Inputs}_B|)^{k_B}}$$

Definition of Terms

Inputs (Is) are defined as "the participant's contributions to the exchange, which are seen (by a scrutineer) as entitling him to rewards or costs." The inputs that a participant contributes to a relationship can be either assets—entitling him to rewards—or liabilities—entitling him to costs.[3]

In different settings, different inputs are seen as entitling one to rewards or costs. In industrial settings, assets such as capital or manual

[2] For a more detailed explication of Equity theory, a review of the wide-ranging and voluminous Equity research, and a more detailed discussion of equity and helping relationships, see Walster, E., Walster, G. W., and Berscheid, E., *Equity: Theory and research*, Boston: Allyn and Bacon, 1978.

[3] The restriction to this formula is that Inputs cannot equal zero.

labor are seen as relevant inputs—inputs that legitimately entitle the contributor to reward. In social settings, qualities such as physical beauty, a dependable character, or kindness are generally seen as assets entitling the possessor to social reward. Social liabilities such as boorishness or cruelty are seen as entitling him to costs.

Outcomes (Os) are defined as "the positive and negative consequences that a scrutineer perceives a participant has incurred as a consequence of his relationship with another." The participant's total outcomes, then, are equal to the rewards he obtains from the relationship minus the costs he incurs.

The exponents k_A and k_B are defined as follows:

$$k_A = \text{sign}(I_A) \times \text{sign}(O_A - I_A),$$

and

$$k_B = \text{sign}(I_B) \times \text{sign}(O_B - I_B).$$

[The exponents are simply a computational device to make the Equity formula "work." The exponents k_A *and* k_B take on the value $+1$ or -1, depending on the sign ($+$ or $-$) of A and B's Inputs and the sign ($+$ or $-$) of their Profits (Outcomes $-$ Inputs). The exponents' effect is simply to change the way Relative gains are computed; if $k = +1$, then we have $(O - I)/(|I|)$, but if $k = -1$, then we have $(O - I) \times (|I|)$. (Without the exponent k, the formula would yield meaningless results when a participant's Inputs and Profits have opposite signs (i.e., when a participant's Inputs are *less* than zero and his Profits are *greater* than zero, or when his Inputs are *greater* than zero and his Profits are *less* than zero.) For a complete description of the assumptions underlying Equity theory and its derivation, see Walster *et al.*, 1978.]

Who Decides Whether a Relationship Is Equitable?

In Proposition II, we argued that societies develop norms of equity and teach these systems to their members. Thus, within any society there will be a consensus as to what constitutes an equitable relationship. However, the Equity formulation makes it clear that, ultimately, equity is in the eye of the beholder. An individual's perception of how equitable a relationship is will depend on *his* assessment of the value and revelance of the various participants' inputs and outcomes. Participants themselves, even after prolonged negotiation with one another, often do not agree completely as to the *value* and *revelance* of various inputs and outcomes. For example, a wife—focusing on the fact that she is trapped in the house with toddlers all day, works long hours, and is constantly engulfed by noise, mess, and confusion—may feel that her relative outcomes are extremely low. Her husband—focusing on the fact that she can get out of bed whenever she pleases in the morning and can see whom she wants, when she wants—may disagree.

If participants do calculate inputs and outcomes differently—and it is likely that they will—it is inevitable that they will differ in their perceptions of whether or not a given relationship is equitable. Moreover, "objective" outside observers are likely to evaluate the equitableness of a relationship quite differently than do participants.

> Proposition III: *When individuals find themselves participating in inequitable relationships, they become distressed. The more inequitable the relationship, the more distress individuals feel.*

According to Equity theory, both the person who gets too much and the person who gets too little feel distressed. Theorists have labeled their distress reactions in various ways. The exploiter's distress may be labeled "guilt," "shame," "dissonance," "empathy," "conditioned anxiety," or "fear of retaliation." The victim's distress may be labeled "anger," "shame," "humiliation," "dissonance," or "conditioned anxiety." (Austin and Walster [1974] review the evidence that exists in support of Proposition III.)

> Proposition IV: *Individuals who discover they are in an inequitable relationship attempt to eliminate their distress by restoring equity. The greater the inequity that exists, the more distress they feel and the harder they try to restore equity.*

There are two techniques by which individuals can reduce their distress:

1. *Restoration of actual equity.* One way participants can restore equity to their unjust relationship is by allowing the exploiter to compensate his victim. Many studies indicate that a harmdoer will often exert considerable effort to make restitution. (See, for example, Berscheid & Walster, 1967; Schmitt & Marwell, 1972; Walster & Prestholdt, 1966.) Parallel evidence indicates that a victim's first response to exploitation is to seek restitution (Leventhal & Bergman, 1969; Marwell, Schmitt, & Shotola, 1971). If the exploiter refuses to make restitution, the victim may settle for "getting even" by retaliating against the exploiter (Ross *et al.*, 1971; Thibaut, 1950).

2. *Restoration of psychological equity.* Participants can reduce their distress in a second way. They can distort reality and convince themselves (and perhaps others) that their ostensibly inequitable relationship is in fact perfectly fair. Individuals use several techniques to rationalize exploitation. A number of studies demonstrate that harmdoers may rationalize their harmdoing by derogating their victim, by denying responsibility for the act, or by minimizing the victim's suffering (Brock &

Buss, 1962; Glass, 1964; Sykes & Matza, 1957). There is even some sparse experimental evidence that, under the right circumstances, victims will even justify their own exploitation (Austin & Walster, 1974; Leventhal & Bergman, 1969).

At this point, Equity theorists confront a crucial question. Can we specify when a person will try to restore actual equity to his relationship or when he will settle for restoring psychological equity instead? From Equity theory's Propositions I and IV, we can make a straightforward derivation: A person should follow a cost–benefit strategy in deciding how he will respond to perceived inequity. Whether an individual responds to injustice by attempting to restore actual equity, by distorting reality, or by doing a little of both has been found to depend on the costs and benefits a participant thinks will be associated with each strategy. (For example, see Berscheid & Walster, 1967; Berscheid et al., 1968; Weick & Nesset, 1968.)

THE APPLICATION OF EQUITY THEORY: THE HELPER'S RESPONSE TO EXPLOITATIVE, RECIPROCAL, AND ALTRUISTIC RELATIONSHIPS

Equity theorists would begin an analysis of helping behavior by classifying the relationship between the giver and the receiver of help into one of three categories:

1. *Exploitative or excessively profitable relationships.* There are two types of relationships here, and we will discuss them in order. Professional "philanthropists" are often fully aware that the best way to help themselves is to "help" others. For example, the Foundation president may know that his charitable donations will increase his relative gains (via tax write-offs) more than the recipient's. The professional fundraiser may know that his charitable solicitations will benefit him. This is an *exploitative relationship.*

Sometimes a person becomes aware that in the past he has received far more, and his fellow man has received far less, than deserved. The person helps in an effort to *partially* remedy the inequity; his recipient accepts it as such. In such situations, the helper is not a helper in the usual sense; a helper–recipient relationship of this type is probably best labeled an *excessively profitable relationship.*

2. *Reciprocal relationships.* Sometimes, participants alternate between being a donor and a recipient. In such relationships, equity is maintained over the long run, and helper–recipient relationships of this type are best labeled *reciprocal relationships.*

3. *Truly altruistic relationships.* Sometimes, the helper is truly a helper. He offers the recipient greater benefits than the recipient can ever hope to return. We will label relationships of this type *altruistic relationships.*

Although in day-to-day conversation all three are commonly labeled "helping" relationships, they are, in fact, strikingly different.

From the preceding discussion, it should be clear that if Equity theory is to make predictions about a potential helper's response to a helping opportunity, two facts are important: (*a*) Does the potential helper perceive that he is in a relationship with the recipient? (*b*) *At the start* of the helper–recipient interaction, does the potential helper perceive that he is overbenefited, equitably benefited, or underbenefited relative to the recipient?

Does the potential helper perceive that he is in a relationship with the recipient? Equity theory deals with the behavior of individuals enmeshed in equitable or inequitable relationships. To calculate Equity, we must know what inputs participants perceive they and their partners are contributing to their relationship and how much profit they are deriving from it. Unfortunately, in much of the research that is available researchers did not ascertain whether or not participants perceived themselves to be in a relationship. This problem is especially acute in the research on innocent bystanders and victims. We simply do not know if, when a bystander observes someone in a burning building, he thinks of himself as being in a relationship with the victim. One could well argue that he does *not.* However, for purposes of this discussion, let us assume that the participants in helping situations *do* see themselves as participants in a relationship with their fellow man, since the assumption is necessary for equity theory to be applied at all.

Does the helper perceive that he is overbenefited, equitably treated, or underbenefited? Most of the time, when we consider others' research, we will feel fairly confident that we can guess how the potential helper and recipient felt. We can guess whether they would classify their relationship as an exploitative, reciprocal, or altruistic one. Sometimes, however, we will not be so sure. For example, in the multifaceted bystander situation, we will often find it impossible to guess how the bystander felt about things. When the bystanders compared their relative gains to the victim's, they *might* have concluded that they were overbenefited and that he was underbenefited. On the other hand, they might also have felt that things were perfectly fair as they stood. Under these conditions, if the bystander were to volunteer to help, his would be a truly altruistic act.

Let us now consider the three different types of so-called "helping" relationships in greater detail.

Exploitative and Excessively Profitable Relationships

These two types of relationships can be diagrammed as follows:

$$\frac{(O_A - I_A)}{(|I_A|)^{k_A}} > \frac{(O_B - I_B)}{(|I_B|)^{k_B}}$$

(Philanthropist)   (Recipient)

Earlier we pointed out that, in an exploitative relation, although the public may label it "philanthropic," the participants in the relationship may see things quite differently. In some situations, both the "philanthropist" and the benefactor may correctly perceive that the philanthropist is using the recipient. Since such exploiter–victim relationships have been fully discussed elsewhere (see, for example, Walster et al., 1978), we will not consider them further in this chapter.

*   *   *

In some settings, potential helpers are uncomfortably aware that—by design or accident—they are partially responsible for the initial or continued suffering. For example, the night watchman who sneaked out for an unauthorized smoke may feel he is at least partially responsible for the theft of equipment from his employer's factory. Or the Kew Gardens residents who neglected to call the police while Kitty Genovese was stabbed may to this day feel they are responsible for her death.

What does Equity theory have to say about such relationships? In analyzing the bystander–victim relationship, we will organize our discussion chronologically, in the way an emergency unfolds. First, we will discuss variables that seem to determine how distressed the bystander will become by the emergency. Then, we will discuss the determinants of how the bystander responds to the emergency, by helping, derogating the victim, or fleeing.

Sources of a Bystander's Distress on Observing an Emergency

The bystander who observes a victim's suffering may feel emotionally and physiologically aroused for two entirely different reasons, empathy reasons and equity reasons.

When the bystander is forced to see another person suffer, he may empathize and become emotionally and physiologically upset (Piliavin & Piliavin, 1971, 1973; Piliavin, Rodin, & Piliavin, 1969).

If the bystander feels that he and the victim are in an inequitable relationship, he should experience distress. There are at least three variables that should intensify the not-quite-innocent bystander's concern on observing an emergency. They are (a) his perceived responsibility for the emergency; (b) the severity of the emergency; and (c) the bystander's personality characteristics.

Responsibility. According to Equity theory, the more responsible a participant is for an inequity, the more distress he should feel. A not-quite-innocent bystander may well experience both self-concept distress ("I am a bad person") and fear-of-retaliation distress ("I will be punished").

There is some evidence that the more responsible the bystander feels for the victim's plight, the more likely he is to help. Schwartz and Ben David (1977) recruited men from the Hebrew University of Jerusalem to participate in a "biofeedback" study. Ostensibly, the men had two jobs, to train rats to modify their heart rate by administering carefully regulated shocks and to train themselves to control *their own* heart rates. While describing the dual training procedure, the experimenter casually warned the men that the rat they had been asked to train was wild and uncontrollable and was terrified of the procedures. When the experiment was well under way, an "emergency" occurred. There was a crash, followed by a single cry from the experimenter; the content of this cry was systematically varied: (a) Sometimes the experimenter blamed the bystander for her plight (She cried: "What did you do?! The rat escaped! What did you do? . . ."); (b) Sometimes she attributed the plight to chance ("What happened?! The rat escaped! What happened? . . ."); and (c) Sometimes she exonerated the bystander and blamed herself ("What did I do?! The rat escaped! What did I do? . . ."). As predicted, the student was most eager to help when he had been blamed for the emergency. He was slowest to help when the experimenter had blamed herself. Similar effects on likelihood of intervention were obtained by Tilker (1970) in a Milgrain obedience paradigm study.

Severity. Piliavin and Piliavin (1971) proposed that a bystander's arousal will increase as the perceived severity and danger of the emergency increases. The louder and more numerous the screams, the more the blood, the higher the flames, the more aroused the bystander will become. Piliavin and Piliavin (1972) provide some support for this contention. These authors staged an emergency in the Philadelphia subway. On each run a male confederate, who pretended to be an invalid with a cane, collapsed. In half of the trials, the victim simply collapsed in the moving subway car; in the other half of the trials, he produced a thin trickle of very real-looking fake blood from the corner of his mouth as he fell. If the emergency was not too severe (i.e., the man merely collapsed), panicky behavior did not occur. On several of the "blood" trials, however, quite emotional and panicky behavior did occur. Other evidence (Lazarus, Opton, Nomikos, & Rankin, 1965) indicates that the heart rate of observers of a film depicting several industrial accidents accelerates more to the sight of a man being impaled by a flying board and dying than to a man losing a finger.

Severity of emergency in Equity theory terms would be equated with the size of the disparity between the gains and losses of the participants. A factory worker who learns that a co-worker doing comparable work makes 10% less than he does should experience less distress than one who discovers a 50% differential. Similarly, a bystander who observes that a person much like himself is being mildly harassed should experience less distress than a bystander who watches a victim being tortured or mutilated. Evidence exists to support the contention that the greater the inequity that exists, the more distress participants will feel (Leventhal, Allen, & Kemelgor, 1969; Leventhal & Bergman, 1969). Parallel evidence also exists to support the contention that the more a victim suffers, the more a bystander will derogate him (Lerner & Simmons, 1966).

Personality Factors. Finally, the bystander's personality should combine with the situational factors just discussed to determine the degree to which he becomes distressed when he encounters a suffering human being. The individual who has a strong self-concept should experience more distress when he causes or contributes to another's suffering than should a person who thinks little of himself (see Glass, 1964). The person who has been taught that exploitative behavior brings swift retaliation from Man and God should experience more distress when he contributes to another's suffering than would the more leniently reared child (see Aronfreed, 1961).

Responding to the Inequity

Once a participant faces the fact that his relationship with another is inequitable, Equity theory makes specific predictions as to how he will respond to the injustice. The bystander can restore *actual* equity to the unfair relationship (he can make reparation to the victim) or he can restore *psychological* equity (he can distort his perceptions of the emergency situation).

The Equity paradigm's conceptual alternatives are essentially that the person gets, or tries to get, help for the victim, reevaluates the situation as one not requiring action, or leaves the scene (see Piliavin *et al.*, 1969).

A bystander cannot, of course, eliminate inequity by leaving the scene. The bystander knows that he was *once* in a relationship and that it was an unfair one. However, "out of sight *is* out of mind," and, in fleeing, a bystander *can* reduce the salience of an inequity. Equity theorists have observed that avoidance does occur when it is more costly to restore equity to a relationship than to abandon it.

Equity theorists and students of bystander behavior seem to agree on how individuals *can* respond to inequity. What determines which of these many potential responses an observer *will* make? Equity theory proposes two principles for predicting how a person will respond to a needy victim: How a bystander responds will depend on the *cost* for the alternative techniques available, and their *adequacy*.

The Cost of Helping. A derivation from Proposition I of Equity theory states that: *Other things being equal, the more costly a person perceives an available equity-restoring technique to be, the less likely he will be to use this technique to restore equity.* Piliavin and Piliavin (1971) wrote that:

> An observer is motivated to reduce his arousal state as rapidly as possible, incurring in the course of his actions as few costs and as many rewards as possible. That is, his response will be determined by the outcome of a more or less rational decision process in which he weighs the costs and rewards attendant upon each of his possible courses of action [p. 6].

There is considerable evidence in support of the contention that rewards and costs are important in determining how a bystander will respond to an emergency. What are the potential rewards for helping in an emergency situation? They include the feeling of competence, self-congratulations, thanks from the victim, praise and admiration from bystanders, money, and fame. The potential costs include the following: personal danger, effort, expenditure, time lost, embarrassment, exposure to disgusting or sickening experiences (such as the sight of or contact with blood or other body fluids, wounds, deformities, seizures), and feelings of inadequacy or failure if help is ineffective. Rewards for *not* helping consist of the rewards associated with maintaining personal freedom, freedom to continue doing what you like without "getting involved," and lack of "involvement." Potential costs for *not* helping include: self-blame, public censure, and—in some situations—criminal prosecution (Radcliffe, 1966).

Piliavin and Piliavin (1972) provide suggestive evidence that cost *is* an important determinant of whether or not bystanders will come to the aid of victims. In the study referred to above, an "invalid" with a cane collapsed. In some cases, he was *not* bleeding from the mouth. In others he was. The "invalid" lay there until someone came to his aid. The assumption was that it is less costly to approach an unbloody person than a bloody one. And, as predicted, bystanders *were* more likely to help the "sanitary" victim than the bloody one. Piliavin, Piliavin, and Rodin (1975) studied bystanders' willingness to help a "normal" victim versus a "costly-to-approach" victim (i.e., a victim who was made up to have an unattractive "port wine stain" birthmark). Again, bystanders were slower and less likely to help the victim with the disfiguring birthmark. In the case of both blood and birthmarks, the presumed costs are psychological; there is revulsion or at least distaste on the part of many individuals toward both blood and disfigurement.

Finally, Darley and Batson (1973) found that people are more reluctant to assist a person slumped by the side of the road when they are in a hurry (and "time is money") than when they have "time to kill."

The Adequacy of Available Equity-Restoring Techniques. A second derivation, from Proposition IV of Equity theory, states that a bystander's reaction to an emergency should depend on how adequate he perceives the alternate available techniques for restoring actual or psychological equity to be: *Other things being equal, the more adequate an individual perceives an available equity-restoring technique to be, the more likely he is to use this technique to restore equity.*

Compelling anecdotal evidence that bystanders take the costs and adequacy of help into account when deciding whether or not to help others comes from Lerner (1971a). In public demonstrations, Lerner has a simple technique for graphically illustrating why bystanders are often insensitive to even the most intense suffering of others. First, Lerner reminds his audience that many Americans and Canadians are suffering and desperately need help. He then hands each member of the audience a folder containing a single case history from the active file of the University Hospital. Each case history describes an American or Canadian family—in serious need of help—who for one reason or another cannot be helped by any official welfare agency. Each of the families lives under degrading conditions. The family needs money for food, clothes, soap, medicine to eliminate intestinal worms and heal sores, etc. The family is starving. Lerner points out that if the person will donate $100 a month he can help this family avoid this primitive kind of human suffering; all that will be required of the affluent members of the audience is to give up a significant part of the money they spend each month on entertainment, liquor, movies, dining out, etc. As we might anticipate, few members of the audience agree to help.

With great sensitivity, Lerner explains why it is that individuals are so unwilling to help: (a) The potential cost of such help is high; if the audience member contributes money this time, where can he stop? Can he and his own family enjoy their lives only when their lot is not better than that of the rest of mankind? (b) The potential adequacy of such help is low. By paying $100 a month, the audience member can only help *one* family. Millions of victims remain. He cannot help them all. Perhaps if he were offered the chance to vote for an equitable tax system that, using his $100 a month, would alleviate the suffering of *all* people, he might be far more willing to help.

Reciprocal Relationships

$$\frac{(O_A - I_A)}{(|I_A|)^{k_A}} = \frac{(O_B - I_B)}{(|I_B|)^{k_B}}$$

Any relationship that endures for very long soon evolves into a reciprocal relationship. Neighbors take turns manning car pools, college students take notes for one another, colleagues exchange advice. In such stable relationships, participants alternate between helping others and being helped themselves.

In *The Gift*, Mauss (1954) analyzes the impact of such reciprocal gift-giving in primitive societies. His observations are equally applicable to our semiprimitive society.

Mauss uses the Melanesian institution of ritual gift exchange—the *kula ring*—as a framework for discussing reciprocal relationships. In the Massim area of the Pacific, tribal chiefs are linked in the *kula,* in which participants travel from island to island doling out and receiving gifts. By custom, a tribal chief is assumed to be a donor on one occasion and a recipient on the next.

Dillon (1968) observes that in the *kula*—as in our own society—"People who receive, want to give something in return. Both are involved in the quest for reciprocity [p. 15]." He points out that the reciprocal exchanges are a source of social stability—they breed good feeling, liking, and cooperation. Experimental evidence supports Dillon's contention that *kula*-type reciprocal exchanges solidify social bonds. For example, Nemeth (1970), Berkowitz (1972a,b), and Gross and Latané (1973) provide evidence that reciprocal helping relations stimulate friendly feelings. Other experiments suggest that kindness generates

not only liking,but also a desire to reciprocate(Greenberg, 1968; Gross&
Latané, 1973; Pruitt, 1968). The responses of participants in a reciprocal relationship will be dealt with in our section dealing with the *recipient's* response to the various types of relationships.

Altruistic Relationships

$$\begin{array}{cc} (Philanthropist) & (Recipient) \end{array}$$

$$\frac{(O_A - I_A)}{(|I_A|)^{k_A}} < \frac{(O_B - I_B)}{(|I_B|)^{k_B}}$$

For most people, the "true" altruistic relationship—the relationship in
which the philanthropist gives more to his fellow man than his fellow
man is entitled to or can ever hope to return—is evidence of Man at his
best. Yet, when we consider the social pressures that propel people to
action and the social rewards and punishments they encounter once they
have acted, it seems evident that—as Equity theory suggests—"altruists"
must have mixed feelings about their sacrifices, and mixed reactions to
them. Why should this be?

Society Tells People They Should Behave Altruistically . . . Sometimes

One of society's most perplexing problems is to decide how the
"needy" should be treated. On the one hand, the U.S. Government defines need as a legitimate input that entitles a citizen to the minimum
outcomes necessary for survival. We collectively acknowledge that if
our fellow human being is so young, so disabled, so sick, or so old that
he is unable to care for himself, society should care for him. We feel we
should give to a plethora of deserving causes—The United Way, Save
the Children Fund, Planned Parenthood, Committee for Voter Registration, etc. (see Berkowitz, 1972a; Berkowitz & Daniels, 1963; Gouldner,
1960; Lerner, 1971b; Leventhal, Weiss, & Buttrick, 1973; Pruitt, 1972).
On the other hand, people do not consider "need" to be an *entirely*
legitimate input. They often complain that they should not be obligated
to help *everyone* who finds himself in sad straits. At best, many be-
leaguered givers feel that any help they do cede should be considered
not a gift, but a loan. Most of us feel that we are at least entitled to the
recipient's gratitude when we provide help. Thus, societal norms provide
competing pressures: They say people should behave altruistically toward
those in "need"—but that they are entitled to some recognition and
thanks for doing so.

Society Rewards People for Behaving Altruistically . . . Sometimes

Generally, society encourages altruistic behavior. The altruist and the hero who have internalized society's norms may reward *themselves* for their "unselfish behavior." (See Rosenhan, Chapter 5 in this volume.) Their fellows may reward them with love, praise, their names in the paper, medals, and/or flowery epitaphs. Yet, there is often a thin line between being an "altruist" and being a "sap." Sometimes people respond to altruistic acts with ridicule and disdain. For example, Brown (1968, 1970) found that *if people believed others would never know they had been slighted and exploited* they were often quite willing to settle for less than they deserved. However, *if they knew that others might discover their "largess,"* they felt they must "get theirs" lest they be thought "less of a man," or become a target for subsequent exploitation. The competitive nature of our society undoubtedly contributes to this.

Since society's reactions to altruism are mixed, we might expect that altruists would have similarly mixed feelings about their altruism. They may end up feeling good and distressed about themselves at the same time.

Psychologists Believe That True Altruism Does Exist . . . at
Least a Few Do

A few scientists believe that man does act unselfishly under very special circumstances. For example, Aronfreed (1970) contends that any time a person's behavior is controlled by empathetic processes, his behavior should be labeled "altruistic." Aronfreed and Paskal (1966) point out that sometimes people place themselves in the shoes of a person needing assistance. They vicariously experience the other's disappointment at not getting what he desires. In such circumstances, a person may sacrifice his own interests for another. Hornstein (Chapter 3 in this volume), using a Lewinian framework, suggests essentially the same thing. Under conditions in which a person perceives a "we-ness" between himself and the victim, he will act to complete an act not completed by the other. Other theorists observe that, under some highly arousing, unambiguous emergency situations, bystanders often perform literally death-defying acts of rescue that could not possibly follow a cost–reward calculus (see, for example, London, 1970).

On the other hand, the majority of scientists—Equity theorists included—are fairly cynical. They interpret apparent altruism in cost–benefit terms, assuming that individuals, altruists included, learn to perform those acts that are rewarded . . . and to avoid those acts that are not. Either self-congratulation or external reward, then, must support apparently altruistic behavior. As Blau (1968) observes:

> To be sure, there are men who selflessly work for others without thought of reward and even without expecting gratitude, but these are virtually saints, and saints are rare. Other men also act unselfishly sometimes, but they require a more direct incentive for doing so, if it is only . . . social approval [p. 453].

Sometimes, then, psychologists view altruism in a favorable light; most often, however, scientists attribute apparent altruism to more selfish motives.

In view of the conflicting pressures on the altruist, it is not surprising that the person who voluntarily contributes more than his share to a relationship often feels pride—mixed with distress. And it is no wonder that altruists are often tempted to reduce that distress by restoring actual or psychological equity.

THE RECIPIENT'S RESPONSE TO EXPLOITATIVE, RECIPROCAL, AND ALTRUISTIC RELATIONSHIPS

Exploitative or Excessively Profitable Relationships

We noted earlier that philanthropic acts may be less generous than they appear on the surface. Sometimes the wily philanthropist is, in fact, cheating the recipient—or returning only a portion of the benefits he owes him. Although the public may label such relationships *helping* relationships, the participants know better. Such relationships are probably best labeled *exploitative* or *excessively profitable* relationships. Since such exploiter–victim relationships have been fully discussed elsewhere (see, for example, Walster *et al.*, 1978), we will not consider them further in this paper. (The category has merely been presented for the sake of completeness.)

Reciprocal Relationships

It has been pointed out that reciprocal relations are the most pervasive and the most stable of social relationships. They breed good feelings, liking, and cooperation. Data from the social sciences make it clear that when an acquaintance offers to help "out of the goodness of his heart " our reaction is an immediate one: We feel gratitude and affection; we resolve to return his kindness. If, on the other hand, an acquaintance makes it brutally clear that he expects a return with interest, we are far less touched by the generosity and less concerned about repaying the "kindness."

Why, in equity terms, should a recipient have different reactions to the giver whose gift was voluntary and spontaneous as opposed to the giver whose gift was involuntary and even "ulterior"? First, the recipient may feel that "goodness" and "unselfishness" in and of themselves are positive inputs to a relationship. Thus, he may feel that a "good" benefactor deserves a bigger return than a "bad" person who performed the same act. Second, the recipient may be more eager to maintain a relationship with a "good" person (who acted out of the goodness of his heart) than with a "bad" person (who acted for selfish reasons). Thus, he may be especially willing to treat the other equitably by repaying his kindness.

Thus there is evidence that recipients' reactions to donors are influenced by their answers to two questions: (a) Was the donor's help intentional? and (b) Was it unselfishly motivated?

Common sense and experimental research suggest that a recipient should have a stronger desire to restore equity by reciprocating if he was intentionally helped than if he had been accidentally or reluctantly helped (Garrett & Libby, 1973; Goldner, 1965; Goranson & Berkowitz, 1966; Greenberg, 1968; Greenberg & Frisch, 1972; Gross & Latané, 1973; Leventhal, Weiss, & Long, 1969).

Schopler (1970) contends that the helper's motives are also important, that, if a recipient of help believes that the benefactor was genuinely motivated, he will be appreciative and likely to reciprocate. If, however, he believes the person was selfishly motivated, he will be less appreciative and less likely to reciprocate. Data in support of this contention come from Heider (1958), Leeds (1963), Brehm and Cole (1966), Lerner and Lichtman (1968), Schopler and Thompson (1968), and Krebs (1970).

Altruistic Relationships

It is easy to see that an altruist might have mixed feelings about helping others. A little thought, however, makes it clear that his recipient may be equally ambivalent about his benefits. On one hand, the recipient knows that the altruist is showering him with more love and material benefits than he is entitled to; he cannot help feeling grateful. On the other hand, the recipient cannot help feeling uneasy about his undeserved benefits. There are three reasons for this: The helper–recipient relationship is (a) inequitable; (b) potentially exploitative; and (c) potentially humiliating.

When the benefactor bestows benefits on a recipient, he places the recipient in an inequitable relationship. As indicated in Proposition III, inequitable relationships are unpleasant relationships. As Blau (1968) put it, "Giving is, indeed, more blessed than receiving, for having social credit is preferable to being socially indebted [p. 453]."

When a philanthropist provides benefits that his recipient cannot repay, the recipient may well feel that he has become obligated to reciprocate his benefactor in unspecified ways for an indefinite period. The recipient might reasonably fear that his benefactor may attempt to extract a greater repayment than the recipient would have been willing to give had he been warned of the conditions of the exchange ahead of time. Throughout time and geography, observers have noted that persons often demand repayment at unsurious interest.

Dillon (1968) provides a compelling example of how the exploitational gift syndrome works. He describes a French industrialist's (Mr. B) warm relationship with an Arab worker as follows:

> In June, 1956, an Arab worker at B's factory asked the *patron* for permission to leave work for two days to attend to problems of burying a brother, Ahmed .... B. responded by offering to pay for the burial, by arranging to have an Arabic-speaking French *officer des affaires indigenes* (an ex-colonial officer) notify the kinsmen in Algeria, and by hiring an *imam* (Moslem prayer leader) to conduct the services. On July 16, 1956, the end of Bastille Day demonstrations by Algerians at the Place de la Republique, B. summoned Kazam and asked: 'If your comrades tell you to go on strike during the vacation, when you are alone guarding the factory, what will you do, Kazam?' The *patron* told him that he was aware he would run the risk of being knifed (*coup de couteau*) by other Algerian members of an Islamic fraternal organization who were organizing sympathy strikes to protest French resistance against Algerian rebellion.... The *patron*, in describing this understanding with Kazam, his oldest Algerian worker, said:
> 'We depend on each other. He has worked for me almost 12 years. Without him I could not count on the work of the other Algerians. He is top man and, being the oldest, I depend on him to control the others ... Kazam knows that he can depend on me when he is in trouble.' [p. 6061]

When the industrialist offered his favors, he did not state that the "price" was to risk one's life. *Had* the Arab known, he may well have concluded that that exchange was not a profitable one. This is the essence of an exploitative relationship.

The recipient may be hesitant to accept "help" for still another reason: He may fear that the gift will establish the benefactor's moral and social superiority. He may be unwilling to accept such menial status. Observational evidence suggests that recipients' fears are probably well-founded. Social observers have noted that gift-giving and humiliation are linked. Homans (1961) notes that "anyone who accepts from another a service he cannot repay in kind incurs inferiority as a cost of receiving the service. The esteem he gives the other he foregoes himslf [p. 320]." In her analysis of beneficence among East European Jews, Joffe (1953) notes:

> For a society within the Western cultural tradition, East European Jewish culture exhibits a minimum of reciprocal behavior. Wealth, learning and other tangible and intangible possessions are fluid and are channeled so that in the main they flow from the 'strong,' or 'rich,' or 'learned,' or 'older,' to those who are 'weaker,' 'poorer,' 'ignorant,' or 'younger.' Therefore, all *giving* is downward during one's lifetime.... The concept of the good deed, the *Mitzvah*, is not voluntary—it has been enjoined upon every Jew by God.... It is shameful ... to receive succor of any sort from those who are inferior to you in status. To receive any (return gifts) implies that you are in a position to be controlled, for the reciprocal of the downward giving is deference [pp. 386–387].

These three factors, then, mean that most recipients of help will have serious reservations about having been so "blessed." This analysis sheds new light on the perplexing finding that recipients sometimes come to resent their dependence and/or despise themselves and their benefactor (see also Lenrow, Chapter 13 of this volume).

Reciprocal Relations versus Altruistic Ones

> Benefits are only acceptable so far as they seem capable of being requited; beyond that point, they excite hatred instead of gratitude [Tacitus, *Annals*, Book IV, sec. 18].

We have focused on two types of helping relationships—reciprocal and altruistic ones. From our comparison of these contrasting types of relationships, it is clear that a single factor seems to have a critical impact on the reaction of recipients to the relationship; namely, the beneficiary's ability to make restitution.

Researchers who have investigated the interactions of Christmas gift givers, members of the *Kula* ring, and the kindness of neighbors have dealt with donors and recipients who knew that eventually their helpful acts would be reciprocated in kind. Researchers who have investigated the interactions in such dyadic relations as welfare workers and their clients, developed and underdeveloped nations, and the medical staff and the physically handicapped have dealt with recipients who know they will never be able to repay their benefactors. The differing reactions of participants in reciprocal and nonreciprocal relations underscores the importance of the recipient's "ability to repay" in determining how help affects a relationship. Ability to repay seems to determine whether the doing of favors generates pleasant social interactions or resentment and suffering. Research supports the following conclusion: *Undeserved gifts produce inequity in a relationship. If the participants know the recipient can and will reciprocate, the inequity is viewed as temporary, and thus it produces little distress. If the participants know the recipient cannot or will not reciprocate, however, a real inequity is produced; the participants will experience distress* (Proposition IV). Evidence in support of this conclusion comes from three diverse sources: ethnography, the laboratory, and survey research.

On the basis of ethnographic data, Mauss (1954) concluded that three types of obligations are widely distributed in human societies in both time and space: (*a*) the obligation to give; (*b*) the obligation to receive; and (*c*) the obligation to repay. Mauss (1954) and Dillon (1968) agree that, whereas reciprocal exchanges breed cooperation and good feelings, gifts that cannot be reciprocated breed discomfort, distress, and dislike.

In support of their contention, the authors survey a number of societies that have an exchange system in which everyone can be a donor *and* a receiver. (The *Kula* ring is such an example.) Harmonious stable relations are said to be the result. They contrast these societies with those in which no mechanism for discharging obligations is provided. For example, Dillon (1968) notes:

> Instead of the *kula* principle operating in the Marshall Plan, the aid effort unwittingly took on some of the characteristics of the potlatch ceremony of the 19th Century among North Pacific Coast Indians in which property was destroyed in rivalry, and the poor humiliated [p. 15].

Volatile and unpleasant relations are said to be the result of such continuing inequities (see also Blau, 1955; Smith, 1892).

There is evidence that a benefactor is liked more when his beneficiary can reciprocate than when he cannot. Gergen and his associates (Gergen, 1969) investigated American, Swedish, and Japanese citizens' reactions to reciprocal and nonreciprocal exchanges. Students were recruited to participate in an experiment on group competition. Things were arranged so that during the course of the game the student discovered that he was losing badly. At a critical stage (when the student was just about eliminated from the game) one of the "luckier" players in the game sent him an envelope. The envelope contained a supply of chips and a note. For one-third of the students (low obligation subjects), the note explained that the chips were theirs to keep, that the giver did not need them, and that they need not be returned. One-third of the students (equal obligation subjects) received a similar note, except that the giver of the chips asked the student to return an equal number of chips later in the proceedings. The remaining students (high obligation subjects) received a note from the giver in which he asked for the chips to be returned with interest and for the subject to help him out later in the game.

At the end of the game, students were asked about their attraction toward various partners. Those partners who provided benefits without obligation or who asked for excessive benefits were both judged to be less attractive than were partners who proposed that the student make exact restitution later in the game.

Gergen et al. (in preparation) conducted a variation of the preceding study. Just as subjects were about to be eliminated from a game because of their consistent losses, another "player" in the game loaned the subject some resources. The donor loaned the chips with the expectation that they would be paid back. However, in subsequent play, only half of the subjects managed to retain their chips, so that half were unable to return the gift. In subsequent evaluations of the donor, recipients who were unable to repay the donor evaluated him less positively than did recipients who were able to repay. These results were replicated in both Sweden and the United States. Other evidence in support of this contention comes from Gross and Latané (1973).

There is also survey evidence reported by the same authors that individuals *prefer* gifts that can be reciprocated to gifts that cannot be repaid. Gergen and Gergen (1971) questioned citizens in countries that had received U.S. aid as to how they felt about the assistance their country had received. They found that international gifts accompanied by clearly stated obligations are preferred to gifts that are not accompanied by obligations or are accompanied by excessive "strings."

There is evidence that individuals are more willing to *accept* gifts that can be reciprocated than gifts that cannot. Berkowitz and Friedman (1967), Berkowitz (1968), Greenberg (1968), and Morris and Rosen (1973) provide support for the contention that people are reluctant to ask for help they cannot repay. For example, Greenberg (1968) told students that they would be participating in a study of the effects of physical disability on work performance. On an initial task, students were given a temporary "handicap"—their arm was placed in a sling. This restriction made it almost impossible for them to perform the task they were assigned. The incapacitated student knew, however, that, if he wished, he could solicit help from a fellow worker. Half of the students believed that the fellow worker would need *their* help on a second task and that they would be able to provide assistance. Half of the students believed that the fellow worker would *not* need their help and that, in any case, they would *not* be able to provide much help. The students' expectations about whether or not they could reciprocate any help strongly affected their willingness to request help. Students in the nonreciprocity condition waited significantly longer before requesting help than did those in the reciprocity condition. Greenberg and Shapiro (1971) replicated these findings.

SUMMARY

In this last part we explored three kinds of helping relationships. Although all three relationships are commonly labeled "helper–recipient" relationships, the dynamics of the three are actually quite different.

First of all, we considered exploitative or excessively profitable relationships—relationships in which the ostensible donor helped others merely because that was the most profitable way to help himself. In this section, we considered a very special kind of relationship—the not-quite-innocent bystander–victim relationship. We considered the case of the bystander who realizes that by his actions or inactions he has contributed to another's suffering. We reviewed factors that determine whether the not-quite-innocent bystander would make actual restitution to the victim, justify his suffering, or leave the situation.

Next, we considered a second type of relationship—reciprocal relationships. Such exchanges seem to breed good feelings, probably due to the desire and capacity to repay.

Finally, we considered the public's epitome of a "good" relationship—the altruistic relationship. We reviewed factors that determine whether such relationships breed good feelings—or, as they more frequently do, breed hostility, humiliation, and alienation.

REFERENCES

Aronfreed, J. The nature, variety and social patterning of moral responses to transgression. *Journal of Abnormal and Social Psychology*, 1961, *63*, 223–240.

Aronfreed, J. The socialization of altruistic and sympathetic behavior: Some theoretical and experimental analyses. In J. Macauley & L. Berkowitz (Eds.), *Altruism and helping behavior*. New York: Academic Press, 1970, Pp. 103–126.

Aronfreed, J., & Paskal, V. Altruism, empathy, and the conditioning of positive affect. Study reported in the meetings of the American Psychological Association, New York, 1966.

Austin, W., & Walster, E. Reactions to confirmations and disconfirmations of expectancies of equity and inequity. *Journal of Personality and Social Psychology*, 1974, *30*, 208–216.

Berkowitz, L. Responsibility, reciprocity, and social distance in help-giving: An experimental investigation of Englsh social class differences. *Journal of Experimental Social Psychology*, 1968, *4*, 46–63.

Berkowitz, L. Beyond exchange: Ideals and other factors affecting helping and altruism. Unpublished manuscript, University of Wisconsin, Madison, 1972. (a)

Berkowitz, L. Social norms, feelings and other factors affecting helping behavior and altruism. In L. Berkowitz (Ed.), *Advances in experimental social psychology*, Vol. 6. New York: Academic Press, 1972, Pp. 63–108. (b)

Berkowitz, L., & Daniels, L. R. Responsibility and dependency. *Journal of Abnormal and Social Psychology*, 1963, *66*, 429–436.

Berkowitz, L., & Friedman, P. Some social class differences in helping behavior. *Journal of Personality and Social Psychology*, 1967, *5*, 217–225.

Berkowitz, L., & Walster, E. (Eds.). Equity theory: Toward a general theory of social interaction. *Advances in experimental social psychology*, Vol. 9. New York: Academic Press, 1976.

Berscheid, E., Boye, D., & Walster, E. Retaliation as a means of restoring equity. *Journal of Personality and Social Psychology*, 1968, *10*, 370–376.

Berscheid, E., & Walster, E. When does a harm-doer compensate a victim? *Journal of Personality and Social Psychology*, 1967, *6*, 435–441.

Blau, P. M. *The dynamics of bureaucracy: A study of interpersonal relations in two government agencies*. (Revised edition.) Chicago, Ill.: University of Chicago Press, 1955.

Blau, P. M. Social exchange. In D. L. Sills (Ed.), *International encyclopedia of the social sciences*, Vol. 7. New York: Macmillan Co., 1968, Pp. 452–457.

Brehm, J. W., & Cole, A. H. Effect of a favor which reduces freedom. *Journal of Personality and Social Psychology*, 1966, *3*, 420–426.

Brock, T. C., & Buss, A. H. Dissonance, aggression, and evaluation of pain. *Journal of Abnormal and Social Psychology*, 1962, *65*, 197–202.

Brown, B. R. The effects of need to maintain face on interpersonal bargaining. *Journal of Experimental Social Psychology*, 1968, *4*, 107–122.

Brown, B. R. Face-saving following experimentally induced embarrassment. *Journal of Experimental Social Psychology*, 1970, *6*, 255–271.

Darley, J. M., & Batson, C. D. From Jerusalem to Jericho: A study of situational and dispositional variables in helping behavior. *Journal of Personality and Social Psychology*, 1973, *27*, 100–108.

Dillon, W. S. *Gifts and Nations*. The Hague: Mouton, 1968.

Garrett, J. B., & Libby, W. L., Jr. Role of intentionality in mediating responses to inequity in the dyad. *Journal of Personality and Social Psychology*, 1973, *28*, 21–27.

Gergen, K. J. *The psychology of behavior exchange*. Reading: Addison-Wesley, 1969.

Gergen, K. J., & Gergen, M. K. International assistance from a psychological perspective. In *The yearbook of international affairs*, Vol. 25. London: London Institute of World Affairs, 1971, Pp. 87–103.

Gergen, K. J., Seipel, M., & Diebold, P. Intentionality and ability to reciprocate as determinants of reactions to aid. (In preparation)

Glass, D. C. Changes in liking as a means of reducing cognitive discrepancies between self-esteem and aggression. *Journal of Personality*, 1964, *32*, 520–549.

Goldner, F. H. Demotion in industrial management. *American Sociological Review*, 1965, *30*, 714–724.

Gouldner, A. The norm of reciprocity: A preliminary statement. *American Sociological Review*, 1960, *25*, 161–178.

Goranson, R. E., & Berkowitz, L. Reciprocity and responsibility reactions to prior help. *Journal of Personality and Social Psychology*, 1966, *3*, 227–232.

Greenberg, M. S. A preliminary statement on a theory of indebtedness. In M. S. Greenberg (Chem.), *Justice in social exchange*. Symposium held by the Western Psychological Association, San Diego, Sept., 1968. (Oral presentation)

Greenberg, M. S., & Frisch, D. M. Effect of intentionality on willingness to reciprocate a favor. *Journal of Experimental Social Psychology*, 1972, *8*, 99–111.

Greenberg, M. S., & Shapiro, S. P. Indebtedness: An adverse aspect of asking for and receiving help. *Sociometry*, 1971, *34*, 290–301.

Gross, A. E., & Latané, J. G. Some effects of receiving and giving help. Unfinished manuscript, 1973.

Heider, F. *The psychology of interpersonal relations*. New York: John Wiley & Sons, 1958.

Homans, G. C. Social behavior: Its elementary forms. New York: Harcourt, Brace & World, 1961.

Hornstein, H. A., Fisch, E., & Holmes, M. Influence of a model's feeling about his behavior and his relevance as a comparison other on observers' helping behavior. *Journal of Personality and Social Psychology*, 1968, *10*, 222–226.

Joffe, N. F. Non-reciprocity among East European Jews. In Margaret Mead & Rhoda Matraux (Eds.), *The study of culture at a distance*. Chicago: University of Chicago Press, 1953, Pp. 386–387.

Krebs, D. Altruism: An examination of the concept and a review of the literature. *Psychological Bulletin*, 1970, *73*, 258–302.

Lazarus, R. S., Opton, E. M., Nomikos, M. S., & Rankin, N. O. The principle of short-ciricuiting of threat: Further evidence. *Journal of Personality*, 1965, *33*, 622–635.

Leeds, R. Altruism and the norm of giving. *Merrill-Palmer Quarterly*, 1963, *9*, 229–240.

Lerner, M. J. Deserving vs. justice. A contemporary dilemma. Department of Psychology, University of Waterloo, Waterloo, Ontario, Canada: Research Report #24, May 15, 1971. (a)

Lerner, M. J. Justified self-interest and the responsibility for suffering: A replication and extension. *Journal of Human Relations*, 1971, *19*, 550–559. (b)

Lerner, M. J., & Lichtman, R. R. Effects of perceived norms on attitudes and altruistic behavior toward a dependent mother. *Journal of Personality and Social Psychology*, 1968, *9*, 226–232.

Lerner, M. J., & Simons, Carolyn H. Observers' reaction to the "innocent victim": Compassion or rejection? *Journal of Personality and Social Psychology*, 1966, *4*, 203–210.

Leventhal, G. S., Allen, J., & Kemelgor, B. Reducing inequity by reallocating rewards. *Psychonomic Sciences*, 1969, *14*, 295–296.

Leventhal, G. S., & Bergman, J. T. Self-depriving behavior as a response to unprofitable inequity. *Journal of Experimental Social Psychology*, 1969, *5*, 153–171.

Leventhal, G. S., Weiss, T., & Buttrick, R. Attribution of value, equity, and the prevention of waste in reward allocation. *Journal of Personality and Social Psychology*, 1973, *27*, 276–286.

Leventhal, G. S., Weiss, T., & Long, G. Equity, reciprocity, and reallocating the rewards in the dyad. *Journal of Personality and Social Psychology*, 1969, *13*, 300–305.

London, P. The rescuers: Motivational hypotheses about Christians who saved Jews from the Nazis. In J. Macaulay & H. Berkowitz (Eds.), *Altruism and helping behavior*. New York: Academic Press, 1970, Pp. 241–250.

Marwell, G., Schmitt, D. R., & Shotola, R. Cooperation and interpersonal risk. *Journal of Personality and Social Psychology*, 1971, *18*, 9–32.

Mauss, M. *The Gift: Forms and functions of exchange in archaic societies*. Glencoe, Illinois: Free Press, 1954.

Morris, S. C. III, & Rosen, S. Effects of felt adequacy and opportunity to reciprocate on help-seeking. *Journal of Experimental Social Psychology*, 1973, *9*, 265–276.

Nemeth, C. Efforts of free versus constrained behavior on attraction between people. *Journal of Personality and Social Psychology*, 1970, *15*, 302–311.

Piliavin, I. M., Piliavin, J. A., & Rodin, J. Costs diffusion and the stigmatized victim. *Journal of Personality and Social Psychology*, 1975, *32*, 429–438.

Piliavin, I. M., Rodin, J., & Piliavin J. A. Good Samaritanism: An underground phenomenon? *Journal of Personality and Social Psychology*, 1969, *13*, 289–299.

Piliavin, J. A., & Piliavin, I. M. Bystander behavior in emergencies. Proposal submitted to the National Science Foundation, July, 1971.

Piliavin, J. A., & Piliavin, I. M. The effect of blood on reactions to a victim. *Journal of Personality and Social Psychology*, 1972, *23*, 353–361.

Piliavin, J., & Piliavin, I. The Good Samaritan: Why does he help? Unpublished manuscript, 1973.

Pruitt, D. C. Reciprocity and credit building in a laboratory dyad. *Journal of Personality and Social Psychology*, 1968, *8*, 143–147.

Pruitt, D. G. Methods for resolving differences of interest: A theoretical analysis. *Journal of Social Issues*, 1972, *28*, 133–154.

Radcliffe, J. M. (Ed.). *The Good Samaritan and the law*. Garden City: Doubleday and Co., 1966.

Ross, M., Thibaut, J., & Evenbeck, S. Some determinants of the intensity of social protest. *Journal of Experimental Social Psychology*, 1971, *7*, 401–418.

Schmitt, D. R., & Marwell, G. Withdrawal and reward reallocation as responses to inequity. *Journal of Experimental Social Psychology*, 1972, *8*, 207–221.

Schopler, J. An attribution analysis of some determinants of reciprocating a benefit. In J. Macaulay & L. Berkowitz (Eds.), *Altruism and helping behavior*. New York: Academic Press, 1970, Pp. 231–238.

Schopler, J., & Thompson, V. D. Role of attribution processes in mediating amount of reciprocity for a favor. *Journal of Personality and Social Psychology*, 1968, *10*, 243–250.

Schwartz, S. H., & David, A. B. Focus of blame, defense against responsibility, and helping in an emergency. *Sociometry*, 1977, *10*, 406–415.

Smith, A. *The theory of moral sentiments*. London and New York: Cr. Bell and Sons, 1892.

Sykes, G. M., & Matza, D. Techniques of neutralization: A theory of delinquency. *American Sociological Review*, 1957, *22*, 664–670.

Tacitus. *Annals*, Book IV, sec. 18.

Thibaut, J. W. An experimental study of the cohesiveness of underprivileged groups. *Human Relations*, 1950, *3*, 251–278.

Thibaut, J. W., & Riecken, H. W. Some determinants and consequences of the perception of social causality. *Journal of Personality*, 1955, *24*, 113–133.

Tilker, H. A. Socially responsible behavior as a function of observer responsibility and victim feedback. *Journal of Personality and Social Psychology*, 1970, *74*, 95–100.

Walster, E., & Prestholdt, P. The effect of misjudging another: Overcompensation or dissonance reduction? *Journal of Experimental Social Psychology*, 1966, *2*, 85–97.

Walster, E., Walster, G. W., & Berscheid, E. *Equity: Theory and research*. Boston: Allyn and Bacon, 1978.

Weick, K. E., & Nesset, B. Preferences among forms of equity. *Organizational Behavior and Human Performance*, 1968, *3*, 400–416.

7

A Cognitive-Developmental
Approach to Altruism

DENNIS KREBS

Wesley G. Morgan opened an article entitled "Situational Specificity in Altruistic Behavior" with the following assertions:

> Little support is available for those wishing to account for an individual's behavior on the basis of broad generalized response dispositions or traits (Mischel, 1968). Latané and Darley (1970) found that seemingly appropriate personality tests were able to account for remarkably little variance in helping behavior and suggested that characteristics of the situation may have a more important influence on how a person behaves than does his personality or life history [Morgan, 1973, p. 56].

It is generally accepted that personality characteristics have contributed little to the explanation of altruism and that altruistic behavior is determined mainly by situational forces. I would like to question the conclusion that altruism is externally controlled and to attempt to point out general limitations in the explanatory power of situational research.

Ultimately I will outline a cognitive–developmental approach for the investigation of altruism and argue that it is uniquely equipped to elucidate some particularly significant aspects of the phenomenon.

THE SITUATIONAL APPROACH TO THE STUDY OF ALTRUISM

The general conclusion that Morgan's (1973) study appears to support is at least as old as the conclusion that Hartshorne and May (1930) drew from their monumental study of character: "There is little evidence of united character traits" that predict prosocial behavior, and prosocial behaviors (called "service" by Hartshorne and May) are mainly "products of fortunate situations [p. 755]." The implications of these conclusions are far-reaching and profound. The same forces that mediate generosity, charity, and helping in emergencies—situational forces such as the behavior of models and the dictates of authority—will cause people to be aggressive toward one another (Harris, Liguori, & Joniak, 1973) and shock one another severely (Milgram, 1963). From a purely situational point of view, all you need to know about a person are the external forces that impinge upon him. For the purpose of predicting behavior, all people are the same. They are as good or as bad as the situations that influence them. References to personality traits like altruism are overused and misleading at best and, at worst, mythical. As Hartshorne and May showed a half century ago, just about everyone will help in some situations; just about nobody will help in other contexts; and the same people who help in some situations will not help in others.

AN EVALUATION OF THE SITUATIONAL APPROACH TO THE STUDY OF ALTRUISM

One of the main sources of support for the situational approach to altruism comes from the negative contribution of research on the relationship between personality and altruism. I have reviewed the relevant research elsewhere (Krebs, 1970), and it has been reviewed more recently by Bryan (1972), Gergen, Gergen, and Meter (1972), and Midlarsky, Suda, and Dressel (in press). There is little basis for resisting Gergen *et al.*'s characterization of personality research on altruism as "a quagmire of evanescent relations among variables, conflicting findings, and low order correlation coefficients [Gergen *et al.*, 1972, p. 113]." However, the conclusion that existing research has failed to support any consistent relationship between personality and altruism should not read as support for the idea that altruism is externally determined. It is obvious that the predictive inadequacy of personality variables may be due to methodological and conceptual inadequacies of the studies that employ them. The average amount of variance accounted for by both situational and personality variables is dismally small. The latest general estimate is 10.3% for situational variables and 8.7% for personality variables (Sarason, Smith, & Diener, 1975). It is difficult to see how any approach could be judged as more or less viable on the basis of a 1.6% advantage in predictive ability, when about 90% of the variance is still left unaccounted for.

Even if situational variables had a significantly greater ability than personality variables to predict behavior, it would not necessarily establish the epistemological superiority of situational explanations of altruism. Although social psychologists generally agree that the goal of research is to predict and control behavior, predicting behavior is not tantamount to understanding that phenomenon. Investigators who adopt a large-scale shotgun predictive approach may be able to discover variables that predict the behavior in which they are interested without in any way increasing their understanding of the processes that determine the behavior. This holds true for both situational and personality predictors. In Morgan's (1973) study, for example, the presence or absence of a moustache predicted opposite-sex compliance to requests for the names of passersby; but without more explanation this finding is quite meaningless. Similarly, a popular test of empathy (Hogan, 1969) contains the true or false alternatives "I am afraid of deep water' and "I prefer a shower to a tub bath." The answers people give help predict empathic behavior, but they probably have a closer conceptual relationship to water safety than to empathy.

In most social psychological research on altruism, specific external variables are manipulated or measured, and their effects on specific helping responses are recorded. However, investigators rarely confine the interpretation of the results precisely to what they have found. If Morgan (1973) had stuck to a strictly situational interpretation of results, he would have produced only a highly descriptive list that would read something like a police report: In Knoxville, Tennessee, in the winter of 1971, 18–44 year-old female undergraduate students who weighed from 90–185 lbs and wore their hair short received more compliance when they asked male passersby for their name than.... Instead, Morgan (1973) interprets his results in terms of general relationships: the effect of location of request, sex, and personal appearance on altruistic behavior. It is fair to wonder how many studies it would require to test all the situations necessary to validate the general concepts employed and whether the procedure supplies a viable way of advancing knowledge.

The questions raised by Morgan's 1973 study are more or less relevant to most of the situational research on helping behavior. Consider, for example, the conclusion of a recent review of research on helping behavior in children, that "few studies have assessed the impact of determinants of helping across time or space. Thus, generalization from the findings of one experiment to other behaviors presumably reflecting the same concept, or to the same behavior at a much later date, or to the same behavior in a somewhat different context cannot be made with assurance [Bryan, 1972, p. 88]." Bryan (1972) also noted that

> few of the studies have been concerned with the degree to which various measures of helping behavior are correlated . . . the few studies that have included more than a single measure of donations or rescuing have failed to find a significant correlation between them. . . . Generalization to the determinants of various forms of helping behavior other than those which have been employed in the particular experiment may well be fallacious [p. 88].

There is a considerable gap between *predicting* helping *behavior* and *explaining* altruism. In Morgan's (1973) study, for example, altruism is operationally defined as giving passersby the time or telling them your name. Significantly, Morgan uses the term *compliance* interchangeably with the term *altruism*. Is giving your name to a stranger altruistic? Without getting into a long definitional debate, it should be easy to agree that not all helping behavior is altruistic and that we have to know more about an incident than a behavioral outcome before we can decide whether or not it is altruistic. Studies, like that of Morgan, that claim to investigate "altruistic behavior" are often guilty of false advertising. If a female student stopped me on the street and asked me for my name I would probably give it to her, but not because I felt altruistic.

The classical issues associated with altruism are motivational. Do people help others out of concern for the others, or are they ultimately motivated to maximize their own gain? A purely situational approach does not concern itself with motivation, but most situationally oriented research appeals to the motivational assumptions of behavioristically oriented learning theory. Inasmuch as situational research subscribes to the principle of reinforcement, it lends itself most readily to the inference that people help others because it is rewarding to them. However, Rosenhan (Chapter 5 in this volume) notes that to speak of learning theory in relation to altruistic prosocial behavior is to speak of a profound paradox; for learning involves reward, and altruism appears to involve none. I shall not explore this issue in detail here because I have done so elsewhere (Krebs, 1975), but I do want to suggest that it is an issue with which anyone who employs the concept of altruism should contend.

MULTIVARIATE INTERACTIONS OF PERSONALITY AND SITUATIONAL APPROACHES TO THE EXPLANATION OF ALTRUISM

The most obvious way to respond to the empirical limitations of personality research and the practical and conceptual difficulties of situational research is to acknowledge the influence of both the person and the situation and to explore the nature of their interaction. Indeed, although social psychological studies that employ only situational variables still outnumber studies that include personality variables, the number of studies that include both has been increasing steadily in the past few decades (Sarason et al., 1975).

Gergen, Gergen, and Meter (1972) came to the defense of person-specific sources of prediction and outlined what I shall call a multivariate interactional position. Basically, Gergen et al. argued that past investigations failed to find consistent relationships between personality variables and helping behavior because they incorrectly assumed that personality traits should predict helping behavior in any or all situations, when, in fact, specific personality traits relate to helping behavior in specific situations. To understand helping behavior, we must attend to the interaction between situational and person-specific variables. Gergen et al. conclude that there are two viable approaches to the investigation of the relationship between personality and helping behavior: (a) to investigate situations of critical social significance in great detail; and (b) to employ a multivariate approach, using techniques like factor analysis, cluster analysis, and multiple regression to capture the complexity of the interrelationships among personality dispositions and the variables that comprise the situation.

A recent series of studies by Staub and his colleagues (Staub, 1974) support and extend the general position of Gergen et al. Staub found that the ability to predict helping behavior was considerably improved when personality variables were considered in interaction with situational variables. For example, only subjects who were assigned to Kohlberg's (1969) major or minor Stage 5 of moral development and who were given permission to enter a room adjoining theirs consistently helped a stooge when he began to "moan and groan" in the other room. Subjects at other stages of moral development and Stage 5 subjects in different situations failed to help more than did control subjects. Similarly, subjects who scored high on a measure of social responsibility (Berkowitz & Lutterman, 1968) and low on a measure of Machiavellianism (Christie & Geis, 1968) helped more than did other subjects, but only in the situation in which the experimenter gave them permission to enter the stooge's room.

At a methodological level, the advantages of the multivariate approach seem indisputable. From a quantitative behavioristic perspective, the multivariate strategy has the greatest predictive potential because it includes more variables. At a theoretical level, the measurement of internal events supplies a way of extending the description of specific causal sequences that characterize the situational approach and begins to supply some basis for broader and more integrated explanations. When we go beyond the finding that $N\%$ of a subject sample volunteered for an experiment on altered states of consciousness and learn that the subjects who volunteered tended to have a high need to seek sensation (Gergen *et al.*, 1972), we acquire some clue as to *why* they volunteered and what their behavior means.

Despite the obvious advantages of the multivariate approach, it is limited. It is better and more inclusive than a purely situational approach, but it maintains what I believe are a limited set of assumptions about the nature of knowledge, as well as a limited set of methodological tools. The multivariate approach is essentially a quantitative extension of the situational approach. Gergen *et al.* (1972) acknowledge some of the practical limitations to the multivariate approach when they wonder whether large numbers of variables and all the interactions among these variables should be assessed. Staub (1974) too asks whether this suggests that "our task (or hope) of finding meaningful personality-situation-behavior relationships is hopeless, because every personality characteristic will relate differently to every kind of helping behavior in each different situation [pp. 329–333]." Although Staub answers this question in the negative, it is fair to wonder whether anyone will ever approach measuring the forces that interact to affect helping behavior in the millions of constantly changing situations of life.

The practical problems with the multivariate approach reflect what I believe to be basic epistemological limitations. Like situational studies, most multivariate studies manipulate discrete and measurable units of analysis—dependent and independent variables—even though they employ more of them and make some attempt to attend to the relationships among them. The problem is that the variables that are easiest to measure are usually the most superficial. They represent only the most external and concrete characteristics of the social world. In employing easily quantifiable variables like how someone is dressed, whether he is stationary or moving, or how he scores on various personality tests, investigators ignore the more general, abstract, and significant aspects of situations and people, such as the *meaning* of asking for the time or asking for someone's name, the implicit rules of politeness that guide social behavior, and the normative structure of social expectations.

The multivariate approach often employs personality characteristics as variables without attending to the theoretical context in which the measures of personality variables are rooted. Some personality tests are essentially atheoretical—they are constructed to enhance our ability to predict particular behaviors. However, other personality tests are rooted in theoretical contexts that are inconsistent with the epistemological assumptions of the situational approach. One of the implications of treating all personality variables as quantitative predictors is that they all obtain equal conceptual status. In Staub's (1974) study on bystander intervention, for example, subjects' stage of moral development is treated like a quantitative variable similar to social responsibility or Machiavellianism; but, in Kohlberg's theory, Stage 5 represents one of six general, pervasive stages of moral development. It is *qualitatively* different from the other stages. People who are at Stage 5 do not have more of the same thing (morality) than people who are at Stage 4; they have a qualitatively different conception of morality.

It might seem that the problems I have been discussing are necessary problems of psychological research, characteristic of all approaches. However, I believe that, although they are common, they are not unavoidable. I would like to outline an approach that I believe solves some of the problems of traditional behavioristic research. The approach is probably familiar to most as a leading position in developmental psychology. It is commonly called the cognitive developmental or structural approach and is associated most closely with the work of Jean Piaget and Lawrence Kohlberg.

THE COGNITIVE-DEVELOPMENTAL APPROACH

As the label implies, cognitive-developmental theory is concerned with the development of thought. It is, however, only incidentally concerned with the content of thought, the accumulation of facts, or, in general, what people think. It is more concerned with the organization of thought, the structure of reasoning, or *how* people think. The concept of cognitive structure is illusive to most empirically oriented scholars. Structure refers to the way thought is organized, how finely concepts are differentiated and integrated, and how logically connections among ideas are made. When we talk about a cognitive structure, we refer to a platform or basis from which inferences are made, a point of view, an organized set of working assumptions.

According to cognitive-developmental theory, the central motivating force of existence is a general tendency to grow. However much our behavior is modified by pleasure, pain, and "payoffs," we still possess a pervasive disposition to make sense out of things. In fact, pain and pleasure are at least as significant as sources of information as they are affective controls.

Piaget has traced the growth of knowledge in children. Infants are born into a complex environment ("situation"), but they have only limited mental faculties. From the beginning, children understand their worlds by assimilating information into nascent systems of thoughts or "schemas," not by internalizing it onto blank slates. Cognitive schemas grow by "accommodating" to the incoming information. We understand things in terms of what we already understand. It is easy to see that an infant or a young child does not "see" what we see, even though we are looking at the same thing. This is true for the social world as well as for the physical world, and for adults as well as for children. When I look at the blackboard of one of my colleagues, who is a statistician, I see only a meaningless mess of numbers. Apparently, he sees more. People react differently to the same social situation even though it consists of the same physical stimuli. Nowhere is this more apparent than in matters of morality and values. The meaning of social acts—having an abortion, giving money to beggars, pulling the plug on a kidney machine, going to war—has little to do with the sequences of behavior that comprise them. The meaning is assigned by people on the basis of differing conceptions of their social and moral worlds.

Ways of knowing, or cognitive structures, are not static or canned points of view like needs, attitudes, values, or personality traits. They are procedures or operations for making sense out of the world. They change with experience, but not like the personality traits that Gergen et al. (1972) describe. There is a direction to their change—they grow, develop, and become more sophisticated and more adequate.

The most controversial postulate of cognitive-developmental theory is that the structures of reasoning undergo a number of *qualitative* transformations as these structures develop. In effect, they organize themselves under a given logic until they outlive it; then they change. When the system becomes maximally well-organized or "equilibrated," it serves as the platform for an entirely new system that eventually subsumes it. Thus, we can associate the pattern of everyone's thought with one more or less dominant form of reasoning, and we can place everyone at a step in the developmental hierarchy. Kohlberg summarizes the cognitive-developmental conception of stages as follows:

> In summary, the kinds of age change relevant to a stage model are restricted to those implied by the distinctions between quality and quantity, competence and performance, and form and content. In addition to focusing upon quality, form, competence, a cognitive-developmental stage concept has the following additional general characteristics (Piaget, 1960):
> 1. Stages imply distinct or qualitative differences in structures (modes of thinking) which will serve the same basic function (e.g., intelligence) at various points in development.
> 2. These different structures form an invariant sequence, order or succession in individual development. While cultural factors may speed up, slow down, or stop development, they do not change its sequence.
> 3. Each of these different and sequential modes of thought forms a "structured whole." A given stage-response on a task does not just represent a specific response determined by knowledge and familiarity with that task or tasks similar to it; rather, it represents an underlying thought-organization.
> 4. Stages are hierarchical integrations. Accordingly, higher stages displace (or, rather, reintegrate) the structures found at lower stages [Kohlberg, 1973, p. 498].

I hope that I have said enough about cognitive-developmental theory to show how it supplies a resolution quite different from the one suggested by Gergen et al. (1972). The structure of social reasoning serves a type of executive function in personality akin to that of intelligence. It is true that "dispositions that are imported into a situation modify one's perception of the situation," and at the same time that "situational manipulations affect personal dispositions [Gergen et al., 1972, p. 126]," but this is through the constant, pervasive, and dynamic process of assimilation and accommodation, not through the interaction of specific personality traits like the need for sensation with specific situations like an experiment on altered states of consciousness. Cognitive-developmental theory agrees with Gergen et al. when they suggest that we must attend to the relationship among internal events and avoid considering events in isolation. However, cognitive-developmental theory is concerned with the *structure* of pervasive, qualitatively-distinct patterns of reasoning that define stages of cognitive development. These types of organization cannot be represented in multivariate statistics. There is a world of difference between the predictive overlap between a need for autonomy and a need for sensation and the structural organization of social reasoning. From the cognitive-developmental point of view, most of the internal events that psychologists measure are *products* of mental work, general interpretations, or conclusions about the way the world is constructed and how we fit into it. Cognitive-developmental theory is concerned with the mental work that gives rise to the content of thought.

In order to understand a person's attitudes, we must know what they mean to the person who possesses them. This entails discovering how they fit in with and follow from their interpretation of relevant situations. One of the reasons why investigators who employ specific products of mental operations as units of analysis fail to find consistent relationships with behavior is that they impose their interpretive scheme on the answers that their subjects give rather than explore the antecedents of their subjects' own reasoning. The problem with this practice is that the same answers can mean quite different things to different people. Moreover, different answers can mean the same thing to different people. As long as we employ answers as units of analysis from the outside without exploring the processes from which they were derived, we are bound to obtain only superficial results. Imagine that we are taking a test of social responsibility and that one of the questions is "Is it wrong to steal?" We all know the right answer—that it is wrong to steal. Four-year-old children know that it is wrong to steal. If they took a test of social responsibility, they would receive one point for a correct answer, just as we would. Conventional tests of social responsibility do not ask their subjects *why* they hold such attitudes. For one thing, it is not practical to explore the reasons behind responses. For another, most tests assume that beliefs and attitudes exist in the outside social world somewhere as self-contained packages that people "internalize" in the same way in which they swallow pills.

For the sake of this argument, I asked my four-year-old daughter why it was wrong to steal. She said, "Because it isn't a very good thing." I asked her to elaborate. She said, "Because when people find out, they have to find someone to get their things back, and that's a lot of trouble; and it costs a lot of money to get their things back." One of my daughter's friends thought it was wrong to steal because "you'll get put in jail if you get caught" and another thought it was wrong "because your mom will be mad." I need not belabor the point that although the content-based answers the children gave were the "same" as yours and mine, they were, in cognitive reality, different.

Actually, I must confess that I do not really believe that it is wrong to steal. I believe that it is right to steal when, for example, the reason for stealing is to save someone's life. My daughter and I disagree on that point. She believes it is always wrong to steal, with no exceptions.

When I reminded her that a consequence of not stealing could be to let someone die, she said "That's all right, just let them die. They will go up and be a fairy." I dropped the point because I do not want the neighbors to think that I am corrupting my children by encouraging them to steal.

The strategy of comparing the reasoning behind my daughter's response with the reasoning behind my own was not serendipitous—it is an essential characteristic of the methodology of the cognitive-developmental approach. The differences among people that are of greatest concern are not the context-based differences measured in most tests of "individual differences." Rather, they are the structural developmental differences in maturity.

The cognitive-developmental approach supplies a solution to the practical problems of measuring all aspects of people and all aspects of situations. It attempts to decipher the logic of the intervening agency or process that gives both personality and situational forces meaning. It supplies a basis for inferring that if a person who thinks in a particular way is in a particular situation, he will interpret it in a particular way. Moreover, it supplies a basis for understanding the most broad, generalized response disposition there is—the disposition to respond in ways that follow from organized ways of interpreting the social and physical world.

A COGNITIVE-DEVELOPMENTAL APPROACH TO ALTRUISM

I have suggested that most research on helping behavior cannot legitimately claim to study altruism. The typical study begins by supplying a dictionary-like definition of altruism, such as "behavior carried out to benefit another without anticipation of rewards from external sources [Macauley & Berkowitz, 1970, p. 73]," or "regard for the interest of others without concern for one's self-interest [Wispé, 1972, p. 4]," then proceeds to operationalize the concept in terms of quantifiable incidences of helping behavior. Wispé (1972) has supplied a summary of the types of helping behavior that have been investigated. They vary from hiding Jews during the war (London, 1970) to making paper boxes for a supervisor in a psychological experiment (Berkowitz & Daniels, 1963). There is rarely anything in the studies to establish the validity of the conceptual definition, the operational definition, or the relationship between them. It might be argued that the task of supplying a conceptual definition of altruism should be left to philosophers, that such tasks are beyond the pale of empirical science, and that the task of psychology is to predict and control behavior. But, as I argued earlier, predicting behavior that appears to be altruistic does not explain altruism. Supplying conceptual definitions of behaviors and assigning behaviors to overriding categories is of little concern to mainstream behavioral psychology. This is as much the case for the study of aggression as it is for the study of altruism.

The cognitive-developmental approach takes the investigation of ideas seriously. It supplies a way of defining concepts like altruism without lapsing into the empirically irrelevant conceptual debates characteristic of philosophy. Philosophers attempt to determine the definition of phenomena like altruism as end products and absolutes. Cognitive-developmental psychology investigates the rules that give rise to ideas like altruism as they fit with ways of thinking that are characteristic of people in various stages of their lives. Cognitive-developmental theory treats concepts like altruism as products and tools of reasoning. The idea of altruism exists because it symbolizes a set of social phenomena. People's ideas about altruism evolve with cognitive development. The meaning and significance of altruism changes as they develop more elaborate theories of the social world. Conceptions of altruism are tied to conceptions of self, human nature, and moral obligation. The concept of altruism is a part of most people's system of values, and it cannot be understood out of context.

This is not the place to present an elaborate account of the development of the meaning of altruism, but it should help exemplify and extend my point to sketch out some ways in which we would expect the meaning of altruism to change with the growth of moral sophistication. I will borrow from the theory and research of Lawrence Kohlberg (e.g., 1969, 1972) for this purpose.

In Kohlberg's theory of moral development, altruism is one of several "aspects" of morality that arise in the social lives of all people everywhere (examples of other aspects are rules, duty, and justice). Structures of moral reasoning give rise to points of view that pervade the aspects of morality. For example, children at the first stage of moral development (i.e., children whose moral point of view is most primitive) generally believe that rules should be obeyed to the letter; duty entails doing what you are told to do by people in authority; justice means an eye for an eye and a tooth for a tooth; and altruism is a matter of helping when you are told to help or helping in order to obtain a reward and avoid a punishment. These attitudes have a number of characteristics in common that reflect the structure of reasoning from which they arise. They are concrete, physicalistic, specific, and heteronomous; and they are egocentric. The young child does not weigh subjective events like the intentions behind an act when he evaluates it, because he does not possess the cognitive sophistication to take the role of other people. His egocentricity is part of his concrete and physicalistic cognitive orientation—he can only entertain one point of view at a time, usually the one that is most salient and physically concrete.

In Kohlberg's scheme, conceptions of altruism change as cognitive development advances. At Stage 2, children adopt a somewhat broader orientation toward altruism—they believe that it is right for all people to advance their own welfare, but they also believe that it is in people's best interest to make and keep bargains with others. At this stage, children have the cognitive sophistication to comprehend the concept of reciprocity, but only in a concrete way. Thus, when asked to interpret the Golden Rule, they say that it means "doing unto others as they do unto you." Altruism is rooted in the idea of helping those who help you.

It is at the third stage of moral development outlined by Kohlberg, which people generally reach in late elementary school and which is characteristic of a sizable portion of the adult population, that concerns about altruism become most salient. At Stage 3, moral obligation is defined in terms of ideal (versus concrete) reciprocity—"Do unto others as you would have them do unto you." The Stage 3, orientation is maximally attentive to doing one's part in social groups, living up to the stereotyped demands of social roles, and, in general, fitting in, conforming, and maximizing social approval. It has been called the "good boy, good girl" moral orientation.

When it comes to the salience of altruism, the fourth stage of moral development seems, superficially, more like the second stage than the third stage. People at Stage 4 do not characteristically interpret moral obligations in terms of ideas like altruism. Concerns about altruism are subsumed at Stage 4 under larger concerns like maintaining social welfare. One of the defining characteristics of Stage 4 is the tendency of the people who possess the orientation to place the welfare of society above the welfare of friends, relatives, and individuals who need help. Thus, to take one example, it would be more consistent with Stage 4 than with Stage 3 reasoning to argue that we should not give money to beggars because giving money to them reinforces a behavior that is contrary to the best interests of society. The structure of Stage 2 reasoning might lead to the same conclusion, but for different reasons. A person employing Stage 2 reasoning might argue that it was stupid to help beggars because they never pay you back.

I hope I have said enough to supply a flavor for the ways in which the meaning and significance of altruism would be expected to change with the evolution of moral reasoning. If cognitive-developmental theory is correct, the conceptions of altruism (embedded, of course, in a more general moral orientation) that characterize late stages are more adequate than the conceptions that characterize earlier ones. These are not arbitrary attitudes; they are a part of increasingly sophisticated cognitive perspectives.

It is probably not obvious why people at Stage 3 who are concerned with altruism would also be concerned with social roles, social approval, conformity, and affectional relations, although research has established a consistent correlation among these attitudes. Cognitive-developmental theory explains these correlations of content as logical products of the structure of the third stage of moral reasoning. In one sense, the task of the cognitive-developmental researcher is to decipher the logic of the relationship between the products of thought and the structure of reasoning that produced them. Why then do people tend to manifest correlated attitudes at particular points in their lives? A large part of the answer is supplied by the structural changes that take place in the ability of people at this stage to take the role of others. At Stage 2, people are capable of adopting the point of view of other people one at a time. They can understand that another person would like them to behave helpfully, but they understand the other side of the equation even better—they want the best deal for themselves. There is little in this perspective to justify self-sacrifice except to foster reciprocity and equal exchange. It is not difficult to see how their role-taking perspective would give rise to the concretely reciprocal Stage 2 definition of the Golden Rule. At Stage 3, people become able to adopt the point of view of groups of other people, or "generalized others." Moral obligation is not defined in terms of one point of view versus another, but in terms of the general point of view implicit to the ideal reciprocity of behaving as you would like others to behave. The Stage 3 point of view subsumes the two points of view contained in Stage 2 and supplies a way of deciding between them when they come into conflict, which is why it is more advanced.

The altruism, conformity, approval-seeking, and stereotyped conceptions of social roles follow quite naturally from the role-taking perspective of Stage 3. They are all part of one concern—to fulfill the generalized expectation of people in one's reference group, which, of course, often entails sacrificing self-interest in order to further the welfare of the group. The expectations of others are formalized in social roles. There are duties associated with being a father, mother, son, daughter, wife, husband, teacher, or friend, and these duties often entail helping people in reciprocal roles. At Stage 2 the point of view of the self must compete only with the point of view of other individuals. At Stage 3 the point of view of the self must compete with the point of view of all the people who occupy roles in reference groups and, indeed, with the types of social expectations that are part of the normative structure of society.

I would predict a fairly consistent relationship between changes in the values that people endorse throughout their life-span and changes in the structure of their moral reasoning. I would expect values relating to equal exchange to peak at Stage 2, values relating to altruism to peak at Stage 3, and values relating to the maintenance of society to peak at Stage 4. However, I would also predict that people's conceptions of various values change with development. Although the words that define the values (altruism, equality, freedom, autonomy) remain the same, people's understanding of the social phenomena that they symbolize grows more sophisticated. At Stage 2, altruism might mean returning favors, and autonomy might mean the freedom to do what one pleases. At Stage 5, altruism might mean fostering the greatest good for the greatest number, and autonomy might relate to the obligation of individuals to oppose unjust laws in their society.

In order to understand the Stage 3 peak in concern about altruism, we must recognize the senses in which it is both more advanced than the concerns at Stage 2 and less advanced than the concerns at Stage 4. Although the idea that it is right to sacrifice one's welfare for the good of the group is generally considered better than the idea of helping those who will help you back, the Stage 3 equation of altruism and morality is also limited. It is often wrong to help others, even though the group endorses it. This is most clear when helping conflicts with other more abstract duties and when the cause to which the help is given promotes injustice. It is wrong to help another when you are helping him harm others. It is wrong to help your family or friends advance their own welfare at others' expense. In general, it is wrong to help people who do not deserve to be helped. There are principles that supersede, guide, and limit the prescription of altruism; but these principles are only understood at high stages of moral development. It is right to behave justly, to treat all people equitably, and to treat people in a way that one would have all other people treat others, even if it means on occasion not helping, or even hurting, others. The confusion between helping others and behaving morally is one of the defining aspects of Kohlberg's Stage 3 moral development.

Undoubtedly, there is a lot more to be learned about the development of conceptions of altruism. I have focused mainly on the significance of altruism as an aspect of moral obligation. The idea of altruism is also closely connected to the development of conceptions of self and society, as described by symbolic interaction theorists such as G. H. Mead, C. H. Cooley, and J. M. Baldwin (cf. Manis & Meltzer, 1972).

A COGNITIVE-DEVELOPMENTAL EXPLORATION OF ALTRUISTIC BEHAVIOR

I began by critically evaluating the approaches to the investigation of altruism that characterize contemporary psychology. I argued that they shared the goal of predicting and controlling behavior. How does the cognitive-developmental approach fare when evaluated from the point of view of contemporary behavioristic research? Does knowledge of a person's stage of, say, moral reasoning help us predict the types of operationally defined helping behavior that psychologists customarily investigate?

Cognitive-developmental theory recognizes that behavior is determined by countless forces. Indeed, in my opinion, the force of "irrational" determinants of behavior such as genetically determined action patterns, hormones, and basic chemical mediators has been greatly underestimated. I believe that some of the ethological work, research on nonverbal communication, and recent findings on sex-typing are convincing on this point. Cognitive-developmental theory also does not deny the effect of learning and conditioning on behavior, as defined by behavioristically oriented learning theory. But it cannot be denied that we possess what I would term basic emotional dispositions from our evolutionary past that exert a powerful influence on our behavior. Although it is obvious that these dispositions interact with, modify, and are modified by higher-order cognitive acquisitions, no one understands very well how this occurs. I am not going to attempt to review here all the determinants of behavior. I want to discuss only one—the structure of reasoning at various stages of moral development.

First let me pursue some implications of viewing social behavior from a *cognitive* and *developmental* perspective. Age and intelligence are the two person-specific variables that have best predicted helping behavior in children in specific situations. We might ask ourselves why age and intelligence would relate positively to helping behavior. The most obvious answer would be that *within the age range investigated* helping behavior is a product of cognitive maturity. This makes some intuitive sense, because generally we think of selfish people as immature and egocentric and altruistic people as more advanced developmentally and socially. A large part of our conceptions of altruism is evaluative, and a large part of our social evaluations are developmental. When we criticize people, we accuse them of being immature and childish and advise them to "grow up." When we speak of altruism, we generally contrast it with selfishness. When we speak of selfishness, we equate it with egocentricity. Perhaps, then, we could find a route to understanding altruism by tracing developmental changes in egocentricity.

From a cognitive-developmental point of view, it is more informative to observe a wide variety of naturally occurring behaviors than to observe the specific responses to specific stimuli that are customarily measured in psychology labs. This is an important point, because it entails a different method for investigating determinants of behavior from the ones we are accustomed to. It implies that, although specific situational influences (the independent variables of experimental research) affect specific behaviors in specific situations, general dispositions (stage of moral development) exert a general effect on a wide variety of behaviors across a wide variety of situations. People do not passively wait for situations to affect them; they actively seek out and construct situations that are appropriate to their level of development. It is integrated patterns of behavior that characterize people, not isolated acts.

If we were to map the behavioral domain of helping in young children, I believe that we would find that the types of help they give correspond to the way they interpret their world. People at different stages of development will behave differently because they interpret differently the situations they encounter and pursue. More specifically, people at higher stages will understand more situations, more completely, and more precisely than people at lower stages. This fact becomes most obvious through observing children. Young children have little appreciation for the needs of others. Characteristically, they feel most generous when they give what *they* would like. When I took my 3- and 5-year-old daughters shopping for birthday presents for their mother, they bought her a box of crayons, a roll of Scotch tape, some colorful ribbons, and a tropical fish.

The quantity of helping would not necessarily increase at each stage. However, if cognitive-developmental theory is correct, the quality of helping should improve at each stage. It should become more exactly attuned to the needs, rights, and duties of individuals as they relate to the needs, rights, and duties of other individuals in the social order.

One implication of sensitivity to developmental changes is described by Jane Loevinger as it relates to ego development. Her points exemplify and extend the points I have been attempting to make. Loevinger (1966) makes a distinction between two types of behaviors: "milestone sequences" and "polar aspects." One milestone sequence is conformity. The only way it can be understood is as a qualitative variable in a developmental context; "Conformity to generally accepted social standards becomes increasingly characteristic of behavior up to a point, but beyond that point with increasing maturity becomes progressively less compelling . . . [p. 202]." In contrast, polar aspects are quantitative variables that decrease systematically with ego development. Tendency to stereotyping is a polar aspect. Milestone sequences are "observable at a minimal inferential level, while polar aspects are not themselves observable but must be inferred from patterns of behavior [p. 204]." Loevinger claims that "ultrabehavioristic" researchers often select as data aspects of behavior that are "observable at a minimal inferential level" (i.e., part of a milestone sequence) and treat them as polar aspects (i.e., attempt to measure them with quantitative methods). In Loevinger's words,

> No useful purpose will ever be served by classing together in regard to conformity those who have not yet grown into it, those who are not willing to conform, and those who have outgrown the stage . . . [p. 203]. The ultrabehaviorists is doomed to deal in trivialities in the personality field, for he approaches the area with a predelection at once for observing behavior at a minimal inferential level and for quantitative variables [p. 204].

By now we have come almost full circle. I would like to close by examining the ability of cognitive-developmental "variables" to predict *specific* helping behaviors in *specific* situations—to, in effect, compete with behavioristic research on its own ground. To determine the predictive power of cognitive-developmental variables, we need simply turn to the literature. Ironically, cognitive-developmental variables have fared better in this task than any other person-specific characteristics.

Some years ago, Kohlberg (1969) made the following rather audacious statement: "Honesty is a meaningless construct, even though my test is really an excellent measure of this meaningless construct." Kohlberg might well have said the same thing about the relationship between his test and the concept of altruism. To date, almost all investigators who have tested the relationship between moral development and helping behavior have obtained positive results (Emler & Rushton, 1974; Rubin & Schneider, 1973; Ruston, 1975). Only one reported study (Schwartz, Feldman, Brown, & Heingartner, 1969) failed to find a reliable relationship between moral development and helping, and the relationship it found approached statistical significance. Ironically, the positive findings of this type of research are problematic for cognitive-developmental theory. Consider the following points: (*a*) Cognitive-developmental tests are not designed to predict behavior; (*b*) The cognitive-developmental tests that were used in the studies were designed to measure the structure of moral reasoning in general, not reasoning about altruism per se; and (c) outdated versions of cognitive-developmental tests are frequently employed.

Let us consider in detail, for example, the study by Emler and Rushton (1974). The study is a perfectly good study of its type; indeed, I have selected it because it is exemplary. Sixty children in the age range 7–13 were given two tests of role taking and two tests of moral judgment. The tests of moral judgment, employed by Piaget in 1932, consisted of two stories about distributive justice. The children were required to play the bowling game so frequently used by learning researchers (Bandura & Walters, 1963; Rosenhan & White, 1967; Staub & Sherk, 1970). They were given an opportunity to contribute their "winnings" to a "Save the Children Fund." Half of the children were made to feel "sympathetic" by hearing the experimenter describe a child in a poster as having no parents, few clothes, no toys, etc. The other half (in the "nonsympathetic" condition) heard the child described in "neutral" terms. Emler and Rushton found that generosity, moral development, and role-taking ability increased with age. Children who scored high in moral judgment gave more to charity than children who scored low (across both sympathy conditions). The investigators failed to find a significant relationship between role-taking and helping behavior.

Although findings such as those of Emler and Rushton appear to support cognitive-developmental theory, they do not really supply a good test of it. Consider the following points: Two Piagetian tests of moral judgment are insufficient to determine the structural characteristics of moral reasoning that comprise the subject matter of cognitive-developmental theory; Piaget's tests of moral judgment are outdated and inexact (Kohlberg, 1964); Piaget's three-stage outline of moral development has been revised by Kohlberg (1964); there is no a priori reason in cognitive-developmental theory for children high on moral judgment to donate more of their winnings to charity than children low on moral judgment; and the behavior of children in one experimental situation is an inadequate basis on which to make the generalization that moral judgment mediates generosity. To put the point somewhat extremely, the results force us to ask how a study that employs a questionable measure of moral judgment can support a hypothesis that cognitive-developmental theory does not make with methods that it does not endorse from a theoretical framework with which it is inconsistent.

Studies like that of Emler and Rushton adopt the type of approach that Gergen et al. (1972) attributed to personality researchers—they attempt to test a general relationship between moral judgment and generous behavior without attending to the interaction between the specific structures of moral reasoning of the children they test and the structure of the specific situation in which generosity is elicited. Further, they treat qualitative differences quantitatively. Although the investigators acknowledge that Piaget identified three stages of moral development, they classify all children as either high or low. However, the purpose of cognitive-developmental tests is not to assign a number that represents the quantity of characteristics like morality that people possess; it is to identify the overriding ways they reason about moral issues. In order to test the relationship between moral judgment and helping behavior in specific situations and from a cognitive-developmental point of view, one must be sensitive to the structure of specific stages of moral development as they would logically be expected to relate to the structure of the specific situation in question.

In the Emler and Rushton situation, we must ask what the Piagetian tests measured and why this would be associated with differences in helping behavior. Emler and Rushton selected children at an important transitional age—7–13. It is between these ages that children generally change from preoperational to concrete operational thought, from the ability to take the role of individual others to the ability to reflect on their behavior from a more general point of view, and from preconventional (Stage 2) moral development to conventional (Stage 3) moral development. It is possible that the Piagetian tests employed by the investigators supplied a rough distinction between the cognitively immature and the cognitively mature children. The cognitively mature children gave more to charity, but we do not really know precisely why. It could have been because they were more sensitive to the demands of the experimental situation, the authority of the exprimenter, the plight of the poor children, or the moral obligation to give. The conclusion that it was moral development per se that determined the helping behavior is not tenable, because the test used to measure it was questionable and because, according to cognitive-developmental theory, advanced role-taking ability is a necessary prerequisite to advanced moral development. You cannot have one without the other, as reported by Emler and Rushton. In order to *explain* the behavior, we must understand the way in which the differences in moral development affected the children's interpretation of the situation and, through it, their behavior. Only then do we have a basis on which to label the behavior as altruistic or whatever else we choose to call it.

It is somewhat disconcerting to wonder how much the results of social psychological research that purports to test the effects of any number of relationships on subjects in this age range are determined by the milestone tendency that occurs at this time to want to please the experimenter, behave like a good subject, and fit into what is going on. It is interesting to compare the results of Emler and Rushton's study with those of Saltzstein, Diamond, and Belenky (1972). The latter investigators found that children who employed Stage 3 moral reasoning were more likely to conform in an Asch-type group influence situation than children at Stage 2 or Stage 4. Saltzstein *et al.* called the behavior "conformity," but it probably stemmed from the same source as Emler and Rushton's "altruism." Saltzstein *et al.* interpret their results in the following way: "It is the tendency to *confuse* one's liking for others and the need for their approval with issues of *adherence to truth and fulfilling commitment* (e.g., sense of obligation to the experimenter) and not the intensity of the need *per se* that leads to the decision to conform [p. 335]." As we have seen, the structure of reasoning at Stage 3 is characterized by precisely this confusion. They go on to say, "For the higher level children, particularly those at Stage 4, the feeling of obligation to the experimenter-authority to remain accurate may have overridden any duty to the group to conform . . . [p. 335]." What the authors do not state, but should, is why the Stage 2 children also did not conform. It is important to note that the behavior of the Stage 2 subjects was the "same" as the behavior of the Stage 4 subjects. A straight quantitative analysis would result in confusion—how could Stage 3 children be more "moral" than Stage 2 children but less moral than Stage 4 children when Stage 2 children and Stage 4 children did the same thing? In order to understand the behavior of the subjects, we must understand the relationship between the structure of moral reasoning at each of their stages and the structure of the situation to which they responded. We need to understand the qualitative difference in moral reasoning between Stage 2 and Stage 4 children. The Stage 4 subjects probably resisted the pull to conform because they were guided by concerns like honest representation and the authority of the experimenter; but the Stage 2 subjects probably failed to conform because they were concerned about themselves.

CONCLUSION

I have gone on at some length about the differences between the traditional approaches to the investigation of helping behavior and the cognitive-developmental approach. I am sure it will seem to some that I have belabored the differences between the two approaches, that I have been unnecessarily critical of the former and inexcusably kind to the latter. I would like to close by defending myself against the first two charges and by pleading guilty to the third. I believe that most of us have been raised in an epistemological tradition that slants our perspective naturally toward the traditional behavioristic approach that I have criticized. Because the traditional approach is the context from which the cognitive-developmental approach is often viewed, it seemed to me that the latter approach would be best elucidated in contrast to the former. It is undeniable that the approach of Piaget and Kohlberg has been misunderstood and misinterpreted by many, if not most, North American psychologists. It is radically different from the traditional approach, and the differences must be recognized before it can be understood on its own grounds. So I have stressed the differences, and, in so doing, I have attempted to point out some of the deficiencies in the traditional approach, deficiencies to which I believe we ought to attend. In effect, I have attempted to accomplish two goals in one—to raise some questions about the traditional approach and to present an alternative. My hope has been that each goal would be advanced better in confluence than separately. I believe that the questions I have raised about the traditional approach are significant ones and, even if sometimes made somewhat pointedly, are questions that must be answered. However, I have been inequitably kind to the cognitive-developmental approach. It too has problems, ones that I intend to explore in future writings.

REFERENCES

Bandura, A., & Walters, R. H. *Social learning and personality development*. New York: Holt, Rinehart and Winston, 1963.

Berkowitz, L., & Daniels, L. Responsibility and dependency. *Journal of Abnormal and Social Psychology*, 1963, *66*, 429–436.

Berkowitz, L., & Lutterman, K. G. The traditionally socially responsible personality. *The Public Opinion Quarterly*, 1968, *32*, 169–187.

Bryan, J. Why children help: A review. In L. Wispé (Ed.), Positive forms of social behavior. *Journal of Social Issues*, 1972, *28*, 87–104.

Christie, R., & Geis, F. (Eds.). *Studies in Machiavellianism*. New York: Academic Press, 1968.

Emler, N. P., & Rushton, J. P. Cognitive-developmental factors in children's generosity. *British Journal of Social and Clinical Psychology*, 1974, *13*, 277–281.

Frederickson, N. Toward a taxonomy of situations. *American Psychologist*, 1972, *27*, 114–124.

Gergen, K., Gergen, M., & Meter, K. Individual orientations to prosocial behavior. In L. Wispé (Ed.), Positive forms of prosocial behavior. *Journal of Social Issues*, 1972, *28*, 105–130.

Harris, M., Liguori, R., & Joniak, A. Aggression, altruism, and models. *The Journal of Social Psychology*, 1973, *91*, 343–344.

Hartshorne, H., & May, M. A. *Summary of the work of the character education inquiry in religious education*, 1930, October, 754–762.

Hogan, R. Development of an empathy scale. *Journal of Consulting and Clinical Psychology*, 1969, *33*, 307–316.

Kohlberg, L. Development of moral character and ideology. In M. L. Hoffman (Ed.), *Review of child development research*, Vol. 1. New York: Russell Sage Foundation, 1964.

Kohlberg, L. Moral judgment and moral action. Paper presented at the Institute of Human Development, Berkeley, Calif., 1969.

Kohlberg, L. Stage and sequence: The cognitive-developmental approach to socialization. In D. A. Goslin (Ed.), *Handbook of socialization theory and research*. Chicago: Rand McNally, 1969, Chapter 6.

Kohlberg, L. From is to ought. In T. Mischel (Ed.), *Cognitive development and epistemology*. New York: Academic Press, 1972.

Kohlberg, L. Stages and aging in moral development—Some speculations. *The Gerontologist*, 1973, *Winter*, 497–502.

Krebs, D. L. Altruism—An examination of the concept and a review of the literature. *Psychological Bulletin*, 1970, *73*, 258–302.

Krebs, D. L. Empathy and altruism. *Journal of Personality and Social Psychology*, 1975, *32*, 1134–1146.

Latané, B., & Darley, J. M. *The unresponsive bystander: Why doesn't he help?* New York: Appleton-Century-Crofts, 1970.

Loevinger, J. The meaning and measurement of ego development. *American Psychologist*, 1966, *21*, 195–217.

London, P. Motivational hypotheses about Christians who saved Jews from the Nazis. In J. Macauley & L. Berkowitz (Eds.), *Altruism and helping behavior*. New York: Academic Press, 1970, Pp. 241–250.

Macaulay, J. R., & Berkowitz, L. *Altruism and helping behavior: Social psychological studies of some antecedents and consequences.* New York: Academic Press, 1970.

Manis, J. G., & Meltzer, B. N. *Symbolic interaction.* Boston: Allyn and Bacon, 1972.

Midlarsky, E., Suda, W., & Dressel, S. *Some antecedents and correlates of altruism in children: A review of theories and empirical research.* In L. D. Nelson (Ed.), *The social process of helping and sharing.* (In press)

Milgram, S. A behavioral study of obedience. *Journal of Abnormal and Social Psychology*, 1963, *67*, 371–378.

Mischel, W. *Personality and assessment.* New York: Wiley, 1968.

Morgan, W. G. Situational specificity in altruistic behavior. *Representative Research in Social Psychology*, 1973, *4*, 56–66.

Piaget, J. The general problem of the psychobiological development of the child. In J. M. Tanner & B. Inhelder (Eds.), *Discussion on child development*, Vol. 4. New York: International Universities Press, 1960.

Rosenhan, D. Learning theory and prosocial behavior. In L. Wispé (Ed), Positive forms of social behavior. *Journal of Social Issues*, 1972, *28*, 151–164.

Rosenhan, D. L., & White, G. M. Observation and rehearsal as determinants of prosocial behaviour. *Journal of Personality and Social Psychology*, 1967, *5*, 424–431.

Rubin, K. H., & Schneider, F. W. The relationship between moral judgment, egocentrism, and altruistic behavior. *Child Development*, 1973, *44*, 661–665.

Rushton, J. P. Generosity in children: Immediate and long term effects of modeling, preaching, and moral judgment. *Journal of Personality and Social Psychology*, 1975, *31*, 459–466.

Saltzstein, H. D., Diamond, R. M., & Belenky, M. Moral judgment level and conformity behavior. *Developmental Psychology*, 1972, *7*, 327–336.

Sarason, I. G., Smith, R. E., & Diener, E. Personality research: Components of variance attributable to the person and the situation. *Journal of Personality and Social Psychology*, 1975, *32*, 199–204.

Schwartz, S. H., Feldman, K. A., Brown, M. E., & Heingartner, A. Some personality correlates of conduct in two situations of moral conflict. *Journal of Personality*, 1969, *37*, 41–57.

Staub, E. Helping a distressed person: Social, personality, and stimulus determinants. In L. Berkowitz (Ed.), *Advances in experimental social psychology*, Vol. 7. New York: Academic Press, 1974, Pp. 294–341.

Staub, E., & Sherk, L. Need for approval, children's sharing behavior, and reciprocity in sharing. *Child Development*, 1970, *41*, 243–252.

Wispé, L. Positive forms of social behavior: An overview. In L. Wispé (Ed.), Positive forms of social behavior. *Journal of Social Issues*, 1972, *28*, 1–20.

8

Psychoanalysis, Sympathy, and Altruism

RUDOLF EKSTEIN

At the end of World War I, Freud (1955) addressed a psychoanalytic congress and wondered what only a handfull of us could do to bring psychoanalytic, scientific insights to the masses. This problem still holds true. The field of psychoanalytic investigation is so different from ordinary academic psychology, so dependent on "experiments in nature," so full of uncertainty and lack of clarity, that it sometimes seems difficult to move from passionate overstatements to actual scientific work. But I am forced to wonder whether this has not always been true of all the behavioral sciences.

I remember the first contribution by Sears (1943) in which he summarized objective studies of psychoanalytic concepts. I recall my first reaction to Sears' paper. I agreed with Freud. Freud did not believe that Freudian theories and hypotheses need proof through experimental psychology—a thought he expressed in a famous note to Saul Rosenzweig (1937). Although Sears' conclusions were pessimistic, his example nevertheless pushed many in the fields of psychology and psychoanalysis toward serious methodological considerations. He tried to build a bridge between the experimental, academic tradition and what is called the psychoanalytic method. I believe that psychoanalysis has since then moved forward in the development of these interests.

During the very beginning, creative phase of psychoanalysis, in the days of the psychoanalytic "movement," and with the world against it, isolation was probably unavoidable. And although I am not now in favor of a melting pot of different scientific endeavors, I am in favor of bridges among the different disciplines. I would not want this virtue, if such it be, to stem from the reaction formation or from altruistic surrender, but rather I would hope that it is the expression of a mutuality that does not destroy individuality.

In what follows I shall try to discuss the etiology of sympathy and altruism—the ontogenic development of positive forms of behavior, if you will—from a psychoanalytic point of view. But first I must confront what appears to me to be a fundamental difference between academic, experimental psychology on the one hand and psychoanalytic theory and practice on the other; namely, the problem of values.

THE PLACE OF VALUES IN THE WORLDS OF PSYCHOLOGY AND PSYCHIATRY

The very attempt to establish "positive" and "negative" forms of behavior brings us into the position of having to make value judgments. Psychology has tried to free itself from such issues. What is valuable? What is the right kind of ethics? What is moral behavior? It has tried to free itself in order to achieve testable hypotheses. But there is the other side of the choice: the demand for social participation, assumption of social responsibility, application of our findings, and the building of research in the applied field.

This dilemma has always been with the psychoanalyst. From the very beginning, the analyst's search for new insights was tied to therapeutic application, to the restoration of the patient's capacity for "love and work"—Freud's classic definition of mental health. (One might even think of the work of the analyst as a form of sublimated altruism, research in the service of healing.) It is interesting that despite these therapeutic endeavors, definitely based on value judgments as to what the analyst ought to do, early psychoanalytic writings were concerned with the attempt to prove that psychoanalysis was not a *Weltanschauung* and that it was free, itself, of value considerations. Freud (1933 [1932]) made that abundantly clear. Hartmann (1960) dealt with the issue of *Psychoanalysis and Moral Values,* and he differentiated between the realm of science and the one of ultimate personal positions. But in applying psychoanalytic theory, for example in education, the goals are in part based on personal convictions and commitments as to what we believe to be positive attitudes and behaviors. In short, although both experimental psychology and psychoanalysis disavowed values, value judgments were probably always a part of psychoanalytic thinking. So for psychoanalysis the problem of values may conceivably involve slightly less defensive maneuvering than for experimental psychology.

ALTRUISTIC BEHAVIOR AND BEYOND

In order to appreciate fully the depth of the problem of altruism, one must keep in mind that a psychoanalytic consideration of the concept will indeed have to go beyond the mere behavioral expressions of it. In the present volume Krebs has broadened his view, but in his otherwise excellent examination of this concept (1970), as well as in his review of the literature, he and others do not fully evaluate, I believe, certain analytic considerations that are concerned not merely with behavior but also with its deeper meaning—what analysts would call its intrapsychic dynamics characterizing the psychic apparatus. Much of the past psychoanalytic literature looked at certain excesses of altruism, generosity, and love as symptoms of inner struggle. Although apparently socially valuable, expressions of positive behavior were actually expressions of illness that in the long run would prove dysgenic. For example, Lewinsky (1951) described a case of pathological generosity that had its roots in pregenital fixations. Instead of the direct satisfaction of a greed for love, a desire for a penis, etc., the illusion of ultimate reciprocity was introduced. Generosity was used as a kind of magic. Anna Freud (1936) also described a case of altruism in which old desires, rather than having been repressed, were projected onto the recipient of the patient's quasi-altruism. The literature describes other cases in which positive behavior patterns have to be understood as being in reality reaction formations, defenses against impulses of greed and sadism. Anna Freud claimed that much generosity could frequently be understood as an offering of treats in order to avoid tricks, so that much altruism could be considered as avoidance of, or masking of, aggression. She discussed many aspects of the altruistic character features of childhood and adolescent behavior in terms of the development of mechanisms of defense, such as turning an unconscious impulse into its opposite overt counterpart. A good example is her discussion of altruistic surrender, in which individual interests are subordinated to those of others as a form of resolution of inner conflict, which then leads to symptom formation and character distortions of various sorts. These observations, of course, can often be applied to children. Even on a large social scale, however, many areas of charity, rather than being *charitas*—expression of genuine love—turn out to be condescending pity, secret hostility, tragic guilt, or self-advertisement (see Hatfield, Walster, & Piliavin, Chapter 6).

Very few examples can be found in psychoanalytic literature that deal directly with positive forms of behavior and do not focus primarily on the aspects of unresolved conflict. Sperling in his *Psychoanalytic Study of Social Mindedness*, however, offers one such exception. He studied patients in whom socialmindedness was a pronounced character trait. He suggested that "In genuine social-mindedness a highly sublimated form of love is directed toward an abstract object, for instance society as a whole, or toward the underprivileged [1955, p. 257]." From the discussion of certain neurotic aspects of socialmindedness in his patients, Sperling attempted to differentiate between genuine and spurious socialmindedness. He saw true socialmindedness as based on object-libidinal cathexis, whereas spurious socialmindedness was motivated by narcissism, exhibtionism, and masochism. He suggested that the psychoanalyst, in actual observations in practice, would see that genuine and spurious socialmindedness differ only in the relative quantities of their constituent factors. Genuine socialmindedness would not be free of narcissistic or aggressive components, but he suggested that the principal cathexis would be object-libidinal. Here is an area ripe for exploration. Here there are possibilities for experiments of nature as well as for experiments with formal designs and adequate controls (see Rosenhan, Chapter 5).

But, of course, this can present another kind of problem. Much genuine concern for the underprivileged, a deep commitment to their welfare, a true love for them and wish to be helpful, often has led to a philosophy in which the end justifies the means. Object-love for the underprivileged may easily be transformed into indiscriminate and ideological hate for the oppressor. What was originally altruism may find expression in violent, destructive action (Hacker, 1971). Christian and other religious ideas, as well as struggles for national identity and for equality and freedom, although originally based on a capacity to love, on empathy with the suffering, and on a commitment to altruism and to social participation, may easily lead to inquisition and religious persecution, to racism disguised as patriotism, or to a dictatorship thinly disguised as liberation of a suppressed class of people. This issue—more complicated, of course, than my sentence suggests—which is to lead us toward the consideration of positive social change, brings to mind Waelder's (1967) thesis that violent attempts to overthrow an authoritarian society have usually led in world history to a totalitarian victory. Our consideration of the facilitation of positive behavior is stimulated by the question of whether the dialectics of social change allow for modes of social change that are truly humanitarian and that are based on altruism and rooted in the capacity for sympathy and empathy. The very attempt to forge psychological tools toward this end indicates that we have hopes, even though at this time we have no strong historical evidence to support them.

THE GENESIS OF ALTRUISM AND SYMPATHY

The germ of this nonsymptom orientation to positive behavior can be found in Freud's early writings. For example, there is a comment by Freud written in 1895 (Freud, 1954), couched partly in neurological language but representing the basic model concerning the origin of human understanding (a poor translation for the German *Verstehen*). Freud suggested that

> At early stages the human organism is incapable of achieving this specific action. It is brought about by extraneous help, when the attention of an experienced person has been drawn to the child's condition by a discharge taking place along the paths of internal change (e.g., by the child's screaming). This path of discharge thus acquires an extremely important secondary function—viz., of bringing about an understanding (*Verstehen*) with other people, and the original helplessness of human beings is thus the primal source of all moral motives [1954, p. 379].

Although not alone in this suggestion, I would like to note that this comment is the first insight into the theory of object relations. Here Freud refers to the beginning of the child's capacity to feel understood by others, to understand the mother, and to achieve basic trust. Erikson (1964, 1968) refers to the acquisition of basic hope, that first ego virtue, which, if maintained, seems to be the most powerful ingredient in positive behavior. These first preverbal cues between mother and infant, this first struggle between waiting and satisfying one's self, are the external organizers of later empathic understanding and of sympathy and altruism.

Good mothering, analysts maintain, makes for good empathy. Empathy is the forerunner of the capacity for imitation, for identification, and for internalization. We know the meaning of a patient's phrase when he says that he does not feel understood; namely, that he is not loved. Early understanding is to be loved, and it is based on emotional contact more than on reason. The first understanding is emotional agreement, as in the illustration above, rather than the kind of understanding that leads toward intellectual insight. One might say that empathy and insight are siblings in the sequence of emotional and intellectual growth. There is an endless variety of contributions in psychoanalytic literature concerning the socialization of the child based on early positive mothering. Gertrude Schwing (1954), an early psychoanalyst, speaks not only of the child's need for mother-love but also of the capacity for motherliness. Good mothering depends on motherliness, which is only available to a mature woman whose love allows the child to grow up as a separate human being. Such a mother's concept of mother-love does not see the baby as property, and her intimate reactions to the child allow for the kind of distance that makes growth possible. The inner psychological structure of such a mother allows for a certain equilibrium, a capacity for self and object constancy, which is the prerequisite for true mothering. As Bettelheim (1950) notes, "Love is not enough." A good mother, then, would use the intimacy of her love for developing the child's capacity for individuation and separation (Mahler, 1968). Olden (1958) describes the first period of unity, in which the mother unconsciously senses the child's needs as well as the child's selfish demands, which are only slowly transformed into its first true love relationship. These relationships have also been described by Benjamin (1959), Brody (1956), Anna Freud (1965), Spitz (1957, 1965), and Winnicott (1957).

And then—finally, perhaps—love leads to reason. It is this early capacity for love, or, if you will, trust in others and trust in one's self, that permits the building of reason that is not overwhelmed by destructive and hopeless cynicism and by obsessive and devaluating doubt. This equilibrium between faith and reason, trust in others and self-reliance, sociability and individualism, must be understood in terms of its genesis in the mother–infant tie. It is only during the last 20 or 30 years that we have called attention with more precision on the two sides of the genetic point of view, the contributions of maturation and of development (Hartmann, 1958; Hartmann & Kris, 1945). We differentiate now between internal readiness as described by the epigenetic scheme (Erikson, 1950) and the positive and negative contributions of the environment.

Perhaps the most important contribution that psychoanalysis has made, comparable in the affective domain, I think, to Piaget's contributions to the field of cognitive learning, has been to point out that positive behavior patterns and their development have a history in society that is repeated to a large extent in the development of the growing child.

Erikson (1964, 1968) speaks about a schedule of virtues. He defines them as ego virtues. These virtues do not come about all at once; they follow the epigenetic scheme, and they permit us to describe ego strength in qualitative terms. He speaks about hope, will, purpose, and competence as the beginning of virtue developed in childhood. He sees fidelity as the virtue that is brought about in a successful adolescence. He describes love, care, and wisdom as the essential virtues of adulthood. Each of these virtues is acquired through the resolution of a psychosocial crisis, and each allows for cognitive and emotional maturation. These virtues are bound together by sympathy and empathy, love and understanding, but they are not absolutes, and they find different forms in different times and in different cultures. The capacity for adaptation is the outgrowth not only of the resolution of inner conflicts but also of the availability of appropriate social apparatuses to be set in motion at the right time.

I gave examples earlier that indicated that each virtue may easily deteriorate under stress. Under the impact of regressive personal or social forces, virtues can turn into neurotic conflicts and thus become nonadaptive defensive devices. The maturational capacity of the child can be undercut by a nonresponsive environment, by a society filled with anxiety and hate, and by an overindustrialized or depersonalized society.

Finally, it should be noted in concluding this section that, although, as Wispé (1968) has suggested, sympathy and empathy are related to identification and imitation, full identification would destroy empathy. Empathy is a kind of inbetween stage, a sort of temporary identification. It is the most important tool of the psychotherapist who is to understand a patient that he or she identify with the patient temporarily on a trial basis but also maintain his or her own identity. It seems to me that true altruistic feelings based on genuine sympathy will, in the same way, reach a mature level only when the altruistic person, therapist, or parent is capable of avoiding overidentification and is able to maintain helpfulness based on differences rather than on fusion. Parents, teachers, and therapists who are capable of this kind of sympathy, who maintain difference and at the same time empathic understanding, will enable the child, by means of identifying with these very traits, to acquire not only hope based on trust in others but also hope that he/she can develop strength and positive qualities.

PSYCHOANALYSIS AND EDUCATION

Early psychoanalytic writing was more concerned with the underlying negative aspects of man and society, those that interfered with mental functioning. It is understandable, considering education at that time, that the interest of analysts in education, which is nearly as old as psychoanalysis itself, was aimed primarily at discovering the faults of the parents, the repressive nature of the educational system, the lack of honesty in society, the deliberate withholding of information from children, the suppression of sexual knowledge, and the attempt of the educators to destroy the child's initiative and individuality (Ekstein & Motto, 1969). Education was seen as suppressive and hateful, a superego structure creating an internal repressive establishment. Education was seen as training, as a kind of conditioning, a taming of the instincts, rather than as an opportunity for self-realization and for the mobilization of positive kinds of behavior. Analysts at that time were forced to consider the destructive forces rather than the forces that hold together, heal, and educate.

At that time, education was subsumed under the Freudian concept of reality and was seen more in terms of frustration than in terms of nurturance. Freud was quoted as speaking about the struggle between the reality principle and the pleasure principle, but he was understandably misunderstood because of the prevailing social climate. In fact, Freud realized that there are to reality not only frustrating aspects but supportive aspects as well. Education not only tames, it also helps to liberate and to widen the individual's options. In the *New Introductory Lectures to Psychoanalysis* (1964), Freud expressed his hope that psychoanalysis might eventually be applied to the problems of understanding and reshaping the educational process.

In a recent study (Ekstein & Motto, 1969) we trained teachers in psychoanalytic principles and surveyed a variety of modes of learning, learning by repetition, by rewards and punishments, by interpersonal identification, and by cognitive and emotional insights. In this work we tried to follow Erikson's (1950) epigenetic scheme in order to teach more effectively the ever-changing patterns of learning readiness. We chose as a title our basic theme: *From Learning for Love to Love of Learning* (1969). We thus implied the different theoretical components of psychoanalytic psychology, the instinctual and gratifying aspects as well as those adaptive aspects of development and maturation that are comparatively conflict-free. Learning for love and gratification, which is a kind of passive surrender, leads to identification with parents and teachers or, on a higher level, leads to identification with certain values and expertise that the adult generation brings to the child. It is hoped that this will also lead to the love of learning, to the love of enriching internal and external options, to the commitment for growth, and to the commitment to the development of one's individuality as well as one's special responsibilities.

Teachers, with an empathic understanding of the child, must continue the work of the mother and create in the children an empathic understanding of their social environment. Much of that, of course, is lost in a society that is in turmoil and has serious pockets of poverty. In a recent study, for example, Coles and Piers (1969) described the training of black teacher-mothers in Mississippi. They tried to teach these mothers to use their feelings in the early relationship to promote affective as well as intellectual learning. They also stressed the relationship between identification and learning.

The point to be made here is that the mechanism transmitting value is the child's identification with the adult generation. The survival of value rests on available opportunities for their fulfillment. Our school system is the institution that must provide the opportunity and the techniques for identificatory learning and offer the skills and the knowledge that will maintain the continuity of the individual and the society within our value system.

CONCLUSION

In the beginning, psychoanalysis was primarily a psychology of unconscious conflicts, and the task of therapy was seen as the resolution of these conflicts. As psychoanalysis developed, the emphasis moved from a psychology of unconscious conflicts to a notion of the human mind that stressed the balanced acquisitions of the capacity for one's own adaptation to the environment and for the adaptation of the environment to one's needs. Today psychoanalysis will make the greatest contribution toward an understanding of positive qualities and the techniques that are to facilitate their growth if it goes beyond the study of therapy and beyond the problems of therapeutic resolution of inner conflicts to questions of child rearing and the study of informal and formal education.

REFERENCES

Benjamin, J. D. Prediction and psychopathological theory. In L. Jessner & E. Pavenstedt (Eds.), *Dynamic psychopathology in childhood.* New York: Grune & Stratton, 1959.
Bettelheim, Bruno. *Love is not enough.* Glencoe, Illinois: Free Press, 1950.

Brody, S. *Patterns of mothering; Maternal influence during infancy.* New York: International University Press, 1956.

Coles, R., & Piers, M. *Wages of neglect—New solutions for the children of the poor.* Chicago: Quadrangle Books, 1969.

Ekstein, R., & Motto, R. L. *From learning for love to love of learning.* New York: Brunner/Mazel, 1969.

Erikson, E. H. *Childhood and society.* New York: W. W. Norton, 1950.

Erikson, E. H. *Insight and responsibility—Lectures on the ethical implications of psychoanalytic insight.* New York: W. W. Norton, 1964.

Erikson, E. M. *Identity—Youth and Crisis.* (1st ed.) New York: W. W. Norton, 1968.

Freud, A. *The ego and the mechanisms of defense.* Vienna: Internationaler Psychoanalytischer Verlag, 1936. (Published in English: New York: International Universities Press, 1946, Pp. 136–137.)

Freud, A. Normality and pathology in childhood: Assessments in development. *The Writings of Anna Freud,* Volume 6. New York: International Universities Press, 1965.

Freud, S. From the history of an infantile neurosis. *Sammlung kleiner Schriften zur Neurosenlehr,* 1918, 4, 578–717. (Published in English: *The Standard Edition.* London: Hogarth, 1955, 17, 13–122.)

Freud, S. Lines of advance in psychoanalytic therapy. *Internationale Zeitschrift für arztliche Psychoanalyse,* 1919 [1918], 5, 61–68. (Published in English: *The Standard Edition.* London: Hogarth, 1955, 17, 159–168.)

Freud, S. *New introductory lectures on psychoanalysis.* Vienna: Internationaler Psychoanalytischer Verlag, 1933 [1932]. (Published in English: *The Standard Edition.* London: Hogarth, 1964, 22, 5–182.)

Freud, S. *The origins of psychoanalysis—Lectures to Wilhelm Fliess, drafts and notes: 1887 to 1902.* New York: Basic Books, 1954.

Hacker, F. *Sublimation revised.* Unpublished paper, 1971.

Hartmann, H. *Ego psychology and the problem of adaptation.* Translated by David Rapaport. New York: International Universities Press, 1958.

Hartmann, H. *Psychoanalysis and moral values.* New York: International Universities Press, 1960.

Hartmann, H., & Kris, E. The genetic approach in psychoanalysis. *The Psychoanalytic Study of the Child,* 1945, 1, 11–30.

Krebs, D. L. Altruism—An examination of the concept and a review of the literature. *Psychological Bulletin,* 1970, 73, 258–302.

Lewinsky, H. Pathological generosity. *The International Journal of Psychoanalysis,* 1951, 32, 185–189.

Mahler, Margaret S. *On human symbiosis and the vicissitudes of individuation.* In collaboration with Manuel Furer. New York: International Universities Press, 1968.

Olden, C. Notes on the development of empathy. *The Psychoanalytic Study of the Child,* 1958, 13, 505–518.

Rosenzweig, S. The experimental study of psychoanalytic concepts. *Character and Personality,* 1937, 6, 61–71.

Schwing, Gertrude. *A way to the soul of the mentally ill.* New York: International Universities Press, 1954. (Translated by R. Ekstein & B. Hall, 1940.)

Sears, R. R. *Survey of object studies of psychoanalytic concepts.* (A report prepared for the Committee on Social Adjustment.) New York: Social Science Research Council (Bulletin 51), 1943.

Sperling, O. E. A psychoanalytic study of social-mindedness. *The Psychoanalytic Quarterly*, 1955, 24, 256–269.

Spitz, R. A. *No and yes on the genesis of human communication.* New York: International Universities Press, 1957.

Spitz, R. A. *The first year of life: A psychoanalytic study of normal and deviant development of object relations.* New York: International Universities Press, 1965.

Waelder, R. *Progress and revolution.* New York: International Universities Press, 1967.

Winnicott, D. W. *Mother and child: A primer of first relationships.* New York: Basic Books, 1957.

Wispé, L. G. Sympathy and empathy. In *International Encyclopedia of the Social Sciences.* The MacMillian Company and The Free Press, 1968, vol. 15, 441–447.

9

Promotive Tension and Prosocial Behavior: A Lewinian Analysis[1]

HARVEY A. HORNSTEIN

Kurt Lewin joined the University of Berlin's faculty in 1921 as a *Privatdozent*. In this capacity he was permitted to lecture but received no fixed salary. *Privatdozents* received a portion of student fees, and their income depended on the popularity of their lectures. Alfred Marrow (1969), Lewin's biographer and friend, tells us that he fared reasonably well in this environment despite his shortcomings as an orator. He was intellectually stimulating, and his enthusiasm fired student imagination.

In time, Lewin became the intellectual mentor of a small group of

[1] Preparation of this chapter and the conduct of a considerable portion of the research with which it is concerned were partially supported by National Science Foundation Grants GS-2773 and BNS76-07697. I am indebted to my wife, Madeline Heilman, and to my colleagues and friends, the students and faculty who populate the Social Psychology Laboratories at Teachers' College, Columbia University. Their work and guidance have been essential ingredients in the development and progress of the program of research reported in this chapter.

students. They met regularly at the Schwedishe Cafe, which is located near the university and where they sat hour after hour, drinking coffee and discussing psychology. It was here that Lewin entertainingly demonstrated the workings of a psychological principle that is central to the theoretical framework presented in this chapter.

I must assume that it was an ordinary day. People ordered their coffee and cakes and discussed psychology. After a while, someone requested the bill. Without keeping a written record and despite the time that had passed and the variety and number of items ordered, the waiter provided a precise reckoning. This might have been attributed to the individual skill of a competent waiter, but Lewin saw more in the event. Thirty minutes later he called the waiter back and asked him to recount the tally he had made earlier. It was impossible, the waiter claimed; they had already paid the bill. He could not be expected to remember.

Lewin's demonstration lacked scientific precision, but it was a clever illustration of the way in which a construct that he called "tension" operates in everyday life. While the waiter's goal of having the bill paid was uncompleted, goal related tension remained aroused. It caused him to think about relevant issues: the items that were being ordered. And it would have caused him to actively seek payment at an appropriate moment. Once the bill was paid, however, goal attainment was complete, and the tension was dissipated. The items could no longer be recalled.

These ideas, captured so casually by Lewin's ingenious illustration, were also at the core of a serious and scholarly controversy that he was having with a psychologist named Ach (1910) about the conditions mediating recall of paired nonsense syllables. The controversy had profound consequences (Deutsch, 1969). For, in the course of it, Lewin (1917, 1922a, 1922b) began to articulate the concept of a tension system; this concept was to play a central role in the development of field theory. In its most basic form, the concept is related to a common assumption of other dynamic theories in psychology that holds that organisms strive to maintain equilibruim. Need-related tensions disrupt equilibrium, and attainment of appropriate goals restores it.

Lewin's formulation abides by these basic assumptions. Within individuals, he reasons, tension corresponds to the existence of a psychological need or intention (sometimes called a quasi-need). Tension, says Deutsch (1969), has two properties. It is a state of a region or system that tries to change itself to become equal to the state of surrounding regions, and it involves forces at the boundary of the region. If in the psychological environment goal regions exist that are relevant to the tension, psychological forces may lead to actual locomotion as well as to thinking about goal-oriented activity.

Within Lewin's formulation (1935, 1938), psychological forces are a dynamic property of the psychological environment. They are coordinated with tensions that are a dynamic property of the innerpersonal system. Three categories of tension are identified as being the potential correspondents of psychological forces (Lewin, 1951): (*a*) tensions arising from own needs, such as the desire to attend a movie or have sexual intercourse; (*b*) those arising from induced needs, such as might occur when mothers inflict upon their children the necessity of wearing earmuffs; and (*c*) tensions arising from the need to satisfy impersonal demands that are matter-of-fact and situational, such as legal codes.

Direction, strength, and point of application are the common properties of psychological forces (Lewin, 1938). Direction refers to the attraction to positively valenced regions and the repulsion from negatively valenced ones. A force's strength is determined by the region's valence and also by the psychological distance between a person and the region. About point of application, Lewin (1951) wrote:

> Forces may act on any part of the life space. Frequently, the point of application is that region of the life space which corresponds to the own person. The child may, however, experience that the "doll wants to go to bed," or that "another child wants a certain toy." In these cases the points of application of the forces are regions in the life space of a child other than his own person. Such cases are common and play an important part, for example, in the problems of altruism [p. 260].

This quotation temptingly suggests a fourth category of tension to which psychological forces can correspond. This tension does not arise from one's needs, others' wishes for oneself, or impersonal demands but rather from empathically recognizing another's needs, someone else's desire to locomote toward or away from a goal.

Promotive tension is the label given (Hornstein, 1972, 1976) to this fourth category, which is defined as tension coordinated to *another's* needs or goals. As Lewin said, there are times when people reduce this form of tension by engaging in altruism and other less dramatic but more common forms of prosocial behavior.

This chapter's next section is concerned with the dynamic properties of promotive tension. The central questions in this section are: "Do people experience tension coordinated to *another's* goals?" and "Are there circumstances when one is aroused by *another's* needs almost as if they were one's own?" I believe that these experiences do occur, and, in order to support this claim, I report research evidence that demonstrates that behavioral and psychological indicators of promotive tension display patterns that precisely parallel those observed in classical research on the dynamic properties of tension systems that are aroused by one's own needs (Deutsch, 1949a,b; Horwitz, 1953; Lewin, 1935, 1936, 1938, 1951; Lewis, 1944; Lewis & Franklin, 1944; Ovsiankina, 1928; Zeigarnik, 1927).

Of course, promotive tension does not arise on all the occasions when one is in the presence of another who has unfulfilled needs or goals. Everyday experience and newspaper headlines clearly show that there are times when one simply does not give a damn. Apathy, not altruism, is the result. In the second and third sections of this chapter, I explore some social conditions that determine whether an individual develops tension systems coordinated to another's goals. In the first of these, I discuss how specific information about another's beliefs and attitudes affects the formation of relationships that provide a basis for promotive tension arousal. Xenophobia and prejudice, both of which reflect constraints in the ability to form these relationships, are also discussed in this section. And in the third and final section, I report research that illustrates how nonparticularistic information about the community at large affects one's sense of relatedness to others and one's readiness to engage in prosocial behavior vis-à-vis total strangers.

PROMOTIVE TENSION

Lewin's conceptions about the dynamics of tension systems have been heuristic. Among the many experiments they stimulated are a series concerned with the recall and resumption of interrupted activities (Lewis, 1944; Lewis & Franklin, 1944; Ovsiankina, 1928; Zeigarnik, 1927). Their findings suggest that: (a) the tendency to recall interrupted tasks is greater than the tendency to recall completed ones; (b) the tendency to resume interrupted tasks is greater than the tendency to resume completed ones; and (c) the tendency to recall interrupted tasks is greater when the task is interrupted near its end. These findings are consistent with Lewin's notion that the strength of a psychological force increases as the psychological distance between a person and a valenced region decreases and, depending on direction, can be graphically presented as an approach or an avoidance gradient. Also (d), the tendency to recall interrupted tasks is less than when the tasks are completed by a cooperating partner but is not affected if they are completed by a noncooperatively linked other.

These last findings (Lewis, 1944; Lewis & Franklin, 1944) are especially relevant to the issue under discussion. They suggest that tensions arising from own needs are reduced if someone else enters an appropriate goal region. Not *everyone* else can reduce these tensions, just those who are related in special ways. In these instances, the relationship was between cooperating partners. Deutsch (1949a,b) obtained additional evidence about the effects of cooperative relationships that corroborates these earlier findings.

In a sense, the major concern of this chapter is the reverse of the one explored by Lewis, Franklin, and Deutsch. They illustrated that tension arising from one's own incomplete goal attainment can be reduced by another's successful goal attainment. The concern in this chapter is with proving that individual tension arousal and subsequent goal-directed activity (e.g., prosocial behavior) are coordinated with *another's* incomplete goal attainment. A closer approximation of this concern is to be found in Horwitz (1953). Examining the findings of previous research, he observed that they leave a critical question unanswered: Given a group goal, does an individual develop tension systems coordinated to the group's reaching its goal?

In Horwitz's experiment, teams of five female volunteers were told that they were competing with other teams in a test of group cooperativeness, using jigsaw puzzles that the group selected. A Zeigarnik-type test for recall demonstrated that more interrupted than completed tasks were recalled, supporting the earlier work of Zeigarnik. More importantly, however, the motivational effect of goals agreed upon by the group was demonstrated, in that interrupted tasks were relatively less likely to be recalled if subjects believed that their group preferred to abandon rather than to complete the task. These data were interpreted as supporting the notion that tension systems that will be "coordinated to" group agreed-upon goals, can be aroused in individual group members.

Strictly speaking, Horwitz's experiment is not an investigation of whether an individual's tensions can be coordinated to another's goal attainment, nor was it intended to be. Subjects in his experiment were members of cooperating groups and fully participated in the selection of group goals. Consequently, his conclusion that tension systems coordinated to *group goals* can be aroused is appropriately qualified.

A related study aimed at investigating the dynamic properties of promotive tension was conducted by Marton, Sole, and Hornstein (in preparation). In one sense, this study is a reversal of Lewis's (1944) and Lewis and Franklin's (1944) studies. In these earlier studies a subject worked to complete a series of Zeigarnik type tasks. Sometimes they were interrupted by the experimenter and obliged to leave a task uncompleted. When these uncompleted tasks were completed by a co-worker, subjects exhibited no tendency to recall uncompleted tasks with a greater frequency than they recalled completed ones. When the tasks were completed by someone who was not classified as a co-worker, there was no substitutability (Deutsch, 1949a,b), and the Zeigarnik effect remained evident inasmuch as subjects were more likely to recall uncompleted than completed tasks. Lewis (1944) says that "tension systems aroused by the tasks could be and were . . . resolved by the activity of another person, the cooperative worker [p. 119]."

In essence, Lewis' work concerned the effects of social relationships on the *dissipation* of tension that was initially aroused by one's *own* goal related activity. Marton's, Sole's, and Hornstein's study concerned the effects of social relationships on the *arousal* of tension coordinated to *another's* goal related activity. The common dependent variable in these studies is recall. In Lewis's work, subjects attempted to recall tasks that they themselves completed or left uncompleted. In Marton's, Sole's and Hornstein's research, the tasks were ones being worked on by *another* person. Specifically, subjects in this study watched another person's hands on a video screen as the other tried to complete a different puzzle in each of 12 20-second work periods. The puzzles contained pictures of familiar objects, and subjects were made aware of what they would be, if completed (e.g., a teapot, scissors, a table, and fish). By varying the interdependence of payoffs for each completed puzzle, the subject and the bogus other were interrelated in one of three possible ways: cooperatively (subject and other earned 50¢ for each completed puzzle); competitively (subject lost 50¢ for each one completed by the other and earned 50¢ for each one left uncompleted); and individualistically (subject and other were financially unaffected by each other's successes or failures).

Cooperative social conditions, as compared to competitive or individualistic ones, were expected to provide a basis for the arousal of promotive tension, that is, tension coordinated to another's goal related activity. Therefore, in this condition, as compared to the two others, another's uncompleted tasks would be recalled with greater frequency than would their completed ones. The *"Zeigarnik effect"* is the label ordinarily applied to instances in which recall of uncompleted tasks exceeds recall of completed ones. To be accurate, we might say that Lewis was examining Zeigarnik effects, whereas Marton *et al.* were examining socially mediated Zeigarnik effects.

The findings confirm the hypothesis, but, before examining these data, another aspect of this study that helps to pinpoint promotive tensions as the explanatory principle must be presented.

One-half of the subjects believed that the other would be allowed to resume work on the uncompleted puzzles sometime after the 12 20-

second work periods were concluded. The opportunity to resume work on uncompleted puzzles was expected to be tension-arousing for competitively linked subjects, because more completions meant less money (i.e., they would be carried into a negatively valanced goal region), but tension abating for cooperatively linked subjects, because, by comparison to those conditions in which no resumption could occur, the tasks were not psychologically uncompleted. Thus, insofar as the comparative recall of uncompleted to completed tasks was concerned, an interaction effect was predicted: In competitive conditions, an opportunity for resumption was expected to produce Zeigarnik effects with greater frequency than in a condition in which no opportunity for resumption occurs, whereas in cooperative conditions the opposite was expected to occur. The data confirm this prediction. In the cooperative condition, if there were no expectations for resumption 68% of the subjects recalled the tasks, as opposed to 28% of the subjects if they expected the other to resume work. By contrast, in the competitive condition the respective results were 28% with nonresumption and 48% with resumption.

By discounting an important alternative explanation, data from an additional control condition further support the idea that promotive tension is mediating these effects. One might argue that these data reflect differential attention of subjects to another's work. Therefore information, not recall, is producing the pattern. Following Lewin, Zeigarnik, and Lewis, an additional group of subjects in the cooperative nonresume condition were told that the study's principal objective was to measure their ability to recall the puzzles. (Of course, they learned this after observing the simulated video material.) Although the predisposition to recall uncompleted tasks had been greatest in the cooperative-nonresumption condition (68% showed a Zeigarnik effect), with this ego-involving goal set before them, only 32% of the subjects showed this predisposition. Overall, they tended to recall more items, and they recalled uncompleted and completed ones in equal numbers. Attention and learning are not the answers. The pattern of recall reflects the motivational consequences of tension arousal coordinated to another's goal related activity.

Admittedly, these findings, like Horwitz's, must be appropriately qualified, because subjects in this study were certainly not impartial about another's goal attainment. It affected their well-being directly. Thus, neither Horwitz's experiment nor this one indicate that promotive tension is aroused when one has no stake whatsoever in another's goal attainment. The limiting conditions of these two studies were removed in a series of experiments by Hornstein (Hodgson, Hornstein, & Siegel,

1972; Hornstein, Masor, Sole, & Heilman, 1971) that had the double aim of further investigating dynamic properties of promotive tension and of exploring its relationship to prosocial behavior.

In these experiments, subjects held no membership in a group in which member goals were economically interdependent, nor did they participate in group-setting. The subjects in the first of these experiments (Hornstein et al., 1971) were 175 pedestrians in Brooklyn, New York. Each of these people found two open envelopes belonging to some stranger. One envelope contained the stranger's pro- or anti-Israeli response to a "Harcourt Public Opinion Service" questionnaire that contained a single question about the Mideast crisis. As pilot work demonstrated, this manipulation easily induced a subject to have positive or negative sentiment toward the stranger. Pedestrians in the heavily Jewish section of Brooklyn where this work was conducted almost uniformly liked strangers who hold pro-Israeli views and disliked them when their views were anti-Israeli. A second envelope contained a contribution to the "Institute for Research in Medicine." A sender was either close to or far from completing his goal of 10 contributions.

In contrast to the social relationships created in earlier experiments (e.g., Horwitz, 1953; Lewis, 1944; Lewis & Franklin, 1944; Marton et al., in preparation), positive or negative sentiment—created by manipulating the similarity of a stranger's opinion about an important topic—was the only social link between a subject and the stranger whose goal attainment had been interrupted. It was assumed that positive but not negative sentiment would be sufficient to provide a basis for promotive tension arousal. On the basis of this assumption and Lewin's notion regarding the strength of psychological forces, it was hypothesized that the interrupted goal attainment of liked others would be completed (i.e., the contribution for the institute would be mailed) more often when they were close to completing their goal of 10 contributions; for disliked others, nearness to goal was expected to be irrelevant. In essence, if promotive tension is mediating subjects' behavior in the like conditions, then evidence of an approach gradient should be observed.

Implicit in this prediction is an assumption that the goal region is postively valenced for both a subject and the stranger. As subsequent research demonstrated, contributions to medical research satisfied this condition. Of course, Lewin's notions also provide a framework predicting the effects of negatively valenced goal regions, an aim of a second experiment that is reviewed later. But the results of the first experiment confirmed our expectation of an approach gradient. In the "like" condition, 87% of the subjects who found the materials in which the sender was close to completing his contributions mailed it, whereas only 53% of those whose materials showed that the sender was still a long way from completing his 10 contributions did so. In contrast, in the "dislike" condition, the respective results were 45% later (close to completing goal) and 54% earlier (far from completing goal).

The late-like and late-no-information conditions were significantly different from the early-like and early-no-information conditions, confirming the prediction that for liked others the frequency of this kind of help is greater when they are close to completing their goal. (Prior to the experiment, pilot work demonstrated that subjects evaluated the other in the no-information and like conditions with equal favor.) An additional prediction, that for disliked others nearness to goal is irrelevant, was also confirmed: There were no statistically significant differences between the early and late dislike conditions.

In addition to forwarding the contribution, subjects in the like and dislike conditions also had an opportunity to complete the interrupted mailing of the Harcourt Public Opinion Service questionnaire. No specific predictions were made with regard to the return of these questionnaires, although it is not unresonable to expect positively cathected questionnaire responses to be forwarded more often than negatively cathected ones. In fact, this was what occurred ($p < .05$), with 80% of the finders in the close to goal condition returning the questionnaires, as opposed to only 57% in the distant from goal condition. It should be noted that, in the like conditions, of the subjects who forwarded the contribution all but one also mailed the questionnaire. In the dislike conditions, however, 11 fewer subjects forwarded the questionnaire.

The relatively high return rates in the late-no-information (86%) and late-like (87%) conditions are interpreted as confirming the expectation that positive sentiment toward a stranger provided a basis for tension arousal coordinated to his goal attainment. Negative sentiment did not establish a relationship to provide a basis for the arousal of such tension. (Note that this is not equivalent to saying that negative sentiment toward a stranger stimulates an aversive response, i.e., a desire to harm.) Using the returns as evidence for the magnitude of arousal, there is evidence of an approach gradient: For liked others, arousal was greater when goal-directed activity was interrupted at a point relatively close to completion.

The framework being used for interpreting these findings encourages speculation about other conditions that affect the magnitude of promotive tension arousal. Following Lewin's notions, it is reasonable to expect that any condition that alters the valence of a goal region will affect the strength of psychological forces coordinated to tension resulting from interrupted attainment of that region. In a second experiment, two such conditions were: (a) the other's attraction to the goal region as perceived by the subject—defined by the strength of the other's self-reported desire for goal attainment; and (b) the subject's cathexis of the goal region—defined in terms of his sentiment for the object it represents, for example, the Institute for Research in Medicine (Hodgson, Hornstein, & Siegel, 1972). In this experiment 475 subjects participated in a procedure similar to the earlier one, with the exception that, for one-half of the subjects, a stranger was contributing to the International Tuberculosis Foundation, whereas for the other half he was contributing to the International Nudist Foundation. Elaborate pretesting established that the Tuberculosis Foundation was viewed far more positively ($p < .001$) than the Nudist Foundation. Although the latter may appear comical, as a stimulus it satisfied several major criteria; in addition to holding a somewhat homogeneously negative opinion about such institutes, the population did not identify it with any redeeming social qualities, nor did they feel personally threatened by completed contributions—as might be true if the stimulus object were some terrorist group.

Attached to each contribution form was a card on which the stranger clearly identified on a 5-point scale the strength of his desire to contribute. Pretesting also confirmed that this manipulation produced the proper image in the subject's mind ($p < .001$). A plausible cover story suggested that the information was needed in order to plan future fundraising campaigns.

Sentiment toward the stranger and his distance from the goal region were manipulated as discussed earlier. Data were analyzed within a factorial design which manipulated positive versus negative goals, strong versus weak desire, positive versus negative sentiment, and close versus distant stage of completion. These data provide support for our theoretical framework. Positive goals produced more returns than negative ones. More importantly, subjects were most likely to complete the interrupted goal attainment of a liked stranger strongly attracted to a positive goal if he was close to completion (70% of the subjects). With negative goals, the opposite was true (37%). When a liked stranger was close to a disapproved goal (30%), helping was less likely than when he was distant (40%). These data replicated the earlier experiment by illustrating the existence of approach gradients. They also demonstrated promotive tension arousal corresponding to avoidance gradients: Subjects were actually more likely to help complete a liked other's attainment of goals that they disapproved of themselves when the other was *distant rather than close to goal completion.*[2]

[2] The analysis of the binomial data obtained in these two experiments and in several that follow involved a method, originally published by Dunn (1961), that permits the simultaneous analysis of predetermined contracts. The joint confidence interval for all the separate analyses reported in this chapter were set at .95.

Although some data in this second experiment were anomalous, they were not inconsistent with the interpretation being offered. Two sets of findings in particular should be noted: the relatively high return rates in the Positive Goal $\times$ Weak Desire $\times$ Positive Sentiment conditions and those in the Positive Goal $\times$ Strong Desire $\times$ Negative Sentiment conditions.

Although there were no overall differences between the weak and strong desire conditions, evidence for both approach and avoidance gradients was confined to conditions in which a liked other's desire to reach a goal was strong. Perhaps different mediating psychological processes occurred in the weak conditions. After all, despite the requirements of the experimental design, it may have been incongruous to find that someone was contributing without enthusiasm to an organization. To resolve this incongruity, subjects may have reinterpreted the importance of helping this organization. Thus, with all the perversity of attribution processes, if a liked stranger is not enthusiastic about making a contribution to a positively evaluated organization but is doing so anyway, subjects might reason that help is especially deserved. (For similar explanations of helping, see Hornstein, 1970b and Schopler, 1970).

The relatively high rate of return for disliked others moving toward positively evaluated goals may be explained within the context of the theoretical framework being developed here. Negative sentiment for another in this context does not provide a basis for promotive tension arousal. This is *not* the same as saying that it creates avoidance tensions. Consequently, subjects in this condition simply responded to the goal region's valence and returned contributions. One reason that this high return rate was not evidenced in the previous study is that this organizational stimulus used previously was not viewed as positively as the present one (means of 6.8 for this study and 7.5 for the previous one).

Despite these few anomalies, the data provide a dramatic demonstration of the way in which an individual's tension can be coordinated to the interrupted goal attainment of another. In this case, positive sentiment provided a basis for the arousal of promotive tension, and other factors, like a goal region's valence and the distance to it, determined the strength and direction of psychological forces operating on subjects.

These findings are consistent with the earlier work of Lewis (1944), Lewis and Franklin (1944), Deutsch (1949a,b), and Horwitz (1953). The properties of promotive tension seem entirely consistent with dynamic concepts in field theory advanced by these investigators as well as by Lewin. In contrast to their earlier work, however, the paradigmatic situation for this research represents a major reversal of perspective. Earlier investigators were concerned with identifying the social conditions under which one person's goal attainment reduced a second person's goal-related tensions. My research has been concerned with examining social relationships that cause one person's tensions to be aroused by another's interrupted goal attainment. It is obvious from these investigations that only some social relationships provide a basis for the arousal of such tensions. The common elements of these "promotive" social relationships will be discussed in the next section.

PROMOTIVE SOCIAL RELATIONSHIPS

The experiments by Horwitz (1953), Hodgson et al. (1972), Hornstein et al. (1971), and Marton et al. (in preparation) can be examined from a perspective other than the one that I have been using. Up to this point, findings of these studies have been used to illustrate that the indicators of promotive tension (i.e., recall and helping) display patterns that are akin to those observed in classical research on the dynamic properties of tension arising from one's own uncompleted goal attainment. In these same experiments, however, there are repeated indications that not all social conditions heighten tension for individuals who witness the interrupted strivings of their fellows.

Related to these findings is a series of studies on empathy that demonstrate that perceived similarity between self and others heightens one's arousal when witnessing another's plight, whereas perceived dissimilarity dampens it. Using physiological indicators such as palmar sweating and vasoconstriction, Stotland (1969), for example, has shown that first-born children in particular were more aroused when witnessing another's distress if they believed that they and the other were similar rather than dissimilar. Krebs (1970) has demonstrated the same effect. He found that people who believed that they and a victim were similar were most aroused and, subsequently, were also more likely to act altruistically. A line of inquiry is suggested; we might ask under what social circumstances one person's tension will be aroused by another's interrupted goal attainment.

Lewin once commented (1951) that "Friendship as distinguished from enmity includes the readiness to accept and to back up the intention of the other person [p. 295]." The insight is germane to this inquiry, but imprecise. Amity and enmity have many causes. Time and social circumstance determine who is identified as "friend" and who is not. Nonetheless, Lewin's insight is revealing and easily identified in everyday experience. On some occasions human beings experience a sense of community, a feeling of oneness with their fellows. As the famed sociologist Charles

Horton Cooley (1909) once wrote: "Perhaps the simplest way of describing this wholeness is by saying it is a 'we'. . . . It involves the sort of sympathy and mutual identification for which 'we' is the natural expression."

In some circumstances human beings experience others as "we," not as "they." When this happens, bonds exist that permit one person's plight to become a source of tension for his or her fellows. Seeking relief, they reduce this tension by aiding a fellow we-grouper. In forming we-groups, men and women are joined with other fellows, and some distinctions between self and other are transcended. When an other with whom one is in union needs aid, then self-interest is served and tension is reduced when one acts on the other's behalf. Through a formation of "we" self-interest is fused together with a concern for others, and the basis of promotive tension and selfless behavior is born.

Three different social conditions seem as if they might provide a basis for the formation of promotive social relationships: those in which social structure creates *promotive interdependence* among individual goals (e.g., subjects in experiments by Lewis, 1944, Deutsch, 1959, and Horwitz, 1953), relationships in which individuals are linked only by *opinion similarity and interpersonal attraction* (e.g., subjects in Hornstein, 1970a), and relationships in which individuals share *common membership in a social category*. The second and third categories are marked by an apparent absence of promotive interdependence among individual goals.

In the following review of literature I intend to make it evident that a more parsimonious, general statement may be substituted for this listing: Promotive social relationships are characterized by an absence of negative sentiment and an understanding that others in the relationship hold dispositions that are concordant with one's own beliefs, values, and self-interests (Hornstein, 1976).

Promotive Interdependence

In the experiments by Lewis, Deutsch, and Horwitz, the feeling of belonging together was elicited by manipulating the structure of work rules and/or goals. These experimental manipulations are consistent with Lewin's (1948) and Deutsch's (1969) definitions of group. In all three experiments interdependence was established by objectively interlocking a subject's fate with the behavior of others. Subjects all had "cooperatively linked partners" whose behavior could determine their success or failure in goal attainment. In this context, a partner's goal attainment had the effect of reducing a subject's goal related tension.

Following these early leads, Marton *et al.* (in preparation) clearly established that this means of establishing interdependence provides a basis for promotive tension arousal, but additional findings illustrate that such arousal is not limited to social relationships in which individual goals are promotively interdependent.

Opinion Similarity and Interpersonal Attraction

In Hornstein's experiments (Hornstein *et al.*, 1971) and in Hodgson *et al.* (1972), opinion similarity on an important topic and consequent interpersonal attraction were interpreted as being sufficient to provide a basis for promotive tension. By a stretch of imagination, however, one might argue that similarity of opinions can give rise to the assumption of promotive interdependence—which, in turn, is what provides a basis for promotive tension. Through a process of inference, for example, people who perceive themselves to be similar along some attitudinal dimensions may infer that their fates are promotively interdependent along other relevant dimensions. In fact, although Lewin was not directly concerned with promotive tension, it is clear that in considering a related issue, that is, the preconditions for establishing a social group, he was making this very argument, as the following quotation shows:

> One should realize that even a definition of group membership by equality of goal or equality of an enemy is still a definition by similarity. The same holds for the definition of a group by the feeling of loyalty or of belongingness of their members. However, such an equality, as well as equality of goal or of enemy, constitutes sometimes, also, a certain interdependence of the persons who show these similarities. Therefore, if one wishes to use the feeling of belonging as the criterion of a group, one can do so if one points to the interdependence established by this feeling. However, one should realize that loyalty for feeling of belongingness is only one variety of possible types of interdependence which may constitute a group (others are economic dependence, love, living together in a certain area). The kind of interdependence of the members (what holds the group together) is equally as important a characteristic of a group as the degree of their interdependence and the group structure [1951, p. 147].

Following similar lines of reasoning, Deutsch and Stembridge (1971) have completed an experiment investigating some aspects of the relationship between similarity and interdependence. Their data demonstrate that when similarity of preference was a cue for competitive rather than for promotive interdependence, subjects worked to one another's disadvantage. When similarity of preference signaled promotive rather than competitive interdependence, however, subjects worked for one another's benefit. Accepting the observation that opinion similarity is more often associated with promotive than with competitive interdependence, these findings add some weight to the argument that Hornstein's manipulation of opinion similarity and interpersonal attraction was mediated by inference of promotive interdependence. Evidence of pro-Israeli attitudes may have easily led subjects to conclude that the other subscribed to associated and corresponding goals that directly affected a subject's self-interests. The research by Deutsch and Stembridge raises this possibility, but provides no conclusive answers. It does not identify the conditions under which opinion similarity and interpersonal attraction lead to inferences of promotive interdependence. Nor does it specify which of these two variables is operating to produce this effect. My previous research was also inadequate in this respect. Whether opinion similarity or interpersonal attraction or both might have been operating in the experiments that he and his colleagues conducted is an open question. Indeed, the question may be meaningless, for Byrne (1969) has found that attraction to a stranger ordinarily bears a linear relationship to the proportion of similar attitudes attributed to him. One implication is that similarity and attraction together are a sufficient condition for the arousal of promotive tension.

Common Social Category Membership

Work done by Tajfel (1970; Tajfel et al., 1971) and Dion (1973) suggests that social categorization based on similarity may be a sufficient condition for the formation of promotive social relationships. Moreover, Tajfel's data, together with other findings by Billig (1972) and Deutsch et al. (1971), can be interpreted as suggesting that discriminatory social behavior, favoring people in categories similar to one's own, is practiced in the absence of competitive incentives and without any associated differences in attraction for similar or dissimilar others. From these findings it can be argued that people will frequently use available criteria to organize their world into "we" and "they," into in-groups and out-groups. Such dichotomies then give rise to behavior that facilitates or hinders another's goal attainment. Additional research by Deutsch and his students (Deutsch et al., 1971) and by Chase (1971) using essentially the same format as Tajfel suggests that social discrimination does not occur unless the experimental world of the subject is *clearly* and *unambiguously* dichotomized into "we" and "they."

In Hornstein's previous research we can safely assume that the subject's experimental world was sharply dichotomized. In his experiments, a stranger was *clearly* placed on one side of the Arab-Israeli conflict.

Such an experimental manipulation may reasonably be interpreted as producing a "we–they" distinction for many of the Jewish citizens of Brooklyn, New York, but certain important questions are left unanswered. When individuals are confronted with *several* opinions expressed by a stranger, will their tendency to help the stranger increase with increases in the proportion of similarity of opinion? Will helping relationships be established where the boundaries are unclear (see Deutsch *et al.*, 1971, for example), where the stranger belongs to the individual's "we-group" along some dimensions but must be excluded when considered along other dimensions? What is the effect of different levels of importance of the opinions expressed?

In an attempt to investigate these issues, three studies were conducted employing experimental contexts that were essentially the same as those used in Hornstein's previous research (Sole, Marton, & Hornstein, 1975). A subject, an unsuspecting pedestrian, "chanced" to find a packet containing two envelopes that, it appeared, were lost by another person who had intended to mail them. As before, one envelope contained its owner's anonymous $2.00 contribution to a charity, and the other contained a sheet revealing the owner's opinions. In the experiments reported here, the owner had expressed opinions on *four issues*. In the *first* experiment, the four issues were of uniformly *high importance* for subjects. In the *second* experiment they were of uniformly *low importance*. The *third* experiment provided the subject with issues of *mixed importance;* that is, two of high importance and two of low importance. Since four opinions were used, five levels of the proportion of similarity of opinion could be created in each of the experiments: 0%, 25%, 50%, 75%, and 100%.

The opinions expressed by the stranger in the first experiment were of uniformly high importance. In this experiment, a single dissenting opinion was sufficient to cause significantly lower rates of helping. In fact, one dissimilar opinion was as detrimental to the rate of helping as was *total* dissimilarity of opinion. The dramatic stepwise pattern of these data support the supposition that subjects divided their world and then granted help only to those strangers who were included in what can be described as their "we-group." Partial or complete dissimilarity of opinion prevented this inclusion. These findings are in accord with a theoretical position expressed earlier in this chapter. *Unclear boundaries, where others may belong to the subject's "we-group" along some dimensions and to one or more "they-groups" along others, are not likely to provide a basis for promotive tension.*

It is by comparison with the attraction data that the pattern of helping becomes most interesting. The helping data's clear stepwise pattern is in marked contrast to the attraction data's smooth monotonic increase. Just as Byrne (1971) has argued, there was no single point of disruption in attraction for a stranger as the proportion of dissimilarity of opinion increased. There was, instead, a gradual diminution in attraction to the stranger as he expressed a greater proportion of opinions opposed to those held by the subject. By themselves, these data cannot be used to discount the mediating role that attraction might be playing. It is entirely possible that a threshold of attraction is required for helping to occur with any frequency. Although plausible, the inference necessary to make this explanation seems excessive and is, in fact, contraindicated by data from the second experiment.

In marked contrast to Byrne's findings, increased agreement about trivial matters did not lead to increased liking for a stranger, but it did lead to increase in helping. Previous research by Banikiotes, Russell, and Linden (1972) is confirmed by these findings. In field settings, the importance of the issues upon which interpersonal judgments are based seems to be a major factor in determining the relationship between similarity and attraction.

It is clear then that when knowledge about another includes only opinions of lower importance, similarity, not attraction, is the better predictor of helping.

In the third experiment, subjects were presented with opinions of two levels of importance. Based on the findings of the experiment with issues of low importance, it seems reasonable to expect that trivial information will become truly irrelevant when viewed in a context of items of greater importance. More specifically, the likelihood of helping was hypothesized to be greatest in conditions of total, or unambiguous, similarity of opinion of those items that were of high importance. The results support this conclusion. With 100% similarity of opinion on items of high importance, there was a significantly greater rate of helping ($p < .05$) than for all other conditions (57%). There was no statistically significant differences among the conditions in which there was less than 100% similarity on the issues of high importance ($p < .05$). Therefore, 50% opinion similarity based on issues of high importance is not better than total disagreement, and opinion similarity based on issues of low importance is of no benefit whatsoever.

As in the first experiment, the high importance items caused subjects to sharply dichotomize their worlds. The tendency of subjects to withhold help from those who disagreed with them on the items of high importance suggests that subjects acted as if they were placing these others "outside" some imaginary boundary that momentarily separated their "we-group" from their "they-group." This critical decision was barely influenced by the trivial information with which the subjects were also provided. Their tendency to help was governed primarily by their perceptions of similarity or dissimilarity of opinion on items of high importance. In combination, these three experiments suggest the following:

1. Agreement about trivial issues seems to be critical only when that is all there is to agree about (as in Experiment II or Tajfel's laboratory procedure). Even then the effect is comparatively slight. In everyday affairs, people are not likely to act on the behalf of another when their only bonds are rooted in a shared belief about inconsequential matters.

2. Attraction may be a common correlate of opinion similarity (Byrne, 1971), but it is not a necessary condition for the formation of promotive social relationships. The bonds of "we" that provide an essential basis for the arousal of promotive tension exist when human beings recognize others as holding beliefs and values that are concordant with their own beliefs, values, and self-interests.

Further evidence in support of these claims is presented in this chapter's concluding section. Before examining that material, however, let us consider the social malady known as *xenophobia*, which emanates from the human ability to distinguish between *we* and *they*.

Xenophobia

Human beings are possibly the only creatures on earth capable of examining their social universe and, by using abstract cues like race, religion, and political sentiment, of deciding that others are "we" or "they." Intellectual ability combines with irrational prejudices and stereotypes born of individual experience and social influence in order to give these cues meaning. Most people escape the extreme pathological consequences that the labels "xenophobia" and "xenophilia" imply, but few grow up free of a tendency to evaluatively judge those who are identified as "we" or "they." It is an unintended by-product of socialization. In the course of social development, the self incorporates attributes to which it is exposed. Surrounding social entities are sources of influence simply because they are there. The habits, patterns, and beliefs of our communities become part of us. "We" and "they" become important social categories because they are symbolically related to self-identity and our earliest and most profound emotional ties. In essence, this process lies at the core of the most ordinary tendency toward xenophobia, which involves a disposition to sharply distinguish between "we" and "they," between in-groups and out-groups.

Classification of others as "we" is withheld when information about the other unambiguously indicates, either directly or through implication, that no social category memberships are shared (as was the case for Tajfel's subjects, Deutsch's in the "alone" condition, and Sole's, Marton's, and Hornstein's in the zero similarity conditions) and when information indicates that the other occupies memberships in social categories that violate minimum criteria for a "we" relationship. (This may have been the case for my pro-Israeli subjects who were confronted with a pro-Arab other, and it certainly appears to have been the case for Sole's, Marton's, and Hornstein's subjects who learned that an other disagreed with their views on a single *important* topic.) When faced with the problem of facilitating the goal attainment of a stranger, either one or both of these conditions may operate to lesson the likelihood of promotive tension arousal.

One small bit of evidence for this argument was obtained in the study by Hornstein, Fisch, and Holmes (1968). One-half of the subjects, midtown Manhattan pedestrians, found a wallet that was ostensibly being returned to its owner by someone who characterized himself as a foreigner. A letter to the wallet's owner stated: "Dear Mr. Erwin, I visit you country and you ways strange and not familiar. But I find you wallet which I here return." (Additional information in the letter, written in the same broken English, is not relevant here.) The remaining subjects found a letter that was exactly similar in terms of information but contained no broken English or self-characterization as a foreigner.

Retrospectively, it can be argued that letters from foreign nationals are more likely to produce inferences of noncommon social category membership and violations of minimum criteria for establishing a "we" relationship than are letters whose authors are not so characterized. The data can be interpreted as supporting this post hoc explanation. Subjects were relatively less likely ($p. < .05$) to facilitate the interrupted goal attainment of foreigners.

Some cross-cultural evidence of this effect is available in a series of studies by Feldman (1972). In each of his investigations the general situation was the same: A native of some city was in a position to aid a stranger who was either a countryman or a foreigner, potentially either a "we" or a "they." In one investigation, unsuspecting natives of Boston, Paris, and Athens were asked for street directions. In another they were asked by a stranger to mail a letter. In a third, they were given a chance to be honest by a passerby who dropped some money. Honesty was also tested in a fourth investigation in which cashiers were overpaid. And a fifth study was concerned with whether or not taxicab drivers take the most direct route to a destination. Feldman summarizes his findings by saying: "In general, when a difference was observed, the Athenians treated a foreigner better than a compatriot, but Parisians and Bostonians treated compatriots better than foreigners [p. 31]." Does this mean that Parisians and Bostonians abide by the propositions that I have been developing but that Athenians do not? On the contrary, the data provide a neat confirmation of these propositions. As Feldman mentions, research by Triandis, Vassiliou, and Nassiakou (1968) explains the seemingly anomalous behavior of Athenians. After examining the in-group, out-group concepts of Greeks, these researchers concluded that the Greek in-group includes family, friends, friends of friends, and *tourists*. Other Greeks are out-group and, therefore, "they."

As the behavior of Greeks demonstrated, who is "we" and who is "they" is not decided on the basis of superficial indicators of similarity. Cues of similarity and dissimilarity take on for people special meaning that is not always apparent to dispassionate observers. Indeed, there are circumstances in which it appears as if "we" has become "they" and "they" has become "we." When aspects of self are disapproved of, even hated, people with similar attributes are condemned to "they" and their plight is of no concern. In a sense, "you" may be "they" because you possess attributes that are similar to those parts of me that I dislike. When this occurs, a xenophilac pattern of prosocial behavior may emerge.

Lewin (1951) describes a similar process in discussing "marginal men," people who stand on the boundary between two groups:

> If the person is partly successful in establishing relationships with the privileged group without being fully accepted, he becomes a marginal man, belonging to both groups but not fully to either of them.... The marginal man shows a typical aversion to the less privileged members of his own groups. This can be noted in the hostile attitude of some subgroups of the Negroes or other races against members of their race [p. 143].

Data relevant to an examination of xenophilac patterns of prosocial behavior can be found in three experiments that are often cited as either investigations in which people tend to help members of the same race or illustrations of white prejudice toward blacks (Gaertner & Bickman, 1971; Pilliavin, Rodin, & Pilliavin, 1969; Wispé & Freshley, 1971). Using their data for these two purposes is justifiable but neglects another important outcome of these experiments. Race was critical only to white subjects in Pilliavin *et al.* who helped someone who had flopped to the floor feigning illness or drunkenness. Blacks, in fact, show a slight tendency toward helping white victims more frequently. The same occurred when Gaertner's and Bickman's bogus victim explained to people over the telephone that he had dialed a wrong number and had no more change and then asked them to call "Ralph's garage" for him. And, when Wispé and Freshley pulled their broken bag caper in front of super-markets, whites provided whites with decidely more enthusiastic help than they provided blacks, but blacks showed no within-race preference. The pattern is clear; blacks tended to show either no preference or a sliight preference for helping whites.

Other data confirm this pattern. Between 1966 and 1968 approximately 1,000 wallets were dropped across the length and breadth of Manhattan Island (Hornstein, 1976). The wallet's owner was identified as a white or a black male in his mid- or late twenties. Observers recorded whether the finder was white or black. Whites showed a slight prference for returning wallets owned by whites. Blacks showed no preference for helping other blacks.

In a study of ethnic relations in Israel, Yochanan Peres (1971) also found evidence of "we becoming they." Oriental Jews share a cultural background with Israeli Arabs; European Jews do not. Yet a question-naire study of Oriental Jews revealed that they, more than the European ones, wanted to maintain social distance between themselves and Arabs. They were less willing to marry them, be friends with them, or live in a neighborhood with them. They were more likely to endorse prejudicial statements. Peres comments that "the Orientals feel that they must reject the remaining traces of their Middle Eastern origin to attain the status of the dominant European group." Importantly, the anti-Arab sentiment was most pronounced among those Oriental Jews whose appearance and accent most resembled those of Arabs.

If "we" can become "they," then the process can also be reversed. In the early 1970s the wallet-dropping investigation was repeated (Horn-stein, 1976). Much had happened since the time of the early investiga-tion that had nearly coincided with those of the other authors. By and large, the civil rights movement turned inward in the hope of establishing a black identity. As before, wallets were placed on the sidewalks of Manhattan. Things had changed. Overall, blacks returned more wallets than before, and there was a slight tendency for them to return wallets to other blacks more frequently than to whites. We can hope that this change is an indication of alteration in self-concept, that for blacks "we" is no longer "they."

Individual Readiness to Form Promotive Relationships

Prejudiced people possess stringent minimum criteria for establishing promotive relationships. These criteria include either nonmembership in specific social categories (e.g., no Jews or blacks) or membership in specific categories (e.g., only Christians or anti-war advocates). By definition, prejudice restricts the range of people with whom one will form promotive relationships.

As the number of minimum criteria increase, the potential for forming promotive relationships decreases: A man or woman who only forms promotive relationships with white Anglo-Saxon Protestants has less such potential than one who can form them with any Protestant. And this second person has less potential than a third who can form such relationships with either whites, Anglo-Saxons, or Protestants. A reasonable conjecture to be drawn from these ideas is that authoritarian personality types, staunch chauvinists in any cause, and dogmatic thinkers are all persons with relatively low potential for experiencing promotive tension. Philanthropes, of course, have relatively high potential. (For discussions of analogous issues, see Berkowitz, 1970, Friedrichs, 1960, and Sorokin, 1954.)

The case against authoritarians is captured in data collected by Mitchell and Byrne (1973). These investigators had subjects judge the guilt or innocence of one William Davidson, who was charged with theft of an examination. Part of the information that they received about Davidson led them to believe that his attitudes on five issues were either concordant or discordant with their own. Subjects' tendencies toward authoritarianism were assessed prior to the study.

Authoritarians discriminated between similar and dissimilar Williams more than their egalitarian counterparts did. When asked "How positively or negatively do you feel about the defendant?" egalitarians liked the similar William and the dissimilar one almost equally. But with authoritarians this was not the case. They liked similar Williams but disliked dissimilar ones. The same pattern emerged when judgments of guilt and punishment were examined. For authoritarians, the boundaries of "we" and "they" were intolerantly and narrowly drawn. Mindful of every difference, they were more prone to judge a dissimilar William as guilty and to punish him severely.

There is also evidence to support the "other side of the coin," so to speak. Helping and altruism have been empirically related to social extroversion, affiliative tendencies (gregariousness), sociability, and attractiveness as a friend (Cattell and Horowitz, 1952; Friedrichs, 1960). After reviewing the available evidence on the relationship between personality traits and altruism, Krebs (1970) concludes that

> altruistic children seem to be better adjusted socially than others—they are less aggressive, quarrelsome, and competitive, and they are more emo-

tionally stable. . . . College-age female altruists are socially oriented—they are cyclothymic and have social (versus political or economic) values. They are nurturant people with low needs for achievement or dominance. College-age male altruists also tend to be socially oriented; they are free from neuroticism, and tend to think that they control their fates [p. 285].

It appears that there is sufficient cause to believe that individuals differ in their readiness to experience themselves as part of a social unit and to form promotive relationships with "all sorts and conditions of men [Allport, p. 411]." In this light, prosocial behavior may be viewed as a by-product of one's readiness to experience a sense of relatedness to other human beings.

A SENSE OF COMMUNITY

In the research discussed earlier in this chapter, promotive relationships were induced either by providing subjects with explicit information about a specific stranger or by altering aspects of the social structure. In modern mass society, however, people are frequently in situations in which they are required to make decisions affecting the lives of nameless, faceless others about whom they have no personal information whatsoever. With only a little introspection, it becomes evident that each of us is capable of acting like an actuary who takes a sampling of the social universe and projects estimates of the extent to which its members subscribe to beliefs and values that are either concordant with or antithetical to our own beliefs and values and self-interests. It seems reasonable to assume that these estimates alter inferences about particular strangers and either foster or suppress the development of a promotive relationship. Further, it may be assumed that for each individual these estimates remain fairly stable until from time to time some especially presuasive bit of information causes shifts toward more favorable or unfavorable social conceptions (e.g., Murray, 1933; Wrightsman & Noble, 1965).

A series of experiments stimulated by this view of humanity as being composed of incorrigible subjective pollsters focused on how knowledge of remote *social* events affects promotive relationships and prosocial behavior. I will report the findings of these experiments. But first I am going to summarize the essential details of the experimental procedure that we have used. It varied slightly from experiment to experiment, but these were variations on a common theme.

Each subject was individually escorted to the door of the experimental room by a female assistant, who first checked a bogus schedule sheet in order to determine their "assigned" room and to create the illusion that more than one room was in use. While music played from a radio located at the front of the room, a second assistant, the experimenter, met each subject by the door, instructed him or her not to talk during the study, and led each to a cubicle-desk, partitioned so that a subject could see very little else besides the front of the room, the experimenter, and the radio. The experimenter then turned off the radio and played tape-recorded instructions that explained the task in which the subject was going to engage.

After a brief delay the experimenter announced: "We're a little early. We'll have to wait for the other room to be ready." The radio was then switched on, and 60 seconds of music was followed by a news broadcast and an additional 30 seconds of music, at which point a confederate entered and said "The other room is ready." The experimenter turned off the radio, and subjects engaged in a task that was designed to obtain our dependent variable measure. After this task was completed, subjects were debriefed and paid equally for their participation.

Prior to the experiment, pretests were conducted on a number of stories in order to establish prosocial and antisocial news broadcasts. Potential stories were adapted from *actual news reports* and were ranked by naive judges in a way that allowed preselection of news stories that were clearly prosocial or antisocial.

In the first experiment in this series, after hearing the news report, subjects played one round of a moderately high-stakes, two-choice non-zero sum game. The news stories were expected to affect a subject's views about strangers and, correspondingly, their relationship to him; that is, a "good" news story was expected to increase the likelihood that subjects would perceive a stranger as someone who was promotively oriented toward them. Consequently, they were predicted to act on the other's behalf and expect the other to do the same for them. A "bad" news story was expected to decrease the likelihood of strangers' being perceived in this way, and subjects were not expected to exhibit or antici-pate cooperative behavior.

The expectations were confirmed. Subjects who heard a prosocial radio newscast played the non-zero sum game more cooperatively and expected their opponent to play cooperatively and have cooperative goals more often than those who heard an antisocial radio newscast (Hornstein, LaKind, Frankel, & Manne, 1976).

In a second experiment we were concerned with obtaining more direct evidence about the presumed mediator of this behavior. Spe-cifically, we wanted to investigate our previously stated prediction that news events that symbolize "human goodness" cause subjects to hold inflated estimates of the distribution of promotive social dispositions among the general public, that is, that they would believe that a relatively higher percentage of people subscribe to beliefs and values that concern them with the well-being of others and are therefore concordant with each subject's self-interest. On the other hand, news events that symbolize "inhumanity" cause inflated estimates about the percentage of people who subscribe to beliefs and values that are essentially antithetical to the well-being of others, including the subject's.

In this experiment, after overhearing the news report, subjects answered nine questions on an instrument called the "Population Estimates Questionnaire." This was, in reality, a substantially altered edition of a portion of Wrightsman's *Philosophies of Human Nature Scale* (1964) and included such questions as "What percentage of people are basically honest?" "What percentage of people would risk his or her own life or limb to help someone else?"

As expected, subjects who heard a prosocial radio newscast, in contrast to those who heard an antisocial one, were more inclined to believe that a relatively high percentage of people subscribed to beliefs and values that concerned them with the well-being of others (Hornstein, LaKind, Frankel, & Manne, 1976). Compared to males, females in this sample subscribed to a more favorable view of humanity. The average prosocial percentage estimates for females was 49%, whereas for males it was only 41%. Females were clearly less affected by the newscasts. For females there was only a 9 percentage point difference between the pro- and antisocial conditions, whereas for men the difference was 12 percentage points in the direction of a more favorable view of humanity after hearing the prosocial broadcast. For females, the difference falls just short of the traditional .05 level of significance, but for males the differences are more dramatic and are well within the range of statistically significant differences.

In a third experiment using these same broadcasts, we had subjects complete the Nowlis Mood Adjective Checklist. It turned out that subjects who heard the prosocial radio newscast did not react differently than those who heard the antisocial newscast. In order to understand this finding, one must recognize that, in comparison to other research using the Nowlis MACL, from the subjects' perspectives this experimental manipulation was subtle, inasmuch as the news report was incidental and totally unrelated to the experiment or the experimenter's interest. Simply stated, subjects were not directed to listen to the news broadcast before receiving the Nowlis MACL, whereas in other experiments they had been directed to attend to certain inputs. This may have produced a certain transparency in previous research. One is forced to wonder whether the experimental manipulation would produce so-called "mood changes" if the experimental instructions more closely paralleled those explicit instructions used by Aderman (1972) and others. In order to explore this possibility, a study was conducted using Aderman's instructions (with word changes to suit our content), which *specifically directed* subjects to attend to the news broadcast. Now the effect on mood became obvious. Scores on all twelve clusters for both sexes indicated "better" moods after exposure to the "good" new broadcast, and many were statistically significant. On the basis of these findings it seems reasonable to conclude that previous findings involving direct measures of mood reflect the demand characteristics of the experiments.

This might tempt one to conclude that mood is unrelated to helping, but that seems excessive. Mood cannot be dismissed as a potential mediator of one's views about people. Intuition suggests that it is common for "good" moods to be associated with predispositions to favorably evaluate the social community and for "bad" moods to be associated with the opposite. But only a little imagination is necessary to think of events that produce "bad" moods while simultaneously heightening favorable conceptions of humanity—some unexpectedly heroic efforts that end in tragedy, for example. Similarly, victories over an unusually ruthless and prevasive foe may produce "good" moods but at the same time may produce narrowed and comparatively unfavorable conceptions of humanity. To explore the relationship between mood and these beliefs about others, it is necessary to manipulate these two independently in a single investigation.

LaKind (1978) did just that using Pennsylvania housewives as subjects. She created four stories that covaried social conception (favorable versus unfavorable) and mood (elated versus depressed). In order to check the manipulation of social conception, LaKind replicated the experiment using the Population Estimates Questionnaire, the revision of Wrightsman's Human Nature Scale. Her results were the same as those previously obtained. In order to check manipulation of mood, LaKind repeated the first experiment using the Nowlis MACL, in which explicit directives to attend to the news stories were omitted. Statistically significant results emerged, demonstrating that the four stories yielded four verifiably different combinations of social conception and mood: favorable conceptions with either elated or depressed moods, and unfavorable conceptions with either elated or depressed moods.

For her dependent measure LaKind had different groups of subjects judge the guilt or innocence of defendants involved in hypothetical litigation. Newscasts that produced positive social conceptions of humanity caused more merciful judgments to be given than did those that produced negative social conceptions. Mood accentuated the effect but, by itself, was unrelated to subjects' judgments. The data compel one conclusion: Mood alters prosocial behavior only when it is caused by or stimulates cognitions or associations that are relevant to the formation of promotive relationships. These relationships are erected or eroded when people have reason to believe that others are "for them" or "agin them." Sometimes these decisions about others rest on hard data about their opinions and values. Sometimes, however—perhaps too often—they rest upon inferences that have been jaundiced by the misdeeds of strangers. Thus, the news is not psychologically neutral. It is an important yet subtle source of influence on assumptions about others and behavior toward them. By changing one's general conception of people, news reports play a critical role in shaping specific inferences about strangers. They act as a bias, creating expectations that predispose us to classify complete strangers as "we" or "they."

REFERENCES

Ach, N. *Uber den Willinsakt und das Temperament: Eine experimentelle Untersuchung.* Leipzig: Quelle und Meyer, 1910.

Aderman, D. Elation, depression and helping behavior. *Journal of Personality and Social Psychology*, 1972, 24, 91–101.

Allport, G. *The nature of prejudice.* Cambridge: Addison-Wesley, 1954.

Amir, Y. Contact hypothesis in ethnic relations. *Psychological Bulletin*, 1969, 71, 319–342.

Banikiotes, P. G., Russell, J. M., & Linden, J. H. Interpersonal attraction in simulated and real interactions. *Journal of Personality and Social Psychology*, 1972, 23(1), 1–17.

Berkowitz, L. The self, selfishness, and altruism. In J. Macaulay & L. Berkowitz (Eds.), *Altruism and helping behavior.* New York: Academic Press, 1970, Pp. 143–157.

Billig, M. G. Social categorization and intergroup relations. Unpublished doctoral dissertation. University of Bristol, England, 1972.

Bruner, J. S. On perceptual readiness. *Psychological Review*, 1957, 64, 123–152.

Bryan, J. H., & Test, M. J. Models and helping: Naturalistic studies in aiding behavior. *Journal of Personality and Social Psychology*, 1967, 6, 400–407.

Byrne, D. Attitudes and attraction. In L. Berkowitz (Ed.), *Advances in experimental social psychology*, Vol. 4. New York: Academic Press, 1969, Pp. 36–89.

Byrne, D. *The attraction paradigm.* New York: Academic Press, 1971.

Byrne, D., London, O., & Griffith, W. The effect of topic importance and attitude similarity–dissimilarity on attraction in an intrastranger design. *Psychonomic Science*, 1968, 11, 303–304.

Cartwright, D., & Zander, A. *Group dynamics: Research and theory.* Evanston, Ill.: Row-Peterson, 1960.

Cattell, R., & Horowitz, J. Objective personality tests investigating the structure of altruism in relation to source traits. A. H. and L. *Journal of Personality*, 1952, *21*, 103–117.

Chase, M. Categorization and affective arousal: Some behavioral and judgmental consequences. Unpublished doctoral dissertation, Teachers' College, Columbia University, 1971.

Clore, G. L., & Baldridge, B. Interpersonal attraction: The role of agreement and topic interest. *Journal of Personality and Social Psychology*, 1968, *9*, 340–346.

Cooley, C. H. *Social organization*. New York: Scribner, 1909.

Deutsch, M. An experimental study of the effects of cooperation and competition upon group processes. *Human Relations*, 1949, *2*, 81–95. (a)

Deutsch, M. A theory of cooperation and competition. *Human Relations*, 1949, *2*, 129–152 (b)

Deutsch, M. Some factors affecting membership motivation and achievement motivation. *Human Relations*, 1959, *12*, 81–95.

Deutsch, M. Field theory in social psychology. In G. Lindzey & E. Aronson (Eds.), *The handbook of social psychology*. (2nd ed.) Reading, Mass.: Addison-Wesley, 1969, Pp. 412–487.

Deutsch, M., & Stembridge, B. The effects of similarity and sharing upon behavior in a prisoner's dilemma game. Unpublished manuscript, Teachers' College, Columbia University, 1971.

Deutsch, M., Thomas, J. R. H., & Garner, K. A. Social discrimination on the basis of category membership. Unpublished manuscript, Teachers College, Columbia University, 1971.

Dion, K. L. Cohesiveness as a determinant of ingroup–outgroup bias. *Journal of Personality and Social Psychology*, 1973, *28*, 163–171.

Dunn, O. J. Multiple comparisons among means. *Journal of the American Statistical Association*, 1961, *56*, 52–64.

Feldman, R. Responses to compatriot and foreigner who seek assistance. In L. Bickman, & T. Henchy (Eds.), *Beyond the laboratory: Field research in social psychology*. New York: McGraw-Hill, 1972, Pp. 44–55.

Festinger, L., Schachter, S., & Back, K. *Social pressures in informal groups: A study of a housing project*. New York: Harper, 1950.

Friedrichs, R. W. Alter vs. ego: An explanatory assessment of altruism. *American Sociological Review*, 1960, *25*, 496–508.

Gaertner, S., & Bickman, L. Effects of race on the elicitation of helping behavior: The wrong number technique. *Journal of Personality and Social Psychology*, 1971, *20*(2), 218–222.

Hodgson, S. A., Hornstein, H. A., & Siegel, E. Socially mediated Zeigarnik effects as a function of sentiment, valence and desire for goal attainment. *Journal of Experimental Social Psychology*, 1972, *8*(5), 446–456.

Homans, G. *The human group*. New York: Harcourt, Brace, 1950.

Hornstein, H. A. Experiments in the social psychology of prosocial behavior. Final report, NSF Grant 1715, 1970. (a)

Hornstein, H. A. Social models and interpersonal helping behavior. In J. Macaulay & L. Berkowitz (Eds.), *Altruism and helping behavior*. New York: Academic Press, 1970, Pp. 29–42. (b)

Hornstein, H. A. Promotive tension: The basis of prosocial behavior from a Lewinian perspective. *Journal of Social Issues*, 1972, *28*(2), 191–218.

Hornstein, H. A. *Cruelty and kindness: A new look at aggression and altruism.* New Jersey: Prentice-Hall, 1976.

Hornstein, H. A., Fisch, E., & Holmes, M. Influence of a model's feeling about behavior and his relevance as a comparison other on observer's helping behavior. *Journal of Personality and Social Psychology,* 1968, *10,* 222–226.

Hornstein, H. A., LaKind, E., Frankel, G., & Manne, S. The effects of knowledge about remote social events on prosocial behavior, social conception and mood. *Journal of Personality and Social Psychology,* 1976, *32,* 1038–1046.

Hornstein, H. A., Masor, H. N., Sole, K., & Heilman, M. Effects of sentiment and completion of a helping act on observer helping: A case for socially mediated Zeigarnik effects. *Journal of Personality and Social Psychology,* 1971, *17,* 107–112.

Horwitz, M. The recall of interrupted group tasks: An experimental study of individual motivation in relation to group goals. *Human Relations,* 1953, 7, 3–38.

Krebs, D. Altruism—An examination of the concept and a review of the literature. *Psychological Bulletin,* 1970, *73,* 258–302.

Kounin, J. S. Experimental studies of rigidity: I. *Character and Personality,* 1941, *9,* 251–272. (a)

Kounin, J. S. Experimental studies of rigidity: II. *Character and Personality,* 1941, *9,* 273–282. (b)

LaKind, E. Expanding and contracting *we*-group boundaries: The effects of news broadcasts on philosophy of human nature and juridic decisions. Doctoral dissertation, 1978. Teachers' College, Columbia University.

Lewin, K. Die psychische Tätigkeit bei der Hemmung von Willensvörgangen und das Grundgesetz der Assoziation. *Zeitschrift für Psychologie,* 1917, *77,* 212–247.

Lewin, K. Das Problem der Willensmessung und das Grundgesetz der Assoziation. *Psychologische Forschung,* 1922, *1,* 191–302. (a)

Lewin, K. Das Problem der Willensmessung und das Grundgesetz der Assoziation. *Psychologische Forschung,* 1922, 2, 65–104. (b)

Lewin, K. *A dynamic theory of personality.* New York: McGraw-Hill, 1935.

Lewin, K. *Principles of topological psychology.* New York: McGraw-Hill, 1936.

Lewin, K. The conceptual representation and measurement of psychological forces. *Contributions to Psychological Theory,* 1938, 1, No. 4.

Lewin, K. *Resolving social conflicts.* New York: Harper, 1948.

Lewin, K. *Field theory in social science.* New York: Harper, 1951.

Lewis, H. B. An experimental study of the role of the ego in work: I, The role of the ego in cooperative work. *Journal of Experimental Psychology,* 1944, *34,* 113–126.

Lewis, H. B., & Franklin, M. An experimental study of the role of the ego in work: II, The significance of task orientation in work. *Journal of Experimental Psychology,* 1944, *31,* 195–215.

Lippitt, R., & White, R. K. The "social climate" of children's groups. In R. G. Barker, J. S. Kounin, & H. F. Wright (Eds.), *Child behavior and development.* New York: McGraw-Hill, 1943.

Marrow, A. J. *The practical theorist: The life and work of Kurt Lewin.* New York: Basic Books, 1969.

Marton, J., Sole, K., & Hornstein, H. A. Socially mediated Zeigarnik effects: An experimental investigation of the effects of group structure and promotive tension. Teachers' College, Columbia University. (In preparation)

Mitchell, H. E., & Byrne, D. The defendant's dilemma: Effects of jurors' attitudes and authoritarianism on judicial decisions. *Journal of Personality and Social Psychology*, 1973, *25*(1), 123–129.

Murray, H. A. The effects of fear upon the estimates of maliciousness of other personalities. *Journal of Social Psychology*, 1933, *4*, 310–328.

Ovsiankina, M. Die Wiederaufnahme von untersbrochenen Handlungen. *Psychologische Forschung*, 1928, *11*, 302–379.

Peres, Y. Ethnic relations in Israel. *American Journal of Sociology*, 1971, *76*, 1021–1047.

Perlmutter, H. V. Correlates of two types of xenophilic orientation. *Journal of Abnormal and Social Psychology*, 1956, *52*, 130–135.

Pettigrew, T. *Profile of the Negro American*. Princeton: Van Nostrand, 1964.

Piliavin, I. M., Rodin, J., & Piliavin, J. A. Good Samaritanism: An underground phenomenon? *Journal of Personality and Social Psychology*, 1969, *13*, 289–299.

Rabbie, J., & Horwitz, M. Arousal in ingroup–outgroup bias by a chance win or loss. *Journal of Personality and Social Psychology*, 1969, *13*, 269–277.

Schopler, J. An attribution analysis for some determinants of reciprocating a benefit. In J. Macaulay & L. Berkowitz (Eds.), *Altruism and helping behavior*. New York: Academic Press, 1970, Pp. 231–240.

Seeman, M. The urban alienations: Some dubious theses from Marx to Marcuse. *Journal of Personality and Social Psychology*, 1971, *19*, 135–144.

Sherif, M., & Sherif, C. *Groups in harmony and tension*. New York: Harper, 1953.

Sole, K., Marton, J., & Hornstein, H. A. Opinion similarity and helping: Three field experiments investigating the bases of promotive tension. *Journal of Experimental Social Psychology*, 1975, *11*, 1–13.

Sorokin, P. A. *Forms and techniques of altruistic and spiritual growth*. Boston: Beacon Press, 1954.

Staub, E. A child in distress: The effects of focusing responsibility on children on their attempts to help. *Developmental Psychology*, 1970, *2*, 152–153. (a)

Staub, E. A child in distress: The influence of age and number of witnesses on children's attempts to help. *Journal of Personality and Social Psychology*, 1970, *14*, 130–141. (b)

Staub, E. Helping a person in distress: The influence of implicit and explicit rules of conduct on children and adults. *Journal of Personality and Social Psychology*, 1971, *17*, 137–144.

Stotland, E. Exploratory investigations in empathy. In L. Berkowitz, (Ed.), *Advances in experimental social psychology*, Vol. 4. New York: Academic Press, 1969, Pp. 271–313.

Tajfel, H. Cognitive aspects of prejudice. *Journal of Social Issues*, 1969, *25*(4), 79–99.

Tajfel, H. Experiments in intergroup discrimination. *Scientific American*, 1970, *223*, 96–102.

Tajfel, H., Flamant, C., Billig, M. G., & Bundy, R. P. Social categorization and intergroup behavior. *European Journal of Social Psychology*, 1971, *1*(2), 149–178.

Triandis, H. C., Vassiliou, V., & Nassiakou, M. Three cross-cultural studies of subjective culture. *Journal of Personality and Social Psychology Monograph Supplement*, 1968, *8*(4), Part 2.

Wispé, L., & Freshley, H. B. Race, sex, and sympathetic helping behavior: The broken bag caper. *Journal of Personality and Social Psychology*, 1971, *17*, 59–65.

Wrightsman, L. Measurement of philosophies of human nature scale. *Psychological Reports*, 1964, *14*, 743–751.

Wrightsman, L., & Noble, F. C. Reactions to the President's assassination. *Psychological Reports*, 1965, *16*, 159–162.

Zander, A., & Havelin, A. Social comparison and intergroup attraction. *Human Relations*, 1960, *13*, 21–32.

Zeigarnik, B. Über den Behalten von erledigten und unerledigten Handlungen. *Psychologische Forschung*, 1927, *9*, 1–85.

10

Aspects of a Transnational Theory of Prosocial Behavior

HELMUT E. LÜCK

According to the late Bertrand Russell (1927), "Animals studied by Americans rush about frantically with an incredible display of hustle and pep, and last achieve the deserved result by chance. Animals observed by Germans sit still and think, and at last evolve the solution [p. 30]." From this one would expect to see German studies in the field of prosocial orientations and behavior marked by a national bias toward deep thinking, hypercritical meditation, and sophisticated problem solving. There are probably many early and even a few present-day studies of this kind, but the majority of recent studies show few discernible marks that fit the national stereotype. Modes of research in social psychology have apparently become internationally standardized. At present some German authors are comparing their prosocial results to previous American studies, but without discussing national differences that may have been operating in their studies. The same neglect of cultural differences can be seen in research conducted in the United States. With few exceptions (Berkowitz, 1966; Feldman, 1968), most researchers have failed to study culture as an independent variable—defining "culture" here in terms of different nations. There are many studies of race and class as to how these affect helping behavior, but these studies can hardly be used to speculate about cross-cultural or transnational differences. And anthropologists, even when they have shown a little interest in so-called "prosocial" behavior, have not studied it experimentally (although the two Graves's [1976] work is an important exception). Thus, most of the prosocial research and theorizing has been done in America, and it is not known how well these conclusions will generalize to other cultures.

This chapter will consider transnational studies of prosocial behavior. Unfortunately (with the exceptions already noted), most of the studies that have tried to replicate prosocial results and to consider cultural and transnational differences theoretically have so far been done mostly in Germany. Since German theories of sympathy were very influential, both on German research and in other respects, I will begin with a short analysis of these theories. I shall then turn to some current research on linguisitic aspects of prosocial concepts, and later discuss early and more recent empirical studies of prosocial helping behavior.

GERMAN THEORIES OF SYMPATHY

In Germany, sometimes called "the nation of poets and thinkers," philosophical studies on sympathy and helping were very much associated with poetry and literature—particularly in the nineteenth century. German *Geisteswissenschaften* (literally, 'sciences of the mind') and *Weltanschauung* ('world view') were still and still are largely determined by the work of Johann Wolfgang von Goethe (1749–1832), Friedrich von Schiller (1759–1805), and Friedrich Wilhelm Nietzsche (1844–1900), among many others. All three mentioned wrote about moral values and sympathy and were poets and philosophers. This is quite different from the situation in England and America, where philosophy and psychology for a long time had stronger ties to the natural and economic sciences. Wispé (1968) has made that quite clear in discussing Adam Smith (1723–1790), Charles Darwin (1809–1882), and Lester F. Ward (1841–1913). American pragmatism and behaviorism made rats "rush about frantically," whereas German *Idealismus, Verstehenspsychologie, Denkpsychologie*, and *Gestaltpsychologie* made German rats "sit still and think."

To distill the philosophy and psychology of moral and prosocial orientations out of the German literature of the nineteenth and twentieth centuries would probably be a lifelong task, particularly since fact and fiction are densely interwoven. I shall therefore limit myself to an analysis of the concept of sympathy, using brief and exemplary description of a few works. The topic of sympathy (*Mitleid*) has been selected because it has been the focus of the German studies and because this kind of analysis in terms of prosocial behavior is, to the best of this author's knowledge, nowhere else available.

The German concept *Mitleid* (literally translated as 'with-suffering,' *Mit-leid*) has been used only since the seventeenth century and is thus of relatively recent origin. It is a more or less literal translation of the Greek *sympátheia* and the Latin *compassio*. Although English uses sympathy and compassion with only slightly different meanings, the German language distinguishes *Mitleid* from *Sympathie*, which in former times had the meaning of compassion but nowadays has more or less the meaning of attractiveness, fondness, social appeal, or attraction. *Mitleid* was a concept introduced into everyday language by the mystics to denote God's compassion with the pains of mankind as well as men's suffering with Christ's Passion. Interestingly, it can be seen that *Mitleid* is a concept that is now becoming more and more old-fashioned. Recent handbooks in psychology, sociology, and education do not even list the term, despite the fact that German psychologists and philosophers like Wilhelm Wundt (1892), Theodor Lipps (1891), Wilhelm Stern (1903), Ludwig Klages (1910), Max Scheler (1913, 1923), Otto F. Bollnow (1947), and Albert Wellek (1950), among many others, have significantly contributed to the analysis of the phenomenon of sympathy.

Among the German writers who studied *Mitleid* I shall concentrate particularly on Immanuel Kant (1724–1804), Arthur Schopenhauer (1788–1960), and Friedrich Wilhelm Nietzsche (1844–1900), whose positions are quite irreconcilable.

Kant wrote that human behavior has moral value only if the will to act is directly determined by the moral law. This moral law is given by common sense and influences the free, completely autonomous will of man. Kant's Categorical Imperative, which prescribes that man should act in such a way that the maxim of his will every time and simultaneously could serve as a principle of a common law (1788, p. 54), makes the law, or a form of the law, superior to human will.

Kant sees sympathy as a "warm and charitable feeling" that is "beautiful and gracious" but has "not the dignity of virtue." The reason for Kant's relatively restricted estimation of sympathy can be seen in the fact that sympathy for him is only a mood, a feeling, and acts based on feelings can bear the marks of egoism and other propensities. The only "moral" propensity is respect for the moral law. Morality is seen in behavior that originated from obedience to the moral law, that is, from "duty." In Kant's opinion, a human act that was instigated by sympathy (or any other feeling) can only have "legality" (that is, if it is in accordance with the moral law—more or less by chance), but it cannot have "morality," since in this case the law has not been the primary cause for the act (1788, p. 127).

Sympathy has a low value in Kant's eyes, because it is a mood, not a virtue. Only if it is paired with the rational moral norm is it regarded as a virtue, an "adopted virtue," as he says. Helping out of sympathy, therefore, would be different than moral-normative helping.

Arthur Schopenhauer was influenced by the French Sensualists, by Goethe, who was 40 years his senior, and by Kant, whose work he "thought through to its conclusion," as he said.

Schopenhauer does not see the moral law as a given basis of moral behavior. For him the Categorical Imperative is an empty, abstract rule. Man is will, not reason. His approach is to evaluate the origins of human will, in which he sees three basic propensities: egoism, spite, and sympathy. He sees sympathy as "the only origin for altruistic acts and therefore as the true basis of morality [1860, p. 246]." Since sympathy is a very direct participation in the sorrow, suffering, and hurt of men and animals, it is not understandable and cannot be understood. Schopenhauer is well aware that his position is in contradiction to the philosophy of the Stoics and to that of Spinoza and Kant. However, he gives J. J. Rousseau as evidence and points to the fact that empathy was considered by the Chinese as the first of the five principal virtues and that in the *agora* in ancient Athens an altar was erected in honor of sympathy. Schopenhauer's inclusion of these and several other historical sources is typical, for in his philosophy he tried to incorporate ancient wisdom into a lively defense of his position.

Whereas in his earlier works sympathy was seen as true love (*agape*, *caritas*), Schopenhauer later sees sympathy as the basis of justice and love for mankind. The balance of justice evolves because sympathy is the counterpart of egoism; love of mankind becomes salient, since sympathy makes people act for others.

Schopenhauer's influence on Friedrich Nietzsche was very strong. Although Nietzsche was 31 years younger, he was also of a romantic and erratic temperament, pessimistic and socially isolated. Nietzsche studied philosophy and literature. At the age of 24 he became a professor of philology at the University of Basle. Though educated as a Protestant, Nietzsche denied Christian virtues like sympathy. He sees the striving for power as the strongest human desire and sees empathy not as a virtue but as a weakness and a disease. His passionate philosophical poem *Also sprach Zarathustra* ('Thus Spoke Zarathustra'), published 1833–1891, is sometimes seen as a forerunner of Nazi ideology. He solemnly proclaims the need for the *Über-Mensch*, the 'super-man,' as the man of the future. Sympathy is seen as a weakness and a danger for mankind. "God is dead; he died from his sympathy with mankind." Whoever wishes to create the future man must be tough and should not be moved by the sorrow of others. "Sympathy is the deepest abyss: As deep as man looks into life, so deep he looks into sorrow." Sympathy is seen as a danger, since it hinders man from loving the man of the future, the *Über-Mensch*.

The progression from the *Mensch* to the *Herrenmensch* to the *Über-Mensch*, with its departure from Christian morality ("the morality of the weak") and its claim that man will become healthier, stronger, more self-reliant, is one of the eloquently formulated demands that fascinated Nietzsche's readers.

From the preceding account it has probably become clear that Nietzsche's philosophy, in particular, is not stringent. It is contradictory in many aspects, and, of course, it has been criticized for its "reversal of values." Still, empathy can humiliate the recipient, and it can be a gentle emotion without instigation to action. Was that what he wanted to say in poetical form?

In Germany these three extreme positions, Kant's emphasis on reason as the foundation of morality, Schopenhauer's insistence on sympathy as the foundation of morality and justice, and his student Nietzsche's rejection of Christian morality and sympathy, were raised within a fairly short period of time. These thinkers had great influence in their times and they all wrote lucidly about sympathy, but, if we try to find their traces in modern psychology, we will be disappointed. There is a branch of philological psychology in Germany, but the majority of psychologists are experimentally oriented and follow the trends determined mainly by Americans. Since American psychologists apparently no longer have close links with German philosophy, which is probably in part due to language difficulties, only rarely is the concept of sympathy mentioned, even in helping research, whether German or American. Certain earlier exceptions have been interesting. Gordon Allport, who spent a year in Germany, incorporated his knowledge of Spranger and other German authors into his personality theory (Allport & Vernon, 1931). J. F. Brown and R. B. MacLeod both spent student days in Germany, and German philosophy, as well as German psychology, influenced their works. But for prosocial orientation and helping studies, no such apparent links exist.

COMPARISONS OF STUDIES OF MORAL
REASONING AND DEVELOPMENT

Given the concern in Germany about the role of morality and reason, an early interest in moral reasoning and conduct is not surprising. Empirical studies of criminals around 1900 suggested that intelligence and moral development were different personality dimensions. The question was how to test for moral reasoning and development separately from intelligence. Cimbal (1909) outlined several ways to test intelligence and moral development. His test consisted mainly of anamnesis items, but he also included such tasks as explaining jokes, proverbs, historical events, the Commandments, etc. in order to evaluate the "moral competence to judge."

Another strong impetus for the study of moral reasoning was given German research by G. G. Fernald, the creative doctor at the Massachusetts Reformatory in Concord. Hugo Marx (1912), a doctor in a Berlin prison, published a vivid report of his visit to several prisons in America, and his description of Fernald's work inspired German scientists to develop comparable standardized instruments. Several years later Jacobsohn (1919, Jacobsohn-Lask, 1920) published two extensive studies on the modified Fernald method that then became known in German literature as the Fernald–Jacobson method (see, e.g., Huijts, 1969, p. 142 ff.). Fernald's test consisted of 10 described offenses that had to be rank-ordered for severeness by the subjects, and a second part consisting of control rankings of positive deeds. Jacobsohn improved this technique by using actual cases from the juvenile law court, presented on separate sheets to be rank-ordered. It was necessary to explain the order and defend it in a subsequent interview. In his first studies (1919), Jacobsohn reported data and interviews with boys aged 12–18, some of them delinquents (delinquent boys ranked their own crimes, as well). In his second article, he gave data for several groups tested additionally as baseline data.

The Fernald–Jacobsohn method was adopted by many psychologists, clinicians, and psychiatrists. In his summary of current tests, Sander (1920) said that it "promises the best results." Yet criticism was close behind. In 1925, Quadfasel pointed out that Fernald was misunderstood by Marx and his followers. Other authors, among them Piaget, said that each case, however described, was seen in a different way, that the subjects were fatigued by too many details, and that everything had to be kept in mind until a final rank-order was established. Soon the problem of moral norms came up; What is the normal, what the ideal, what the correct rank? Some researchers relied on data from "moral leaders" for comparison, others used "normal people" as a standard. But, naturally, the lack of external validity finished off these kinds of tests of morality. They probably measured knowledge of formal law, but the method was "too much conceptualized parallel to intelligence tests [Huijts, 1969, p. 145]."

Psychologists were also interested in the study of moral development in children. Both educational and criminal psychologists were interested in the age at which young people reached moral maturity. The Simon and Binet concept of *mental age* was transferred to such concerns and was accordingly spoken of as *moral age* (Riebesell, 1917; Schaefer, 1913). Schaefer studied 1,250 normal and disabled children who had to compose an essay entitled "Why is it forbidden to steal?" The essays were categorized according to a system elaborated by the author and his colleague Levy-Suhl using a typology developed by Arthur Schopenhauer. The five categories Schaefer used have great similarity to Piaget's (1932) and even more so with Kohlberg's (1969) stages, because he saw "concentric circles or stages" starting from the "ego" and going to the family, then the social community, and on to the state. (See Chapter 7 by Krebs for a further discussion of Kohlberg.) It was found that religious motives declined with advancing age, whereas personal and socioethical motives increased. Very similar to Piaget's work (1932), Schaefer (1913) found that "egoistic" thinking declined with age and that the socioethical reasoning of normal children increased starting from about age 14 or 15. Schaefer gives tables with norms and even draws developmental trends strikingly similar to those given by Kohlberg (e.g., 1963, p. 16). As far as the present author knows, these studies were not known, or at least they were not cited, by Piaget and Kohlberg. Somehow it seems to be typical that the early German studies drew upon Schopenhauer and other philosophers, whereas a few years later the connection between philosophy and empirical research was lost. To legitimate his work the psychologist now quotes other psychologists.

Summing up these very early German attempts to study moral development, justice, and social responsibility, one sees their philosophical roots very clearly, but one hardly ever finds psychoanalytic, sociopsychological, or sociological theorizing. At about the same time, the concept of moralization (later socialization) was popular in America. But in Germany there was no Cooley, Baldwin, or Giddings, and their works, if known, were probably misunderstood. On the other hand, the intensive and often insightful research in Germany was not taken up by Piaget and his co-workers, nor later by American social psychologists like Kohlberg. Once again, the review of this literature confirms that the history of psychology is, in part, a history of "missed opportunities"

(Anger, 1965). Eventually the results of these earlier investigations were forgotten, even by German psychologists.

These early attempts to understand moral development were strongly influenced by several practical concerns: by questions of legal responsibility, by efforts to educate for social responsibility, and by theological concerns about moral conduct. After the 1930s, as far as the present writer knows, there were few attempts to develop reliable and valid tests in this field, and not much else was done. Recently, however, there has been a reawakened interest in transnational aspects of moral values and moral development. For example, several surveys on moral values and their presumed importance in education (see Lück, 1975, p. 36) show only slight differences among several subgroups of respondents classified according to age, sex, social status, and religion. Compared to American data, there is still a stronger emphasis on ideals like obedience, orderliness, and industriousness; however, "obedience" has declined since the 1950s. In general, these studies are in accordance with the cross-cultural study of Almond and Verba (1963) that showed that generosity and considerateness were values estimated lower in Germany than in America and (particularly) in Great Britain.

Several studies have been conducted to corroborate and extend Piaget's findings of a moral development from heteronomous to autonomous moral (Danne, 1965; Kemmler, Windheuser, & Morgenstern, 1970; Pongratz, 1964; Schmitt, 1963). In all of these studies, multiple-choice questionnaires with items of projective contents were used to determine the moral stage of the respondents. The studies revealed that moral judgment is only slightly or not at all correlated with intelligence (Danne, 1965; Kemmler et al., 1970). A significant difference, however, was found for children of the same age with different family backgrounds (Kemmler et al., 1970); that is, children from white-collar families had higher moral scores. This agrees with several American studies.

In this study, the testing appears to have been improved by subdividing "moral" into three meaningful aspects leading to three different subscores, namely, "distributive versus retaliative justice," "dissolving from authority," and "bias towards punishment." Yet even this questionnaire with its 12 stories lacks the usual test criteria and cross-validations. According to Kemmler (personal communication, 5th August, 1974), no further studies have been conducted using this questionnaire.

Within a sociological context, Döbert and Nunner-Winkler (1976) intensively interviewed 9 conscientious objectors, 15 volunteers for an officer's career, and 14 drug addicts to test the hypothesis that the development from conventional to postconventional structures of moral consciousness is caused by a striking crisis in adolesence (i.e., a serious conflict with parents or friends, a phase of drug addiction, suicidal attempts, etc.). Interview statements were rated by independent judges,), and the hypothesis was considered as partly confirmed. Although only half of the postconventionals had had a serious identity crisis, hardly any of the persons who have had a crisis argued on a conventional level. The authors suggest that a crisis may be a sufficient but not necessary condition for the acquisition of postconventional structures of morality (à la Piaget). Despite its flamboyant style, the preliminary nature of the study, and the low level of internal and external validity, this is an interesting study because an unusual hypothesis was tested by age groups rarely studied in developmental psychology.

PERSONALITY TESTS AND MOOD SCALES

After the early Fernald–Jacobsohn studies, it took some decades before fresh attempts were made to develop German tests on moral–social orientations. Joerger's Group Test for Social Attitudes, S-E-T (1968), using photographs as stimuli for projective answers, was a first and rather sophisticated attempt to measure social attitudes and personality in children and adolescents.

Recently, Lichtenberg (1974) worked on an adaptation of Rotter's (1967) trust scale, the sympathy scale of Wispé (personal communication, 1971), the nurturance scale of Murray (1938), and the social responsibility scale of Berkowitz and Daniels (1964). All items were translated independently by two experienced translators. For each item the best translation was taken, and, for control reasons, the new scales were translated back into English by a third translator. If necessary, corrections were made (for this method of test adaptation, see Schwebcke, Lück, & Jandron, 1973). These scales, together with the German version of the Crowne–Marlowe social desirability scale (Lück & Timaeus, 1969) and several items for the check of internal validity, were administered to 211 students for the purpose of item analysis. After the elimination of inappropriate items, the scale reliabilities (r_{tt} between $+.70$ and $+.85$) were satisfactory. The scales were, however, considerably intercorrelated, and most of them correlated highly with social desirability, particularly the social responsibility scale. Table 10.1 gives the scale-intercorrelations and the correlations with the C–M social desirability scale.

All scales were moderately related to biographical data and internal validity questions. For example, students with divorced parents showed less responsibility ($p < .05$), less sympathy ($p < .05$), and less nurtur-

TABLE 10.1

Scales	Authors	Number of items in revised German version	Reliability (r_{tt})	Correlations with social desirability
Nurturance	Murray	20	.84	.55
Sympathy	Wispé	28	.85	.44
Responsibility	Berkowitz/ Daniels	22	.70	.69
Interpersonal trust	Rotter	25	.81	.50

ance ($p < .05$) than students with nondivorced parents. Female students showed more nurturance ($p < .005$) and more sympathy ($p < .005$) than male students. However, the pattern of these relations was sometimes unpredictable. In some way the data were parallel to those of Gergen, Gergen, and Meter (1972).

Since many social psychologists doubt the predictive value of personality tests on prosocial orientations and since the question of the variances in behavior of different persons in very similar situations has not been answered, perhaps the use of mood scales would be more fruitful. (However, see Wispé, Kiecolt, & Long, 1977.)

Hecheltjen and Mertesdorf (1973) have developed a German mood questionnaire (MSF) containing 12 different standardized subscales. The principal method for obtaining the subscales was factor analysis. The results were similar to those of Nowlis (1965). A very clear factor of social affection (*Anteilnahme*) emerged. No systematic research on prosocial moods that can compare with studies using films (e.g., Reykowski & Jarymowicz, 1975; Wispé, Kiecolt, & Long, 1977), success of positive reinforcement (e.g., Isen, 1970), or reading of mood statements (e.g., Adermann, 1972) has yet been carried out in Germany.

So far, the more recent studies on moral development, moods, and personality offer only a few opportunities for cross-cultural comparisons. Studying cross-cultural differences in prosocial motivations, however, could (*a*) serve to reveal cultural differences in social norms, educational styles, and psychodevelopmental patterns; (*b*) help us to understand other nations and thus enhance cross-cultural training; and—most important—(*c*) provide an opportunity to test the generality of theories on prosocial behavior, as well as the corresponding research methods and strategies. To illustrate this third point with an example: Studies that tried to confirm Kohlberg's stages of moral development in different cultures (e.g., Gorsuch & Barnes, 1973) served to corroborate the generality of this theory.

With these latter considerations in mind, I became concerned with the possible semantic differences in the terms used in prosocial research in Germany and in America. For an empirically oriented researcher, hermeneutic aspects of prosocial concepts may be a rather dissatisfying concern. One cannot fail to recognize, however, that the supposedly similar concepts used elicit different meanings and connotations. And this undoubtedly has its effects.

CONNOTATIONS OF PROSOCIAL CONCEPTS

We selected for evaluation six prosocial concepts: *Leidensgefährte* ('companion in misfortune'), *Leidensgenosse* ('fellow sufferer'), *Leid* ('sorrow'), *Mitleid* ('compassion,' 'sympathy'). *Hilfeleistung* ('help,' 'assistance'), and *soziales Engagement* ('social [or prosocial] engagement'). These terms are important and are probably the ones used most frequently in both German and American theories of sympathy and helping. In one of the studies, these six concepts were rated by 48 students on 18-item semantic differentials. Here Ertel's (1965) Standard-Differential was used, with the well-known dimensions: evaluation, potency, and activity as described by Osgood *et al.* (1957). Each dimension consisted of six bipolar items arranged in a seven-point scale. Table 2 shows the arithmetic means for the six concepts on evaluation, potency, and activity.

It is quite apparent that *Leidensgefährte* is evaluated more positively than *Leidensgenosse*. *Soziales Engagement* is considered as more active and stronger. *Hilfeleistung* has higher scores on the evaluation items. These data confirm the results of intensive interviews carried out earlier with another group of subjects in an attempt to study the connotations of these concepts.

Means for all items of each concept were computed, and the similarity of concepts was estimated by Spearman rank-order correlations of the profiles. These correlations, too, are in accordance with the interview results. The highest similarity was revealed in *Hilfeleistung* and *soziales Engagement* ($r = +.91, p = .01$). Leid has a stronger relation to Liedensgenosse ($+.91$) than to *Leidensgefährte* ($+.16$), probably since *Leidensgefährte* is evaluated more positively. These relationships were further clarified when the profiles were correlated with Ertel's (1965) data. His data for very characteristic concepts have quite extreme positions within

TABLE 10.2
Evaluation, Potency, and Activity Ratings by Forty-Eight Students for Six Prosocial Concepts

Prosocial terms	Evaluation	Potency	Activity
Companion in misfortune (*Leidensgefährte*)	25.46	23.00	20.85
Fellow sufferer (*Leidensgenosse*)	20.55	21.50	20.90
Sorrow (*Leid*)	15.54	19.64	20.19
Compassion, sympathy (*Mitleid*)	24.38	22.67	23.38
Help, assistance (*Hilfeleistung*)	31.73	30.69	30.50
Social or prosocial engagement (*soziales Engagement*)	28.85	32.73	33.02

the semantic frame and thus can well be used for purposes of comparison. *Leidensgenosse* and *Leidensgefährte* correlate positively with exhaustion, faintness, and tiredness and correlate negatively with temperament and obstinacy. *Leid* correlates with submissiveness (+.81), dirt (+.69), exhaustion (+.65), and weakness (+.65). *Hilfeleistung* and *soziales Engagement* show very similar positive relations to determination, temperament, authority, and obstinacy. Both concepts correlate negatively with faintness, weakness, and tiredness. In addition, the data were factor analyzed (principal component analysis with Varimax rotation after Scree test). The three well-known factors, activity, evaluation, and potency, clearly emerged. *Hilfeleistung* and *soziales Engagement* had the highest loadings on the first factor, whereas *Leidensgefährte* had the highest loadings on the second factor.

In this study, although only a few concepts were studied, the method employed indicates a way to clarify the emotional meaning of relevant concepts frequently used in research in prosocial studies. But this study makes an important contribution to increasing cross-cultural understanding. It shows how different groups of people feel about what may be similar concepts. Too little work of this kind has been done. Hofstätter (1957) tired to show that in America *lonesomeness* elicits much more pessimistic reactions than *Einsamkeit* does in Germany. The correlation between the Semantic Differential data for German and American students was $r = .40$, much lower than for other concepts. But the step was in the right direction.

We know very little about the modifications of such concepts within certain limits of time. To me, it seems as if prosocial terminology comes and goes with unusual rapidity. In Germany, for example, *Hilfeleistung* is not as up to date as *soziales Engagement*. In America, "sympathy" has given way to "prosocial behavior" and a host of other terms. So it is not surprising to see that the German Red Cross now makes great use of promptings based on the concept of *soziales Engagement* to win young people as volunteers or blood donors. Good old *Einfühlung* is old-fashioned compared to *Empathie*. In recent German articles one finds *Empathie*, apparently to let the reader know that the writer is familiar with Anglo-Saxon research on *empathy!* Finally, Osgood's Differential seems to be an appropriate instrument to test cross-cultural differences, changes in time, and the growing or fading of cultural similarities.

FIELD STUDIES

We turn now to several field studies that attempted as exactly as possible to replicate in the Federal Republic of Germany works conducted in America and Australia. These studies were chosen because of their potentially lower level of reactivity. (For a further discussion of the theoretical aspects, see Chapter 9 by Hornstein.)

Several experiments using the "lost letter" technique (Milgram *et al.*, 1965) were conducted. Among them was a replication of the very first experiment conducted by Merritt and Fowler (1948) on the "pecuniary honesty of the public at large." In that study addressed, stamped, and sealed letters were "lost" to see whether they would be mailed by a passerby. In the original study some of the letters contained lead pieces in the shape of a 50¢ coin. In the replication in Germany, pieces in the weight and shape of 2 DM were used. The results were that 54% of the letters reached their addresses in the United States and 69% in Germany. Very similar results were also obtained using the "Medical Research Associates" and "Mr. Walter Carnap" addresses Milgram used. The lost letter technique, however, did not lead to meaningful results when it was used to predict elections. In several detailed studies in which subjects finding the "lost" letters were filmed and rated and in which subjects were interviewed after finding a letter, we were able to evaluate several reasons for the restricted usefulness of the technique. For example, we found that the decision to mail the letter was very frequently a social process. In about one-third of all cases the letters were found by groups of people who immediately discussed what to do. Thus, the lost letter technique is of limited applicability, and quite definitely it is not always a valid, nonreactive method in attitude research, as Milgram (1969) suggests. (See Lück & Manz, 1973 for further discussion and a review of the literature.)

The "wrong number" technique (though ethically doubtful, like many of the nonreactive research techniques; Silverman, 1975) concerns the willingness of subjects (Ss) to help a victim (stooge) with a broken car. The Ss are requested to call a garage to get help for "the stranded motorist." We replicated the original Gaertner and Bickman study (1971) to test difference in helping behavior of Ss with different and same sex of the victim. No such differences or interactions were found. The social status of the victim was also manipulated. In one condition, he (or she) said that he (or she) had to go to shift work, in the other condition he (or she) said that he (or she) had to attend a conference. Again, no difference was found. Compared to the data of Gaertner and Bickman, our helping rates were considerably and significantly higher (90% versus 65% for white victim and white $Sp < .01$). Our explanation would be that in Germany, where considerably fewer people have telephones than in the United States, a greater informal obligation exists to help people under such circumstances.

Another study used the Darley and Latané (1970) "request for time" technique, in which passersby in New York were asked, "Excuse me; I wonder if you could tell me what time it is? In the original, 84% helped. We replicated this experiment using German male and female confederates as well as a Greek student appearing as an immigrant worker in Germany. We asked German Ss as well as immigrant workers from southern European countries for the time. Our surprising result was not a single refusal among the 171 Ss. This 100% helping response is again considerably more than the American 84%. One possible explanation could be lesser density of population in German cities as compared to New York (cf. Milgram, 1970).

In another study we used a victim appearing as an immigrant worker in order to replicate Wispé's and Freshley's (1971) "broken bag" study. In the original study a white and a black female confederate were the victims whose bags of groceries broke in a supermarket parking lot. The behavior of male and female, black and white Ss (passersby) was tested. In one of our studies we used a German male and a German female confederate, which led to a significantly higher helping response in favor of the female. In a second study we used a German female and a south European female S appearing as an immigrant worker. (Both young ladies were previously rated as equals in age and attractiveness.) Our Ss were male and female German shoppers. As in the original study, no overall differences for the two victims were found, and, as in the original study, men helped more frequently than women, this difference being particularly prominent as regards the foreign victim. Thus, comparable behavior patterns were found in both studies.

We also used the "request for a room" technique in our studies on helping behavior directed toward immigrant workers from south European countries, and so far we have not found any strong prejudices. It is well-known and documented by several facts that this group of people suffers from numerous social disadvantages. Possibly, the manipulated requests cost so little that prejudice was not operating (Campbell, 1963). In a very simple way, Bochner (1972) has studied reactions toward aborigines in Australia just by submitting newspaper ads ostensibly placed by a couple searching for an apartment. In one advertisement the couple described itself as "aborigines"; in another no hint was given. The difference between the number of offers was significant in the expected direction. We replicated this experiment with *Gastarbeiter* ('immigrant workers') as the essential stimulus word. To the two *Gastarbeiter* ads we received no offers, but for the two plain "couple" ads we received six different offers apiece. The only offer for the "immigrant worker" was a mimeographed leaflet from a real estate agent, whereas to the "couple" ad the offers were mostly private and personal. The ratio of reactions is comparable to that of Bochner, who received five phone calls for the aboriginal couple and 17 for the (presumably) white couple.

CONCLUSION

Cross-cultural and transnational studies in prosocial motivation and behavior provide a test of the generality of theories of sympathy, altruism, and helping. Transnational and cross-cultural studies also provide interesting opportunities to evaluate research techniques and methodologies. Although the cultural differences between Germany and America are presently probably smaller than those between many other countries—thus limiting the generality of the replications—this particular comparison provided its own kind of insights. For example, it is not generally known in America that about 70% of the German behavioral scientists emigrated for political reasons during the 1930s. From the end of World War II to the present, therefore, Germany (the Federal Republic as well as the German Democratic Republic) has been trying very hard to regain international standards. It has been to this end that many German psychologists have been replicating American studies that appeared to be theoretically fruitful. Different American methodologies have also been tried to see if they "work" in another culture. Other German psychologists have concentrated upon reviews of the literature and integrative theories and have generated research on this basis. Keeping all these factors in mind, then, it is not surprising that the German replications have added so little that is new and different. On the other hand, this overview was provided the opportunity, serendipitously perhaps, for the author and the reader to examine the sociopolitical implications of transnational replications. The first conclusion is probably that simple cross-cultural or transnational replications in which culture is not systematically included from the outset may be of limited value. Studies like Feldman's (1968) ingenious field experiments on foreigners who sought assistance in Paris, Athens, and Boston and Berkowitz's (1966) studies of dependency and helping in English and American schoolboys are the exceptions rather than the rule in transnational prosocial research, but they should be models.

It is also worth pointing out that American behavioral science may have influenced German science, especially German psychology, in yet another way. Research activities in Germany today are very decentralized. In contrast with, for example, Poland, where a team of 15 psychologists under the direction of Janusz Reykowski (1977) are studying cognitive processes in prosocial behavior, in Germany research is scattered throughout the country.

Social change is a second matter to be considered seriously in cross-cultural replications. Timing is important. For example, in 1975 we found that 69% of the passersby mailed the letters containing what appeared to be a coin. The original study was done in 1948. Would 69% of the German passersby have mailed the letter then? Probably not. Social attitudes, including the readiness to help, change with increasing rapidity. Also, the attitude toward obeying social norms changes. This was shown quite dramatically by Wormser (1975), who replicated in Munich the well-known study of pedestrian violations of traffic signals originally conducted in Austin, Texas (Lefkowitz, Blake, & Mouton, 1955). In contrast with the original study, in which more pedestrians followed a well-dressed young man, Wormser found that only 16.2% of the men and women in Munich followed a young man dressed as an air force officer when he violated the norms, whereas 32.9% followed a sloppily dressed hippy when he walked "against the light." Had Wormser conducted his replication in the 1950s, probably the reverse would have been found. A second conclusion is that cross-cultural comparisons in times of rapidly changing attitudes, values, and norms can only be meaningful if conducted simultaneously and in close cooperation.

Finally, it should be noted that replication in Europe of American studies (unfortunately, the reverse has hardly ever happened) is very much handicapped by American publication policies (see Cartwright,

1973), which cause a time-lag of at least 3 years. Apart from the research implications, publication policies influence transnational studies in yet another way: Replication studies are no more rewarding for an academic career in Germany than they are in America!

REFERENCES

Alderman, D. Elation, depression, and helping behavior. *Journal of Personality and Social Psychology*, 1972, 24, 91–101.

Allport, W., & Vernon, P. E. A test for personal values. *Journal of Abnormal and Social Psychology*, 1931, 26, 231–248.

Almond, G. A., & Verba, S. *The civic culture*. Princeton: Princeton University Press, 1963.

Anger, H. Sozialpsychologies. In E. V. Beckerath *et al.* (Eds), *Handwörterbuch der Sozialwissenschaften*, Vol. 12. Stuttgart, Tübingen, and Göttingen: Fischer, Mohr, and Vandenhoeck & Ruprecht, 1965, Pp. 636–650.

Berkowitz, L. A laboratory investigation of social class and national differences in helping behavior. *International Journal of Psychology*, 1966, 1, 231–242.

Berkowitz, L., & Daniels, L. Affecting the salience of social responsibility norms: Effects of past help on the response to dependency relationships. *Journal of Abnormal and Personality Psychology*, 1964, 68, 275–281.

Bochner, S. An unobtrusive approach to the study of housing discrimination against aborigines. *Australian Journal of Psychology*, 1972, 24, 335–337.

Bollnow, O. F. *Einfache Sittlichkeit*. Göttingen: Vandenhoeck & Ruprecht, 1947.

Campbell, D. T. Social attitudes and other acquired behavioral dispositions. In S. Koch (Ed.), *Psychology, a study of a science*. Vol. 6. New York: McGraw-Hill, 1963, Pp. 94–172.

Cartwright, D. T. Determinants of scientific progress: The case of research on the risky shift. *American Psychologist*, 1973, 28, 222–231.

Cimbal, W. *Taschenbuch zur Untersuchung nervöser und psychischer Krankheiten*. Berlin: Julius Springer, 1909.

Danne, A. Über die Eigenart moralischer Werturteile und deren Beziehungen zur intellektuellen Reif bei Zehnjährigen. Masters thesis, University of Münster, 1965.

Darley, J. M., & Latané, B. Norms and normative behavior: Field studies of social interdependence. In J. Macauley & L. Berkowitz (Eds.), *Altruism and helping behavior*. New York and London: Academic Press, 1970, Pp. 83–101.

Döbert R., & Nunner-Winkler, G. Zum Zusammenhang von Adoleszenkrisenverlauf, moralischem Bewussein und Wertorientierung. In M. R. Lepsius (Ed.), *Zwischenbilanz der Soziologie*. Stuttgart: Ferdinand Enke, 1976, Pp. 296–310.

Ertel, S. Standardisierung eines Eindrucksdifferentials. *Zeitschrift für experimentelle und angewandte Psychologie*, 1965, 12, 22–58.

Feldman, R. E. Response to compatriot and foreigner who seek assistance. *Journal of Personality and Social Psychology*, 1968, 10, 202–214.

Gaertner, S., & Bickman, L. Effects of race on elicitation of helping behavior: The wrong number technique. *Journal of Personality and Social Psychology*, 1971, 20, 218–222.

Gergen, K., Gergen, M. M., & Meter, K. Individual orientations to prosocial behavior. *Journal of Social Issues,* 1972, *28,* 105–130.

Gorsuch, R. L., & Barnes, M. L. Stages of ethical reasoning and moral norms of Carib youths. *Journal of Cross-Cultural Psychology,* 1973, *4,* 283–301.

Graves, T. D., & Graves, N. B. Demographic changes in the Cook Islands: Perception and reality, or where have all the *Mapee* gone? *Journal of the Polynesian Society,* 1976, *85,* 447–461.

Hecheltjen, K. G., & Mertesdorf, F. Entwicklung eines mehrdimensionalen Stimmungsfragebogens (MSF). *Gruppendynamik,* 1973, *4,* 110–122.

Hofstätter, P. R. *Gruppendynamik, Kritik der Massenpsychologie.* Hamburg: Rowohlt, 1957, 2. ed., 1971.

Huijts, J. H. *Gewissensbildung.* Köln: J. P. Bachem, 1969 (translated from the Dutch).

Isen, A. M. Success, failure, attention, and reaction to others: The warm glow of success. *Journal of Personality and Social Psychology,* 1970, *15,* 294–301.

Jacobsohn, L. Gibt et eine brauchbare Methode, um Aufschluss über das sittliche Fühlen eines Jugendlichen zu bekommen? *Zeitschrift für die gesamte Neurologie und Psychiatrie,* 1919, *46,* 285–347.

Jacobsohn-Lask, L. Über die Fernaldsche Methode zur Prüfung des sittlichen Fühlens und über ihre weitere Ausgestaltung. *Zeitschrift für angewandte Psychologie (Leipzig),* 1920, Beiheft 24.

Joerger, K. *Gruppentest für die soziale Einstellung (S-E-T).* Göttengen: Hogrefe, 1968.

Kant, I. *Critik der practischen Vernunft.* Riga: Johann Friedrich Hartknoch, 1788.

Kemmler, L., Windheuser, H. J., & Morgenstern, F. Gruppenanwendung von "Piaget"–Geschichten zum moralischen Urteil bei acht- bis neunjährigen Jungen im Vergleich mit einigen anderen Variablen. *Zeitschrift für Entwicklungspsychologie und Pädagogische Psychologie* 1970, *2,* 113–124.

Klages, L. *Prinzipien der Charakterologie.* Leipzig: Barth, 1910.

Kohlberg, L. The development of children's orientations toward a moral order, I: Sequence in the development of moral thought. *Vita Humana,* 1963, *6,* 11–33.

Kohlberg, L. Stage and sequence: The cognitive developmental approach to socialization. In D. A. Goslin (Ed.), *Handbook of socialization theory and research.* Chicago: Rand McNally, 1969, Pp. 347–480.

Lefkowitz, M., Blake, R., & Mouton, J. Status factors in pedestrian violation of traffic signals. *Journal of Abnormal and Social Psychology,* 1955, *51,* 704–706.

Lichtenberg, R. P. Die Adaption von vier amerikanischen Persönlichkeitsskalen zur Prognose prosozialen Verhaltens. Unpublished masters thesis, University of Cologne, 1974.

Lipps, T. *Der Streit über die Tragödie.* Hamburg: Leopold Voss, 1891.

Lück, H. E. *Prosoziales Verhalten. Empirische Untersuchungen zur Hilfeleistung.* Köln: Kiepenheuer & Witsch, 1975.

Lück, H. E., & Manz, W. Die Technik der verlorenen Briefe—Ein neues Instrument verhaltensbezogener Einstellungs messungen? *Zeitschrift für Soziologie,* 1973, *2,* 352–365.

Lück, H. E., & Timaeus, E. Skalen zur Messung manifester Angst (MAS) und sozialer Wünschbarkeit (SDS-E and SDS-CM). *Diagnostica,* 1969, *15,* 134–141.

Marx, H. Reiseeindrücke eines Gefängnisarztes in den Vereinigten Staaten. *Vierteljahrschrift für gerichtliche Medizin und öffentliches Sanitätswesen,* 1912, *13,* 166–193, 395–412.

Merritt, C. B., & Fowler, R. G. The pecuniary honesty of the public at large. *Journal of Abnormal and Social Psychology*, 1948, *43*, 90–93.

Milgram, S. The lost letter technique. *Psychology Today*, 1969, *3*(1), 30–33, 66–68.

Milgram, S. The experience of living in cities. *Science*, 1970, *167*, 1461–1468.

Milgram, S., Mann, L., & Harter, S. The lost-letter technique: A tool of social research. *Public Opinion Quarterly*, 1965, *29*, 437–438.

Murray, H. A. *Explorations in personality*. New York: Oxford, 1938.

Nietzsche, F. *Also sprach Zarathustra. Ein Buch für Alle und Keinen*. (4 parts) Leipzig: Naumann, 1899.

Nowlis, V. Research with the mood adjective check list. In S. S. Tomkins & C. E. Izard (Eds.), *Affect, cognition, and personality*. New York: Springer, 1965, Pp. 352–389.

Osgood, Ch. E., Suci, G. J., & Tannenbaum, P. H. *The measurement of meaning*. Urbana, Illinois: University of Illinois Press, 1957.

Piaget, J. *The moral judgment of the child*. New York: Harcourt, Brace, 1932.

Pongratz, J. M. Zur Ontogenese des sittlichen Urteils in besonderer Anknüpfung an die einschlägige Theorie Piaget's. Doctoral thesis, University of Heidelberg, 1964.

Quadfasel, F. Die Methode Fernald–Jacobsohns, ein Methode zur Prüfung der moralischen Kritikfähigkeit—und nicht des sittlichen Fühlens. *Archiv für Psychiatrie und Nervenkrankheiten*, 1925, *74*, 1–18.

Reykowski, J. Cognitive development and prosocial behavior. *Polish Psychological Bulletin*, 1977, *8*, 35–45.

Reykowski, J., & Jarymowicz, M. Elicitation of the prosocial orientation. Paper presented at the general meeting of the European Association of Experimental Social Psychology, April 1975, Bielefeld (Germany).

Riebesel, P. Untersuchungen über das Moralitätsalter. *Zeitschrift für pädagogische Psychologie*, 1917, *18*, 376–385.

Rotter, J. B. A new scale for the measurement of interpersonal trust. *Journal of Personality*, 1967, *35*, 651–665.

Russell, B. *Philosophy*. New York: W. W. Norton & Co., 1927.

Sander, H. Die experimentelle Gesinnungsprüfung: Ihr Aufbau und ihre Methodik. *Zeitschrift für angewandte Psychologie*, 1920, *17*, 59–109.

Schaefer, M. Elemente zur moral-psychologischen Beurteilung Jugendlicher. *Zeitschrift für pädagogische Psychologie*, 1913, *14*, 47–59, 90–98.

Scheler, M. Zur Phänomenologie und Theorie der Sympathiegefühle und von Liebe und Hass. Halle: Max Neimeyer, 1913. Later published as *Wesen und Formen der Sympathie*, Bonn: Friedr. Cohen, 1923.

Schmitt, R. Uber Verlauf und Bedingungen der Entwicklung des moralischen Urteils bei Kindern vom Lande und aus der Stadt. Masters thesis, University of Münster, 1963.

Schopenhauer, A. *Preisschrift über die Grundlage der Moral*. Frankfurt A. M.: Joh. Christ. Hermannsche Buchhandlung, 1841. Second ed. Leipzig: Brockhaus, 1860.

Schwebcke, A., Lück, H. E., & Jandron, E. Probleme und Erfahrungen der Adaptation fremdsprachiger Tests. *Psychologische Beiträge*, 1973, *15*, 434–470.

Silverman, J. Non-reactive methods and the law. *American Psychologist*, 1975, *30*, 764–769.

Stern, W. *Das Wesen des Mitleids*. Berlin: Dümmlers, 1903.

Wellek, A. *Die Polarität im Aufbau des Charakters: System der Charakterkunde.* Bern and München: Francke, 1950.

Wispé, L. Sympathy and empathy. In D. L. Sills (Ed.), *International encyclopedia of the social sciences,* Vol. 15. New York: Macmillan, 1968, Pp. 441–447.

Wispé, L. Positive forms of social behavior: An Overview. *Journal of Social Issues,* 1972, *28,* 1–19.

Wispé, L., & Freshley, H. Race, sex, and sympathetic helping behavior: The broken bag caper. *Journal of Personality and Social Psychology,* 1971, *17,* 59–65.

Wispé, L. G., Kiecolt, J., & Long, R. E. Moods and helping revisited: A failure to confirm. *Social Behavior and Personality,* 1977, *5* (in press).

Wormser, R. Nicht-verbale Kommunikation. *Psychologie heute,* 1975, *2*(7), 50–53.

Wundt, W. *Ethik.* Stuttgart: Enke, 1892. 2nd rev. ed.

11

Prosocial Behavior
and Its Discontents[*]

SASHA R. WEITMAN

The central point that will be elaborated on in this chapter is that the broad category of activities that I call *social behavior properly so-called (PSC)*[1]—and that includes, among others, the kinds of "prosocial be-

[1] The term "social" means one thing in ordinary English and quite another in the lingo of American social scientists. In ordinary English, "social" connotes gregariousness, affability, accessibility, neighborliness, friendliness, hospitality, warmth, concern for the welfare of others—in brief, qualities that facilitate association or result from it. In the terminology of American social science, on the other hand, the concept has been diluted and transformed beyond recognition to encompass all interactions and products thereof involving "meaningful mutual orientation" on the part of those involved. (Note, first, that in this peculiar social science sense virtually *all* human interactions and their products are "social," with the possible exception of traffic accidents, which result precisely because of absence of meaningful mutual orientation. Note, secondly, that in this same sense no interaction between animals can ever be social, since they are incapable of meaningful orientations.)

To distinguish between these two meanings, I refer to social behavior *properly so-called* by the "PSC" suffix.

229

* I wish to thank *Archives Européennes de Sociologie* for kindly allowing me to reprint certain (edited) sections from "Intimacies: Notes toward a Theory of Social Inclusion and Exclusion," 1970, *11*, 348–367.

havior" with which this book is concerned—is composed of activities all of which are profoundly and inescapably paradoxical and are therefore problematic. This paradoxical nature of social behavior PSC, and the social problems to which it gives rise, stem from its characteristic *multivalence*.[2] That is, the valence of social behavior PSC to those for whom it is intended is very different from its valence to those for whom it is not intended. Not only are these valences different in absolute value, they are even of opposite sign. Thus, social behavior PSC that is positive to those for whom it is meant is ipso facto negative—or, at the very least, potentially negative—to others who were not taken into account. If so, it follows that "prosocial behavior" is not the unambiguously positive social good it is often assumed to be. Nor is it at all simple to practice it in such a way as to avoid boomeranging effects of one type or another.

A pair of examples should suffice to illustrate the point. On the interpersonal level, anyone who has brought up siblings knows that it is by no means easy to do something nice on behalf of one of them without automatically causing the other(s) to feel jealous and to react accordingly.

The vicissitudes of prosocial behavior at the societal level are not as plainly distinguishable, but they are potentially far more devastating. To take a famous example, the revolutionary unrest that swept through French society during the latter part of the eighteenth century and was capped by the Great Revolution of 1789 was *not* stirred up, as is still widely assumed, by a reactionary regime's callous unresponsiveness to the miseries of its people. Quite on the contrary, the Great Revolution was preceded by successive socially responsible royal cabinets that tried by all manners and means to alleviate the misery of the people, to spread the burden of taxation more equitably, to improve social services, and so forth. Instead of achieving these objectives, however, the socially melioristic activism of the royal government resulted mostly (a) in awakening in the lower classes unrealistic expectations that the old regime could not begin to fulfill; (b) in bringing out in the open and exacerbating beyond hope of reconciliation conflicts that had hitherto been more or less latent, such as those between town and country, between nobility and upper bourgeoisie, between Paris and the provinces, between the upper and the lower clergy, and so forth; and finally (c) in

---

[2] The term *multivalence* is used to avoid confusion with the psychoanalytical term *ambivalence*, which refers to inner conflicts and is limited to two valences, pro and con. *Multivalence* refers to an objective, external reality: the constellation of feelings *others* harbor toward a given conduct or person. The term multivalence also allows for as many kinds of valence as there are relevant others.

causing the entire ship of State to be brought to a condition of total discredit and virtual paralysis. It is thus that social reforms, instead of averting revolution, may become their principal cause (de Tocqueville, 1856/1955).

Likewise, though closer to home, the dismal failure of most of the "Great Society" programs of the Kennedy–Johnson era and the extraordinary social turmoil to which these programs gave rise resulted largely from government reformers' ignoring this basically multivalent nature of what, to them, must have also seemed unambiguously "prosocial"—and therefore unquestionably positive—policies. But it was clear at the outset that the massive and spectacular publicity with which the federal administration sought to extend compensatory privileges to hitherto disenfranchised sections of the American public (in particular to blacks) was bound to arouse, as indeed it did arouse, passionate expectations and rancorous animosities in other sections of that public. For example, some, such as Puerto-Ricans and Chicanos, American Indians, women, homosexuals, prison inmates, and the physically handicapped, felt grossly neglected by the new social policies. Others felt unjustly taken advantage of, such as Italian Americans, Irish Americans, American Jews, etc., and still others felt directly threatened by the new social policies, like Southern whites, of course, but also middle-class suburbanites in general, the unionized crafts, etc. As a consequence, the overall impact of all those prosocial federal programs on behalf of the black minority resulted in (a) considerable frustration coupled with relatively little material benefit for that minority; (b) the arousal of increasing numbers of increasingly intransigent groups and subgroups whose strident demands could be neither met nor even muffled; and, worst of all, (c) a generalized revulsion on the part of the public at large against all this social ferment as well as against the prosocial reforms that had provoked it, a reaction that was clearly expressed in the election, and in the subsequent landslide reelection, of a crypto-fascist national leadership.

Additional examples of prosocial efforts gone sour could be multiplied at will and can be gleaned from virtually every sphere of life, from the most modest to the loftiest. The important thing about all these examples is *not* to draw the wrong conclusions from them. The wrong conclusion would be to think that all melioristic efforts at reform are doomed, that since humans are inveterately ungrateful creatures bent, like the proverbial snake, on biting the hand that feeds them, there is therefore no point in doing anything positive on their behalf. Such a conclusion would be not only nihilistic but also thoroughly fallacious. A more appropriate conclusion, the one I propose should be drawn from this paper, is that no matter how well-intentioned, prosocial behavior is *liable* to be as upsetting and destructive as is "antisocial" behavior. Consequently, *great care must be exercised to introduce it and to manage it in such a manner as to minimize the chances of its backfiring.* Put differently, successful prosocial policies and successful prosocial behavior *are* possible, but on condition that their essentially multivalent nature be properly understood and duly taken into account.

Porcupines, it has been said, must make love *very carefully.* The point of the examples given is that we humans can ill afford to be any less careful in our own effusions. The pages that follow will attempt to explain why this is so and what precautions must therefore be taken.

AN ELEMENTARY THEORY OF SOCIAL BEHAVIOR PSC

French ethnologists have conceptualized social bonds and, indeed, the whole of social life PSC as created and continually maintained by repeated acts of generosity, even by sacrificial acts (Lévi-Strauss, 1949–1969; Mauss, 1967). The most spectacular illustration of this proposition is provided by the potlatch of the Indians of northwestern America—those Indians of Alaska and of the Vancouver region whom Lévi-Strauss describes as evincing "a genius and exceptional temperament in their treatment of the fundamental themes of a primitive culture." But, he is quick to point out, we also continually reaffirm, reenact, and reillustrate in a myriad ways the profound truth of this general proposition. We do this, for example, when we send holiday presents to our relatives, when we send greeting cards to our neighbors and acquaintances, when we invite friends into our homes and treat them to extraordinary meals, and when we socialize our earnings in the form of taxes and voluntary donations. But above all else, he adds, we live out this principle when we raise our own children so that only others may profit from their labor and so that only others may enjoy them as friends, lovers, and spouses.

What I said in an earlier paper about intimacies (Weitman, 1970) bears a direct relationship to this general phenomenon. In effect, the strict prohibition against public displays of intimate affections resembles the taboo on incest, just as it resembles the norm against unrestrained exhibitions of extreme personal happiness in public places. The latent sentiment expressed by these and other such taboos and proscriptions may be called a "socialist" sentiment. This sentiment, the dynamics and potency of which have been far better understood and appreciated by those who lead men than by those who study them, is embodied in the principle that excess good fortune ought to be socialized, that the larger community should be allowed to share in it as well. The failure to heed this muffled yet extraordinarily powerful *demand for inclusion* is liable to arouse collective indignation, anger, and punitive retaliation. As Lévi-Strauss (1949–1969) put it with regard to the commission of incest, "the violent reaction of the community is the reaction of a community wronged." To which I would only add that this reaction is so automatic, so passionate, and potentially so devastating not just because any social norm has been broken, but because the particular norm that has been violated happens to be the norm against gratuitous acts of social exclusion. Or, to be a little more precise still, the norm that has been violated is the norm against acts that make others *feel* excluded, the significant nuance here being—sociological "realists" of the orthodox Marxian variety notwithstanding—that men become more furiously aroused by the ostentatious display of acts of social exclusion than by the existence per se of such acts.[3] In the case of intimacies, therefore, the community appears grudgingly to recognize the right of every member to indulge in exclusive affectionate relationships, but what it expects from him on such occasions—in fact, what it demands from him—is that he refrain from parading his ecstasy in the presence of others, so as spare them the vivid reminder of the relative misery of their own lot. Hence the moral distinction between high- and low-intensity acts of affection and the impassioned insistence that the former be scheduled in time and be segregated in space in such a manner as to be insulated from view and from hearing.

Let us elaborate what has just been stated into an elementary theory of social behavior PSC.

Proposition One (The Social Passions)

Proposition One of this theory is that human passions, particularly the social passions (that is, the passions whose objects of consummation are other people), tend to be aroused by, and in their turn tend to give rise to, processes of social inclusion and exclusion. Let me define the principal terms of this proposition before proceeding to elaborate it.

Passions are here defined as sentiments that distinguish themselves by their extraordinary intensity, their automaticity, their capacity to overwhelm, and their escalatory propensities. The extraordinary intensity of

---

[3] Marx and Engels subscribed to the absolute deprivation theory of revolution as well as to the relative deprivation theory, although they espoused them at different times, the former in 1848 and the latter in 1849, as shown by James Davies' article (1962).

passionate sentiments is what prompted Emile Durkheim (1933) to refer to them as *des états forts de la conscience*—potent mental states. Under their spell, men have a tendency to behave, to paraphrase Pascal's famous aphorism, as though the heart follows reasons that reason itself cannot follow. Passions are aroused *automatically*, which is to say that a deftly administered flattery, insult, or caress will activate them at once and in force, even against the recipient's better judgment. (It is this type of *sui generis* dynamism that Durkheim [1933] tried somewhat clumsily to convey through the adjective "mechanical.") Once passions have been activated, the urge for their expression or consummation is so *overwhelming* that they are likely to monopolize one's thoughts, to take command over one's mental faculties, and, on occasion, even to assume control over one's overt actions. Hence the common and rather disparaging designation of behavior carried out under their sway as "irrational" behavior.[4] Finally, passions, and the social passions in particular, distinguish themselves by their *escalatory propensities*, by which I mean that when people who feel them are provoked to action, the magnitude of the response these passions tend to call forth is not equivalent to that of the stimulus but is much larger. It is thus that a casual remark by A prompts B to riposte with a nasty insult that so stings A that he, in turn, cannot contain himself and slaps B across the face, which triggers such a rage in B that he assaults A with "intent to do bodily harm," as the lawbooks put it, and so on and so forth.

Passions, I said, tend to be aroused by acts of social inclusion or of social exclusion. By *acts of social inclusion* are here understood those activities whereby a person or group communicates to another person or group one or more of the following messages: "What I am (or have or do), you too may be (or may have or may do)"; or "The best of what I have is not good enough for you"; or "You are more worthy or (more attractive) than you or others think"; or "Let us join together and form a new entity, more integral and self-sufficient than either of us is without the other."

Processes of social inclusion consist of more or less complex sequences of mutual penetration and incorporation and are variously expressed in such familiar social activities as flirting, complimenting or flattering, honoring, introducing, initiating or debuting, exchanging gifts or secrets, promoting or electing to high office, taking into one's confidence, dancing together, hosting, eating together, playing together, corresponding,

---

[4] Passions have but one aim: their own exhaustion (Durkheim, 1933, Book 1, Chapter 2). Or, as Lewis Coser put it, they provoke conflicts (which he calls "nonrational") that "are not occasioned by the rival ends of the antagonists, but the need for tension-release of at least one of them [1956, p. 49]."

caressing, making love, singing, marching, traveling or vacationing together, marrying, living together, and so forth. One thing all these activities have in common is that they make people—or, rather, they are designed to make people—feel as though they have free and privileged access to certain highly valued social activities.

Conversely, the expression *acts of social exclusion* is used to denote the myriad ways and means that people throughout the ages have devised to make other people feel as though they have no access, or at best have only very restricted access, to these highly valued activities. More specifically, they consist of acts that communicate one or several of the following meanings: "What I am (or have or do), you are not and may not be (or do not and may not have, or cannot and may not do)"; or "What is good enough for me is too good for you"; or "You are less worthy or (attractive) than you and others think"; or "Go away (or I am leaving you): I am better off without you (or with someone else)."

Among the most common and least subtle of these processes of exclusion is, on the one hand, the entire gamut of *acts of expulsion*, such as demotion, dismissal, ceremonial degradation, execution, humiliation, excommunication, exile, imprisonment, mutilation, ostracism, insult, defamation, and commitment to a mental institution. And, on the other hand, there is the equally variegated range of *acts of obstruction to entrance*, as expressed, for example, in the withholding of appropriate keys or passwords; in the erection of walls, fences, barricades, and the display of signs that say things like "Private Property," "Beware of Dog," "No Loitering," and "Trespassers Will Be Prosecuted"; in the posting at entrances of border guards, policemen, immigration and customs officials, dogs, automatic alarm systems, bouncers, and concierges; in the imposition of age, citizenship, examinations, and other formal entrance requirements; and so on and so forth *ad nauseam*.

Now that the terms of Proposition One have been defined, let us return to it and make it more explicit. What this proposition maintains is that two of the fundamental kinds of processes through which the social passions are aroused are the processes of social inclusion and those of social exclusion. More specifically, what I am suggesting is that *processes of social inclusion tend to activate the associative passions*— which might also be called the "passions of social attraction," the "sympathetic passions," or the "prosocial passions," and under which are here subsumed, among others, such emotions as erotic love, filial and parental love, loyalty, friendship, patriotism, and fraternity. *Processes of social exclusion, on the other hand, tend to arouse the dissociative passions*—that is, the types of passions that could also be called the "passions of social rejection," the "antipathetic passions," the "anti-social passions," or the "passions of hostility," all of which subsume such emotions as contempt, detestation, repugnance, spite, hatred, alienation, resentment, envy, and jealousy.

Proposition Two (The Multivalence of Social Behavior)

We now come to Proposition Two of the theory, which derives from the observation that acts of social inclusion and acts of social exclusion are as inseparable as the two faces of a coin. More precisely, what Proposition Two claims is that *the very same activities that are, for those privileged to partake in them, unambiguous acts of social inclusion are at the same time liable to represent for those who are not so privileged equally unambiguous acts of social exclusion.* Thus, whenever colleague A invites colleague B for supper, he thereby runs the risk, unless he takes adequate precautions, of alienating his other colleagues, C, D, and E. Likewise, a person's love for his or her mate, insofar as it is an exclusive love, deprives other equally worthy mates of some of this love. (The same, incidentally, can be said of our relationship to our children.) When we bestow a medal on a soldier, we are thereby choosing not to bestow that medal on other soldiers who may think themselves no less brave and deserving. When we elect a candidate for office, we are thereby automatically rejecting his opponents. When we single out a friend and take him into our confidence, we are thereby deliberately choosing not to confide in our other friends.[5] This particular property, which seems to be unique and distinctive of acts of social inclusion, is what I referred to as the intrinsic *multivalence of human bonds.*

[5] Proposition Two may strike the reader as highly overstated. Various examples of acts of inclusion that do not on their face appear to also represent acts of exclusion may come to mind. The reader may conceivably be right. But, before I agree to such a conclusion, I would argue, first, that a pointed analysis of acts of inclusion would reveal that just about all such acts of inclusion are exclusive in one form or another, to some degree or another. Thus, even the most universalistic of the proselytizing religions (especially Christianity and Islam) require of their new members that they undergo a formal conversion that usually consists of reneging on membership in their previous religious group and of taking an oath of allegiance to their new faith. Second, I would argue that if so many acts of inclusion are indeed commonly carried out without provoking the antipathies of the excluded, it is only because the actual manner and context in which such acts of social inclusion usually take place are richly endowed with various and sundry palliative devices, most of which (like walls, for example) we take so much for granted as to be virtually blind to them, and all of which serve essentially the same function: to avoid creating "hard feelings" among those who have been left out. This theme is elaborated on in the next section.

Proposition Three (The Social Dysfunctions of Solidarity)

We now have all the elements needed to derive our third and, for the purposes of this paper, our central proposition. Because acts of social inclusion may also be acts of social exclusion (according to Proposition Two) and because these are liable to kindle and fan the meanest and most destructive of human passions (according to Proposition One), Proposition Three is now advanced to suggest that prosocial behavior in particular and *acts of social inclusion in general are potentially just as provocative of hostile retaliation as are "naked" acts of social exclusion.* Acts of social inclusion are therefore potentially just as dangerous. They can be dangerous, first of all, to insiders (that is, those included) in so far as they run the risk of being assaulted and injured by outsiders (that is, those excluded). Second, they can be dangerous to outsiders because any assault on insiders may well provoke, given the escalatory propensities of the passions, a much more devastating retaliatory blow by the insiders and their allies. Finally, acts of social inclusion can also be dangerous to the larger collectivity because the ever-widening circle of conflict they are liable to produce may disrupt ongoing cooperative activities of major importance as well as jeopardize the chances of future cooperative activities on which the collectivity's welfare, prosperity, and security might depend.[6]

SOCIETAL MANAGEMENT OF THE SOCIAL PASSIONS

With this last proposition I have reached the point at which my argument must either wander off into absurdity or else pay off with sociologically meaningful insights and propositions. I say wander off into absurdity because, if my theory is correct—if, in other words, simple acts of love and solidarity are really as fraught with perils as I have made them seem—then the next claim I might perhaps be expected to make is that the human species as we know it is unviable and that the fearsome combat of all against all is bound sooner or later to stop—indeed, that it should have stopped a long time ago—if only because of a lack of live combatants left to carry it on.

Although I am not prepared to make quite such a claim, I am prepared to suggest on the basis of the theory that *it is precisely because of the explosive potential of acts of social inclusion and exclusion that societies everywhere and at all times have developed an extraordinarily dense*

---

[6] This danger is especially present in segmentary-lineage societies, as is shown by Lloyd A. Fallers (1968).

network of prophylactic measures designed to prevent such acts from occurring and to bring them under control if and when they do occur. The types of mechanisms involved so pervade and structure life as we live it from day to day and are so intimately and profoundly enmeshed in even the most elemental of our habits that social scientists—to say nothing of ordinary laymen—implicitly assume them to be part of "human nature" and rarely think of seriously questioning their *raisons d'être.* However, neither our familiarity with these patterns of conduct nor their dismissal by public opinion as trivial constitute good grounds for ignoring their existence, taking them for granted, or discounting their sociological significance. Their importance was unmistakably recognized decades ago by Sumner, Durkheim, Simmel, and Freud and is now gradually being rediscovered in contemporary American sociology under the combined impact of current events, psychoanalysis, anthropology, and ethology.[7]

What I shall attempt to do, therefore, in the remaining pages of this chapter is to demonstrate, or rather to illustrate, how this theory provides what may be the organizing principle, the explanatory master key to a host of seemingly disparate customs, habits, norms, mores, laws, and institutions, all of which are seen here as mechanisms designed to achieve essentially the same broad functional objective: to prevent, by means of various containment strategies, inclusive–exclusive activities from provoking destructive outbursts of passionate hostilities.

There are, first of all, the various mechanisms of *privatization,* by which I mean essentially the same thing Merton (1957) and Rose Coser (1961) mean by the "insulation from observability of behavior"; these mechanisms consist simply of the removal of certain activities from the perception of those not invited to partake in them. The phenomenon of *intimacies,* alluded to earlier, is a clear instance of a set of activities that are, in one way or another, universally privatized. The *clothing* of nudity—or, rather, of what are believed to be erogenous zones—represents another obvious instance of privatization.

Privacy, I should emphasize, is ordinarily thought of as the right of a person against the encroachment of society. As it is conceptualized in this chapter, it is that, to be sure, but it is also *society's right,* that is to

---

[7] Significantly enough, it was not a sociologist but a "behavior physiologist," Konrad Lorenz, a student of ducks, fish, geese, and the like, who declared on the subject of "good" manners that "we do not, as a rule, realize either their function of inhibiting aggression or that of forming a bond. Yet it is they that affect what sociologists call 'group cohesion'." See his *On Aggression,* translated by Marjorie Kerr Wilson, New York: Harcourt, Brace, & World, 1966, p. 79.

say, *the right of others* not to have to be subjected to the sights and sounds of desirable experiences that they have not been invited to share. In short, walls, fences, curtains, venetian blinds, doors, and, generally, all the partitions erected to ensure privacy are just as necessary for those outside as they are for those inside.

The second category of mechanisms is that of *compensatory inclusion*. These are the numerous little ways by which we occasionally include people into our lives to compensate for our habitual exclusion of them. To this end, *rituals of hospitality* have evolved that command (a) that we invite them into our home at certain intervals; (b) that on such occasions we treat them spectacularly well, that is, substantially better than we would ordinarily treat our own selves at home; and (c) that we assure them before their departure that our home is open to them any time they wish to come by.

Another, no less striking compensatory inclusion mechanism is embodied in the *rituals of salutation*. Chance encounters between acquaintances are punctuated by more or less elaborate greeting rituals that may include (depending on the culture, social occasion, and statuses involved) such varied gestures as bowing, curtsying, kneeling, smiling, hat-tipping, glove-doffing, handshaking, hand-kissing, cheek-pinching, mouth-kissing, shoulder-gripping, bear-hugging, back-patting, ass-slapping, even ball grabbing, nose rubbing, joking, querying about one another's health, about close relatives, about business fortunes, and so forth, after which comes the entire gamut of departure rituals: again, handshakes, kisses, smiles, expressions of pleasure for having met, "good-bye," "shalom," "adieu," "take it easy," "best regards to every-one," and so forth.[8] Like the rituals of hospitality, these salutation rituals can be regarded as acts of temporary inclusion, during which people who are otherwise relatively indifferent to one another take time out, moved by a norm of *humanité oblige*, of ordinary social generosity, to acknowledge each other's existence, to express interest in one another, to honor one another, to wish the best to one another—in brief, to act *familiar* (i.e., inclusive) with one another.[9] It seems to me that the various gift-giving and donation rituals on the occasion of holidays also belong to this class of compensatory mechanisms of inclusion.

There is still another subclass of compensatory inclusion mechanisms

---

[8] For an ethological treatment of human greeting, see Eibl-Eibesfeldt (1968).

[9] For a different treatment of the subject of deference gestures, see Erving Goffman (1956). For an ethological analysis by a prominent anthropologist, see Raymond Firth (1971).

that differ from the ones above in that they belong to the realm of beliefs rather than to that of rituals. Most evident among these are *transcendental religions*—the "opiates of the people"—especially those religions that propound the Myth of Heaven and Hell, the myth that those who are excluded in this miserable world stand a good chance of being the included (the Elect) in the next world, which is, after all, the only important world, since it is the world of Eternal Life. The Hindu Myth of Reincarnation serves a similar sociological function. So does, to some extent, the secular Myth of Revolution. And so do the Jewish Myth of the Messiah and of the Chosen People, the Christian credo that "Blessed Are the Meek for They Shall Inherit the Earth," and the democratic Myth of Universal Equality, as expressed, for example, in the Horatio Alger myth that, with hard work, perseverance, and a little bit of luck *everyone* in America has a fighting chance to become as rich as the Rockefellers.

Closely related to these compensatory inclusion myths is the interesting subset of those that consist of the *glorification of the excluded*. It is thus that, in many modern societies, the lower and working classes—by definition the most excluded people in the society—have occasionally been glorified as the "real people" (*Le Peuple, Il Popolo*), as representing the marrow and essence of the nation, the finest it has to offer. Similarly, there have been numerous attempts to glorify, or at least to romanticize (though more ambivalently than in the case of the lower classes), such excluded categories of the population as armed outlaws (nowadays guerrillas) in their mountain hideouts, madmen confined to asylums, Jews, gypsies, Blacks, Indians, hustlers, bohemians, and so forth.

The third broad category of passion-containment mechanisms consists of *norms against nastiness*, that is, against gratuitous acts of exclusion, particularly when the acts are overt. Norms of this type are so numerous, so varied, and so commonplace that I shall mention only one of them here, the norm—in some societies it has the strength of a taboo—against the uttering of curses and insults. Two things about curses and insults are of particular interest in relation to our thesis. First, they are verbal stimuli whose one and only purpose is deliberately to provoke in others what I called earlier the antipathetic passions. Second, an analysis of these stimuli reveals that most of them consist of symbolic acts of exclusion. "To hell with you!", for example, exiles you to a very unpleasant place, and "son of a bitch!" excludes you (as well as your mother) from the species *Homo sapiens* and reclassifies you as a mere canine.

Fourth in the list of societal ways of managing passions there are the numerous safety-valve mechanisms that have long since been recognized as such by sociologists. These comprise, first of all, *role-reversal holidays and gatherings* such as Purim, Halloween, Queen-for-a-Day, wife-swapping parties, and the like, through which those who are ordinarily excluded become included, whereas those who are ordinarily included are excluded, and during which the former are accordingly licensed to behave as they wish with impunity for a limited period of time, usually a day or less. Second, there are the great *equal-access festivals*, such as the annual *bals masqués* (masquerade parties), Mardi gras celebrations, orgies, carnivals, and bacchanalia, in all of which the norm is for people who are ordinarily accessible to but a very few to become temporarily accessible to the many. Festivals of this sort have been known to last anywhere from one night to several days. Third, there are various *devices of hostility redirection*, the function of which is not so much the abatement of hostile reaction to exclusion, but rather its distraction from the real *agents provocateurs* and its redirection toward targets on which it can be more safely dissipated. Three such hostility-redirection devices are (*a*) competitive games, for instance, participation in sports, that provide one with the chance to exclude others from the rewards of triumph; (*b*) *dramatic spectacles*, whether athletic, theatrical, literary, pictorial, or cinematographic, the function of many of which is deliberately to arouse the emotions under relatively controlled conditions and allow them to be vented for brief stretches of time—the optimum duration for such cathartic exercises in Western societies ranges from 1½ to 3 hours—while at all times maintaining control over the spectators' overt behavior and keeping their passions focused on the symbolic representations of good and evil, rather than on good and evil as they operate on that other and larger dramatic stage on which all of us are actors; and (*c*) scapegoating, a device that provides the masses of the excluded with the twin opportunity to do some excluding of their own and at the same time to justify this cruelty by blaming all their miseries on their victims.[10] *Paranoidism*, that is, the deeply

[10] Jews, as everyone knows, have been the all-time favorite scapegoats of both Christian and Muslim societies. The principal reason for the Jews' extraordinary knack for eliciting the vilest hostilities against themselves is not their religion per se or their alleged historic role as Christ-killers, to say nothing of the other fantastic crimes attributed to them. Rather, their principal "crime" has been, and to this day continues to be, that they impress others as forming *relatively exclusive communities*—a "state within the state," as some of their more sophisticated detractors have been fond of saying. (This expression, incidentally, was coined by Richelieu in reference to Protestants, not to Jews.) Jews are *viewed* as exclusive—and, therefore, sociologically speaking, they *are* exclusive: They speak their own dialect; they follow their own customs; they worship their own God without any attempt at proselytizing their religion (that is, without any attempt at inviting others to join).

ingrained tendency to perceive sinister conspiracies behind every un-
explained contrariety of some importance, is also characteristic of the
systematically excluded and may be seen as a relatively benign form of
scapegoating.

Fifth in our list are the passion-framing mechanisms—the mechanisms of *institutionalization*—which consist of the imposition by the
collectivity of standardized molds on the kinds of passional outbreaks
whose incidence and prevalence are so great as to be generally accepted
as virtually ineradicable. Outbreaks of heterosexual love are thus
ritualized into dating and courtship, formalized into engagement, and
legally framed into marriage.[11] Similarly, grave cases of antagonism and
hostility are hurriedly pressured into the formal harness of duels, jousts,
blood feuds, or legal suits, all of which serve essentially not only to
frame the incipient conflict and prevent it from spreading to other
parties but also (and no less importantly) to pump out of it, via the
insistence on rigid adherence to ritual procedures, much of the emotional fuel that helped ignite it in the first place. This double aim is
achieved, interestingly enough, not by entirely insulating the two
antagonists but by fetching a third ("outside") party and involving him
in the conflict. To be acceptable to the antagonists as well as effective in
resolving their conflict, this third party must be viewed not only as
impartial but also as *emotionally neutral*. Each antagonist, in vying for
the third party's support, must therefore defuse his appeals of their

---

They are also exclusive in that they are endogamous, in that they take pride in
themselves as a nation, and in that they appear to be always ready to assist one
another in times of hardship, without regard to the national and geographical
boundaries separating them from their brethren. In short, and this is the only
reason for this lengthy digression, the tragic fate of the Jewish nation in exile
illustrates, more tellingly than any other historical example I can think of, the
profound perils of social solidarity (see Proposition Three of the theory). This is
the terrible predicament that has plagued and haunted the Jewish people for
centuries and that triggered the rise of the Zionist movement as a self-conscious
and deliberate effort to, if you will, "privatize" Judaism by gathering the scattered
fragments of the Jewish nation and *erecting solid walls around it*—walls that not
only would provide Jews with a fighting chance to repel the onslaughts of anti-
Semites but also should contribute substantially to the removal of the root causes
of anti-Semitism itself. I might add, therefore, that the widely cherished hope, even
among some Jews, that *ignorance* is the root cause of anti-Semitism—and that,
therefore, only the spread of education can stamp it out once and for all—is as
naive and futile as would be the homologous belief that ignorance is at the root of
jealousy and that only a better education can becalm the murderous passions of
the cuckold.

[11] For a marvellously Pirandellian exposition of this process of societal intervention, see Philip Slater (1963).

passional content and base them on general principles acceptable to all.[12] The proliferation of specialized conflict-mediating agencies such as arbitration panels, government-appointed mediators, courts of law (civil as well as criminal), and parliamentary bodies constitutes one of the hallmarks of the modern rational society.

Sixth and last of the mechanisms of passion containment examined in this essay are those that aim at the *devaluation* of the passions. Despite being the most innocuous, or perhaps precisely because they are the most innocuous, these are probably the most reliable and effective of all the mechanisms considered. They consist of all the linguistic, cognitive, and normative devices whereby inclusion–exclusion activities, as well as the passions they arouse and through which they themselves are brought into being, are morally denigrated and intellectually trivialized as "childish," "in poor taste," "degrading," "immature," and "ugly."

It is thus that the most obvious stimulants and methods of love tend to be publicly ignored, as though by some tacit gentlemen's agreement, and that the mere mention of them in public, to say nothing of their actual exposure, is nervously and impatiently dismissed. The ban on them in our culture has been so powerful, in fact, that they are not even legitimate subjects on the agenda of the academic social sciences, on the presumptive grounds that they are, as topics, insignificant at best and vulgar, frivolous, and pornographic at worst. The same applies, though to a substantially lesser degree, to the arts and letters, which prompted no less than Freud to puzzle over the fact that "the genitals themselves, the sight of which is always exciting, are nevertheless hardly ever judged to be beautiful; the quality of beauty seems, instead, to attach to certain secondary sexual characters [1930–1962, p. 30]."

As for the exclusive activities that arouse the antipathetic passions, as well as for these passions themselves, a similar fate befalls them. The man who has been insulted, assailed, and spat upon by another is immediately surrounded and soothed by his friends and subjected to repeated and insistent advice not to make "a mountain out of a molehill," not to "stoop" to the other man's level, not to "get into the gutter" with him. In a word, he is enjoined to realize that the spittle on his face is not so much his problem as it is the other man's. Restraints of this type are, it is true, particularly potent in contemporary middle-class circles, but they do, nevertheless, seem to operate to one degree or another in all societies.

---

[12] The classic treatment of the sociological significance of the third party is, of course, in Georg Simmel (1950).

LESSONS FROM THE THEORY:
THE MANAGEMENT OF PROSOCIAL REFORMS

The two main lessons to be drawn from the preceding analysis with regard to prosocial behavior are the following. First, in order to be effective, the application of prosocial behavior must take into account the potentially exclusionary interpretations to which it is predictably liable in certain quarters. It follows, second, that serious prosocial efforts, whether on a modest or on an ambitious scale, *require* for their success that they be coupled with appropriate mechanisms of passion-containment of the kind that societies themselves have spontaneously evolved through the millennia, including those that were discussed in the preceding section.

These lessons are not particularly original, and they have been intuitively well understood by most ruling classes. Traditional aristocracies, for example, have benefited from substantial exclusive privileges. As everyone knows, the maintenance of these privileges is dependent not just, nor even mainly, on the aristocracy's police powers. Of far greater significance is the *tacit acceptance* by most of the public (that is, by the excluded) of these exclusive privileges.[13] How is this acceptance achieved and maintained? Precisely by means of the unsparing use of a host of passion-containment mechanisms of the sort that were just discussed. It is thus that the vast array of aristocratic privileges are carefully *insulated* (physically of course, but also cognitively), elaborately *justified* (e.g., by myths of racial superiority and by functional theories of stratification), culturally *devaluated* (e.g., by norms that trivialize the significance of material possessions and exaggerate that of spiritual qualities), and symbolically *compensated* (e.g., via competitive sports, role-reversal myths, and rituals).[14]

[13] It was one of Simmel's and Weber's major contributions to sociology that they insisted that the cornerstone (and mystery) of all structures of power lay not in the characteristics of the power-wielder himself or in his conduct, as is widely assumed, but in the ready acceptance by others of the power-wielder's right to command. This ready acceptance, in turn, is not based on fear of negative sanctions, as is also commonly assumed, but on positive belief systems that legitimate and support the power-wielder's right to expect obedience to his commands.

The same principle applies directly to class privileges and to kindred structures of exclusion. The significant thing about social structures in which certain groups benefit from substantial exclusive privileges at the expense of everyone else is that these privileges are accepted—and quite frequently they are actively supported and ardently defended from attack—*by the very people who are excluded from them!*

[14] We are now in a position to clarify the allusion made at the start of this chapter concerning the revolutionary impact of social reforms in France at the end of the old regime. My thesis is not that it was the central government's reformist activ-

What all the preceding suggests, therefore, is that the least we can do for prosocial programs and policies on behalf of the *underprivileged* is to ensure that these programs and policies are just as well coupled with mechanisms of passion-containment as are the programs that benefit the *privileged* classes. To achieve this aim, however, two prerequisites must be met. First, *we must be able to predict the antagonistic reactions to which such programs are liable.* This in turn requires (*a*) that we identify beforehand the relevant persons and groups that are not covered by the prosocial measures is question; and (*b*) that we determine their respective predispositions to construe such inclusive acts on behalf of others as exclusive toward themselves.[15] Second, we must also be able to prevent or at least to control such reactions. For this, however, we need to achieve a better theoretical understanding than we now possess of precisely why, how, and under what conditions specific mechanisms of passion-containment do and do not work. The six types of mechanisms identified in the preceding section are a step in that direction, but they do not constitute a true typology, since they were not derived from the cross-classification of the basic relevant dimensions. Such a typology is

---

ism per se that radicalized French society. What I contend, rather, is that it was the social recklessness of the methods by which the royal ministers tried to push through their reforms that precipitated France toward revolution. Specifically, in their rationalistic zeal to introduce these reforms over and against the resistance of the nobility, the agents of the central government managed to undo the entire fabric of social and ideological mechanisms of passion-containment that had protected the nobility through centuries of (at times unconscionable) exclusionary practices. Conversely, the nobility fought back with equal or even greater social recklessness by exposing for all to see the central government's bureaucratic heavy-handedness, its pervasive corruption, its organizational ineptness and confusion, and so forth. Thus, the nobility in its turn subverted the social and ideological structures of passion-containment that had supported the royal government for centuries. And as a result of this protracted process of mutual discreditation—which grew in intensity and in publicity during the reigns of Louis XV and XVI—*the entire monumental and intricate edifice of social and ideological structures of passion-containment was irreversibly undermined,* and the subsequent collapse of the old regime and the ensuing revolution became virtually foregone conclusions. For an elaboration of this thesis, see Sasha R. Weitman, 1968 (especially chapters 2, 4, and 8).

[15] Just as there are marked differences among individuals in their propensity to be jealous, so it is with groups and even with entire societies. In some, there is a greater likelihood than in others to construe as exclusive acts that are only meant to be inclusive of others. This differential predisposition to paranoid interpretations and responses is a function of at least three factors: (*a*) *a history of exclusion* (on the level of the individual, see Edwin Lemert, 1962); (*b*) *certain structures of domination,* especially the divide-and-rule variety; and (*c*) *the insufficiency and inadequacy of passion-containment mechanisms* to mitigate against the impact of the aforementioned.

yet to be constructed. Likewise, the fit between specific kinds of inclusive–exclusive activities on the one hand, and the corresponding effective passion-containment mechanisms on the other, is to be demonstrated and explicated. These topics will be taken up in subsequent writings.

REFERENCES

Caplow, T. *Two against one: Coalitions in triads*. Englewood Cliffs, New Jersey: Prentice-Hall, 1968.

Coser, L. *The functions of social conflict*. Glencoe, Illinois: Free Press, 1956.

Coser, R. L. Insulation from observability and types of social conformity. *American Sociological Review*, 1961, *26*, 28–39.

Davies, J. Toward a theory of revolution. *American Sociological Review*, 1962, *27*, 5–6.

Durkheim, E. *The division of labor in society* (G. Simpson, trans.). New York: MacMillan, 1933.

Eibl-Eibesfeldt, I. Zur Ethologie des menschliches Grüssverhaltens. *Zeitschrift für Tierpsychologie*, 1968, *25*, 727–744.

Fallers, L. A. Political sociology and anthropological study of African societies. In R. Bendix (Ed.), *State and society: A reader in comparative political sociology*. Boston, Massachusetts: Little, Brown, 1968.

Firth, R. Postures and gestures of respect. In J. Pouillon & P. Maranda (Eds.), *Echanges et communications: Mélanges offerts à Claude Lévi-Strauss*. The Hague: Mouton, 1971.

Freud, S. *Civilization and its discontents* (J. Strachey, ed. and trans.). New York: Norton, 1962.

Goffman, E. The nature of deference and demeanor. *American Anthropologist*, 1956, *58*, 473–502.

Lemert, E. Paranoia and the dynamics of exclusion. *Sociometry*, 1962, *25*, 2–20.

Lévi-Strauss, C. *The elementary structures of kinship* (J. Bell, J. von Sturmer, & R. Needham, eds. and trans.). Boston, Massachusetts: Beacon Press, 1969.

Lorenz, K. *On aggression* (M. Wilson, trans.). New York: Harcourt, Brace, and World, 1966.

Mauss, M. *The gift: Forms and functions of exchange in archaic societies* (I. Cunnison, trans.). New York: Norton, 1967.

Merton, R. The role-set. *British Journal of Sociology*, 1957, *8*, 114.

Schwartz, B. The social psychology of privacy. *American Journal of Sociology*, 1968, *73*, 741–752.

Simmel, G. *The sociology of Georg Simmel* (K. Wolff, ed. and trans.). Glencoe, Illinois: Free Press, 1950.

Slater, P. On social regression. *American Sociological Review*, 1963, *28*, 351–356.

de Tocqueville, A. *The old regime and the revolution* (S. Gilbert, trans.). New York: Doubleday, 1955.

Weitman, S. Bureaucracy, democracy, and the French Revolution. Unpublished doctoral dissertation, Washington University in St. Louis, 1968.

Weitman, S. Intimacies: Notes toward a theory of social inclusion and exclusion. *Archives Europeennes de Sociologie*, 1970, *11*, 348–367.

III

SOME CRITICAL
CONSIDERATIONS

12

The Ethics of Helping People*

B. F. SKINNER

I

We sometimes act for the good of others. We feed the hungry, clothe the naked, and heal the sick. We say that we care for them, provide for their needs, do good to them, help them. But this behavior often has unforeseen consequences that need to be taken into account.

We presumably help people in part for reasons that concern the survival of the species. Maternal behavior is a kind of help that is either part of an organism's genetic equipment or quickly acquired because of a genetic susceptibility to reinforcement; it is obviously important for survival. The human species is presumably more likely to survive if people generally help each other or are naturally reinforced by signs that they have done so. Something of this sort may contribute to the behavioral disposition that is part of what we call love or compassion.

* This article first appeared in *The Humanist* January/February 1976 and is reprinted by permission.

It is more obvious that we learn to help or do good and that we learn because of the consequences that follow. We sometimes help because we find the helplessness of others aversive. We help those who help us in return, and we stop doing so when they stop—when, as we say, they are ungrateful. We often fail to help those who are too weak to reciprocate or to protest effectively when we fail to help. The very young, the aged, the infirm, the retarded, and the psychotic are classic examples of people who have often been not only not helped out also mistreated.

We may also help others because in doing so we further the survival of the group to which we belong. A social environment (a "culture") may induce us to give help even though we gain nothing directly from the advantage for the group. Thus, we may be a Good Samaritan at some personal sacrifice, and the group supplies overriding reasons for doing so, with practices that have been selected simply because they have contributed to its survival. It plays such a role when it steps in to guarantee adequate care for the young, the aged, the infirm, the retarded, and the psychotic. There are few if any behavioral processes that provide for such care in the absence of a disposing social environment, with the possible exception of such genetic considerations as the care of the very young.

The sanctions arranged by a group are often treated in a different way. They are "justified" as defending individual *rights,* as guaranteeing that people shall get what they deserve or what is fair or just. It was perhaps easiest to justify helping those who were most in need of help, but in many cultures people are now said to have the right not only to life, liberty, and the pursuit of happiness, but also to a share in the common wealth. "To each according to his [or her] need" was St. Augustine's program before it was Karl Marx's, and it is still a program rather than an achievement; but it also suggests the extent to which groups are now engaged in the business of making sure that their members help each other. The program is not without problems of an ethical nature. In solving them, all the consequences of an act of help must be considered. The following discussion deals with certain possibly relevant behavioral processes.

II

To begin with a very simple example, we may not really help others by doing things for them. This is often the case when they are learning to do things for themselves. We watch a child tying a shoelace and grow jittery, and to escape from our jitteriness we "help" the child tie the lace. In doing so we destroy one chance to learn to tie shoe laces.

Comenius made this point nearly 400 years ago when he said that "the more the teacher teaches, the less the student learns." The metaphor of "communication," or the transmission and receipt of information, is defective at just this point. We ask students to read a text and assume that they then know what they have read, but effective communication must provide for the so-called "acquisition of knowledge, meaning, or information." A traditional method has been to repeat what is said, as in a verbose text, but new methods in which textual help is progressively withdrawn have emerged in the field of programmed instruction. The aim is to give as little help as possible so that readers say things for themselves.

By giving too much help we postpone the acquisition of effective behavior and perpetuate the need for help. The effect is crucial in the very profession of helping—in counseling and psychotherapy. Therapists, like teachers, must plan their withdrawal from the lives of their clients. One has most effectively helped others when one can stop helping them altogether.

III

More serious unanticipated effects of the good we do to others often arise because goods function as reinforcers. It has long been known that behavior is affected by certain kinds of consequences. That is why rewards and punishments are such well-established social measures. The Utilitarians proposed to quantify consequences in terms of pleasure and pain, for social purposes. For example, the pleasure enjoyed as the reward of unethical or illegal behavior was to be offset by a corresponding amount of pain administered as punishment. Both rewards and punishments were regarded as compensation, and, when they were fairly balanced, the ethical account was closed.

This formulation neglected certain contingent relations between behavior and its consequences that were recognized by the American psychologist, Edward L. Thorndike, in his Law of Effect. By *effects* he also meant feelings, but they were more than compensation; they strengthened the connection between behavior and the situation in which it occurred. The strengthening effect of reinforcement has been an important consideration in the experimental analysis of operant behavior. Extremely complex environments are constructed in which reinforcing consequences are contingent upon both behavior and the setting in which it occurs, and the effect upon the probability that a given instance of behavior will occur upon a given occasion is analyzed.

The fact that strength in the sense of probability of occurrence is an important property of behavior has come to be understood only very slowly. With respect to the present issue, an important point is that strength is not related in any simple way to quantity of reinforcers and therefore not in any simple way to the help we give or the good we do to others, as these are traditionally evaluated. We need to consider the possibility that strength of behavior is more important than the receipt or possession of goods.

IV

Those who are in a position to help others by giving them things can use these things as contingent reinforcers. This is, of course, the point of behavior modification. The right to change the behavior of others in this way has been challenged on ethical grounds, as we shall see, and Carl Rogers has suggested that the help given by the therapist (and one could also say teacher or friend) should be made carefully *non*contingent on the behavior of the recipient. Unfortunately, reinforcers are always temporally contingent on some behavior, and they are effective even though there is no causal connection. Adventitious reinforcements build superstitions. For example, whatever people are doing just before rain falls at the end of a drought they are more likely to do again in another drought. And, since the more conspicuous their behavior, the more effective the adventitious contingencies, a ritual such as a rain dance may emerge and, in turn, a myth to explain it—for example, such a myth as that of the propitiation of a Giver of Rain. The grace of God was defined by St. Paul as noncontingent upon works ("for if by works, then grace is no longer grace"), and Rogers is proposing essentially that therapeutic help should have this divine quality. But there are behavioral processes that cannot be denied, and offerings and sacrifices to the Giver of Help are an important problem for the therapist.

V

Unanticipated consequences that follow when we are said to give people help can be much more serious. In an environment in which such things as food, shelter, and safety are guaranteed as rights, these things are less likely to serve as reinforcers. The recipients of bountiful help are rather in the position of those who live in a benign climate or possess great wealth. They are not strongly deprived or aversively stimulated and hence not subject to certain kinds of reinforcement. Some important forms of behavior are never acquired or, if they have been acquired, are no longer exhibited. But such people do not simply do nothing; instead, they come under the control of lesser reinforcers. No objection is likely to be raised to the classic examples found in art, music, literature, and scientific exploration. Individuals are encouraged to devote themselves to these fields through the kind of help called patronage or grants-in-aid. But these reinforcing consequences are, unfortunately, seldom as immediate or as personally effective as others that have long given the leisure classes a special character. Sweets remain reinforcing to the nonhungry; alcohol and drugs have anomalous reinforcing effects; sexual reinforcement survives because we do not leave satiation to others; certain special schedules of reinforcement (such as those basic to all gambling devices) make weak reinforcers effective; and it is often reinforcing simply to watch other people living seriously or dangerously, as in films and television.

These are the reinforcers, rather than those of art, music, literature, and science, that are more likely to be given free play by any help that preempts the serious business of life, and there is little to be said for them. Some are stultifying, and none leads to the full development of the human genetic potential. One may spend a lifetime reinforced in these ways and undergo almost no important change, and, when these alternative reinforcers lose their power or are suppressed by societal rules, behavior falls to a very low ebb. We call the child who has been given excessive help "spoiled," and the term applies as well to the adult.

VI

Organisms are at least as strongly disposed to take goods away from others as to supply them in the form of help, particularly when unmerited, and this disposition may serve as a natural corrective to excessive help. (We are inclined to speak of the feeling of compassion that accompanies helping others and the feeling of resentment that accompanies taking goods away from those who have not worked for them, but it is the tendencies to act that are involved here.) Aggressive behavior offsets or corrects compassionate help and may have survival value for either species or group if it leads to a more equitable distribution of goods, but *the question is not who should have how much of what but, rather, how they are to get what they have.*

The plight of those who are not often reinforced—because others do things for them, because they have not learned to do things for themselves, or because they are given the things by which they would otherwise be reinforced—is familiar enough. Traditionally, their behavior is attributed to feelings and states of mind. Such people are said to lack initiative, to show little strength of character, to have weak wills, to lack spiritual strength, or to have egos that are not well-developed. They are said to suffer from aboulia (lack of will), acedia (spiritual torpor), apathy (lack of feeling), or boredom. *What they are suffering from is a lack of positive reinforcement.*

It is easy to dismiss that statement as the idée fixe of a behavioral analyst, but strength of behavior, in the sense of the probability that behavior will occur, is a basic aspect of human nature. It is to be attributed to external contingencies of reinforcement rather than to internal deficiencies, and hence it is an aspect about which something can be done. In fact, something *is* being done by those who understand the importance of contingencies of reinforcement.

VII

A good example of the neglect of relevent aspects of the environment is to be found in analyses of incentive conditions in modern industry (Heilbroner, 1975). The "degradation of labor" is said to have begun with the systematic destruction of craft skills. Workers move from craft to industrial conditions for many reasons. Work is usually easier, and, because a task is divided among many workers, each share is simpler and can be learned during a briefer apprenticeship. Workers produce more in less time and can therefore be paid more. Yet, something has been lost. Many interpretations have appealed to feelings and states of mind: the worker has come to think of himself as "a cog in a machine"; he is no longer "the possessor of the accumulated knowledge of the materials and processes by which production is accomplished"; work has been reduced to "a series of bodily movements entirely devoid of meaning"; the worker is separated ("alienated") from the product of his labor; and so on. But why is this degrading? It is true that work on a production line is probably faster than the work of a craftsman without a deadline and, because it has been reduced in scope, necessarily more repetitious and hence likely to yield the fatigue of repeatedly doing the same thing (not to be confused with physical exhaustion). Yet the gambler "works" fast and repetitiously and calls his life exciting, and the craftsman uses machines to save labor when he can and often works with a time-and-motion efficiency that an industrial engineer would give much to duplicate. Craftsmen repeat themselves and work long hours.

The important difference lies in the contingencies of reinforcement. It is often supposed that industrial workers work to get a reward rather than to avoid punishment, but, as Marx and others have noted, they work because to do anything else would be to lose a standard of living maintained by their wages. They work under the eye of a supervisor upon whose report their continued employment depends. They differ from slaves only in the nature of the "punishment" they receive for not working. They are subject to *negative* reinforcement, a condition obscured by the uncritical use of the term "reward."

The craftsman, in contrast, is reinforced at every stage by those conditioned reinforcers called "signs of progress." A particular task may take a day, a week, a month, or a year, but almost every act produces something that will form part of the whole and is therefore *positively* reinforcing. It is this condition of "nondegrading" work that has been destroyed by industrialization, and some of those concerned with incentive conditions have used the principles of behavior modification to restore it.

VIII

A similar correction needs to be made to offset the unwanted by-products of helping others by supplying goods. Unfortunately, it is difficult to see this and to act accordingly just because our behavior in helping others is determined to such a large extent by reciprocal reinforcement. Given a choice between receiving something gratis and the opportunity to work to get it, those whom we help are likely to choose the former, and we are thus more abundantly reinforced when we help by giving them things. It is only in the long run that the advantage of getting rather than of possessing makes itself felt both by them and by us, and what happens in the long run does not often have much of an effect. What a person is said to deserve as a right is subject to a similar bias.

It is just at this point that behavior modification plays a unique role. This term needs careful definition. Behavior has been modified ever since it was modifiable—that is to say, from the beginning. Behavior is modified by the threat of the bully or of the nation with a nuclear stockpile, by incentive tax allowances, by advertising, by religious rituals, by state lotteries and other gambling enterprises, and recently by certain physiological measures and explicit Pavlovian conditioning. The term was introduced, however, to refer to certain applications of the experimental analysis of behavior, particularly through the arrangement of contingencies of positive reinforcement. Behavior modification in that sense helps people by arranging conditions under which they *get* things rather than *receive* things gratis. That is its essential feature, and for that very reason it was inevitable that there should be some conflict with traditional views of helping others—and especially with principles of what is just or fair or to be defended as the rights of the individual.

IX

The issue first arose when behavior modification was used in institutional care. In many cultures food, shelter, clothing, security, and possibly privacy have been made available to those who for any reason cannot obtain them otherwise. Homes for the very young, the aged, the infirm, and the retarded, hospitals for psychotics, and prisons are far from a benign world, but those who live in them characteristically have little reason to work for the basic reinforcers because the reinforcers have been guaranteed as rights. Most of the alternatives, such as gambling, sex, alcohol, and drugs, are not available (except surreptitiously in prisons), and as a result such people suffer all the ills of having nothing to do. They may be reinforced by mild troublemaking, and if possible they escape, but otherwise we say that their behavior tends to be marked by boredom, abulia, acedia, and apathy.

Behavior modification, properly defined as the applied analysis of behavior, is precisely what is needed to correct this shortcoming of institutional life *because it is concerned with establishing effective contingencies of reinforcement.* Actual practices need not be described here, but the behavior modifier usually begins with a search for available reinforcers and then arranges especially clear-cut contingencies, such as those involved with the use of tokens. Contingencies can be programmed to shape complex behavioral topographies and to bring behavior under the control of complex stimuli. For those who will eventually leave the institution, such a program is called educational, therapeutic, or rehabilitative; for those who must remain, the goal is simply a "prosthetic" environment—an environment in which people behave in reasonably effective ways despite deficiencies and in which they take an active interest in life and begin to do for themselves what the institution had previously done for them.

Whether we are concerned with education, therapy, and rehabilitation or with the construction of a prosthetic environment, we need those reinforcers that have acquired special power in the evolution of the species. Yet they are the very things supplied in the act of helping or caring for people—the things guaranteed as rights. In order to make them contingent on behavior in an institutional setting, we must withhold them until the behavior occurs. The individual must therefore be to some extent deprived and will appear to remain unhelped or to be denied certain rights. We cannot avoid this conflict so long as we continue to view help as providing goods rather than as arranging contingencies of reinforcement.

The conflict first came into the open in an attack upon operant reinforcement programs in mental hospitals. One set of proposed regulations contained the following:

> Deprivation is never to be used. No patient is to be deprived of expected goods and services and ordinary rights, including the free movement of his limbs, that he had before the program started. In addition deficit rewarding must be avoided; that is, rewards must not consist of the restoration of objects or privileges that were taken away from the patient or that he should have had to begin with. The ban against deficit rewarding includes the use of tokens to gain or regain such objects or privileges [Lucero, Vail, & Scherber, 1968, p. 232].

The authors insist that they are concerned with the legitimacy of the rationale for using operant conditioning, but it is the rationale of rights that is at issue. Why have these things been guaranteed to the patient? What "should" patients have had to begin with? The mistake is to generalize from those who cannot help themselves to those who can. For the latter, a much more fundamental right—the right to live in a reinforcing environment—must be considered. If the function of an institution is education, therapy, or rehabilitation, all available resources should be used to speed the process, and the strong reinforcers are undoubtedly to be classified as such. For those who will never return to the world at large, a strongly reinforcing environment is equally important.

Under proper contingencies many institutionalized people can engage in productive work, such as caring for themselves, keeping their quarters clean, and working in laundry, kitchen, or truck garden. But when these things have previously been done by paid personnel, suspicion falls on the motives of management. Should not residents be paid the same wages? One answer is that they should unless the contingencies are "therapeutic," but that raises in only a slightly different form the question of "help." Residents are receiving help when being reinforced in a prosthetic environment, although they are not necessarily being "cured." Especially when we consider the economics of institutional care, can there be any objection to an institution in which the residents themselves produce all the goods and services it was once supposed to be necessary for others to give them?

At least one state has recognized the issue. A bill was recently passed in Iowa with the provision that:

> The administrator may require of any resident of the County Care Facility with the approval of a physician reasonable and moderate labor suited to the resident's age and bodily strength. Any income realized through the labor of a resident together with the receipts from operation of the County Farm if one is maintained shall be appropriated for use by the County Care Facility in such manner as the Board of Supervisors may direct [*Behavioral Voice*, p. 18x].

The constitutionality of the bill is being questioned.

The so-called "rehabilitation" of the prisoner raises a special problem. Prisoners usually undergo very little useful change. They have been separated from society for the latter's protection or as punishment and are unable to help themselves only because they have been cut off from the usual means. The destructive changes that follow are well-known, and some promising results have been obtained from the application of an experimental analysis of behavior—for example, in a project at the National Training School for Boys in Washington, D.C. (Cohen & Filipczak, 1971). Unfortunately, experiments of this sort have been confused with efforts to change prisoners with drugs or with the more violent forms of aversive conditioning, and protests against the latter— for example, by the American Civil Liberties Union—have been extended without warrant to efforts to construct more sustaining prison environments.

Like everything else, operant conditioning can be misused. Management may solve some of its problems by arranging contingencies that suppress disruptive behavior and under which a child, a prisoner, or a psychotic may simply sit quietly and do little or nothing all day long. Even so, this may be better than achieving the same result through punishment, but both solutions may be challenged if nothing further is done. Much more can be done through the applied analysis of behavior, once the problem is understood.

X

Some of the same issues arise in the world at large, where helping people takes on a much broader meaning. Very little has ever been achieved by simply supplying goods and services. Governments do not help their citizens by *giving* them order and security—that is the claim only of the police state; they help them by arranging environments in which they behave in orderly and mutually supportive ways. They do not defend the rights of life, liberty, and the pursuit of happiness as things their citizens *possess;* they maintain environments in which people do not threaten the lives and political freedoms of each other. Schools and colleges do not *give* their students information, knowledge, or skills; they are environments in which students acquire informed and skillful behavior. The "good life" is not a world in which people *have* what they need; it is one in which the things they need figure as reinforcers in effective contingencies.

A case history will show how easily the basic issue is missed. After World War II Denmark entered upon a program of "modern reformatory guidance" to raise the standard of living of the Eskimos of Greenland (Jensen, 1973). Thousands of construction workers were sent in to build modern houses and facilities. But the local industry, fishing, could not support these material standards, and an annual subsidy of many millions of dollars will now be needed—indefinitely—for the 50,000 inhabitants. The goods supplied are not contingent on productive behavior, and it is not surprising that a long-established cooperative culture has broken down. Under the surface there is said to be an alarming chaos of human frustration. An antagonistic class society is developing. Good dyadic social relations have yielded to drunken brawls.

It means little to say that a high standard of living was an artifical creation, that it can be made natural by giving each person a more direct influence in government, or that a "strategy of wholeness" is needed. The trouble is that certain basic contingencies of reinforcement have been destroyed. And it is difficult to see how they can ever be restored except by greatly increasing the behavioral repertoires of the Eskimos or by sharply reducing their so-called "standard of living." It will not be enough that the teams of construction workers are now to be followed by teams of social workers. The United States is repeating the experiment on a small scale on the island of Bikini, and it will be interesting to see whether the result is the same.

XI

Even in the restricted sense of the applied analysis of behavior, behavior modification has grown with astonishing speed, and much of that growth has been uncharted and chaotic. Practitioners have ranged from scientists highly skilled in basic analysis to laymen applying a few cookbook rules. But the accomplishments are too substantial to be dismissed—among them, programmed instruction and contingency manage-

ment in the classroom, the design of prosthetic environments for
retardates and psychotics, personal and family counseling in ethical
self-management, educational environments for juvenile delinquents,
and new incentive systems in industry. In retrospect much of this often
seems to be simply a matter of common sense, but people have had
common sense for thousands of years and it has not helped them solve
the basic problem. It has been too easy to put possession ahead of
acquisition and to miss the importance of strength of behavior and its
relation to contingencies of reinforcement. In the classroom, hospital,
factory, prison, home, and the world at large the obvious fact is that
some of the good things in life are in short supply. We are just beginning
to see that a mere shortage is not what is causing trouble and that
people will not necessarily be helped by increasing the supply. Behavior modification through the management of contingencies of reinforcement is a special way of helping people just because it is concerned
with changing the probability that they will behave in given ways.

For just that reason it is now under attack. A recent example is the
report of the Erwin Committee, *Individual Rights and the Federal Role
in Behavior Modification*, based on a 3-year investigation of federal
support of a variety of programs. According to Senator Ervin, "The most
serious threat posed by the technology of behavior modification is the
power this technology gives one man to impose his views and values on
another. . . . If our society is to remain free, one man must not be em-
powered to change another man's personality (Ervin, 1974, p. iii)."
But individuals have always had the power to impose their views on
others; the relevant behavioral processes were not recently invented.
One of the greatest and certainly the most convenient of all reinforcers
is money, and we have recently seen some extraordinary examples of its
misuse. Why does the Ervin Committee not consider constitutional
safeguards against the power that a person can amass by accumulating
money? We have minimum wage laws and other laws restricting some
uses of money, but we have no maximum wage laws restricting the
extent to which money can be acquired for use. And money is only one
of the more conspicuous instruments of control. The experimental
analysis of behavior will, possibly, play its greatest role in forcing an
examination of *all* the ways in which "one man [can] change another
man's personality."

Like any other means of control—say, physical force—behavior modification should be supervised and restrained. The concept of the rights of
the individual is concerned with that problem. Some traditional principles have emphasized freedom from coercive or punitive control, and
they are as badly needed today as they have ever been. Other tradi-

tional principles have emphasized the possession of goods and services, and here a sweeping revision is needed. Neither a capitalist defense of private property nor a socialist program of state ownership as a means of equitable distribution takes into account the full scope of relevant behavioral processes.

It has been suggested that the Gross National Product should be subordinated to "Gross National Happiness" in evaluating a culture, but nothing much would be gained if happiness were identified as a static condition of satisfaction derived from the possession of goods. Indeed, in that case, there would scarcely be a distinction. The greatest good of the greatest number may be the greatest bore, and the Utilitarians lost their case just because they neglected the reinforcing contingencies that build the condition we describe by saying that we are happy.

The intense current interest in ethical, moral, legal, and religious matters is no doubt largely a response to worsening world conditions. A burgeoning population forces us to take another look at birth control, abortion, and selective breeding. Increasing violence, as in bombings, hijackings, and political kidnappings, forces us to look again at legal sanctions, possibly reversing a humane trend against capital punishment. In addition, however, a surprising number of critical issues have to do with what is called "helping" people. "Aid" is a synonym for "help," and foreign aid raises many ethical, moral, and legal problems. In the name of aid the United States has become one of the Zaharoff's of the last half of the twentieth century—one of the great munitions makers who were once held in utter contempt. In the name of aid we rescue some of the starving peoples of the world while allowing others to die, and we refuse to admit that we are practicing triage. With both military and nonmilitary "help" we have nearly destroyed Indochina. And so we begin again to ask to what extent the rich nations of the world are to help the poor or, in domestic affairs, how far a government should go in increasing the help that its rich citizens must give to its poor (see Rawls, 1971 and Nozick, 1974).

But it is a mistake to turn again to certain earlier principles. For reasons that in themselves illustrate a powerful behavioral principle, we have grossly overemphasized the importance of simple possession. Neither happiness nor the survival of the group depends on the satisfaction derived from having things. And the most generous help may fail as ignominiously as the most aggressive despoliation. Something else is needed to achieve conditions under which human beings will show the productivity, the creativity, and the strength, inherent in their genetic endowment, that are essential to the survival of the species.

REFERENCES

Behavioral Voice, Center for Human Development, Drake University, Des Moines, Iowa, Vol. II, Number 2, 1974. (The bill is called "The Redesignation of County Homes as County Care Facilities," HF659. The quotation is from Section 5.)

Cohen, H. L., & Filipczak, J. *A new learning environment*. San Francisco: Jossey-Bass Inc., 1971.

Ervin, S. *Individual rights and the federal role in behavior modification* (Report No. 5270–02620). Study prepared by the subcommittee on constitutional rights. Washington, D.C.: Government Printing Office, 1974.

Heilbroner, R. L. Review of Harry Braverman, *Labor and monoply capital: The degradation of work in the twentieth century* (New York: Monthly Review Press, 1974) in *New York Review*, January 23, 1975.

Jensen, B. Human reciprocity: An arctic exemplification. *American Journal of Orthopsychiatry*, 1973, *43*(2), pp. 447–458.

Lucero, R. J., Vail, D. J., & Scherber, J. Regulating operant-conditioning programs. *Hospital and Community Psychiatry*, 1968, *19*, pp. 232–233.

Nozick, R. *Anarchy, state, and utopia*. New York: Basic Books, 1974.

Rawls, J. *A theory of justice*. Cambridge: Belknap Press of Harvard University Press, 1971.

13

Dilemmas of Professional Helping: Continuities and Discontinuities with Folk Helping Roles

PETER LENROW

Painful dilemmas confront members of the "helping professions." Contrary to popular ideals of help flowing effortlessly from a benevolent authority or coolly dispensed by a technical expert, entering into a relationship with someone in a way that is helpful is fraught with conflicts for the professional as well as for the client. The recurrent experiences of conflict, anguish, and perplexity can sharpen the helper's appreciation of similar experiences of the client. But they can also lead the helper to avoid the dilemmas of his own role and become insensitive to those of other people. Awareness of these problems may permit the helper to recognize when he is trying to escape discomfort in his role rather than serving the client. But besides being aware of the problem, we also need to ask: What are the sources of the dilemmas that face professional helpers? Are they resolvable? Are there ways to redefine professional roles in order to cope more effectively and responsibly with such dilemmas?

After examining available answers to these questions and finding them wanting, I have come to look outside the domain of thinking about professional training and practice in order to bring a larger perspective to such questions. In this chapter, I explore what light we can throw on them by examining helping in ordinary, everyday social interaction. More specifically, I ask to what extent the dilemmas of professional helpers can be understood as common to generic forms of helping as we find them in folk helping roles.

ISOLATION OF THINKING ABOUT
PROFESSIONAL AND FOLK HELPING ROLES

The study of helping has been pursued in two areas in virtual isolation from one another. One is the examination of training and practice in the various helping professions: counseling and psychotherapy, teaching, human relations and organizational consulting, social planning, and health care. The second is the study of helping among "ordinary" people as distinguished from professional helpers.

The study of professional helping includes much unpublished lore and wisdom handed down in training and supervision by experienced practitioners. It is also pursued in a literature that includes systematic theories of helping (cf. Kelly, 1955; Menninger, 1958; Rogers, 1959), hypotheses of more limited scope about crucial processes in helping (cf. Rogers, 1957; Hobbs, 1962; Erikson, 1963; Schein, 1969), research on outcomes of helping efforts (cf. Eysenck, 1952; Rosenzweig, 1954; Marrow, Bowers, & Seashore, 1967; Klaus & Gray, 1968), attempts to identify and illustrate helping processes in particular cases (cf. Freud, 1905; Rogers, 1942; Sarason et al., 1966; Argyris, 1970), hypotheses about psychological processes in the helper (cf. Freud, 1912; Reik, 1937; Schafer, 1959; Truax & Carkhuff, 1969), and speculations about what would be wise in various difficult situations of professional practice (cf. Freud, 1912; Burton, 1959; Strupp, 1960; Jones, 1968).

The study of folk helping is much older, including as it does inquiries into the nature of altruism and sympathy in Classical Greece (cf. Plato, 1945; Aristotle, 1925) and since the Enlightenment (cf. Smith, 1759; Kant, 1785; Spenser, 1870; Scheler, 1922; Sorokin, 1950). Seminal cross-cultural studies on the exchange of gifts (Lévi-Strauss, 1949; Mauss, 1964) and rare naturalistic inquiries describing helping on the part of young children (Isaacs, 1933; Murphy, 1937) have been joined in the past 15 years by a wide variety of laboratory experiments (cf. Lenrow,

1965; Lerner & Simmons, 1966; Bryan, 1970),[1] experiments in field settings (cf. Bryan & Test, 1967; Macaulay, 1970; Darley & Latané, 1970; Wispé & Freshley, 1971), and case studies (London, 1970).

The isolation of the two areas of thinking stems mainly from unexamined assumptions implicit in the two areas of inquiry.[2] In much of the discussion about the helping professions there is an assumption that the problems faced by professionals are peculiar to their lot as professionals. This makes it less likely that professionals will look outside their work roles for explanations of their problems. In much of the work on everyday helping, there is an assumption that such inquiry gets at basic human capacities and that, when such knowledge is refined, it can eventually be "applied" by professional helpers, planners, policy makers, or other activists. Since such refined knowledge is not yet at hand, this assumption makes it unlikely that these researchers will give attention to what they see as problems of application by professional helpers.

Overcoming the isolation of these two areas of inquiry would be fruitful for both: Professional helpers may be better able to cope with some of their central concerns by viewing them as generic issues common to folk helping rather than as peculiarly professional problems; researchers on folk helping may find that, by examining professional helping as a special case of more general forms, they can better understand the complexity of the social situations in which helping behavior is embedded.

COMMON DILEMMAS OF PROFESSIONAL HELPERS

Among the value conflicts experienced by professional helpers, some seem specific to the particular circumstances and individuals involved

---

[1] I include laboratory experiments under studies of folk helping in the sense that they are involved with helping as it occurs outside of professional roles and are intended to reproduce certain "everyday" conditions in laboratory situations. By this usage I do not mean to minimize the differences between studies of helping based on contrived laboratory situations and those in natural settings as bases for generalizations about everyday situations.

[2] A growing body of literature examines in nonindustrialized societies roles that seem to serve functions similar to those of professional healers in contemporary American society. With few exceptions (cf. Frank, 1961; Adelson, 1962; Bakan, 1967), the pattern in this literature has been to reinterpret phenomena of folk healing in terms of current ideas derived from psychotherapy, rather than to explore what can be learned from the meaning of folk helping roles to broaden our understanding of contemporary professional roles.

or seem closely tied to the work of a particular professional specialty. But others are recurrent dilemmas that are less situation-specific and cut across professional traditions. The following dilemmas illustrate recurrent concerns reported by professionals varying widely in age, experience, training, sex, ethnic group, and clientele: [3]

1. tension between the necessity of having enough *confidence* about matters of judgment to make choices in face-to-face interactions and the necessity to recognize the inevitable *uncertainty* about what is true or good, which requires one to be tentative and self-critical about one's judgments;

2. tension between the obligations to act on the basis of one's own beliefs about what is good for the client and to respect the client's values and beliefs concerning what is good for him;

3. tension between the obligations to obtain the "informed consent" of the client to decisions that will affect his welfare and to acknowledge to oneself that the client rarely has a basis for understanding the implications of the choice to which he is being asked to "consent" (e.g., he rarely has a realistic assessment of the helper's powers or the risks involved);

4. tension between the obligations to stay with and provide follow-up on a person (or group) in whose life one has initiated changes and to acknowledge one's limitations rather than hang on and continue trying to help where there is nothing more one can do;

5. tension between the obligations to use one's resources in the interests of less powerful persons and groups in the society and to acknowledge the limitations of one's knowledge, beliefs, and affluent social position for effective helping with poor and oppressed people;

6. tension between the obligations to use the specialized knowledge and methods in which one is experienced and competent and to develop knowledge and methods that are appropriate for work with new groups and settings;

7. tension between the obligations to recognize and critically assess one's own viewpoints and choices and to relate to people as friends in relatively unselfconscious ways;

8. tension between the necessity to recognize differences between oneself and others (that make one an outsider) and the necessity to assume similarity with others in some respect in order to understand them at all;

[3] The analysis that follows assumes that these value-conflicts will be recognized by a wide variety of professional practioners as recurrent concerns in their own work. The illustrations are not offered as a systematic sample.

9. tension between the obligations to suspend judgment about others' worth, on the assumption that everyone comes to his beliefs honestly (i.e., in ways that make sense to him), and to make judgments about good and oppose evil without reserve.

EXPLAINING THE DILEMMAS

If we assume that these dilemmas are a fair sample of those experienced by a wide variety of professionals, how can we account for such dilemmas? What sources contribute to the conflicts?

The first general explanation available holds that there is an inherent contradiction in the very idea of a professional helping role. It is important to examine this explanation critically in order to decide whether we need to look elsewhere for sources of the dilemmas.

"Professional Helping": A Contradiction in Terms?

Critics of professional helping typically hold that the more "professional" the helper, the less helpful he is. The detachment cultivated by professional helpers as an aid to impartial, rational analysis of facts is seen as aloof, cold, or uncaring by many people in distress. Professional concern with "having reasons for everything they do" is often perceived as reluctance to make a firm commitment to support the interests of the person in distress. And the professional's questions, unfamiliar language, or assumptions about the situation of the person to be helped may be seen as reflecting the professional's ignorance about everyday life outside the consulting room or the classroom. In short, professional helpers are often seen as unapproachable, unresponsive, and unrealistic.

If such qualities necessarily follow from the nature of a professional role, then it would make sense to say that there is a contradiction between the idea of a professional and the idea of helping.

A second line of criticism of helping professions also views helping as a contradiction in terms, at least in relation to less powerful and less competent people in society. It argues that the values of professionals are in conflict with the best interests of these groups.

This view holds that the helping professions have unwittingly been serving the interests of the more powerful groups in the society (cf. Guttentag, 1970; Ryan, 1971) and legitimizing the separation of people into categories of incompetence in ways that relieve society of the necessity to address one of its most serious problems: the scarcity in this society of meaningful roles in which individuals can experience self-respect and worth in their relations with a larger unit. The helping professions, this argument holds, deal with people in ways that maintain these isolated, stigmatized compartments in thinking about people (cf. Goffman, 1961; Levinson, Merrifield, & Berg, 1967; Hobbs, 1974). By so doing, professionals perpetuate socially irresponsible policies for responding to the inevitable fact of human diversity. In this view, professionals are seen as trying to get clients to adapt to the way things are rather than as helping them to change for the better. For the less powerful people in the society, this is a special disservice.

I believe that there is much merit in both lines of criticism of the helping professions. In order to judge to what extent these defects are inherent in the role of professional helper, we need reasonable definitions of both "professional" and "helper." Because there is much ambiguity in the usage of these terms, we need to be explicit and critical in providing definitions here. We can then ask to what extent present practices and institutionalized policies in the helping professions are faithful expressions or corruptions of the professional role. We can also ask how compatible with helping are professional ideals as well as practices.

Values That Define the Professional Role

Although many professionals are well-described by the preceding criticisms, a very different picture is called for by what might be called the "classical values" of the professional role. By "classical" I mean values that go back to the original "learned professions" of law, medicine, and the clergy but are also appropriate to contemporary professional life. Although members of the professions are no longer drawn primarily from an aristocracy, are paid salaries in many cases rather than client's fees, and may work in large organizations rather than as independent agents, there is a core of values that are as appropriate now as then.

These are the values of impartiality, rationality, empirical knowledge, and ethics committed to the dignity of the individual and to public welfare. Although these values have come to have an increasingly secular coloring consistent with a scientific approach to empirical knowledge rather than a theistic approach to sacred knowledge, they can be said to be enduring ideals of the professions.

Impartial does not mean morally neutral but instead means dispassionate and fair, rather than self-serving. *Rational* means reflective and attentive to the logic and the persuasiveness of alternative arguments, rather than impulsive or arbitrary. *Empirical knowledge* here means beliefs based on experience and open to correction on the basis of new experiences, rather than held with a closed mind. *Respect for the dignity of the individual* means abstaining from covert or coercive manipulation of people as means to one's own ends. And *commitment to public welfare* means taking into account in one's actions what would promote just or healthy interrelationships of all groups, rather than working blindly for a special interest group conceived of in isolation from the rest of the community.

Although popular conceptions of the professional role still attribute expert knowledge and skills, prestige, and a certain amount of authority to the role, the images have become negative in many respects. It seems clear that some of this is due to the ways in which many professionals enact a caricature of the classical values. Instead of being impartial, they are vacillating; instead of rational, they are obsessional; instead of knowledgeable, they are pedantic; instead of concerned about public welfare, they avoid all controversy; instead of respecting individual dignity, they are intrusive, passive, or aloof.

But even if we distinguish optimal professional qualities from those distortions that provide a caricature of the classical professional values, it could be argued that these values are themselves culture- or class-bound. In this view, the particular virtues of a professional role make it unattractive and an object of mistrust for people in the greatest economic and social need.

This view would have to argue that the very nations of impartiality, rationality, and openness to correction on the basis of evidence are culture-bound. This strikes me as stereotyped thinking about poor and oppressed people. It is quite true that impartiality of an aloof, bloodless sort, rationality of a wordy, patronizing kind, scientific outlook of a narrowly technical or elite type, and secular outlook of a morally neutral and faithless cast will repel many people. This may generally be the case outside the narrow circles of people who specialize in intellectual pursuits. But this aversion represents distaste for detachment as a way of life rather than for detachment in particular situations in which the participants see a need for fairness and a sorting-out of evidence. This distaste would signify intolerance for certain styles of expression and ways of living, not necessarily intolerance for the values of impartiality, rationality, empirical knowledge, and the other classical values.

The styles of expression of most professionals may indeed be culture-bound and class-bound. This would argue for recruiting into the helping professions larger numbers of people from diverse cultures and social classes. It would not lead to a conclusion that the essential values of the professional are inherently alien to many people in need.

A Working Definition of Helping

In order to ask how compatible these professional ideals are with helping, we must first define "helping." By *help*, I refer to *uncoerced interaction between two or more people that is intended to benefit at least one of the parties and in which the parties are in agreement about who is intended to benefit.* This definition can cover a variety of helping forms, from cooperation in a work team, in which all parties expect to benefit from their mutual efforts, to a unilateral donation of resources by one person to benefit another person. It excludes such frequent events as an action by one person who characterizes it as a way to benefit a second person but which is perceived by the second person as self-serving or as serving other interests.

The "Internal Contradiction" Explanation Rejected

Since the classical values of the professional role envision someone who is (and has a public obligation to be) especially reflective about his choices, well-grounded in knowledge and skills concerned with human capacities and problems, and responsible in the use of the power that is available to anyone who is presumed to have such resources, they are in no way inconsistent with help as I have defined it.

Although the *idea* of professional helping contains no inherent contradiction, it is clear that much professional *practice* is incompatible with the idea of helping. Since help entails an agreement between the would-be helper and the person who is supposed to benefit from the helping, anything in professional practice that prevents a client from trusting the credibility and helpful intent of the professional becomes incompatible with helping.

But even when we are dealing with professionals whose clients have great confidence in their competence and benevolence, such professionals experience painful dilemmas in the helping role. I conclude from this that the criticisms of the helping professions do not contain an explanation of the dilemmas that are experienced by professionals no matter how faithfully their practice expresses the ideals of the professional role and fits the definition of helping.

An Alternative Explanation: Generic Structure of Helping Roles

Where, then, can we turn for an explanation of the content and persistence of these dilemmas? By comparing professional helping roles with those of "ordinary" people in everyday life, I hope to find more basic sources of these dilemmas then are suggested by criticisms of the helping professions. At the same time, I hope to clarify what contemporary influences lead to distorted interpretations of professional ideals in practice. I also hope to discover clues suggesting affirmative directions in which to reform professional helping.

In pursuing this comparison, I proceed from the premise that the social structure of helping relationships, together with the personalities of the helper and the helpee, are more crucial factors in helping than any particular technique or the individual personality of the helper considered in isolation from his role.

The Structure of Folk Helping Roles

A wide variety of literature on social interaction in American society and in other cultures suggests that it is useful to distinguish between two large classes of helping relationships: *long-term social exchange* and *aid to strangers in distress.*

The first category refers to exchange that is mutually beneficial when considered over long periods of time. This includes cooperation within work parties such as those that tend all the fields in neighboring homesteads in some cultures (cf. LeVine & LeVine, 1963), gift-giving and return-gifts (Mauss, 1954; Cohen, 1972), and the sharing of food under conditions of varying social integration and interdependence (Cohen, 1961).

Aid to strangers in distress refers here to interaction in which one participant has greater power and uses it in the service of what he perceives as the other participant's interests under circumstances that provide no prospect of reciprocation by the person helped. The person to be helped is a stranger in the sense that he is not a member of the helper's network of everyday mutual obligations. They may be from different primary networks (such as kinship groups), different social classes, or different geographic and cultural regions that provide barriers to continuing contact (cf. Rosenhan, 1970). Aid to strangers also includes aid when the helper remains anonymous, as in the case of kidney donors (Fellner & Marshall, 1970), or in situations in which the helper is a covert ally for whom reward from the helpee might even be dangerous, as in the case of Christians who rescued Jews from the Nazis in World War II (London, 1970).

The structural features of help as long-term social exchange are *enduring networks* of *reciprocal obligations* among members who in some basic way have a long-term common fate. In contrast, aid to strangers in distress is based on *temporary relationships* characterized by *asymmetry of power*. The stranger in distress remains in a position of relatively low power compared to the helper.

This distinction based on the studies already cited finds independent confirmation in Titmuss's (1970) cross-cultural study of blood donations. Like Lévi-Strauss (1969) and Mauss (1954), Titmuss distinguishes between economic exchange concerned with marginal utility and social exchange concerned with reciprocal obligations and serving to promote harmonious relationships among individuals and groups. But, beyond this, he distinguishes between exchange among known individuals and groups based on reciprocal obligations on the one hand, and, on the other hand, anonymous giving in which there is no exchange based on reciprocal obligations.

If we assume, then, that long-term social exchange and aid to strangers in distress represent two general and socially viable forms of helping relationships, it is important to consider the extent to which contemporary American society provides conditions under which such relationships could develop or last. The many studies showing us to be a nation of strangers (Reisman, Glazer, & Denny, 1953; Packard, 1972) living in temporary relationships (Bennis & Slater, 1968; Slater, 1970) or in fragmented social networks and vanishing neighborhoods (Gans, 1962; Newman & Oliver, 1967) make it clear that the conditions for help as long-term social exchange are becoming more and more rare. Although help in the form of aid to strangers is not limited to modern societies with fragmented social networks, there is certainly need for such help in contemporary society.

In such a society, how can we understand the relation of professional helping roles to the general forms of folk helping described above?

Continuities between Professional and Folk Helping Roles

Professional helping roles can be understood as continuous in important ways with the two general forms of folk helping. There are also social influences that can make professional practice incompatible with one or both of these generic helping forms. In this section, I examine the continuities and, in a later one, turn to the discontinuities.

The relatively rare phenomenon of the small-town doctor or teacher illustrates a professional role in the tradition of long-term social exchange. The more prevalent professional specialist in urban areas may be seen as continuous with the tradition of help as aid to strangers.

In the former case, the professional helper's work and his life in the community are more integrated with each other, and he has far more interaction with his clients as citizens outside the professional helping role. He is also likely to have less privacy and less ready access to the sophisticated science and technology of his profession than his urban counterpart. The urban professional specialist, on the other hand, defines narrower limits on his competence as a helper and frequently refers people to other specialists. In return for greater privacy in an urban, mass society, he is more anonymous and impersonal as viewed by clients, who typically have no contact with the professional outside the specialized helping relationship. There is little integration of the professional specialist's work and his life outside the office.

In small, relatively stable communities, such as some small towns or urban neighborhoods, the professional helper is thus more a part of a network of social exchange that entails long-term reciprocal obligations. He is subject to social control by the community, including clients, through everyday interactions, rather than through bureaucratic regulations alone. For an example of a professional helper whose work is closely tied to the network of social exchange in an urban neighborhood, see Hentoff's (1966) description of Elliot Shapiro, a New York City school principal (pp. 35–42, 73–82).

In the more typical case of professional helping, social control over the helper is exercised in the form of regulations by bureaucratic organizations that license, insure, and pay him and lobby on behalf of his profession. Control by clients is weakened by the fact that the relationship is isolated from ongoing networks of enduring mutual obligations. Moreover, the professional's power as an expert is made highly salient by the fact that he is known to clients only in his work role and in brief contacts.

It is thus in their structural features—the extent of reciprocity in social interaction and of ties to enduring networks of mutual obligations—that the "small town" professional helper and the more typical professional helper show continuities with the two generic forms of helping.

Does Generic Structure Explain the Dilemmas of Professional Helpers?

Dilemmas and Long-Term Social Exchange   The rare professional who works with clients all of whom are friends or neighbors is not without dilemmas. On the occasions when such a professional helper gives primary allegiance to the beliefs of his professional peers rather than to those of his neighbors, he experiences tension between the value of being a member of the local setting and the value of being in some sense an "outsider." This seems not to be peculiar to professional helping roles, however, nor to helping roles only. Such a dilemma is experienced in small, stable towns and neighborhoods by a person who votes Republican when his neighbors are overwhelmingly Democrat or by a person whose primary identity is that of a Jew, a black, or a Catholic in a town where there is no such local reference group. What neighbors are skeptical about in these examples is the individual's general credibility as a good and loyal "local." It is this that leads to tension in the example of a professional just given, rather than anything peculiar to the individual's credibility as a specialist in helping.

Professionals whose clients are friends and neighbors would also experience tension between the value of spontaneous, un-self-conscious interaction with such clients on the one hand, and, on the other hand, the obligation to be self-conscious and alert to multiple options in one's decision making about their welfare. Such a dilemma is not peculiar to the professional but is common to all who have a bent for reflection, introspection, and responsible choices in their social relationships, yet do not want to live in a detached way. What about a professional in such a setting who is not strongly inclined to be reflective and introspective as a matter of personal style but is so primarily due to the obligation to be especially responsible about his choices in return for the special power and privileges he receives as a professional? In this special and perhaps unlikely case, the individual would experience a dilemma that we would have to say is peculiar to his status as a professional helper.

Dilemmas and Aid to Strangers in Distress   What about the dilemmas experienced by the great majority of professional helpers, who do not have in common with their clients an enduring network of reciprocal obligations, that is, whose clients are strangers?

The fact that such relationships are isolated from any already established network of reciprocal obligations generates ambiguity about how it is appropriate to deal with the asymmetry of power and the temporary nature of the social attachment. In the face of this ambiguity, the helper feels challenged to use his competence to make things better. At the same time, he is concerned that a constructive relationship depends on finding common ground between his values and the unknown values of the stranger. How is the would-be helper to reconcile or balance these contrasting and complex concerns? For the helper, the result is great tension.

Such tensions are inherent in the structure common to both folk and professional roles in helping strangers. Table 13.1 suggests how the two main structural features of aid to strangers interact to produce painful tensions. It remains to ask whether the dilemmas that I initially listed as characteristic of professional helpers can be understood in terms of

TABLE 13.1

Dilemmas Generated by the Social Structure of Aid to a Stranger in Distress

	Temporary relationship: No enduring network of reciprocal obligations	
	Distinctive values of helpee and helper are not initially known to each other.	Norms common to helper and helpee are not initially known to either.
Asymmetry of power:	A	C
Helper maintains greater power than person in distress.	Helper has greater power but is dependent on helpee to learn what will benefit helpee ("Where does it hurt?").	Helper can unilaterally define norms for the interaction, but if they do not appeal to mutually acceptable values, helpee may not cooperate enough for helper to use his power effectively.
	B	D
Legitimacy of helper's use of power depends on the extent to which helper and helpee have common norms about power.	Helper has obligation to take helpee's values into account in exercising power but also recognizes limitations on helpee's understanding of possible consequences of helpee's choices. So helper must also make his own value judgments.	Helper recognizes the limitations of unilateral imposition of norms for assuring that his uses of power will be perceived as legitimate by helpee, but he has to act on the basis of his own norms while trying to discover values they have in common.

such tensions. The value of such a structural explanation of the dilemmas will depend on its usefulness in understanding them as: (a) special cases of a smaller number of problems than those on the original list; and (b) problems that arise from generic features of helping roles, rather than from something peculiar to professionals.

The first two dilemmas reflect the fact that when a helper and the person to be helped are strangers, the helper knows that some of his ordinarily confident judgments about what is good for people may be wrong, since the stranger may have very different beliefs and values. Yet the helper cannot simply rely on the stranger to make choices. This is partly because the stranger is in distress, partly because the helper has greater power in the situation, and partly because, in the end, the helper has to take responsibility for his own choices.

This tension is heightened by the fact that the helper's relatively greater power in the situation gives him a greater obligation to be concerned about the consequences that his judgments have for the other person. The legitimacy of the helper's use of power depends on there being agreement between him and the person to be helped on some norms concerning power. Such norms define limits on what exercise of power is appropriate, fair, and just. Since the helper has greater power in the situation but he and the stranger do not necessarily have any common norms concerning power, the helper has an obligation to be especially cautious in using his power and to try to discover what the other person's values are in order to take them into account in exercising his power. To ignore this obligation is to use his power arbitrarily or coercively, rather than legitimately (cf. Kelman, 1972, 1974; see also all four cells in Table 13.1).

In the third dilemma, the obligation to obtain "informed consent" is stated as a professional obligation, but it is an ethical claim not limited to professionals. It recognizes that, as a stranger, the other person may have very different values and should be permitted and encouraged to maintain some degree of control over what happens to him, especially in view of the helper's greater power in the situation. This reflects an assumption that the person's well-being includes individual dignity and that this entails being in some respects an origin, rather than simply a pawn, of external forces. Yet the person is usually dependent on the helper's greater familiarity with the possible consequences of various choices, particularly when the person to be helped is a stranger to the setting (see Cell B in Table 13.1).

The next three dilemmas (4, 5, and 6) can be understood as variations on a common theme. The greater power of the helper is constrained by the helper's limited competence to benefit a stranger because of the helper's unfamiliarity with the stranger's beliefs and values and because of the uncertainty about whether the helper's skills and knowledge will be apt. The greater responsibility that goes with the helper's greater power in the situation leads him to be especially cautious about intervening in the life of a stranger (see especially Cell A).

In the seventh dilemma, we return to the tension between self-consciousness and spontaneous involvement with other people. Although this tension is experienced by anyone who is reflective and introspective, the effort to help a stranger makes reflection an obligation rather than a matter of personal style. It becomes an obligation as part of being responsible in one's use of power when intervening in the affairs of a stranger in distress. But it is an obligation of anyone attempting to help a stranger, not an obligation peculiar to professional helpers. (This tension is not well represented by Table 13.1.)

The choice in the eight dilemma, how much to assume similarities or differences between oneself and another person, is present in all human communication. The tension involved in this choice is not peculiar to professional roles or to helping relationships. It is, however, intensified in communication with strangers, since one initially has no way of estimating what similarities may exist, yet arriving at some common meanings depends on finding similarities. The tension is further intensified in efforts to help strangers, because greater responsibility for wise choices goes with the helper's greater power in such a situation. (Cell D represents some features of this dilemma.)

The ninth and last dilemma, which is concerned with suspending judgment, seems at first glance to deal with a peculiarly professional attitude. But, on further examination, it, too, seems to be continuous with experiences of ordinary people in everyday life. When one meets a person whose behavior is in conflict with one's own values but who is clearly from a different culture, it is quite common to suspend judgment about the person's worth. There is a mitigating assumption that the person did not know any better in this setting or that the person came by his values in a way that made sense to him in his own culture. Behavior perceived as alien seems to pose less of a threat to the observer because it is not seen as likely to affect one's own world.

When one attempts to aid a stranger, the helper is usually faced with some behavior that is at odds with his own values and evokes tension concerning how it is fair and responsible to react. If the helper deals with the stranger as someone unlikely to affect his own world, he may find no difficulty suspending generalized judgments about the stranger's worth. But in relegating the stranger to an airtight compartment outside his own world, the helper is likely to have great difficulty understanding him or benefiting him. Insofar as a helper regards a stranger as having possible effects on his own world, he is likely to experience conflict between the value of suspending judgment for purposes of understanding and the value of judging the person in defense of the helper's own values. Although this tension is given particular attention by professional helpers, it is not peculiar to a professional helping role but is common to any role in which one tries to aid strangers. (Cell B represents some features of this dilemma.)

With the possible exception of the seventh dilemma, it seems fair to conclude that the structure of aid to strangers makes sense of these dilemmas without appeal to the peculiarly professional aspects of a helping role.

Professional Responsibilities and Continuities with Folk Helping

Does this continuity between folk and professional help for strangers mean that a professional helper has no special problems or responsibilities by virtue of his professional status? Hardly. Because his expertise as a professional is supposed to lie in helping when power is asymmetrical and relations are temporary, the professional is assigned a position of power and privilege in the society. Because of this status, the professional has even greater responsibility than other helpers to recognize the complexities of such relationships and the abuses to which they are vulnerable.

In a sense, when you put together being a professional with the role of helper to strangers, you get a professional who is in much pain. Because of the professional ideals of rationality, self-consciousness about choices, and detachment, he is supposed to be more aware than most people of the inherent tensions in aid to strangers. While being especially reflective, he is also supposed to be especially responsible in his helping efforts.

Because the client's only interaction with the professional is in their brief work contacts, the client is likely to overestimate the professional's power. Client responses, whether positive or negative, to the professional's power are therefore likely to be disproportionate to what seems reasonable or realistic to the professional. The professional helper, therefore, has a special responsibility to take these factors into account in using his power wisely.

Because the client and the professional helper are typically not members of a common, ongoing social network, the client does not have ready access to a system of social control over the helper's conduct. The professional helper has a responsibility to criticize his own ways of coping with the tensions of the role in order to prevent efforts on his part to overcome at the client's expense the limitations of the temporary relationship. For example, if the helper is not rooted in a network of his own that meets a wide range of his needs, he may compensate by seeking intensified temporary intimacy or involvement in the client's social network as a way to gratify his own needs for attachment and social anchorage. The helper's needs may lead to a misinterpretation of those of the client.

It seems fair to conclude that the struggles of professional helpers with recurrent dilemmas in their work may represent efforts to overcome or escape the inherent limitations of their generic role as provider of aid to strangers: the asymmetry of power, the temporary nature of the attachment, and the fact that the relationship is unlikely to change the sources of the stranger's distress, which operate in his own social system.

Given the intensity of the dilemmas experienced by professional helpers, some gravitate toward being less reflective, others toward being less available or helpful to clients. Any way of coping with the predicament leaves one vulnerable to other influences on professional practice that may make it incompatible with helping.

Structural Sources of Discontinuity between Professional and Folk Helping Roles

In arguing that professional helping is continuous with folk helping, I have been describing an ideal professional role. There are also powerful factors shaping professional roles in ways that are discontinuous with folk helping and with the ideals of the professional role.

Bureaucratic Organization

The structural features I refer to here are such things as centralization of authority, division of labor according to function, specialized roles, and hierarchical relations among roles. The ideological features are the priority given to efficiency, consistency, and compliance with uniform procedures.

The results in a particular organization may take the form of regulations restricting the professional's choices of whom to help, how to go about it, within what time periods, in what surroundings, and what other responsibilities compete with the opportunity to help. These regulations may take the form of policies of agencies, government regulations, or duties prescribed by a guild, union, or other association of the professional's peers (cf. Lubov, 1965; Katz, 1971).

When a professional's work is embedded in bureaucratic structure, his role may be incompatible with helping, in the sense that many of his actions are not intended to help and that the clients (or students) do not perceive the professional's actions as intended to help them.

Economic Self-Interest

The structural features I refer to here are roles in which help is defined narrowly as a service for which economic compensation is due. The ideological features have to do with the belief that it is right to provide help on the basis of who can pay for it.

When a professional's decisions are heavily influenced by considerations of economic self-interest, his work may be in conflict with the ideals of the professional role. He may be actively perpetuating a system of institutionalized services that is patently unfair to poor people and thereby harms the public welfare in the sense that this refers to mutually beneficial relations among the interdependent groups in society.

When a professional chooses his clientele primarily on the basis of their ability to pay high fees and when the continuation of services is heavily dependent on the client's continuing ability to do so, these priorities also conflict with the priority given in folk helping to the interests of the individuals to be helped or to the well-being of the community, rather than to the aggrandizement of the helper.[4]

Technological Supremacy

In structural terms I am referring here to the narrow technical focus of professional roles during and after training. These roles institutionalize a belief that competence in dealing with human problems lies in mastery of specialized techniques considered in isolation from the personal meaning systems and integrity of the people using the techniques or affected by them.

Bakan (1967), in discussing psychotherapy, makes the more general point that the dominance of technical considerations is appropriate only when the objectives of an enterprise are clear and unambiguous. As I have tried to show, there is much ambiguity about objectives in helping a stranger, since, as strangers, the helper and the person to be helped start off with neither a common system of reciprocal obligations nor a knowledge of each other's values. Under such conditions, preoccupation with technique or skill works against the development of a common framework within which the would-be helper can benefit the stranger in terms that are meaningful to both.

Nevertheless, the discomfort involved in facing the uncertainty and ambiguity of human distress leads students and faculty in many training programs to give primary attention to technical skills. To the extent that this substitutes action for reflection and tries to escape the uncertainties of human relationships, such a focus abandons the professional ideal of reflection and responsibility in the use of one's power.

---

[4] Decisions by professional helpers to stop participating in oppressive bureaucratic organizations have been a central factor leading to the creation of new settings, such as alternative schools, both public and private (cf. Dennison, 1969; Graubard, 1972; *Harvard Educational Review*, 1972). Similar developments among professionals have taken place periodically in mental health services (cf. Sarason *et al.*, 1966) and in public health settings (cf. Freudenberger, 1974).

Defensive Self-Aggrandizement

Under defensive self-aggrandizement I refer to the hierarchical structure frequently institutionalized among various professional roles and between professional roles and those of nonprofessionals doing similar work. The hierarchies of prestige and power serve to shore up the belief in each profession that it is in some way superior to some other group. This in turn is used to justify each profession in preserving the beliefs, practices, and privileges that define its difference from the others. In this process, certain helping roles are restricted to members of a particular professional specialty, even when there is no evidence that such membership is a criterion of efficacy in helping. To the extent that such hierarchies and regulations are arbitrary rather than based on evidence concerning competence, they are in conflict with the meanings of help, with folk helping roles, and with the professional ideals of impartial, empirically based, and responsible uses of power.

Helping, especially aid to strangers in distress, calls for a high degree of collaboration between the helper and the person to be helped, in which they take into account their respective limitations as well as their particular competencies. It requires of a professional that he distinguish between taking responsibility for those things he is uniquely equipped to do and protecting his privileged position in order to have control over a wide range of decisions that others are equally or better equipped to make.

Ethnocentrism

Here I refer in structural terms to the institutional definition of services that perpetuate beliefs of the dominant group in society about the lives of relatively powerless groups. Ideologically, I refer to the blindness of many middle-class and affluent professionals to the assumptions they make in practice concerning people who are different from themselves.

These include assumptions about motives and the degree of control that other people have over the conditions in which they live. Many of the assumptions are false (cf. Brown, 1965; Desnison, 1969). Ryan (1971) has been especially persuasive in pointing out such patterns among members of the helping professions. One major pattern, "blaming the victim," is a process of attributing to poor or oppressed individuals responsibility for their poverty or oppression rather than looking for ways in which the institutional policies, beliefs, and opportunity-structures in the society interact with individual and group characteristics and victimize people with less power.

As professionals have begun to recognize and respond to the neglected needs of poor people and members of minority groups, they have also found that their position as outsiders is a barrier to helping these potential clients. This is ironic, for historically the fact that the professional helper is outside the primary networks of the client has been regarded as a key condition permitting the client to view the professional as an impartial, disinterested ally. This presumed advantage of being an outsider, a stranger, made sense as long as the professional worked with people who were of similar social class and cultural background. Although he was outside their primary networks, such as the family, he understood and shared many of their values and customs. But since professionals typically do not understand or share many of the values and customs of poor or minority people, they have great difficulty demonstrating that they are credible as allies.

Professional Responsibilities and Discontinuities with Folk Helping

To the extent that professional helping roles have come to include these five factors, it is understandable that many, especially poor and oppressed people, view professional helping as a contradiction in terms. But it is not the *professional* aspects of such roles that are the problems. The problems are inherent in the five more general *structural* factors. This, of course, offers no consolation to people who find professional helpers preoccupied with other considerations than the client's well-being. The professional cannot take refuge in the view that these ordinary folks "don't understand" professional roles. What they may understand all too well is prejudice, pettiness, and preoccupation with bureaucratic, commercial, and technical matters under the guise of helping.

This would suggest that, rather than "deprofessionalizing" their roles, members of the helping professions should be *more* professional and less caught up in the five factors described above. By "professional" I mean more faithful to the classical values that define the professional role.

REDEFINING PROFESSIONAL HELPING ROLES

Limitations of Current Variations in Professional Helping Roles

Relationships that are influenced by both enduring networks of social exchange and temporary, contractual arrangements among strangers are bound to involve tensions that are difficult to understand and to cope with. Yet virtually all relationships in contemporary mass society are of this mixed sort, since we live both in primary networks such as nuclear families and in organizations regulated by contractual arrangements, such as apartments, offices, stores, schools, and hospitals. In response to this ambiguity and tension, professionals have typically defined their helping roles narrowly, in explicitly limited, contractual terms. Partly in reactions against this approach, other professionals have tried to evolve holistic roles as long-term members of primary social networks.

The major advantage of a contractually defined helping role is that its ground rules are relatively clear for both parties. Although the contract is defined primarily by the professional, its explicitness gives it a semblance of fairness based on informed consent. It also gives the professional leverage to point out when the client is being unrealistic about what can be expected from the relationship, and this may be useful to the client in examining unrealistic expectations in other aspects of his life (cf. Freud, 1912; Menninger, 1958; Green, 1964).

A major disadvantage of a contractual approach is that it has been developed largely on the basis of work with middle-class and affluent clients and is likely to be mistrusted by members of poor and oppressed groups. Whereas the more privileged members of society have reason to believe that contracts will protect their interests, the less privileged have expectations based on a history of being excluded from or exploited by contracts among people with power.

In contrast, the long-term approach advocates letting the professional's role emerge from his developing membership in a community group, for example, a daycare collective, a neighborhood improvement organization, or a community-based school (cf. Adams, 1972). Its main advantage is that the potential clients are fellow members of the group, with more power to define the relationship in ways that are comfortable to them. The major disadvantage of such an approach is that the professional feels very vulnerable to conflicts between his professional training and his life in the informal social system where he tries to do his helping.

Many professionals, uncomfortable with both contractually defined roles and "emergent" roles as a member of a community setting, try to develop a role that combines the advantages of each approach while avoiding the disadvantages. Typically, this takes the form of a role as consultant, moving between the professional's own contractually defined institutional base (e.g., mental health center, agency, or university) and a setting in the client's neighborhood or work setting (e.g., local school, parent-run day-care center, service club, or multi-service center; see McIntyre, 1967, Fromm & Maccoby, 1970, and Sarason, 1917).

In such settings on the client's "home turf," the professional in this mixed role tries to discover how to be useful to the setting, rather than beginning with a highly explicit contract in one instance or trying to become a member of the setting in the other instance. But whereas the contractual model provides statisfactions as a clearly structured form of aid to strangers and the holistic-involvement model offers the rewards of membership in an enduring social network, the mixed model is a nexus of all the tensions between these two social forms.

Affirmative Directions for Redefining Professional Helping Roles

Does the analysis of continuities between professional and folk helping suggest directions for coping effectively and responsibly with this predicament? What is needed besides an awareness of the pitfalls of available approaches?

Dialectical Framework

For one thing, the professional would need to struggle continually to generate and refine a conceptual framework with which to make sense of his complex experience and to identify choices consistent with his basic values. To be faithful to the complexity of human experience, it seems crucial to have a framework that postulates both reconcilable aspects of personality and of society and aspects that are inherently in tension. Yet having a complex framework that tolerates apparent contradictions is not enough. There is need for a coherent and comprehensive conceptual framework, not just a continually shifting or piecemeal one. There is, however, no such explicit, systematic, and comprehensive theoretical framework available. But in order to develop a greater measure of integration in one's professional helping role, it does seem crucial to reflect on the day-to-day incidents of practice and to work toward some such framework.

Modest Integration of Contract and Involvement

The complexity of such a problem calls for modesty about the degree of integration that it is possible to achieve between the contractual aspects of one's relationships and holistic involvement in primary networks. A structural expression of such modesty would be to make oneself clearly accountable to the clients for the effects of exercising one's skills. This involves the development of a working relationship in which the clients have the power to define the problem in their own terms, to specify values that must be included in a solution, to use the helper to generate more alternatives from which they can choose, to select other helpers in addition to or instead of a particular professional, and to decide when they no longer need help. The integration of contract and involvement is here reflected in a high degree of *accountability*, along with a greater than usual degree of *symmetry* in the distribution of power between professional and client.

Teams of Helpers as Limited Networks

A second structural safeguard for clients is for the professional to work with at least one partner who is committed to maintaining open dialogue with him about his limitations as they affect the clients. This is in accordance with current methods of guarding against self-deception and disorientation of professional helpers by "peer supervision," "co-counseling," and "teaming," as practiced in some counseling and teaching. The basic idea is to build in a process of criticism and confrontation in order to avoid the ways individual professionals contribute to confusion, role-conflict, and negative side-effects in their well-intentioned efforts.

The challenge here is to build a long-term relationship among several individuals who strive to maintain a balance between affirmation of each other's special talents and confrontation with each other's particular foibles. Because this is conceived of as part of generic helping relationships rather than as an exclusively professional skill, the team members would feel free to engage in such dialogue with each other in the presence of clients, rather than only afterwards in an exclusively professional group.

In terms of the social structure of helping, a network of helpers represents a hybrid between long-term membership in an enduring system of social exchange and a narrow contractual relationship between an isolated helper and strangers. As I envision it, the team of helpers must be an enduring network of reciprocal obligations that go beyond contractual, instrumental relationships. This network is likely to be an extension of the family in many ways, rather than a team for specialized work only. The necessity of knowing each other as whole people and of affirming and confronting each other leads members of such teams to invest themselves more fully in the team than work with strangers would seem at first to call for. At the same time, the tensions within the life of the team mean that areas of privacy and some functional separations between team and family are valued as opportunities for renewal and individual fulfillment.

The team then contracts with strangers to work in the clients' turf, the team's turf, or both, as the situation calls for. The team contracts to explore whether their modes of understanding and coping with sources of distress are viable and useful to the clients' ongoing network, whether that be a family (cf. Speck & Attneave, 1973), an organization such as a school or service agency (cf. Sarason *et al.*, 1966), or a group that is creating a new setting (cf. Goldenberg, 1971).

What is crucial in this approach is the quality of life that the team has developed and its fruitfulness for the particular network that is experiencing problems. The aim of the contract is for the team to support the client network in developing a viable way of living in which the team is no longer needed.

Promoting Networks of Mutual Aid among People Where They Are

Awareness of the structural limitations in the role of helping strangers and modesty about one's personal resources for helping suggest that the more people can help each other in their everyday settings, without an outside helper, the better off they would be. Such a view relegates the professional helper to a role in which he supports individuals in strengthening local resources for mutual aid. This involves encouraging them to take seriously their own knowledge of their neighborhoods and work places and those elements of a system of mutual aid that are already present. It involves helping them to identify what resources they need to meet their needs. This may include such things as police protection, public health nurses, after-hours use of school buildings, information about permits for building a playground in a vacant lot, summer jobs for teenagers, public transportation, housing regulations, and public school resources. The professional's emphasis would be on preventing distress that overwhelms local resources and leads to dependency on outside specialists for relief. The challenge would be to support individuals in using institutions and contractual arrangements on terms that strengthen long-term networks of social exchange.

SUMMARY AND CONCLUSION

Starting from the recurrent and painful dilemmas experienced by professionl helpers, I have explored the extent to which they can be understood in terms of the structure of helping relationships that are more general than professional roles. I attempt to distinguish generic dilemmas of helping from peculiarly professional ones on the basis of the continuity of the former with ordinary, everyday forms of helping. On the basis of a comparison of such folk helping and professional helping roles, I argue that the major dilemmas experienced by professional helpers are built into social life apart from the specifics of professional roles.

I examine criticisms of professional helping that imply that there are peculiarly professional values that make being a professional incompatible with helping. My inquiry suggests that these criticisms refer to institutionalized practices that corrupt the expression of professional ideals, rather than to the basic conception of professional helping.

One implication of this argument is that professional helpers have a responsibility to resist and work toward changing institutionalized values and structures that interfere with their faithful translation of professional ideals into practice.

I argue that if ordinary, everyday helping roles are used as a basis for understanding the conditions under which helping occurs, the perspective gained suggests affirmative and responsible ways to redefine professional roles despite the contradictions of our society.

There is need for some combination of (*a*) being accountable to clients in a way that acknowledges one's limitations in understanding and helping in their life situations; (*b*) promoting structural conditions that can support ongoing helping relationships with a minimum of dependency on outsiders and professional specialists; and (*c*) practicing what one preaches about the importance of helping networks by working in collaborative teams rather than alone. Although such roles will no doubt be as stressful as present ones, they would be more faithful to the concept of help.

ACKNOWLEDGMENTS

I want to thank Jeri Posnick, Gordy Donaldson, Marion Shapiro, Gerry Mohatt, and Hilde Burton for helpful criticisms and comments during the preparation of this chapter.

REFERENCES

Adams, F. Highlander folk school: Getting information and going back and teaching it. *Harvard Educational Review*, 1972, 42(4), 497–520.

Adelson, J. The teacher as model. In N. Sanford (Ed.), *The American college: A psychological and social interpretation of higher learning*. New York: Wiley, 1962, Pp. 396–417.

Argyris, C. *Intervention theory and method*. Reading, Massachusetts: Addison-Wesley, 1970.

Aristotle. *Nicomachean ethics* (translated by W. D. Ross). Oxford: Clarendon Press, 1925.

Bakan, D. Psychotherapist: Healer or repairman? In *On method: Toward a recon-struction of psychological investigation.* San Francisco: Jossey-Bass, 1967, Pp. 122–126.

Bennis, W. G., & Slater, P. E. *The temporary society.* New York: Harper and Row, 1968.

Brown, C. *Manchild in the promised land.* New York: Signet, 1965.

Bryan, J. H. Children's reactions to helpers: Their money isn't where their mouths are. In J. Macaulay & L. Berkowitz (Eds.), *Altruism and helping behavior.* New York: Academic, 1970, Pp. 61–73.

Bryan, J. H., & Test, M. A. Models and helping: Naturalistic studies in aiding be-havior. *Journal of Personality and Social Psychology,* 1967, *6,* 400–407.

Burton, A. *Case studies in counseling and psychotherapy.* Englewood Cliffs, New Jersey: Prentice-Hall, 1959.

Cohen, R. Altruism: Human, cultural, or what? In L. G. Wispé (Ed.), *Positive forms of social behavior. Journal of Social Issues,* 1972, *28*(3), 39–57.

Cohen, Y. A. Food and its vicissitudes: A cross-cultural study of sharing and non-sharing. In *Social structure and personality.* New York: Holt, 1961, Pp. 312–350.

Darley, J. M., & Latané, B. Norms and normative behavior: Field studies of social interdependence. In J. Macauley & L. Berkowitz (Eds.), *Altruism and helping behavior.* New York: Academic, 1970, Pp. 83–101.

Dennison, G. *The lives of children: The story of the first street school.* New York: Random House, 1969.

Erikson, E. H. The golden rule and the cycle of life. In R. W. White (Ed.), *The study of lives: Essays on personality in honor of Henry A. Murray.* New York: Atherton, 1963, Pp. 412–428.

Eysenck, H. J. The effects of therapy: An evaluation. *Journal of Consulting Psy-chology,* 1952, *16,* 319–324.

Fellner, C. H., & Marshall, J. R. Kidney donors. In J. Macaulay & L. Berkowitz (Eds.), *Altruism and helping behavior.* New York: Academic, 1970, Pp. 269–281.

Frank, J. D. *Persuasion and healing: A comparative study of psychotherapy.* Balti-more: Johns Hopkins, 1961.

Freud, S. (1905) Fragment of an analysis of a case of hysteria. In *The complete psychological works of Sigmund Freud* Standard Edition, Vol. 7. London: Hogarth, 1953.

Freud, S. (1912) Recommendations for physicians on the psychoanalytic method of treatment. In *Collected papers,* Vol. 2. London: Hogarth, 1924.

Freudenberger, H. J. (Ed.). The free clinic handbook. *The Journal of Social Issues.* 1974, *30,* No. 1.

Fromm, E., & Maccoby, M. *Social character in a Mexican village.* Englewood Cliffs, New Jersey: Prentice-Hall, 1970.

Gans, H. *The urban villagers.* New York: Free Press, 1962.

Goffman, E. *Asylums: Essays on the social situation of mental patients and other inmates.* Garden City, New York: Anchor, 1961.

Goldenberg, I. I. *Build me a mountain.* Cambridge, Massachusetts: MIT Press, 1971.

Graubard, A. *Free the children: Radical reform and the free school movement.* New York: Pantheon, 1972.

Green, H. *I never promised you a rose garden.* New York: Holt, Rinehart, and Winston, 1964.

Guttentag, M. The insolence of office. *Journal of Social Issues*, 1970, *26*(3), 11–17.

Harvard Educational Review, 1972, *42*, No. 3: Alternative schools.

Hentoff, N. *Our children are dying*. New York: Viking, 1966.

Hobbs, N. Sources of gain in psychotherapy. *American Psychologist*, 1962, *17*, 741–747.

Hobbs, N. *Issues in the classification of children: A sourcebook on categories, labels and their consequences*. San Francisco: Jossey-Bass, 1974.

Isaacs, S. *Social development in young children*. London: Routledge, 1933.

Jones, R. *Fantasy and feeling in education*. New York: New York University, 1968.

Kant, I. (1785) *Foundations of the metaphysics of morals* (translated by L. W. Beck). Indianapolis: Bobbs-Merrill, 1969.

Katz, M. *Class, bureaucracy, and schools*. New York: Praeger, 1971.

Kelly, G. A. *The psychology of personal constructs* (two volumes). New York: Norton, 1955.

Kelman, H. C. The rights of the subject in social research: An analysis in terms of relative power and legitimacy. *American Psychologist*, 1972, *27*(11), 989–1016.

Kelman, H. C. Social influence and linkages between the individual and the social system: Further thoughts on the processes of compliance, identification, and internalization. In J. T. Tedeschi (Ed.), *Perspectives on social power*. Chicago: Aldine, 1974, Pp. 125–171.

Klaus, R. R., & Gray, S. W. The early training project for disadvantaged children: A report after five years. *Monographs of the Society for Research in Child Development*, 1968, *33*, 1–66.

Lenrow, P. B. Studies of sympathy. In S. S. Tomkins & C. E. Izard (Eds.), *Affect, cognition and personality*. New York: Springer, 1965, Pp. 264–294.

Lerner, M. J., & Simmons, C. H. Observer's reaction to the "innocent victim": Compassion or rejection? *Journal of Personality and Social Psychology*, 1966, *4*, 203–210.

LeVine, R. A., & LeVine, B. B. Nyansongo: A Gusii community in Kenya. In B. B. Whiting (Ed.), *Six cultures: Studies of child rearing*. New York: Wiley, 1963, Pp. 015–202.

Levinson, D. J., Merrifield, J., & Berg, K. Becoming a patient. *Archives of General Psychiatry*, 1967, *17*, 385–406.

Lévi-Strauss, C. (1949) *The elementary structures of kinship* (translated by J. H. Bell, J. R. Von Sturner, & R. Needham, ed.). Boston: Beacon, 1969.

London, P. The rescuers: Motivational hypotheses about Christians who saved Jews from the Nazis. In J. Macaulay & L. Berkowitz (Eds.), *Altruism and helping behavior*. New York: Academic, 1970, Pp. 241–250.

Lubov, R. *The professional altruist: The emergence of social work as a career*. Cambridge, Massachusetts: Harvard, 1965.

Macaulay, J. R. A shill for charity. In J. Macaulay & L. Berkowitz (Eds.), *Altruism and helping behavior*. New York: Academic, 1970, Pp. 43–59.

Marrow, A. J., Bowers, D. A., & Seashore, S. E. *Management by participation*. New York: Harper, 1967.

Mauss, M. *The gift: Forms and functions of exchange in archaic societies*. (Translated by I. Cunnison.) Glencoe, Illinois: Free Press, 1954.

McIntyre, D. Two schools, one psychologist. In F. Kaplan & S. B. Sarason (Eds.), *The psycho-educational clinic*. Boston: Massachusetts Department of Mental Health, 1967, Pp. 21–90.

Menninger, K. *Theory of psychoanalytic technique*. New York: Basic Books, 1958.

Murphy, L. B. *Social behavior and child personality*. New York: Columbia University, 1937.

Newman, F. M., & Oliver, D. W. Education and community. *Harvard Educational Review*, 1967, *37*, 61–106.

Packard, V. O. *A nation of strangers*. New York: McKay, 1972.

Plato. *The republic of Plato* (translated by F. M. Cornford). New York: Oxford, 1945.

Reik, T. *Surprise and the psychoanalyst*. New York: Dutton, 1937.

Riesman, D., Glazer, N., and Denny, R. *The lonely crowd: A study in the changing American character*. New York: Doubleday, 1953.

Rogers, C. R. *Counseling and psychotherapy*. Boston: Houghton Mifflin, 1942.

Rogers, C. R. The necessary and sufficient conditions of psychotherapeutic personality change. *Journal of Consulting Psychology*, 1957, *21*, 95–103.

Rogers, C. R. A theory of therapy, personality, and interpersonal relationships, as developed in the client-centered framework. In S. Koch (Ed.), *Psychology: A study of a science*, Vol. 3. New York: McGraw-Hill, 1959, Pp. 184–256.

Rosenhan, D. L. The natural socialization of altruistic autonomy. In J. Macaulay & L. Berkowitz (Eds.), *Altruism and helping behavior*. New York: Academic, Pp. 251–268.

Rosenzweig, S. A transvaluation of therapy: A reply to Hans Eysenck. *Journal of Abnormal and Social Psychology*, 1954, *49*, 298–304.

Ryan, W. *Blaming the victim*. New York: Random House, 1971.

Sarason, S. B. *The culture of the school and the problem of change*. Boston: Allyn and Bacon, 1971.

Sarason, S. B., Levine, M., Goldenberg, I. I., Cherlin, D. L., & Bennett, E. M. *Psychology in community settings*. New York: Wiley, 1966.

Schafer, R. Generative empathy in the treatment situation. *Psychoanalytic Quarterly*, 1959, *28*, 342–373.

Schein, E. *Process consultation: Its role in organization development*. Reading, Massachusetts: Addison-Wesley, 1969.

Scheler, M. *The nature of sympathy*. (1922) New Haven: Yale, 1954.

Slater, P. E. *The pursuit of loneliness*. Boston: Beacon, 1970.

Smith, A. *The theory of moral sentiments*. London: Miller, 1759.

Sorokin, P. A. (Ed.). *Explorations in altruistic love and behavior*. Boston: Beacon, 1950.

Speck, R., & Attneave, C. L. *Family networks*. New York: Random House, 1973.

Spenser, H. *The Principles of psychology*, Vol. 1. (Second edition.) London: Williams and Norgate, 1870.

Strupp, H. H. *Psychotherapists in action*. New York: Grune and Stratton, 1960.

Titmuss, R. M. *The gift relationship: From human blood to social policy*. London: Allen and Unwin, 1970.

Truax, C., & Carkhuff, R. *Toward effective counseling and psychotherapy*. Chicago: Aldine, 1969.

Wispé, L. G., & Freshley, H. B. Race, sex, and sympathetic helping behavior: The broken bag caper. *Journal of Personality and Social Psychology*, 1971, *17*, 59–65.

14

A Legal Look at Prosocial Behavior: What Can Happen If One Tries to Help or Fails to Help Another

JOHN KAPLAN

You are sitting on the edge of a pier, eating a sandwich, and watching the sunset when the fisherman next to you leans too far forward and falls in. He screams to you: "Help! I can't swim. Throw the life preserver." You make no effort to get up to throw the preserver, which is hanging only 5 feet from you, even though you could do this with absolutely no danger to yourself and with only the most minimal effort. Indeed, you sit chomping away on your sandwich and now, along with the sunset, you watch the fisherman drown.

Under the law of essentially every Anglo-American jurisdiction, you are guilty of no tort making you civilly liable to the family of the fisherman you permitted to drown, nor would you be criminally liable in any way for his death (student note, 1952).

This is admittedly a dramatic example, but the fact of the matter is that this hypothetical example is legally accurate (Bohlen, 1905, 1908;

Seavey, 1960).[1] Neither our tort nor our criminal law concerns itself with the good that one does not do, but rather attempts merely to forbid the doing of harm. This can be defended in part on the grounds that under today's social conditions, the law is more than ambitious enough when it tries to prevent people from harming each other or, in a distressingly wide range of cases, from harming themselves (Kaplan, 1971). In fact, the law in the United States does not do very well in preventing armed robbery, burglary, drunken driving, and a host of other offenses in which people harm other people, and it seems to do appallingly badly at preventing people from harming themselves through drug use, gambling, or the like. It is arguable, then, that the law shows a wise economy in avoiding the temptation to try to force people to be good to each other.

In fact, most commentators and courts have not based the well-known principles against liability for omissions on the fact that law enforcement has more urgent tasks that already tax its resources. Rather, they have been based on two other principles.

First is the principle of *individualism*, carried to an extreme in many of the cases. This principle looks at the event from the point of view of the defendant and his right to be "let alone." It regards the fisherman's falling into the water as an imposition upon the freedom of those around him and asks why the law should permit the fisherman, merely by being careless, to impose legal duties on others and to interfere with their freedom to behave as they wish so long as they do not harm anyone.

The second principle is probably more important. It is the "why me" principle and focuses on the enormous difficulty of drawing *standards* in this type of case. Let us say that, instead of falling off a pier next to me, the fisherman had drowned in an ocean surf in full view of several thousand people. Any one who could have saved him with no danger to himself could, if the legal duty were recognized, be prosecuted. However, since it obviously would be beyond the scope of any prosecutor's resources to prosecute all involved, he would have no choice but to pick out just a few as an example. In this case they might very well be able to claim "why me" and not all the other people. For instance, it might very well have been that, although you could have saved the fisherman, several other people in the vicinity who also heard his scream could equally well have saved him, with varying degrees of effort. The problem of standards in directing the prosecutor as to which of these people to prosecute and is directing the courts as to which to convict is

[1] See generally Perkins, R., *Criminal Law* (2nd ed.), 1969, pp. 594–595; Prosser, W., *Law of Torts*, (4th ed.), 1971, p. 338, § 338.

so difficult that the courts have shied away from the whole area, bolstering their view with the arguments in favor of individualism.

It is interesting to note that in cases in which we have a sufficient answer to the "why me" argument we *do* tend to impose liability for failure to behave in prosocial ways. For instance, one answer to the "why me" question could be that you stand in some particular relationship with the victim. For instance, in the event that the victim is your minor son, you certainly do have a duty to save him and can be held criminally liable if you do not. Another possibility is that you stand in a relationship of responsibility to the victim in some contractual sense. For instance, the captain of a ship who makes no effort to save a passenger or the hospital nurse who makes no attempt to aid a dying patient may be and more likely will be held liable.[2]

A somewhat different way of satisfactorily answering the "why me" question arises when you are in some causal sense responsible for the accident. For instance, if the fisherman had first tripped over you and then had fallen into the water, even if only his clumsiness were to blame, you might still have the duty to save him. The answer to the "why me" question could then be that you were the one he tripped over. Note that this is true even if no responsibility could possibly be attributed to you for the actual action that caused the death. In one case, for instance, the defendant motorist had made no effort to remove a sign he had knocked over or to render it less dangerous by giving warning, and the plaintiff motorist, somewhat later and without negligence, ran into the fallen sign and suffered injuries. The court therefore held the defendant liable on the grounds that having caused, even nonnegligently, the obstruction to traffic he was then required, if it could be done safely, to take reasonable precautions lest others be injured.[3]

The final answer to the "why me" question is probably the most interesting. What would have happened had you undertaken to throw one of the life preservers in the fisherman's direction but had cast it so incompetently that he was unable to reach it before he drowned? One way of handling the problem would be to say that the "why me" question could be answered: "Because you undertook to save him." On the

[2] State v. Staples, 126 Minn. 396, N.W. 283 (1914) (parent–child); West v. Spratling, 204 Ala. 478, 86 So. 32 (1920) (innkeeper–guest); L. S. Ayres & Co. v. Hicks, 220 Ind, 86, 40 N.E.2d 344 (1942) (land occupier–invitee); Tubbs v. Argus, 140 Ind. App. 695, 225 N.E.2d 841 (2d Div. 1967) (land occupier–social guest).

[3] See Cal. Vehicle Code § 20003, providing that "the driver of any vehicle involved in an accident resulting in injury . . . shall render to any person injured in the accident reasonable assistance. . . ." The penalty for violation is imprisonment for up to five years, or fine of not more than $5,000, or both (St. Paul, Minn.: West Publishing Co., 1971).

other hand, most courts would hold that this was not enough, on the theory that, although the "why me" question could be answered in some rhetorical sense, no harm had been done to the fisherman by the incompetent cast, inasmuch as he would have drowned just the same had there been no cast at all.[4]

On the other hand, the courts are unanimous in imposing liability if some argument can be made that your bungled attempt to help the fisherman placed him in an even worse position than he was in before you made the attempt. Thus, if other people who might have saved him desisted from their efforts when they saw that you were preparing to cast the life preserver, the case for liability would be fairly clear.

A LAW TO HELP?

These, then, are the principles that govern Anglo-American law as to punishments for failure to perform prosocial activities in general, and the rescue of someone in distress in particular. No one disputes the fact that, should these principles be found wanting, the Legislature may appropriately change them. After all, the Legislature is already placing upon its citizens a steadily increasing number of prosocial duties. For the most part, they involve regulations upon those involved in business. But the duty to perform such prosocial acts as paying income taxes and registering for the draft now falls upon large classes of citizens. There is no statute in our fundamental Constitutional structure that prevents the Legislature from establishing a general duty to rescue in place of the narrow categories that presently obtain (Edgar, 1976; McNiece & Thornton, 1949).

Several arguments have been made that, indeed, our Legislature should do just this. It has been argued that the ancient common law principle, though appropriate for its time, is nonetheless an anachronism today. Indeed, one of the earliest of what might be called the recent wave of attacks upon the Anglo-American law of omissions begins with the acknowledgment that "during the early years of the common law, affirmative wrong doing presented too great a threat to the king's peace for the courts to concern themselves with mere omissions." However, anyone familiar with the problems of urban America might be pardoned for feeling that things have not changed much (student note, 1952).

Second, it is pointed out that many nations have such requirements (Rudzinski, 1966). One major problem is that we know almost nothing

[4] See Devlin v. Safeway Stores, 235 F. Supp. 882 (S.D.N.Y. 1964).

about the enforcement of such laws and whether they actually affect the behavior of citizens. One thing we do know is that, in France, out of over 100,000 sentences to jail passed in the year 1962, only 52 were for failure to rescue. Moreover, apparently the type of case that is most common is one in which the Anglo-American law would provide a duty anyway. Thus, one case discussed by one of the leading French authorities in the field concerns an incident in which "the family of a drunkard had refused to let him in when he came back home late at night. They wanted to give him a lesson. And, the following morning, they found him dead at the door (Tunc, 1966, p. 57–58)."

Another aspect of the French experience is also interesting. Although a number of other nations had adopted before World War II a duty to rescue, the French law was first enacted by the Vichy government. According to Professor André Tunc, "In 1941 after 50 hostages had been killed as a reprisal for the murder of a German officer, a statute was passed... obliging citizens to intervene for the prevention of crimes and rescue of persons in danger (Tunc, 1966, p. 46)." This was seen as part of the complex of laws that imposed upon citizens a duty to inform of crimes and to aid in other ways the Vichy regime. It cannot, of course, be argued that the association of such laws with totalitarian government means that such laws are bad. First of all, they have also been adopted in many nontotalitarian nations. Second, even a clock that is stopped is correct twice a day. Nonetheless, it can be argued that, though in moral terms it makes great sense, the duty to rescue one in danger, even if appropriately limited so as to require no great effort or danger to the rescuer himself, is only one step down what lawyers call the slippery slope toward requirements that citizens aid their government in less clear circumstances, such as informing about or suppressing dissent. One can argue at great length whether in the long run the symbolic effect of establishing under threat of jail man's moral duty to his neighbor in distress plus, of course, any additional forced movement toward a more civilized style of conduct is worth the further elaboration and rigidifying of the principle that the enforcement of men's morals is the duty of government.

And, although the law in some circumstances certainly has an important educational effect, our knowledge of the effect of this type of law is minimal. Perhaps the only information we have on the effect of such a law upon public attitudes concerns a comparison between Germany, where law does provide a duty to rescue—interestingly, one greatly expanded under the Nazi government—and Austria, where there is no such duty (Zeisel, 1966). An opinion study indicated that a far higher percentage of Germans than of Austrians (86% and 26%, respectively) thought that there was a legal duty (and hence were correct) and that a considerably higher percentage of Germans (44%) than of Austrians (33%) felt that criminal punishment is appropriate for failure to rescue. On the other hand, when citizens of both Germany and Austria were asked to estimate what percentage of people would act so as to ignore the plight of one in dire need of rescue, the percentages were almost identical. In short, we simply do not know whether there are any differences between difference nations in such prosocial behavior. Moreover, even if there were sizable differences in the actual percentages of people willing to rescue others, cultural differences in urbanization, income levels, religious adherence, and many other variables might completely dwarf the prosocial effect, if any, of the law.

The final argument for a change in our Anglo-American law is simply that, regardless of whether the law has any effect upon behavior, it should require morality (Minor, 1923). The relationship between law and morality is an extremely complicated one, but there are good reasons why the attempt to compel morality through threats of criminal punishment may do more harm than good. At the very least, such laws encourage a trend that has been shown to be a very dangerous one in various other areas, such as sexual conduct, drug use, and even political attitudes, where moral principles have been invoked in far less noble a cause than the aid of one in distress.

In any event, among the American states only Vermont has attempted to grapple legislatively with the general problem of rescue. An act passed in 1971 provides that:

> (a) A person who knows that another is exposed to grave physical harm shall, to the extent that the same can be rendered without danger or peril to himself or without interference with important duties owed to others, give reasonable assistance to the exposed person unless that assistance or care is being provided by others.
>
> .... (c) A person who willfully violates subsection (a) of this section shall be fined not more than $100.00.[5]

THE GOOD SAMARITAN STATUTE

Actually, the number of fishermen who drown while bystanders look on and make no effort to save them is not large. There is, however, one situation that has received considerable discussion as regards the law on prosocial behavior and has even become a type of political issue.

[5] Vt. Stat. Ann., tit. 12, § 519 (Supp. 1971).

The principle just mentioned that, though one has no duty to aid someone in distress, he will be liable if he does it incompetently and aggravates the injury has generated considerable discontent among the medical profession. The typical case cited as an example of the unfairness of the law is that of a physician driving home after a hard time at the operating, bridge, or dinner table and obviously not in his very best condition. On the way he passes an automobile accident, and, though he could have driven right by, he stops and renders medical attention. Unfortunately, he does so negligently and, by making the victim's condition worse, becomes liable (D'Amato, 1975; James, 1953).

The physician feels that it is unfair to apply the ordinary rules of negligence in such a case and that if he does in good faith try to help he should not be sued. Moreover, it is not so much the case in which he is negligent and is sued that the physician finds disturbing. Rather, he is much more upset by the case in which he is not negligent but is sued anyway. Even if the courts eventually come out with the right result—something that the physician has absolutely no confidence in—he (or, in actuality, his malpractice insurer) will nonetheless have had to endure the expenses of litigation. Perhaps even more important to him is the fact that, if he is sued, he will have to suffer the insults of bad publicity and loss of status among physicians, as well as the injury of a possible increase in his malpractice insurance rates (Chayet, 1969).

As a result, various medical associations have lobbied, often successfully, for specific "Good Samaritan" statutes that shield physicians from liability for their ordinary negligence (Oberstein, 1963) when they voluntarily stop at roadside emergencies.[6]

Subsidy and Status Symbol?

The force of the argument for Good Samaritan statutes lies not only in the assumed fairness of the matter but also in the simple fact that it is impossible to compel the physician to stop and give aid. So, as long as one wants a physician to render medical services in an emergency,

---

[6] The texts of these statutes may be found in D. Louisell & H. Williams, *Medical Malpractice*, 1971, §§ 21.01.1–21.34. Some statutes cover only physicians (e.g., New Hampshire), whereas others include all licensed medical personnel (e.g., Illinois), and still others cover anyone who renders aid (e.g., Georgia). Some statutes restrict coverage to in-state physicians (e.g., Nebraska), and others cover their out-of-state counterparts (e.g., New Hampshire) as well. Most states exclude liability for those acting "in good faith" (e.g., California), and others hold liable those who commit "gross negligence" (e.g., Indiana) or "willfull or wanton negligence" (e.g., Connecticut). Some statutes apply only to services rendered gratuitously (e.g., Kansas) or to those undertaken without "the exception of remuneration" (e.g., Texas); others are silent on this issue (e.g., New Jersey).

one should not allow the specter of liability to deter him. Good Samaritan statutes are one solution to this problem. It might well be that a better one would be to have a social insurance scheme to pay the physician the fair value of his emergency services and to have him remain liable for his negligence to the emergency victim just as he would be to his patients (Godfrey, 1974). This solution avoids a major objection to Good Samaritan statutes—that in essence they provide a subsidy to physicians by releasing them from a liability that is imposed on all other citizens.

Probably the most interesting aspect of the Good Samaritan statute is that, although the issue is hotly debated, so far as we know there has never been a reported appellate case in which a physician has been successfully sued in the situation contemplated by the Good Samaritan laws. And although there appear to have been a few cases in which the physician was unsuccessfully sued, it would seem that this is merely one of the risks of living in a civilized society—and a risk by no means obviated by the Good Samaritan laws, since they usually allow the injured "patient" to recover damages for gross negligence from the physician. In any event, Good Samaritan laws have swept the nation as one state after another has yielded to the entreaties of its medical society. Indeed, some have even broadened the law to afford Good Samaritan protection to nurses. It even seems that, just like evidentiary privileges (accountants, newspaper reporters, social workers, and a host of other occupational groups have argued for a privilege, such as lawyers and physicians now enjoy against disclosure of their communications), Good Samaritan statutes are coming to be prized more as status symbols than for any practical value.

Enforced Helping

It is possible, however, that, having raised the issue, the physician may very well in the long run come to regret it. Other countries apart from the Anglo-American tradition—the Dutch, for instance—do sometimes impose liability for failure to perform prosocial actions that might save lives. And there the parade of horrible examples that we can imagine has not eventuated—perhaps because of the wise use of prosecutorial discretion. It might be that this type of experience will lead to a further broadening of our laws on the issue, and, if it does, one of the most obvious candidates for the imposition of a duty to aid those in distress will be the physician. When one considers that an enormous percentage of the physician's invested capital, the cost of his medical education, has, at least in the last 30 to 40 years, been paid by the public at large, it may very well not be so unreasonable to regard the physician as in some sense in a special category for this purpose.[7]

It might very well be that a strong moral argument—and one without too great theoretical difficulty—could be made in this case. Unfortunately, the problem would remain that the law would probably be unenforceable except on the most hit-or-miss basis. The fact is that no one would be able to prove in the vast majority of cases whether the physician saw the accident, whether he realized his help might be necessary, or whether he was hurrying home to attend to another patient.

The case of the physician and the Good Samaritan statute indicates the intricacies of attempting to compel prosocial behavior—indeed, even the most elementary form of what we would consider decency—through the law. It might very well be that even the advantages in terms of any increase in prosocial behavior that might result from a legal declaration that this was required would not be worth the costs in unfair whimsical prosecution and the like that a change in the law might bring.

IMPETUS FOR PROSOCIAL BEHAVIOR:
THE LEGAL CARROT

Thus far, we have been talking about the stick of the law without mentioning the carrot. With the exception of the inducement provided by the Good Samaritan laws, most of the law we are discussing does act, if it acts at all, as the stick. There are, however, a number of areas where legal doctrine does attempt to provide an impetus for prosocial behavior. There are special statutes that allow rewards for the apprehension of criminals and, in at least one state, one injured in an attempted rescue can be compensated from a general fund set up for that purpose. For the most part, however, it is in the tort law of rescue that we see what little has been done to encourage this kind of altruism (Landes, 1978; Feldbrugge, 1966).

[7] The Australian state of New South Wales has done precisely this. In 1963, after several physicians in a hospital refused medical attention to a dying infant, a statute was passed that provided that a physician is subject to serious discipline if he "refuses or fails, without reasonable cause, to attend, within a reasonable time after being requested to do so, upon a person for the purpose of rendering professional services in his capacity as a medical practitioner in any case where he has a reasonable cause to believe that such person is in need of urgent attention by a medical practitioner but shall not be guilty under this paragraph of such conduct if he causes another medical practitioner to attend as aforesaid." Medical Practitioners Act § 27(2)(c), New South Wales Stat. (Perm. Supp. 1968), amending Medical Practitioners Act § 27(2), New South Wales, Stat. (1960).

You are sitting beside a road when a hiker walking along the road fails to notice a car bearing down on him. As noted before, you have no duty even to shout a warning. Let us say, however, that either the hiker is deaf or that there is not time enough to warn him, so that all you can do if you wish to save him is push him out of the car's path. If you do attempt to push him out of the way and are struck by the automobile, the courts today will hold the driver liable to you for your injuries if he was driving negligently. At one time the view was that, inasmuch as you had risked your life without having any duty to do so, the rescue attempt was your sole responsibility and you therefore could not collect from the driver for your injury even if the hiker could have done so.

The modern rule, however, is that "danger invites rescue" and that the driver's act of endangering the hiker was also a threat to those around who might attempt to rescue the hiker. Regardless of the reason, however, the fact is clear that if you, the rescuer, are injured because the driver was negligent, the fact that you were a voluntary actor will not bar you from recovering damages for your injuries.

Let us assume now that the hiker, not the automobile driver, was the one who was negligent. In that case, if you are injured in trying to save the hiker, you may very well be compensated by him for your injuries (assuming he is insured or can afford it). The theory is that the case is between you and him and that he should pay simply because his negligence with respect to his own life is also negligent with respect to that of anyone who might attempt to save him.

Note how minimal is this encouragement of prosocial behavior. If neither the driver nor the hiker is negligent, you do not generally get compensated, or if the one who is negligent (or each, if both are negligent) is without funds or insurance, the most you get is thanks. And if your rescue attempt was foolhardy, then you cannot collect, even from one who was both negligent and solvent. It is one thing for the law to encourage rescue attempts; it is another thing to encourage foolhardy ones—despite their high moral content.

This then is the encouragement the law provides to prosocial behavior. It is of course inadequate, but so long as our financial reward to one individual must come in the form of a penalty to another, we must not expect too much. It is hoped that, when we learn more about how to structure reward systems to induce desired behavior, we will devote more legal attention to this issue. Even now one might speculate that we know enough to fashion a type of lottery in which people who had done service to others over and beyond what could be required will become eligible for a system of governmental bonuses—either directly or perhaps less expensively in the form of a ticket to a "good citizens lottery."

The idea is intriguing. Perhaps someday some jurisdiction will do it—once they figure out how to make the necessary factual determinations fairly and at a reasonable cost.

Until then, with the legal tools at our disposal it seems that neither the carrot nor the stick of the law is a very effective tool for the stimulation of prosocial behavior. Indeed, if it were, most of the reasons why we consider behavior prosocial might arguably be lessened. If an individual rescues someone in distress because of legal pressure or inducement, is the act any more prosocial than holding down a job, driving carefully, or a host of other things we do for our own selfish—rather than for prosocial—reasons?

REFERENCES

Bohlen, F. The basis of affirmative obligation in The Law of Tort. *The American Law Register*, 1905, 53, 209–239, 293–310, 337–377.

Bohlen, F. The moral duty to aid others as the basis of Tort liability. *University of Pennsylvania Law Review and American Law Register*, 1908, 56 (Old Series), 217–244, 316–338.

Chayet, N. *Legal implications of emergency care*. New York: Appleton-Century-Croft, 1969.

D'Amato, A. "Bad Samaritan" paradigm. *Northwestern University Law Review*, 1975, 70, 798–812.

Edgar, J. The bystander's duty and the law of torts: An alternative proposal. *St. Mary's Law Journal*, 1976, 8, 302–308.

Feldbrugge, F. Good and Bad Samaritans: A comparative survey of criminal law provisions concerning failure to rescue. *American Journal of Comparative Law*, 1966, 14, 630–657.

Fleming, J., Jr. Scope of duty in negligence cases. *Northwestern University Law Review*, 1953, 47, 778–816.

Godfrey, C. Emergency care: Physcians should be placed under an affirmative duty to render essential medical care in emergency circumstances. *University of California, Davis, Law Review*, 1974, 7, 246–269.

James, F. The scope of duty in negligence cases. *Northwestern University Law Review*, 1953, 47, 778–816.

Kaplan, J. The role of the law in drug control. *Duke Law Review*, 1971, *1971*, 1065–1104.

Landes, W. Salvors, finders, good Samaritans, and other rescuers: An economic study of law and altruism. *Journal of Legal Studies*, 1978, 7, 83–97.

McNiece, H., & Thornton, J. Affirmative duties in tort. *Yale Law Journal*, 1949, 58, 1272–1289.

Minor, H. The moral obligation as a basis of liability. *Virginia Law Review*, 1923, 9, 420–431.

Oberstein, N. Torts: California Good Samaritan legislation: Exemptions from civil liability while rendering emergency medical aid. *California Law Review*, 1963, 51, 816–822.

Rudzinski, A. The duty to rescue: A comparative analysis. In J. Ratcliffe (ed.), *The Good Samaritan and the law*. Garden City, New York: Anchor Books, 1966.

Seavey, W. I am not my guest's keeper. *Vanderbilt Law Review*, 1960, *13*, 699–702.

Student Note. The failure rescue: A comparative study. *Columbia Law Review*, 1952, *52*, 631–647.

Tunc, A. The volunteer and the Good Samaritan. In J. Ratcliffe (Ed.), *The Good Samaritan and the law*. Garden City, New York: Anchor Books, 1966.

Zeisel, H. An international experiment on the effects of a Good Samaritan law. In J. Ratcliffe (Ed.), *The Good Samaritan and the law*. Garden City, New York: Anchor Books, 1966.

15

Toward an Integration

LAUREN WISPÉ [1]

It would be very satisfying indeed to be able, in this last chapter, to suggest a new, integrative theory of helping behavior, a theory in which were incorporated the best of Part I, the most exciting of Part II, and the admonitions of Part III. But this is obviously impossible now. Instead, something can be gained from the attempt to ferret out points of agreement and disagreement among the theories, to analyze some implicit assumptions, and to clarify the principal concepts used. Such is the mission of the present chapter. I will first discuss the nature of altruism as it emerges from the various discussions, then the problem of helping motivation, and finally the social role of sympathy and helping.

THE NATURE OF ALTRUISM

The term *altruism* is of recent origin. The attempts to explain the behavior to which the term applies, however, are ancient, as Masters

[1] Portions of this chapter were written while I was a Visiting Fellow at the Battelle Seattle Research Center.

(Chapter 3) points out. It is generally acknowledged that Comte, the French sociologist, invented the term "sociology," but it is not widely known that he also coined the term "altruism." How he came to adapt it from the Italian word for other, altrui, rather than the French, autrui, or the Latin, alter, remains a puzzle.[2] By altruism he meant an unselfish regard for the welfare of others. Despite its sociological origin, the term altruism has not been widely used by behavioral scientists. In the first place, self-sacrificial bravery, as Campbell (1965) notes, is an extreme form of behavior with low rates of occurrence among humans even in warfare. And, in the second place, the study of altruism creates problems for the behavioral scientist. It is the wrong paradigm. Since Adam Smith, the behavioral sciences have preferred an exchange model of social interaction based upon some kind of psychological hedonism, in which certain input contingencies determine output probabilities (Chapter 6). Within this model, obviously, altruism, in which the victims contribute only their misfortune, is hard to handle. Biologists, however, found the term useful, although they gave it a rather special meaning. In the present volume, Wilson (Chapter 1) defines altruism as "self-destructive behavior performed for the benefit of others." Wilson's stark definition of altruism would also include behavior called "heroic," but behavioral sciences have not been interested in heroism either.

The attempts to explain behavior to which the term altruism applies—will use this term in place of the phrase "altruistic behavior"—have revolved around three persistent questions: What is it? Why would anyone do it? and How can it be inherited? We will consider each of these in turn.

What Is Altruistic Behavior?

As suggested previously, the biological sciences and the behavioral sciences use the term altruism differently. The biologists originally used the term to refer to heroic, often self-destructive behavior directed toward the well-being of others. They have more recently begun to consider any behavior that counters the effects of individual selection as altruistic. The behavioral scientists mean by altruism any unselfish behavior that is other-directed. The point of agreement is that both focus on the welfare of the other person or persons. Although there is this

[2] I am indebted to Professor Joseph Katz for calling this to my attention.

basic agreement, there are also at least two distinctions worth noting. In the first place, the term *altruism* seems to be the generic term for all other-directed behaviors. And there are many synonyms for selfless, other-directedness. In the second place, *altruism* refers to actions that have at least the potential for extreme self-sacrifice—a point Campbell correctly stresses (Chapter 2). The self-sacrifice may be self-annihilating, as in Wilson's definition, or it may be merely inconvenient, as when an expert swimmer goes to someone's rescue knowing that the chances are pretty good that he/she will succeed and survive. To sum: Behavior to be designated as "altruistic" must be directed to the well-being of another person or group and must involve at least some nontrivial self-sacrifice.

The preceding discussion suggests some interesting and important attributional problems. For example, how crucial is the self-sacrificial element in the perception of altruistic behavior? And how does the environmental context influence attributions of altruism? The behavior of a fireman entering a burning building, even in the line of duty, would probably be labelled "altruistic" rather than foolhardy. The same behavior by an average person would probably be seen as foolhardy, even if altruistic. On the other hand, a soldier throwing himself over an unexploded grenade in order to save his fellows would certainly be considered altruistic, although his behavior is suicidal as well as foolhardy in the sense that Kaplan suggests in Chapter 14. Taking his hint from the fact that we live in an attributional world, some interesting elaborations are suggested by Trivers (1971). He suggests that people receive social credits for altruistic actions. There is the intriguing social psychological problem of the empirical determination of social credits accruable for each level of altruistic risk; one must bear in mind that the altruist who estimates the risks is the "actor," whereas the determination of social credits is made by the "observer." Trivers' (1971) notion of "reciprocal altruism" in particular depends upon some kind of equity relationship between the actor and the observer such that the observer must set the social benefits high enough for each level of risk so that the actor will be induced to behave altruistically but also must estimate the risk level accurately so that the chances are reasonably good that the outcome for the actor will be a "viable" one (see Jones & Nisbett, 1972).

This raises some interesting questions about the motivation for heroism. There are adumbrations in the last part of Chapter 6 that heroic altruism may be somewhat less self-conscious than helping relationships and perhaps less concerned with an equitable outcome. It may be less a trait than a state. Although heroic behavior, like other behavior, is probably multiply determined, it may be more difficult to predict heroic behavior than helpfulness. We know so little about heroic forms of altruism that we do not know whether heroes generally act altruistically, or under what circumstances. For example, other things being equal, would a man who rushed into a burning building be equally likely to jump into the icy water to rescue someone? Would that person help a handicapped person across the street? Contribute to a worthy cause? Comfort a crying child? We have few comparative studies of the lives of heroes. Perhaps society can tolerate only a limited number of heroes, but it would be interesting to know what instigated their heroism.

Before leaving this section, it is necessary to point out that behavioral scientists have studied altruistic behavior like cooperation (Mead, 1937) and charity (Bryan, 1972), even though they have not studied heroism. Now biologists have devised roughly comparable terms for cooperation and charity, terms like "mutualism" and "commensalism." In *mutualism* both individuals or species benefit, and in *commensalism* one individual or species benefits without harm to the other. At the other extreme from mutualism there is *parasitism* and *spite*, in which benefits are gained at the expense of the other individual or species. Each discipline has used its own terms for what are, in fact, roughly comparable behaviors. Mutualism and commensalism, for example, offer behavioral classification that could be used for lower forms of life as well as for humans, and thereby some continuity in research between the biological and the behavioral sciences might ensue.

Why Would Anyone Do It?

Psychological hedonism is the doctrine that states that persons strive only after pleasure, and the roots of this doctrine run deep in American psychology. The basic assumption of reinforcement learning theories, equity theory, and even psychoanalytic theory is hedonistic. The basic assumption is that reinforcements maintain behavior and that unreinforced behavior drops out of the response repetoire. This assumption is clear in Chapters 5 and 6. My discussion will be limited to the implications of altruistic behavior for reinforcement theories. One should note, however, that, for Pavlovian conditioning, psychological hedonism is not the principle.[3]

The dilemma that altruism and reinforcement theory pose for one

[3] Professor Richard Solomon emphasized this point in our correspondence.

another is clear. If stable behavior must be reinforced, what are the rewards for altruism? On the other hand, if altruistic behavior is completely selfless and noncontingent, then the basic assumption in reinforcement theory is wrong. If our interpretations of reinforcement theory and of purely altruistic behavior are correct, they are incompatible. It is this dilemma that Lester Ward (1883), the first American sociologist, called "the altruistic paradox." The discussion of this "paradox"—so-called—is peculiar to the behavioral sciences, since they are concerned with the conditions under which behavior is acquired and maintained. The biological sciences are more concerned with the transmission of behavior, and so this problem does not arise. For our purposes, however, the paradox is important, because it raises a fundamental question about altruistic behavior, namely, how selfless must it be? All of the authors in the present volume agree that altruistic behavior involves benefits for the other person. And they would probably agree that in altruistic behavior the welfare of the other person takes precedence over the interests of the self. Some, like Hornstein, would maintain that there are times when ego and other blend so that the other's plight arouses tensions in ego. In their way, self-interest is fused with other's welfare. But this is a more cognitive interpretation. For reinforcement theory the problem arises when one tries to decide how freely these benefits must be given. The issue is not a semantic one. If definition were the only problem, then altruism could be operationalized one way or another, and research could proceed accordingly. The issue is whether enduring, completely selfless behavior is possible or if it is only illusory. Because if "true" altruism is possible, then it appears that none of the research to date bears upon it. The question may be unanswerable at this time, but that does not diminish its theoretical importance.

The suggestion made by most reinforcement theorists is that some kinds of internal, subjective events, called "self-rewards," rather than external, material rewards, serve to reinforce altruistic behavior. For many behavioral scientists, however, invoking the idea of self-rewards to explain altruistic behavior creates as many problems as altruistic behavior itself. As Rosenhan (Chapter 5) notes, self-rewards can explain away the paradox of altruism without really increasing our understanding of the phenomenon. In the absence of any visible, palpable rewards and without operational definitions, one can argue that the altruistic behavior is being maintained by self-rewards. But this is circular argumentation, and it explains more than is observed. This is not to deny that one can feel peculiarly good about having performed an altruistic deed. That argument would go beyond the requirements of even the strictest definition of altruism. Self-satisfaction is simply not a criterion. One can feel satisfied about grossly materialistic and violent acts as well.

Behavioral scientists have been ambivalent and in conflict about the possibility of truly altruistic behavior. This is nowhere clearer than in the chapter on Equity theory (Chapter 6). Favorable outcomes in Equity theory terms are those events that are, or lead to, pleasurable sensations. Hedonism is at the heart of Equity theory. Yet in this chapter is cited the parable of the Good Samaritan—the Good Samaritan, who sought neither wealth nor praise, nor was proud or vain. The Good Samaritan, who sought not "favorable outcomes." But the Good Samaritan is a parable, not a fact.

The Genetics of Altruism

Whereas psychologists, at least in this volume, have been concerned with the maintenance of altruistic behavior, biologists have been concerned with its transmission. For psychologists, the controversy revolves around whether external reinforcements are necessary for altruistic behavior. For biologists, the controversy has been between the genetic and the social basis for the evolution of altruism. Given the biologically oriented, self-sacrificial definition of altruism, the question is inevitable: How can genes that lead to less of me (the altruist) lead to more of us (altruists)?

The basic theoretical problem was first examined by Haldane (1932) and Wright (1945). Wilson states it clearly in Chapter 1. How can genes that are involved in possibly self-sacrificial altruism persist in a species to which these genes are possibly disadvantageous? The answer, of course, is that the species is not really disadvantaged so long as the self-sacrificial behavior of the altruist permits the multiplication of the altruism-bearing genes in the population to a degree more than compensated for by the loss of the altruist. Note that, by this explanation, self-sacrifice for one's offspring, the example that springs most readily to the minds of the behavioral scientists, is not defensible biologically, because individual fitness is measured by the number of surviving offspring. The biologists are not talking about a quid pro quo trade-off. Biologically there is no reason for a man to lay down his life for his brother unless the brother more than doubles the representation of altruistic genes in the next generation. The biologists have neatly worked out the arithmetic. An uncle must more than quadruple his contributions to the next generation to make the altruistic sacrifice worth it, and a cousin must augment his fitness eight times. When genetic fitness gets involved, most of the good will is removed from altruism, a point already made by Wilson. Thus, behavioral scientists and biological scientists may be talking about different levels of behavioral analysis, the mechanisms of behavioral transmission and the mechanisms of behavioral maintenance. I shall return later to this point.

Now the fact of the matter is that, notwithstanding the problems altruism creates for the population geneticist, every society has institutionalized the virtues of altruism and cooperation—a point Campbell (Chapter 2) makes very well. Some form of altruism and helping behavior is absolutely indispensable for human society. Anthropologists (see Chapter 4) have repeatedly pointed out that no society has ever existed without institutionalized cooperation in some form. Now, since man has evolved from nonhuman progenitors, either altruism appeared suddenly or it, too, evolved. The latter is the only scientifically acceptable alternative, so the question is *how* altruistic forms of behavior evolved. It is in this connection that Wilson discusses kin and group selection. Recently a spate of models for group selection have begun to appear, many of them refinements of Haldane's (1932) original idea. They provide a more scientific, mathematical basis for group selection, indicating the kinds of boundary conditions that must exist for group selection to be possible. Wilson discusses several of these, with the conclusion that, although the conditions presupposed by these models are rarely met in nature, it is not inconceivable that altruism could evolve where altruists selectively cooperate with one another, producing thereby mutual benefits at the expense of the nonaltruists. But, given our knowledge at this time, Wilson argues that the genetic basis for altruism remains only a theoretical possibility (see also Dobzansky [1973] for a similar conclusion). Wilson's chapter should be read by all behavioral scientists who would like to know more about the current controversy over the biology of altruism. It is probably the clearest statement of population genetics available anywhere.

Given the difficulties seemingly inherent in the genetic explanation for altruism, behavioral scientists have sought elsewhere. Mostly, they have turned to social evolution. Campbell (Chapter 2) and Cohen (Chapter 4), for example, argue that the role of culture is to inculcate behavioral dispositions directly counter to the selfish tendencies produced by individual selection. The behavioral science argument has usually exploited some condition or mechanism allegedly involved in the course of genetic evolution. Campbell, for example, maintains that genetic competition for reproductive success among social cooperators is a most infelicitous occasion for the propagation of altruism. And since some form of competition putatively exists for access to procreative females, altruism must evolve socioculturally. To support his argument, Campbell points to the cultural admonitions against hedonistic gratifications. These exist, he says, to inhibit the egocentric selfishness produced by Darwinian evolution. But, later on in Chapter 14, Kaplan points out that laws, and so presumably cultural commandments, do not contain the passions, prevent crimes, or inhibit cheating. So not only is the case for cultural admonitions weakened because they are inefficacious and therefore have little survival value, but also they fail to demonstrate convincingly that they are a factor in the sociocultural evolution of altruism. Altruism could still be genetically inherited, with counter-hedonic commandments as cultural interpretations for that fact. Campbell's suggestion, nevertheless, contains some intriguing possibilities, although Marxist scientists would offer quite another explanation for the existence of antigratificatory aphorisms. These kinds of adages, the Marxist might argue, provide a rationalization, intended for the proletariat, for the control of libidinal impulses. This argument would maintain that the upper classes, if they preached them, never followed them.

However one interprets the admonitions against lying, cheating, stealing, killing, adulterating, and other self-indulgences, the fact remains that neither the biological nor the social explanation for altruism is without its difficulties. We have already considered some of the limitations on altruism as a product of natural selection. The difficulty with the argument that altruism is a product of social evolution is that it is circular, as Masters points out in Chapter 3. To say that cultural proscriptions against hedonistic gratifications have evolved to counter the traits begot by individual selection is to beg the question. Nor does it help to study ways in which cultures have modified these proscriptions, because cultural differences do not preclude some kind of genetic base.

There is, however, an interesting historical basis for the disinclination among behavioral scientists to accept an evolutionary interpretation of altruism. Ever since Huxley's (1888) execrable but brilliant essay on "The Struggle for Existence in Human Society," in which he extended Darwin's theory to provide an ethic of unlimited competition, there has remained the lingering doubt for most behavioral scientists that the laws of natural selection preclude the evolution of cooperation and altruism— and that the interpretation of social progress could not be entrusted to biologists. Despite Kropotkin's (1902) passionate refutation of the "struggle for life" philosophy, in which he clearly argued that cooperation is just as necessary for survival as is competition, the doubt remains, and the sociopolitical implications are still important (Proshansky & Tobach, 1976).

Conclusion

The conclusion given here must be ineffably frustrating. There is disagreement—the extent is hard to estimate—about what behavioral domain is covered by the term *altruism*, about how selfless altruism must be, and about whether it is propagated socially or genetically. Each of these different questions is important in its own right. Whereas the first two questions may be more theoretical, the last one—about "the nature of human nature"—has great practical significance. The chapters by Campbell, Masters, Cohen, Skinner, and Kaplan make that clear. On the one hand, if altruism is a product of social evolution, then changing the social values—what Skinner in Chapter 12 refers to as the reinforcement contingencies—should increase the rate of altruistic behavior. Perhaps we can, without too much difficulty, produce a more altruistic society. On the other hand, if altruism is less amenable to social manipulations, it may take a little longer.

I have carefully avoided until now the troublesome possibility that human procreation may be different from animal reproduction. Krebs points out in Chapter 7 that people seek out situations appropriate for their cognitive level, situations in which they expect their behavior to be rewarded. Human behavior is probably less fixed than is animal behavior. And so it is not inconceivable that human females exercise more choice in selective fitness than has heretofore been considered, and that this selection may work against the kinds of physical dominance factors discussed, for example, by Campbell. The association of sex and dominance may be a figment of the male reconstruction of our ancestral past. Perhaps human females have known all along that physical dominance does not provide for their needs during pregnancy and early child-rearing and have opted for traits like protectiveness, tenderness, sympathy—and altruism. This possibility is also discussed by Masters.

THE MOTIVATION TO HELP

In the behavioral sciences, research and theorizing have been concerned with the conditions under which people help and their reasons for helping. In this section, we will consider not *why* people help, but *theories* of why people help. Roughly, we can distinguish between two kinds of theorizing. On the one hand, there have been attempts to develop a theory of helping, or some aspect of helping per se. Good examples of this kind of theory are Latané and Darley's (1970) work on bystander intervention, Lerner's (1966) just world hypothesis, and Hornstein's (1976) Promotive Tension theory. On the other hand, there have been attempts to apply more comprehensive theories to helping behavior. Hatfield *et al.*'s chapter on Equity theory (Chapter 6) is a particularly good example of this approach. As a matter of fact, there are many more examples of the latter than of the former. Shortly after the appearance of the first articles on helping behavior (Berkowitz & Daniels, 1963; Daniels & Berkowitz, 1963) and altruism (Campbell, 1965), behavioral scientists turned to a host of existing psychological and sociological theories for explanations. Berkowitz and his co-workers invoked the concept of reciprocity norms (Gouldner, 1960) and then the norm of social responsibility. Other explanations quickly followed, among them guilt (Darlington & Macker, 1966), modeling (Bryan & Test, 1967), sympathy (Aronfreed, 1968), empathy (Aderman & Berkowitz, 1970; Kerbs, 1970; Stotland, 1969), affective states (Isen, 1970; Moore, Underwood, & Rosenhan, 1973), Equity theory (Walster & Piliavin, 1972), and Learning theory (Cialdini & Vendrick, 1976). And this is only a partial list. It omits the excellent work in developmental psychology (see Hoffman, 1976; Mussen & Isenberg-Berg, 1977; Staub, 1975; and others), as well as the work with animals (Epley & Rosenbaum, 1975; Latané & Glass, 1968; Masserman, Wechkin, & Terris, 1964). But the trend has clearly been to incorporate helping behavior into one of the existing theories rather than to theorize about helping, a point to which I will return in the conclusion.

Since good summaries are available of the bystander intervention research (Huston & Korte, 1976) and the Just World hypothesis (Lerner, 1975), these theories were not included in the present volume. They are sufficiently important, however, so that they should be briefly discussed, and to that I shall now turn. After that I shall discuss some points of agreement among Equity theory, Promotive Tension theory, and Social exclusion theory. And finally, in the conclusion to this section, I shall consider critically some of the possible effects of "Big theory" theorizing.

The Just World Hypothesis and Bystander Intervention Research

The basic finding of the Just World hypothesis is that victims who have no control over their fate are derogated for their misfortunes. Contrary to expectations, victims do not receive sympathy and compassion. Why is this? According to the Just World researchers, the explanation is that, in the absence of any other information, observers assume that the victims somehow deserved what had befallen them. In the mind of the observer, there is a "just world" cognition that assumes that this a world where one gets what one deserves and deserves what one gets. The victim, the explanation continues, must be involved with his fate—the victim and his fate are seen in a unit relationship, in balance theory terms—and so the victim is devaluated.

This finding has been confirmed in several laboratories, and there is also considerable sociocultural support for it. For example, playwrights and scriptwriters have always known the motivational appeal of morality plays. The popularity of morality plays and soap operas depends not only upon their reaffirmation of the moral sanctions, but also upon a direct psychological function. Skinner argues in Chapter 12 that helplessness is aversive, and there is some evidence that seeing helplessness is also aversive. Now, since the victim is helpless against his fate, seeing the victim causes the observers some discomfort, whether this occurs while watching a soap opera or while participating in Just World research studies. In the soap opera or the morality play, the agent of evil (and sometimes the victim) is duly punished. In the Just World research, there are no "bad guys," and the questionnaire provides the subject with an opportunity to retaliate against the victim for the discomfort the victim has caused the subject—an opportunity not provided the audience in a morality play. The devaluation of the victim in the Just World research, therefore, can be seen as a form of punishment for the discomfort that person has caused—as well as because of the justice hypothesis.

Whether or not the Just World researchers would agree with the interpretation just given, the Just World theorizing involves essentially a cognitive-evaluational concept. Not only has the Just World research contributed significantly to a developing theory of helping, but it has also reintroduced the concept of justice to experimental psychology. Asd the psychology of justice is now emerging as a researchable area in itself.

Perhaps the largest body of research in the helping area, however, is that on bystander intervention. The "intervention situation" assumes (a) that the victim's predicament is critical; and (b) that it will get worse unless someone intervenes. Although intervention research has been strikingly inventive, the first assumption is obviously difficult to reproduce experimentally. A situation involving physical assault would seem appropriate for intervention. And Darley and Latané's ingenious original research (1968) tried to reproduce a laboratory facsimile of a tragic case of this kind of deadly assault. But one of the obvious deterrants to intervention in a case of physical assault is the fear of retaliation and injury. Since more than 80% of the intervention research has been conducted in college laboratories (Huston & Korte, 1976), this assumption generally goes unmet. It is also unmet in the situation used by Latané and Darley. But, of course, there are other kinds of intervention situations. And, according to these investigators, regardless of the situation the person must first define the situation as an emergency and then decide what he or she will do about it. The most interesting and durable of their findings is that intervention is inversely related to group size when the estimates are based on individual performance.

There have been some reevaluations of bystander intervention research, as well as attempts to extend it. In the first place, the research paradigm lends itself to situational as opposed to personality-type dependent variables. Intervention researchers have tried to find personality factors in those who intervene (Darley & Batson, 1973), but so far without success. In the second place, the theoretical model has been questioned. Whether emergency behavior of this kind is as rational as their model suggests remains to be demonstrated (Wispé, 1972). A recent review (Nisbett & Wilson, 1977) raises serious reservations about this possibility. This review indicates that subjects may make verbal reports amenable to the Latané–Darley rational model, but their actual behavior may have been more impulsive than the subjects realized or were able to report. These concerns notwithstanding, intervention research has indicated a number of factors affecting whether one person will come to the rescue of another; among them, such things as the salience (Clark & Word, 1974) and the seriousness (Piliavin & Piliavin, 1972) of the situation, freedom to enter the field (Staub, 1971), whether another person helps (Bickman, 1971)—and many more.

Although both the Just World and bystander intervention theories employ cognitive mediating explanatory variables, the discerning reader will not have missed an apparent contradiction between them. Why should bystanders intervene in behalf of victims they are derogating? Certainly no one would be strongly motivated to come to the aid of anyone who is implicitly held responsible for his or her own fate. Why risk embarrassment and even injury for someone who is not worth it? Obviously, the Just World hypothesis offers a ready rationalization for anyone who is unwilling or unable to intervene. But the contradiction may be more apparent than real. The explanation may be something like this. Although intervention depends upon many factors—only a few of which were mentioned—both research and observation indicate that interveners are in a distinct minority. Heroes and Good Samaritans are rare in any population. Therefore, the unfortunate tendency to derogate the unfortunate may be one of the psychological factors accounting for low intervention rates. What appears to be a contradiction may, with more research, produce a complementarity of results.

A Comparison of Three Helping Motivation Theories

In the present section, I shall analyze in detail Equity theory (Chapter 6), Promotive Tension theory (Chapter 9), and Social Exclusion theory (Chapter 11). These three theories were chosen because of their apparent dissimilarity. Equity, with its roots in economics, is an excellent example of applying a comprehensive theory to the phenomenon of helping behavior. Promotive Tension theory is clearly Lewinian in origin and is a good example of extending a cognitive psychological theory to include helping. What we are calling here Social Exclusion theory provides a classically sociological analysis of any form of aiding. What, if anything, do these three theories have in common, and what does this commonality tell us about the motivation to help? Let us consider first a comparison of Equity and Promotive Tension theory.

In both Equity and Promotive Tension theory, motivation is, of course, inferred from behavior. In Promotive Tension theory, Hornstein indicates that linked fates, similar beliefs and attitudes, and an absence of negative sentiments promote the formation of "we-bonds" that in turn facilitate helping. Hatfield *et al.* indicate that helping occurs in the absence of negative perceptions—such as seeing the victim as stupid or greedy—and when the cost to the helper is not too great or is not greater than the expected returns. In both theories, therefore, the crucial element is a judgmental one. In Promotive Tension theory, the person must decide whether the other person is included in the "we-group." In Equity theory, the person must judge the cost of the helping in terms of its potential gratifications. In equity theory the person who makes the judgment, the so-called "scrutineer," can be an outside observer, the potential helper, or the victim. In fact, helping research has been concerned primarily with the helper. So in both theories, however different their theoretical assumptions and terminology, the potential helper is in the same phenomenological spot. Although Promotive Tension theory is in one sense "predecisional," Equity theory is "postdecisional"; the former says little about expected rewards, whereas the latter emphasizes them. In both theories the cognitive element is most important.

Equity and Promotive Tension theory also focus on different phases of the helping process. Promotive Tension theory concentrates on the factors involved in the onset of helping; Equity theory is more concerned with the maintenance and termination of a helping interaction. Promotive Tension theory investigates the phenomenology of certain social characteristics that initiate the helping relationship, but, once begun, it is less concerned with the "outcomes" of the relationship. Equity theory assumes that the two people are interacting (even if only potentially). If the two people are not in a relationship, there is no basis for deciding upon the equity of the exchange. Once they are in a relationship, however, then Equity theory explains the nature and the termination of the relationship in terms of input–output ratios.

We might try to summarize this comparison of Equity and Promotive Tension theory by noting that Equity Theory assumes that the potential helper and the victim are already in some kind of relationship and then goes on to explain the progress and the duration of the interaction in terms of input–output ratios. Promotive Tension theory, by contrast, inquires into the conditions that initiated the helping relationships in the first place. It has little to say about the "value" of the help to either person. But despite these important differences, both theories have remarkably similar cognitive components. The importance of this fact for mutual enlargement will soon become clear. But, next, let us include Social Exclusion theory in our analysis.

A comparison of Weitman's Social Exclusion theory with Equity and Promotive Tension theories reveals at least one interesting similarity. The outraged violence that Weitman predicts as a result of being socially excluded depends, in part, upon the person's perception of a situation from which he or she has been "excluded" without "good cause." Now, perceiving oneself as being excluded unfairly is like perceiving oneself as being in the "out-group." And perceiving oneself as being in the "out-group" is similar to other kinds of perceptual categorizings, including perceiving onself in the "in-group." There are judgments, cognitive processes, as is also the perception of "equity."

Now, of course, feelings of being excluded can range from paranoidal delusions to veridical perceptions. Not all situations to which one remains uninvited generate the destructive, moral outrage to which Weitman refers, because other interpretations are possible. In Chapter 8, Ekstein discusses some of the mechanisms by which these kinds of interpretations are made. A guilty person, for example, might interpret such a situation as one to which he or she does not deserve to be invited, thus defusing it. In general, however, Weitman is vague about how such interpretations are made and about what is accomplished by the outraged violence that often follows being excluded. To say that one is passionately aroused by being socially excluded is not an explanation, much less a justification, for violence. But using Equity theory terms, one can reinterpret these outraged feelings following social exclusion as an attempt to restore psychological equity or fairness. Since equity is a compelling psychological motive, the intense reactions to being excluded are not as irrational, nor as inexplicable, as first appeared. Here, the comparison indicates that the various theories of helping behavior mutually support and enliven each other.

Another example of the ways in which this comparison leads to reciprocal enlightenment among the theories involves a further analysis of Equity and Social Exclusion theory. Equity theory has always been disturbingly silent about the factors that determine the judgment of equity. This is crucial to prediction in Equity theory. Social norms cannot be invoked as explanations, because, as Campbell points out in Chapter 2, there are norms for quite diverse behaviors. For example, there is a norm for acting quickly ("A stitch in time saves nine"), but there is also a norm for proceeding cautiously ("Look before you leap"). So, to invoke a normative explanation is merely to restate the problem one step removed. The question then becomes: Why did the person select that particular norm rather than some other one? Now, Weitman's idea of feeling socially excluded may provide a somewhat more interesting, clearer explanation. An "inequitable" exchange would be one in which the subject felt excluded from certain positive things—like love, money, and status—from which he felt he had a rightful claim not to be excluded.

To what extent these reinterpretations would be acceptable to the individual authors is unknown. But even if they are only partly correct, certain developments follow that could lead to more comprehensive theorizing. We have shown that these theories can mutually enrich each other, possibly by virtue of a common cognitive construct used by all three theories. The cruciality of cognition in all these theories is in itself of importance. In addition, although Equity theory offers a powerful reductive model for the complexity of social relationships, it may be a deceptive oversimplification to treat all psychological relationships as economic exchanges. In fact, Equity theory is psychologically rather barren. Now, Weitman's Social Exclusion theory adds to Equity theory a possibly interesting, commensurable psychological dimension. On the other hand, the concept of inequity provides for Social Exclusion theory an explanatory motive that increases the power of that theory at the psychological level. We have already pointed out that Equity and Promotive Tension theory emphasize different aspects of the helping relationship. These comparisons suggest the lines along which these theories need to develop in order to be more adequate. It is hoped that these kinds of detailed comparisons among theories will lead to more testable hypotheses, that, in the end, will lead to a better understanding of helping.

Conclusion

In a burgeoning area, it is natural for investigators to be bold in what they try. Given the necessity for publicizing research, however, they often become timorous in their explanations. Perhaps there is some justification for this. It is probably easier to get new results published if they are interpreted in old ways. This might be called the "safe play" strategy in scientific research, but it comes at a price. The price science pays for the "safe play" strategy is that it subtly inhibits the development of new theories. New methods and new ways of looking at things are discouraged. Existing theories thus expropriate new results and their related methodologies and use these to support their claims to being comprehensive, general theories of behavior. Rather than enriching the conceptual language of science, the new results are transplanted, and any new theoretical speculations are stillborn. The more interesting and exciting the results, the more likely this is to happen.

Something of this sort seems to have happened in the area of helping behavior research. As I noted above, there have been any number of ingenious, careful studies showing that subjects will help if they are made to feel guilty, if they are preceded by a helping model, or if they are reinforced—to mention only a few examples. The question is whether these studies contribute much to our understanding of helping or whether they merely demonstrate, again, the power of guilt, modeling, and reinforcements.

Before concluding this section, it may be worth noting that there is one kind of helping behavior to which the theories above apply somewhat less, and that is the kind of helping that occurs as the fulfillment of certain professional roles: the helping of counselors, social workers, and physicians, for example. Although discussing professional helping roles rather than laboratory research, Lenrow's analysis in Chapter 13 tends to confirm some of the points previously made. In particular, Lenrow notes the disequilibrium inherent in the helping interaction and the need to balance it. This is not dissimilar from Hatfield et al.'s discussion about the need for equity. Lenrow also stresses the importance of perceptual factors between helper and client in terms similar to Hornstein's.

THE SOCIAL ROLE OF SYMPATHY

Part I of the present volume argued for the possibility of some genetic susceptibility for altruism. Wilson's theorizing was more genetic; the remaining chapters were less so. It was noted that there was an audible silence about the conditions under which altruism occurred. Part II presented the most important theories of helping behavior but observed that, although the theories were social and psychological, the majority were not primarily concerned with helping. Further analysis revealed, however, that most of them involved an important cognitive component. Now, in this section, the concept of sympathy (or some variant of it) will be considered as a possible or a partial explanation for helping behavior. Since sympathy is representational, it fulfills the cognitive-motivational aspects discussed in Part II. And since it is counterhedonistic, it fills the selflessness requirement noted in Part I. Finally, it is a concept with a long and honorable, if not always lucid, history in the behavioral sciences, and it is inextricably tied to helping behavior. This is not to say that sympathy motivates helping only, nor that all helping is motivated by sympathy, but rather that helping is one of the dominant responses accompanying the feeling of sympathy.

Nothing in any of the above paragraphs intends a criticism of the excellent chapters on the more comprehensive general theories of behavior, like Learning, Equity, Psychoanalytic, Cognitive-Developmental, or Field theory, in which helping behavior is but one small part. Eventually, one of these may offer the best explanation. What follows is instead intended to stress the importance of the concept of sympathy as it relates to helping.

A Description of Sympathy

The term *sympathy* comes from the Latin *sympathia* or the Greek *sympatheia* and means, literally, with (*syn*) feeling (*pathos*). In general, it has referred to that capacity among men to apprehend and respond to the suffering of another being; this, in turn, is the basis for the social bond. One is inclined to use "sympathy" to refer to feelings and emotions, rather than to actions. The connotations of sympathy are cognitive and affective. By contrast, *altruism* usually refers to actions.

Sympathy refers to inner states or traits that serve to represent or to reflect to the self the point of another person and to move the beholder to try to ameliorate the other person's discomfort. One is constrained to definitional caution, given the current controversy over state and trait theory; but sympathy, in general, has been used to refer to some motivational features within the individual roughly comparable to affiliation, aggressiveness, or achievement. Perhaps there are, in fact, only general dispositions to make certain kinds of responses in particular situations, but sympathy is not usually imputed to persons whose representative behavior over a sample of places, times, and roles fails to meet some minimal, but specifiable, standards of concern for the comfort of another individual.

Some Psychological Factors in Sympathy

In Chapters 4 and 8, Cohen and Ekstein, respectively, discuss some factors in the development of sympathy within the structure of the Western family. Although they approach the problem from different perspectives, they come to some similar conclusions. Since neither anthropology nor psychoanalysis has used the concept of sympathy systematically, these two chapters are signal contributions. Let us turn first to the substance of Cohen's and Ekstein's chapters.

Cohen notes that in European cultures and in their derivatives an intensive affectivity is cathected by the intrafamilial bonds. In Western societies, for the most part these are relatively stable, enduring familial relationships, usually between the child and one or two adults who are in a position to minister to its needs. Usually, but not always, these are the biological mother and father, but Cohen does not discuss the consanguinous basis for parenting. Presumably, any other adult in the same role and similarly endowed with affection and tenderness for the child could perform the same functions with the same results. But this remains an open question. Biologists might object to the assumption that any other adult could be endowed to the same degree as the biological parents with the requisite love and affection. Cohen, understandably, leans toward a sociocultural explanation for the development of sympathy. He argues that deep emotional attachments between the child and those with whom the child interacts are fostered by a situation that promotes durable and frequent parent–child interaction. Now, Adam Smith realized a long time ago that sympathy would be greatest for members of one's own family, next greatest for the next of kin, and so on down the line—just as Wilson would predict. But none of these writers consider the mechanisms that make these developing bonds peculiar in this regard—a point to which I shall return when considering Ekstein's work. Instead, most writers discuss the social consequences of this kind of emotional indoctrination. Cohen, for example, observes briefly that, although these patterns of childrearing foster highly emotional expressions within the family, they also tend to generalize somewhat indiscriminately to social, political, and economic relationships at large. The market place does not lend itself to analysis in terms of affective relationships, but workers nevertheless are said to be "alienated" from their jobs. "Make love not war," one of the slogans of the 1960s, reveals this failure to discriminate politics from passion. Appositing love and war in this manner, besides revealing the sloganizer's unconscious assimilation of sex and aggression, shows the failure to grasp the intensely private nature of certain kinds of emotional relationships. This is directly related to Weitman's discussion in Chapter 11.

Turning now to Ekstein's contribution, it has probably been noted before that psychoanalysis is the preoccupation with intense, primarily familial, emotional relationships. Ekstein outlines some of the conditions that make for the development of sympathy—although he would probably not use that term. "Good mothering" is the generic descriptive phrase for the agent who understands and is able to respond selflessly to the offspring's infantile needs and later childish—including adolescent—demands with compassion, support, and only as much restrictiveness as the situation requires. Although Ekstein might not put it this way, good mothering, like good sex, involves more than passionate surrender. It involves active participation. The interaction is biological, not mechanical. It involves listening to the deeper needs and to the harmonic overtones: An epiphany seen only through loving eyes. Like good lovers, good mothers must know when to say yes and when to say no. If all of this makes "good mothering" seem difficult, if not almost unattainable, do our rising divorce and delinquency rates indicate anything less?

Both Ekstein and Cohen emphasize the importance of the development of interpersonal emotional relationships. Although, as Ekstein notes, psychoanalysis originally studied only the pathogenic aspects of emotional relationships, later it began to study more positive social behaviors and the operation of exactly those forces about which, as we said earlier, almost nothing is known. Many will be constrained to observe that the future of the concept of sympathy is in bad hands. They will object that psychoanalytic theory cannot be tested, that its terms are metaphorical at best, and that its sample of subjects is biased. There is unarguable truth in some of these objections. Ekstein would probably agree. Be that as it may, have already belabored the point that no one else has been tried to develop a theory of sympathy. And it is not inconceivable that interesting research may grow from metaphorical acorns!

We turn now from theory to some research. Hornstein's chapter on Promotive Tension provides a fruitful extension of some of the suggestions in Cohen's and Ekstein's chapters. Although Hornstein does not use the concept of sympathy, certainly an ingeniously simple experimental paradigm in which one person's tension systems are influenced by another person's unfulfilled needs or unmet goals is related to that concept. If this is true, then Hornstein's research represents a decade of sustained investigation—something rare in social psychology—into one aspect of sympathetic helping behavior. In Chapter 9 he lucidly summarizes research on some of the conditions under which sympathy—or promotive social relationships—might arise.

The briefest and broadest description of Promotive Tension theory is that it involves, in ways not yet fully understood, the extension of the self to include the needs of another person. In recent years, "Self theories" have been unpopular in America, and Hornstein, as did Lewin before him, wisely avoids any references to the self. Call it what you will, however, we do respond emotionally to a wide variety of stimuli as if they were a part of the emotionally charged familial nexus discussed previously. One dislikes the car salesman who kicks the tires of one's car in almost the same way as someone who casts aspertion on the honor of one's parents. Examples are too commonplace to need to multiply them here. Conditioning theorists offer one explanation for this phenomenon that certainly contains elements of truth, but overall it may be inadequate. Cognitive theorists have been moving into this area, trying to operationalize the conditions that produce this extension of the self. Hornstein uses the "we-bond" to describe the cognitive structure antecedent to sympathetic helping. Those are helped who are perceived as part of the "we" group; those who are seen as part of the "they" group are not. The antecedent conditions of helping behavior are probably more complicated than that, but, indeed, Hornstein has investigated one important dimension. And this area is exactly where economists (Phelps, 1975; Schneider, 1948) and biologists (Darwin, 1871; Wilson, 1975), as I noted previously, are most deficient. It is an observable fact people extend help beyond their immediate families, but it is doubtful that they calculate the biological fitness to be accrued before undertaking each helpful act. Hornstein asks, therefore, what kinds of psychological conditions provide a basis for helping relationships. The important thing about the work of Hornstein and his collaborators is that they have investigated experimentally the conditions under which helping occurs, and their results are interpretable in terms of a theory of sympathy.

The Dark Side of Helping

Up to this point, no one has cast doubt on the goodness of helping. The implicit assumptions seem to be that, if we knew more about its nature, motives, and development, we could increase the amount of helping. And, further, since one cannot make two responses at the same time, as we increase the rate of helping, we decrease the rate of antisocial behaviors like war, crime, delinquency, etc. Making love is still better than making war. Now along come Weitman (Chapter 11), Skinner

(Chapter 12), and Kaplan (Chapter 14) to raise some embarrassing, counterintuitive questions. Their message is that helping is not always good for society.

Weitman argues cogently and gracefully that every act of helping can arouse hostile reactions based upon wounded feelings. Taking a more sociological position, he agrees with Cohen that a society is maintained in part by acts of generosity and sacrifice. But he suggests that societies should encourage helping in the same way in which porcupines make love—carefully. For any helping act has the psychological effect of making those who have not been helped feel excluded. Although he does not put it just this way, those who are unhelped are in a position of "relative deprivation." They see themselves as discriminated against, and they are easily aroused to acts of passionate outrage. Now, although all societies have institutionalized forms of exclusiveness—affectionate relationships in Western societies are among the most prominent examples—they also have what he calls "passion-framing" mechanisms, like dating and courtship, and institutionalized forms of release, such as bacchanalia, festivals, and games. The function of these carnivals lies in the fact that they tend to democratize and deemphasize the exclusiveness otherwise maintained by certain individuals. In certain instances they provide open access to otherwise privatized interaction, thus, in effect, trivializing them. Making something available makes it unimportant.

This is an intriguing idea, but there is an obvious danger. The danger is similar to that found in the manner in which earlier psychoanalysis, according to Ekstein, approached positive kinds of interpersonal emotions. Some kinds of helping probably do have negative aspects, but all helping relationships are not bad. To his credit, Weitman tries to avoid this pitfall. He does point out that helping behavior is more complicated than psychologists and biologists have indicated. And certain safeguards must be included in most social meliorative programs to improve their effectiveness, a point much the same as that Lenrow makes.

There is another "bad" side to acts of inclusiveness, however, one that neither Weitman nor Hornstein consider, but that Campbell (1965) does. "We-bonds," helping, and whatever else builds a sense of group spirit, also makes wars possible.

Skinner, in Chapter 12, also disapproves of meliorative programs, but for another reason. Given the choice of getting something for nothing or of working for it, Skinner argues, most people still choose the former. But, since in an economic sense value cannot be created without work, if some people get something for nothing, some other people must pay for it. In Hornstein's terms, "they" get something for nothing, and "we" work for it. Since this goes against even a commen-sense notion of equity, how long can it prevail? Skinner argues that helplessness is aversive, and so we help others who are helpless as long as they reinforce us for our helping. And our helping stops as soon as "they" stop reinforcing us; that is, when they become sated, resentful, or too old. In other words, those who probably need the help the most, some of the culturally disadvantaged and the elderly, are the least likely to get prolonged assistance.

So far it is bad enough, but Skinner carries his argument one step further. Helping programs lead to a sense of possession rather than to a sense of acquisition. The emphasis is on "having" rather than on "getting." Reinforcing a sense of acquisition leads people to work for what they need. Reinforcing a sense of possession leads to dependency. And psychological dependency makes political totalitarianism easier. Totalitarian governments guarantee a few simple possessions; democracies guarantee nothing except the freedom to work for them. Even the Constitution does not guarantee happiness; only the freedom to chase it. Whether or not one agrees with Skinner's capstone point, it is hard to deny its importance. And a closer examination shows that the arguments of Skinner, Weitman, and Lenrow are related. In particular Lenrow's criticism of the socially established helping roles comes to the same general conclusion as Skinner. All agree that most social meliorative programs have got to the wrong people with the wrong message.

The Legal Aspects of Helping

The tragic murder of Kitty Genovese in March, 1964 in full view of no less than 38 neighbors aroused public indignation about why helping was such a rare phenomenon in our society. In Chapter 14, Kaplan, trained as a lawyer, discusses some of the legal aspects of helping. Our focus has now shifted from altruistic acts toward a member of one's family and sympathetic intrafamilial bonds to the arena of public behavior. This turns out to be quite a different situation, and heroism gives way to legalism. Kaplan discusses with admirable clarity some of the issues at stake, the first being the "principle of individualism" or the "why me" question. This principle assumes that it is every individual's right to be left alone as long as no harm is being done to others. The need for help, on the other hand, carries with it an inherent limitation on this freedom of others, especially on the freedom of anyone who is able to help. The latter might be called "the responsibility to help"—although that is not Kaplan's phrase. Obviously, the "principle of individualism" and the "responsibility to help" are in conflict. Some countries already have mandatory helping laws, often called "Good

Samaritan Laws." And many people in America, understandably indignant over failures to intervene, such as in the Kitty Genovese case, are urging passage of Good Samaritan Laws without realizing fully the legal implications. Where does one's responsibility end, Kaplan asks, when there are laws making helping mandatory? And he points out how easily Good Samaritan laws can be perverted to include informing on one's neighbors for the good of the state!

As a lawyer, Kaplan is not concerned with programs for improving the moral fiber of the public or with the psychology of heroic intervention, and he makes it clear that the law exists to inhibit and punish wrongdoers, not to encourage do-gooders. Since it has obviously failed to prevent antisocial actions, how can one expect it to promote prosocial behaviors? Still, special interest groups press for passage of Good Samaritan laws. Kaplan seems to doubt whether such laws would be enforceable and whether they would much affect helping behavior. At present, there is little legal encouragement for prosocial behavior. The modern rule, he says, is that danger invites rescue but discourages heroism.

The relationship between the law and psychology is a complicated one. The "why me" question illuminates the difficulty in legislating moral motivation. How can the law make morally compelling a contingency relationship over which the person, by definition, has no control? Perhaps helping behavior can be motivated in response to equity motives, as Hatfield et al., maintain, or perhaps it can happen in response to certain social norms, as Cohen, Weitman, and others would argue; but, considering the enormous effort involved in eliciting what is presented as altruistic behavior in defense of one's country during wartimes, the prospects for making altruistic behavior legally compulsory do not seem promising. The parable of the Good Samaritan exemplifies the good Christian life. But it does not demand it. The Good Samaritan remains a parable, not a commandment.

Finally, as Kaplan notes, if helping is required by law, it is no longer altruistic. If there are laws requiring altruism, there is no altruism!

Conclusion

The historical search for the explanation for man's social unity has oscillated between two antipodal positions, that of those who, like Nietzsche, feel that creativity and superiority derive from chaos and conflict, from the "dancing stars within us," and, on the other hand, that of those who, like Hume, Adam Smith, and Darwin, feel that in man's capacity for sympathy and compassion lies the basis for sanity and society. Our problem has been complicated, because the most in-fluential theories in the behavioral sciences have been about conflict rather than about harmony: Freud and intrapsychic conflict, Marx and class conflict, Darwin–Huxley and the struggle within and between species. The language of the behavioral sciences is richer in synonyms for antisocial than for prosocial activities (Wispé, 1974). We know more about hate, aggression, and prejudice than about love, sympathy, and cooperation. The present volume is a small contribution to redress the imbalance.

It is now generally acknowledged, after more than a hundred years of empirical behavioral science, that every society has some institutionalized forms of "positive" behavior. It is generally accepted that, without these, human life as we know it would be impossible. Nevertheless and notwithstanding, as we have repeated throughout this volume, there have been few theoretical attempts to fathom institutions operating along these lines. One of the concepts most frequently mentioned in this con-nection, however, is sympathy. But the discussions, with the exception of that of Adam Smith (Schneider, 1948), have been unsystematic. In fact, the history of the concept of sympathy is composed of a series of often brilliant episodes tied together by a general disregard for the way in which it functions. In the analysis here presented I tried to present a general description of sympathy and to discuss how it might operate motivationally. I also tried to suggest some factors in the development of sympathy—albeit the term *sympathy* was not always mentioned. And I tried to point to some work that seemed interpretable in terms of sympathy. In the present section, therefore, I tried to advance the case for sympathy as the motivational basis for helping behavior—at least for one form of it.

REFERENCES

Alderman, D., & Berkowitz, L. Observational set, empathy, and helping. *Journal of Personality and Social Psychology*, 1970, *14*, 141–148.
Aronfreed, J. *Conduct and conscience.* New York: Academic, 1968.
Berkowitz, L., & Daniels, L. Responsibility and dependency. *Journal of Abnormal and Social Psychology*, 1963, *66*, 427–436.
Bickman, L. The effect of another bystander's ability to help on bystander interven-tion in an emergency. *Journal of Experimental Social Psychology*, 1971, *7*, 367–379.
Bryan, J. Why children help: A review. *Journal of Social Issues*, 1972, *28*, 87–104.
Bryan, J., & Test, M. Models and helping: Naturalistic studies in aiding behavior. *Journal of Personality and Social Behavior*, 1967, *6*, 400–407.

Campbell, D. Ethnocentricism and other altruistic motives. In D. Levine (Ed.), *Nebraska symposium on motivation*. Lincoln: University of Nebraska Press, 1965, Pp. 283–311.

Cialdini, R., & Vendrick, D. Altruism and hedonism: A social developmental perspective on the relationship of negative mood and helping. *Journal of Personality and Social Psychology*, 1976, *34*, 907–914.

Clark, R., & Word, L. Where is the apathetic bystander? Situational characteristics of the emergency. *Journal of Personality and Social Psychology*, 1974, *29*, 279–287.

Daniels, L., & Berkowitz, L. Liking and response to dependency relations. *Human Relations*, 1963, *16*, 141–148.

Darley, J., & Batson, C. "From Jerusalem to Jericho": A study of situational and dispositional variables in helping behavior. *Journal of Personality and Social Psychology*, 1973, *27*, 100–108.

Darley, J., & Latané, B. Bystander intervention in emergencies: Diffusion of responsibility. *Journal of Personality and Social Psychology*, 1968, *8*, 377–383.

Darlington, R., & Macker, C. Displacement of guilt-produced altruistic behavior. *Journal of Personality and Social Psychology*, 1966, *4*, 442–443.

Darwin, C. *The descent of man and selection in relation to sex*. New York: Appleton, 1871.

Dobzansky, T. Ethics and values in biological and cultural evolution. *Zygon*, 1973, *8*, 261–281.

Epley, S., & Rosenbaum, M. Cooperating behavior in rats: Effect of extinction of shock onset conditions during acquisition. *Journal of Personality and Social Psychology*, 1975, *31*, 453–458.

Gouldner, A. The norm of reciprocity: A preliminary statement. *American Sociological Review*, 1960, *25*, 161–178.

Haldane, J. *The causes of evolution*. London: Longmans, Greene, 1932.

Hoffman, M. Empathy, role-making, guilt, and development of altruistic motives. In T. Likona (Ed.), *Moral development and behavior: Theory, research, and social issues*. New York: Holt, Rinehart and Winston, 1976, Pp. 124–143.

Hornstein, H. *Cruelty and kindness: A new look at aggression and altruism*. Englewood Cliffs, New Jersey: Prentice-Hall, 1976.

Huston, T., & Korte, C. The responsive bystander: Why he helps. In T. Likona (Ed.), *Moral development and behavior*. New York: Holt, Rinehart and Winston, 1976, Pp. 269–283.

Huxley, T. The struggle for existence in human society. *The nineteenth century*, February, 1888. Reprinted in Kropotkin, P. *Mutual aid*. Boston: Extending Horizon Books, 1955, Pp. 329–341.

Isen, A. Success, failure, attention, and reaction to others: The warm glow of success. *Journal of Personality and Social Psychology*, 1970, *15*, 294–301.

Jones, E., & Nisbett, R. The actor and the observer: Divergent perceptions of the cause of behavior. In E. Jones *et al.* (Eds.), *Attribution: Perceiving the causes of behavior*. Morristown, New Jersey: General Learning Press, 1972.

Krebs, D. Altruism—An examination of the concept and a review of the literature. *Psychological Bulletin*, 1970, *73*, 258–302.

Kropotkin, P. *Mutual aid*. Boston: Extending Horizon Books, 1955. First, published London, 1902.

Latané, B., & Darley, J. *The unresponsive bystander: Why doesn't he help*. New York: Appleton-Century-Croft, 1970.

Latané, B., & Glass, D. Social and nonsocial attraction in rats. *Journal of Personality and Social Psychology*, 1968, *9*, 142–146.

Lerner, M. (Ed.). The justice motive in social behavior. *Journal of Social Issues*, 1975, *31*(3), 1–19.

Lerner, M., & Simmons, C. Observer's reaction to the "innocent victim": Compassion or rejection. *Journal of Personality and Social Psychology*, 1966, *4*, 203–210.

Masserman, J., Wechkin, S., & Terris, W. "Altruistic" behavior in Rhesus monkeys. *American Journal of Psychiatry*, 1964, *121*, 584–585.

Mead, W. *Cooperation and competition among primitive people.* New York: McGraw-Hill, 1937.

Moore, B., Underwood, B., & Rosenhan, D. Affect and altruism. *Developmental Psychology*, 1973, *8*, 88–104.

Mussen, P., & Isenberg-Berg, N. *Roots of caring, sharing and helping.* San Francisco: W. H. Freeman, 1977.

Nisbett, R., & Wilson, T. Telling more than we can know: Verbal repots on mental processes. *Psychological Review*, 1977, *84*, 231–259.

Phelps, E. (Ed.). *Altruism, morality, and economic theory.* New York: Russell Sage, 1975.

Piliavin, J., & Piliavin, I. Effects of blood on reactions to a victim. *Journal of Personality and Social Psychology*, 1972, *23*, 353–361.

Proshansky, H., & Tobach, E. (Eds.). *Genetic destiny: Race as a scientific and social controversy.* New York: AMS Press, 1976.

Schneider, H. (Ed.). *Adam Smith's moral and political philosophy.* New York: Harper & Row, 1948.

Staub, E. Helping a person in distress: The influence of implicit and explicit "rules" of conduct on children and adults. *Journal of Personality and Social Psychology*, 1971, *17*, 137–144.

Staub, E. *The development of prosocial behavior in children.* New York: General Learning Press, 1975.

Stotland, E. Exploratory investigations of empathy. In L. Berkowitz (Ed.), *Advances in experimental social psychology*, Vol. 4. New York: Academic, 1969, Pp. 271–313.

Trivers, R. The evolution of reciprocal altruism. *Quarterly Review of Biology*, 1971, *46*, 35–37.

Walster, E., & Piliavin, J. Equity and the innocent bystander. *Journal of Social Issues*, 1972, *28*, 165–189.

Ward, L. *Dynamic sociology: Or applied social sciences as based on statistical sociology and the less complex sciences.* New York: Appleton, 1883.

Wilson, E. *Sociobiology: The new synthesis.* Cambridge, Massachusetts: Harvard University Press, 1975.

Wispé, L. Positive forms of social behavior: An overview. *Journal of Social Issues*, 1972, *28*, 1–20.

Wispé, L. The yin and yang of psychological research: An analysis of studies of "postive" and "negative" forms of social behavior. Paper presented at the American Psychological Association meetings, New Orleans, 1974.

Wright, S. Tempo and mode in evolution: A critical review. *Ecology*, 1945, *26*, 415–419.

Subject Index

A   8
B   9
C   0
D   1
E   2
F   3
G   4
H   5